ILLUSTRATED Hawaiian DICTIONARY

by *Kahikāhealani Wight*

illustrated by *Robin Yoko Racoma*

THE
BESS
PRESS

3565 Harding Avenue, Honolulu, Hawai‘i 96816

Design: Carol Colbath
Typesetting: Island Graphics

Library of Congress Cataloging in
    Publication Data

Wight, Kahikahealani.
    Illustrated Hawaiian dictionary /
Kahikahealani Wight ; illustrations by
Robin Yoko Racoma.
        p.   cm.
    Includes illustrations.
    1-57306-056-9
    1. Hawaiian language – Dictionaries –
English. 2. English language – Dictionaries –
Hawaiian. I. Racoma, Robin Yoko, ill. II.
    Title.
PL6446.W53 1997   499.419-dc20

Printed in the United States of America

ISBN 1-57306-056-9

Contents

Preface

Our aim in creating the *Illustrated Hawaiian Dictionary* has been to create a reference that includes words and definitions most commonly used by beginning students of the language. We have limited the number of words (approximately 2,500 entries in each language) for ease of use by beginning learners of all ages. The meanings are those most often heard in simple daily conversation. Example sentences include lines from well-known Hawaiian songs, *'ōlelo no'eau* (wise sayings), historical references, and current topics of concern to the Hawaiian community, such as the debate about sovereignty.

In planning this book, we quickly became aware of one problem: the difficulty of establishing a one-to-one correspondence between English and Hawaiian words. There is often not just one Hawaiian word that translates an English one. Similarly, many Hawaiian words have several possible English translations that are not necessarily connected with each other in Western thinking. This difficulty in establishing a one-to-one correspondence is partly due to Hawaiian's shorter alphabet, which has only seven consonants plus the *'okina* (glottal stop, considered to be a letter of the Hawaiian alphabet) and partly due to the poetic nature of Hawaiian oral expression, which celebrates a multiplicity of meanings or symbols incorporated into one word.

Therefore, you should be aware that we have included a limited number of meanings for most Hawaiian words, selecting those that are most commonly used today, based on our experience as Hawaiian teachers and students. Alternative meanings are listed in parentheses for most words. However, for some Hawaiian words that have a multitude of possible English translations, we have indicated that there are "many other meanings"; in that case you may want to refer to the Pukui and Elbert *Hawaiian Dictionary* for a full list of possible English meanings.

So also for translation of English words into Hawaiian: we have chosen Hawaiian words that seem to be used most often in Hawaiian conversation to translate the English. You should be aware, however, that there may be other equally valid ways to say the same thing in Hawaiian. Do your grandparents use a different word when they speak Hawaiian? Remember that Hawaiian native speech is a rare and precious gift still passed on in oral tradition, and should be a source of learning for all.

Parts of Speech

Hawaiian does not often assign a particular grammatical function or part of speech to a word. For example, <u>hoaka</u> means "a crescent, brightness" (nouns), "to cast a shadow, to drive away or ward off" (verbs) and "shining, glittering" (adjectives)—and these are only a few of the meanings listed for this word in Pukui and Elbert's *Hawaiian Dictionary*. Most Hawaiian words used as adjectives (placed after the noun they modify) can also be used as adverbs (placed after the verb they modify). *No'eau*, meaning skilled or clever, is used as an adjective in the phrase *hana no'eau* (skilled activity, art or craft). This same word is used as an adverb in the following sentence: *Ulana no'eau ka wahine i ka lauhala.* (The woman skillfully weaves the *hala* leaves.) To avoid "pigeonholing" Hawaiian words, restricting their meanings in ways that run counter to Hawaiian thinking, we have decided not to label parts of speech except where needed for clarity.

Plurals and Pronouns

Hawaiian plurals and pronouns need a brief explanation, since they are markedly different from English plurals and pronouns. Hawaiian pluralizes in two ways: singular nouns with "the" (*ke* or *ka*) pluralize by replacing *ke* or *ka* with *nā*: *ka lole* = the dress, *nā lole* = the dresses.

In all other situations, simply add *mau* before the noun: *kā'u pēpē* = my baby, *ka'u mau pēpē* = my babies.

Hawaiian follows other Polynesian languages in pronoun usage. Unlike English, Hawaiian does not distinguish the sex of the person being referred to: *'o ia* can mean either "he" or "she."

Hawaiian also includes dual pronouns, referring to two people, such as *'olua* (you two).

Perhaps most confusing is the use of four words in Hawaiian for "we," including two words for duals (*kāua* = you and I, *māua* = my buddy and I) and two for three or more people (*kākou* = all of us, *mākou* = my buddies and I). Note that *māua* and *mākou* do not include the person being addressed. See the pronoun chart below for reference.

Pronoun Chart

singular	dual (2 people)	plural (3 or more)
au (I, me)	*kāua* (you and I) *māua* (she/he and I)	*kākou* (us, we all) *mākou* (us, not you)
'oe (you)	*'olua* (you 2)	*'oukou* (you all)
'o ia (he/she)	*lāua* (they 2)	*lākou* (they all)

For dual and plural pronouns, possession of an object is indicated by adding either *ko* or *kā* before the pronoun. Is the item possessed something you cannot help having, a birthright (such as land, ancestors, parents, siblings, feelings, parts of your body)? Is it something you can get into (such as cars, clothes, buildings)? In both instances, use *kō*:

kō lākou hale = their (3) house

kō kāua mau kāma'a = our (your and my) shoes

If, on the other hand, the item possessed is something you can acquire (such as spouses, children, grandchildren, jobs, tools, money, food, drink), use *kā*:

kā lāua mea 'ai = their (2) food

kā mākou kālā = our (us 3, not your) money

As you become more familiar with the language and Hawaiian thinking, the use of *ko* and *kā* will become clearer.

Singular possessive pronouns combine *ko* or *kā* and the pronoun to form one word. You never say <u>*kō au inoa*</u>, but <u>*ko'u inoa*</u> (my name). Likewise, <u>*kā 'o ia hana*</u> becomes <u>*kāna hana*</u> (her/his job, activity). See the possessive pronouns chart for reference.

Possessive Pronoun Chart

singular	dual (2 people)	plural (3 or more)
ka'u/ko'u (my)	*kā kāua/ko kāua* (our, your and my) *kā māua/ko māua* (our, her/his and my)	*kā kākou/ko kākou* (our, us all) *kā mākou/ko mākou* (our, not your)
kāu/kou (your)	*kā 'olua/ko 'olua* (your)	*kā 'oukou/ko 'oukou* (your all)
kāna/kona (his, her)	*kā lāua/ko lāua* (their)	*kā lākou/ko lākou* (their all)

Spelling

Hawaiian is being revived as a spoken language due to the extraordinary dedication of Hawaiian families who have supported the development of Hawaiian language preschools and a growing Hawaiian Immersion program under the Department of Education. New words are being created for science (astronaut = *kela lani*, lit. sky sailor) and new technologies (compact discs = *cēdē, sēdē*). A few old words are being shortened for use in spoken Hawaiian (*pā'ani kinipōpō peku wāwae*, which means "football game, to play football," has being shortened to *pōpeku*). A new reference guide to the latest Hawaiian words is *Māmaka Kaiao,* published by Hale Kuamo'o, University of Hawai'i-Hilo.

While all of us involved in Hawaiian education are thrilled to witness the growth of interest in learning the language, we are aware of the challenges presented by changes in spelling and the use of diacritical marks (*'okina* and *kahakō*). The spellings in this dictionary reflect current usage; however, be aware that you will see variant spellings as you learn more and as the language grows in daily usage.

The Role of Hawaiian Culture

We have chosen to use common *'ōlelo no'eau* (wise sayings) and familiar lines from Hawaiian songs as examples of word usage as often as possible, because wise sayings and songs are an integral part of Hawaiian language and help introduce readers to the poetic nature of Hawaiian thinking. We have identified as many song composers as possible, because they are the skilled poets of our culture. Songs listed as traditional often are older chants that have survived as songs or have been put to melody in modern times.

Translations of the song lines are our own except for a few lines taken from *Nā Mele o Hawai'i Nei, 101 Hawaiian Songs,* by Elbert and Mahoe. We have also included well-known place names on various islands, as well as other names, such as those of winds and rains, since these are another important part of Hawaiian cultural knowledge.

We hope our dictionary will contribute to the practical use of Hawaiian as a living language and provide explanations of basic cultural concepts that clarify areas of difference between Hawaiian and English, such as Hawaiian family terms or the importance of *kalo* (taro) as a symbol for the deep connection Hawaiians feel to our land.

May it also be a first step toward understanding the beauty and subtlety of Hawaiian expression of feelings, which is such as integral part of our language and culture.

E a'o aku, a'o mai i ola nō ka 'ōlelo 'ōiwi o ka 'āina!

Teach and learn so that the native language of the land lives on!

Acknowledgments

No book is ever the work of any one person, no matter whose name is on the cover. In this case, many people worked diligently over many months to help bring the *Illustrated Hawaiian Dictionary* to life.

Robin Racoma provided beautiful illustrations and waited a long time to see them used.

Early contributors included Kau'i Keola of the Hawaiian Immersion program and Hana Pau and friends from the Hawaiian Studies department at Kamehameha Schools.

Hawaiian language students Dr. Houston Wood of the University of Hawai'i-Mānoa English department and Yuka Kimura of Japan helped with editing and feedback, as did Hawaiian language instructors 'Iwalani Koide and Lālepa Koga.

Tracking down song composers proved to be a challenge. Mahalo to Ku'uipo Kumukahi, Gerry Santos, and Ainsley Halemanu for their ongoing *kōkua*.

Thanks to the people at The Bess Press for their patience as we figured out how to do it best. Carol Colbath provided the wonderful design. Revé Shapard spent many hours editing through revision after revision, with the assistance of Jeela Ongley.

Tia Ballantine Berger deserves special credit for her many contributions, including thought-provoking commentary and sharp editing skills. *Mahalo piha, e Tia.*

Mahalo iā 'oukou pākahi a pau.

Thanks to each and every one.

Abbreviations

adj	adjective
ant	antonym
approx	approximately
cap	when capitalized
fig	figuratively
lit	literally
n	noun
pl	plural
syn	synonym
v	verb

Pronunciation Guide

Hawaiian consonants are said the same as they are in English, except for *w*, which is usually pronounced like *v* after *i* and *e*.

Vowel sounds:

a, ā	like *a* in *was: (olonā)*
e	like e in *red: (heʻe)*
ē	like *a* in *baby: (nēnē)*
i, ī	like *e* in *me: (imu, kī)*
o, ō	like *o* in *go: (kalo, kō)*
u, ū	like *oo* in *moon: (hula, pāʻū)*

Hawaiian words are usually stressed on the next-to-last syllable, unless there is a single line over a vowel. This line is called a macron or *kahakō*. It shows that the vowel should be said with stress, or longer and stronger.

Sometimes two vowels go together: *ai, ao, au, ei, eu, oi, ou.* The vowel sounds are rolled together as you say them, with the first one being stronger.

The mark like an upside-down apostrophe (ʻ) is called an *ʻokina*. It marks a glottal stop. It shows that there is a break in the word, as when you say the English *oh-oh*.

Hawaiian-English

a 1. belonging to, of. [*ka puke a Melia*, Melia's book] 2. and (used primarily between sentences). [*Ua holoi 'o Lahela i nā pā a ua kāwele 'o Kele iā lākou.* Lahela washed the dishes **and** Kele wiped them.] Also used before article *he* (a, an) and before object markers *i / iā* [*he kāne a he wahine*, a man **and** a woman] [*Kelepona aku 'o ia i ke kauka a iā 'Ululani.* She phones the doctor **and** 'Ululani.] Note: *A me* also means "and," but is used primarily within a sentence to indicate a second subject or object. [*Ua holoi 'o Lahela a me Kele i nā puna a me nā pahi.* Lahela **and** Kele washed the spoons **and** the knives.] 3. until, up to. [*E kali ana māua a hō'ea mai ke ka'a ho'olimalima.* We (he and I) will wait **until** the taxi arrives. (*a hiki i* = up until, up to, toward [lit., until arrived at]) [*mai Hau'ula a hiki i Hale'iwa,* from Hau'ula **to** Hale'iwa]

ā jaw. (*ā luna* = upper jaw) (*ā lalo* = lower jaw) [*'Eha nō ko ka'u kaikamahine ā lalo i ka niho hu'i.* My daughter's **lower jaw** is very painful due to a sore tooth.]

'ā 1. fiery, burning. 2. turned on (refers to appliances [lit fire]). [*Ua 'ā ka lolouila.* The computer is **on.**] (*ka hale 'ā* = the burning house) (*ho'ā* = to turn on machine, electricity, to light fire) [*E ho'ā i kāu pipa.* **Turn on** your beeper.]

a'a 1. rootlet. (*ke a'a hala* = the *hala* roots) 2. muscle, nerve, vein, artery. (*a'a koko* = vein, artery [*lit.* blood rootlet]) (*a'a lolo* = nerve [*lit.* brain rootlet])

'a'a 1. to dare, challenge. [*E waiho i ka hilahila i ka hale, e 'a'a i ka hula.* ('*ōlelo no'eau*) Leave embarrassment at home, **dare** to dance.] 2. volunteer. 3. intrepid, bold. [*He mau wāhine 'a'a kēlā mau ho'okele.* Those navigators are **intrepid** women.]

'a'ā 1. to burn, glow, blaze. [*'A'ā ka pele.* **Lava** glows.] 2. lava, rough type. [*'Ōkupe ka malihini i ka 'a'ā.* The newcomer trips on the **rough lava rock.**]

'a'ahu costume, garment, clothing. [*He pū nui ko kāna mo'opuna 'a'ahu Heleuī.* His (Her) grandchild's Halloween **costume** is a big pumpkin.]

'a'ai 1. erosion. 2. to erode. 3. malignant. (*ma'i 'a'ai* = cancer) [*He ma'i a'ai ko ko Anuhea kupuna kāne.* Anuhea's grandfather has **cancer.**]

'a'aka 1. grumpy, surly, cranky. 2. wrinkled, peeling.

'a'ala fragrant, sweet-smelling. [*He pua 'a'ala ka pīkake.* The *pīkake* is a **fragrant** flower.]

'a'ali'i 1. native plant, symbol of independent people of Ka'ū. [*'A'ali'i kū makani.* (*'ōlelo no'eau*) The **'a'ali'i** that stands up to the wind. (Ka'ū folks are known to be intolerant of rulers who abuse commoners.)]

'a'ali'i

'ae 1. yes. [*Hau'oli 'oe? 'Ae, hau'oli nō au.* Are you happy? **Yes,** I'm really happy.] 2. to agree, consent. [*'Ae ko ka'u ipo mau mākua i ko māua male 'ana.* My sweetheart's parents **agree** to our (his and my) marrying.]

'a'e to trespass, break *kapu* or violate law, to tread on, step over (*fig.* oppressed). [*Mai* *komo i ka heiau i hoʻolaʻa hou ʻia o* **ʻaʻe** *ʻoukou i ke kapu.* Don't enter the religious site that has been rededicated or else you may all **violate** the sacredness.]

aea to come up from under water, to surface. [*Luʻu iho ka lawaiʻa a* **aea** *aʻe.* The fisherman dives down and then **comes to the surface.**]

ʻaeʻa 1. wandering, shiftless, unstable. (*nā hōkū* ʻaeʻa = the wandering stars; Hōkūpaʻa = North Star, "fixed" star that doesn't move across the sky) (*ʻaeʻa haukaʻe* = homeless wanderer [an insult in ancient days]) (*kanaka ʻaeʻa* = tramp)

ʻae kai edge of sea, place where land and sea meet.

aha what. [*He* **aha** *kēia? He iʻa kēia.* **What** is this? This is a fish.] Note: A variation of this basic question is used to ask for specific type or brand name: *He* **aha** *ke ʻano o* (what is the type/nature of/brand name) + article + noun. [*He* **aha** *ke ʻano o kēia honu? He ʻea ke ʻano o kēia honu.* **What kind of** turtle is this? This kind of turtle is a tortoiseshell turtle.] Note that asking for a personal name (proper noun) requires use of another question word, namely *ʻo wai* (who). [**ʻO wai** *ka inoa o kēia honu? ʻO "Pewa" ka inoa o kēia honu.* **What** is the name of this turtle? "Fin" is the name of this turtle.]

ʻaha 1. meeting, community. 2. general name for cordage made of coconut fiber, sennit. (*ʻAhaʻōlelo* = Congress [*lit.* federal legislature; syn. *ʻAhaʻōlelo lāhui*]) (*ʻahahui* = organization) (*ʻaha mele* = concert)

ahi fire. (*ahi kao lele* = fireworks) (*kinai ahi* = fire extinguisher or firefighter) (*kāhea pau ahi* = fire alarm) (*pau ahi* = destroyed by fire)

ʻahi tuna fish.

ʻahia question word asking "how many?" (a less commonly used variation of *ʻehia,* used in an idiomatic phrase asking "Which of day of the week is it?" [*lit.* what number night?]). [*ʻO ka Pō* **ʻahia** *ʻo nehinei? ʻO ka Pōʻahā ʻo nehinei.* **What** (number) day of the week was yesterday?

Yesterday was Thursday.]

ahiahi evening, time when fires were lit.

ʻahiʻahi to slander.

ʻāhina gray. (syn. *ʻāhinahina, hinahina, hina*)

ʻāhinahina Hawaiian silversword, indigenous plant found on Maui and Hawaiʻi islands.

ʻāhinahina

ʻāhiu wild, untamed (*fig.* shy or unsocial). [*He pilikia nui ka puaʻa* **ʻāhiu** *ma ka wao nahele.* **Wild** pigs are a big problem in the rain forest.]

aho 1. fishing line, lashing, cord, kite string. 2. breath (syn. *hanu*). 3. to breathe (syn. *hanu*). (*paupauaho* = out of breath) 4. idiomatic phrase: *E aho* + verb, "It's better (to do . . .). [**E aho** *ka ʻai ʻana i ka ʻīnika.* **It's better** to eat spinach.]

ahonui 1. patience. [*Ke mālama ʻoe i nā luāhine a me nā ʻelemākule, ʻo ke* **ahonui** *ka mea pono.* When you take care of the elderly women and men, **patience** is the proper thing.] 2. patient. (*ahonui ʻole* = impatient)

ahu 1. pile, mound, mass, cairn. 2. shrine, altar.

ahulau epidemic. [*Nui nā Hawaiʻi i hala i nā* **ahulau** *i kēlā kenekulia aku nei.* Many Hawaiians died in **epidemics** in the last century.]

ahupuaʻa traditional land division encompassing a piece of land from mountains to sea (*lit.* pig mound, pile of stones where pig image or offering marked boundary of land division).

ʻahuʻula feather cloak, a symbol of high rank worn by male chiefs. [*He* **ʻahuʻula** *mamo ko Kamehameha ʻekahi.* Kamehameha I had a *mamo*-**feather cloak.**]

ahuwale prominent, in clear view, obvious.

ʻahuʻula

ai 1. sexual intercourse. (syn. *hana ai, hana ei*) (*nā maʻi hana ei =*

sexually transmitted diseases) 2. to have sexual relations.

'ai 1. food, especially plant or vegetable; sometimes refers specifically to poi or taro. (*ka 'ai me ka i'a* = fish and poi) [*Ua lawa mākou i ka pōhaku, ka 'ai kamaha'o o ka 'āina.* Rocks, the astonishing **food** of the land, are enough for us. (song, "Kaulana Nā Pua," by E. Prendergast)] 2. score, points in a game. [*He aha ka 'ai pōpa'ilima?* What's the volleyball **score**?] 3. to eat, taste, bite. [*Mai, mai e 'ai.* Come, come in and **eat.** (traditional greeting; all passersby were welcomed to eat and rest)]

'ā'ī neck. (*lei 'ā'ī* = neck *lei*, necktie)

aia there. [*aia i ka uka a'o Pi'ihonua,* **there** in the uplands of Pi'ihonua (song, "Kimo Henderson Hula," by H.D. Beamer)] Note: *Aia* is essential in Hawaiian to indicate location in time or space, but is often not translated into English. Both *'ō* and *laila* are used to mean "over there." *'Ō* is used to indicate a general direction; *laila* is used when the exact location is already known. [*Ua kipa aku 'olua i Kahana? Mālie 'o laila.* Have you (two) visited Kahana? It's peaceful **over there.**] (*ma 'ō a ma 'ane'i* = everywhere [*lit.* over there and over here])

aia i hea where. [*Aia i hea ka hālāwai ma kēia lā? Aia ka hālāwai ma ka hōkele hou.* **Where**'s the meeting today? The meeting is in the new hotel.]

'aiana 1. clothes iron. 2. to iron.

'ai'ē 1. debt. 2. to owe.

'aiha'a hula style with low stance.

'aihue 1. thief, theft. 2. to steal. [*Ua 'aihue 'ia ko kona 'ohana ka'a ma ka pāka.* Her family's car was **stolen** at the park.]

'aikalima (from English) ice cream.

'aila 1. oil, fat. 2. greasy, oily, fatty. (*'aila iki* = low fat) (*'aila hamo* = massage oil, ointment, salve)

'aina meal. (syn. *pā'ina* [also means party, to eat, to party]) (*'aina ahiahi* = dinner) [*E 'ai kākou i ka 'aina ahiahi ma ka hale 'aina 'o Wisteria!* Let's eat **dinner** at the Wisteria restaurant!] (*'aina awakea* = lunch) (*'aina*

kakahiaka = breakfast)

'aina kakahiaka

'āina land, earth (*lit.* that which feeds spiritually and physically, implying sacredness of land). (*ke aloha 'āina* = patriotism, love of the land) (*'āina hānau* = native land, birthplace; *one hānau, lit.* birth sands, is also frequently used) (*'āina ho'opulapula* = Hawaiian Homestead land) (*'āina nui* = mainland) (*'āina puni 'ole* = continent) (*'āina panoa* = desert) (*nā 'āina 'ē* = foreign lands)

a i 'ole or (*lit.* and if not). [*Hiki iā ia ke hula a i 'ole ho'okani 'ukulele?* Can she dance hula **or** play the ukulele?]

āiwaiwa mysterious, inexplicable. [*He mea āiwaiwa ka huaka'i pō.* The night marchers are a **mysterious** thing.]

aka 1. shadow. 2. reflection, image. (*ili i ke aka* = to cast a shadow)

akā but. [*Huhū ka 'ōhua, akā mālie ke kalaiwa ka'a 'ōhua.* The passenger is angry, **but** the bus driver is calm.] (*akā na'e, akā nō na'e* = however) [*Ua hao mai ka makani; akā na'e 'a'ole nui loa nā 'ale o ka moana.* The wind was blasting; **however,** the ocean swells weren't really big.]

'aka'aka 1. laughter. [*Ua hū ka 'aka'aka.* **Laughter** burst out.] 2. to laugh. [*Mai 'aka'aka mai ia'u!* Don't **laugh** at me!]

'aka'akai onion. (*'aka'akai lau* = green onion) (*'aka'akai poepoe* = round onion)

akāka clear, luminous, distinct, intelligible. [*Akāka wale ko lāua wehewehe 'ana.* Their (two) explanation is **clear.**]

'ākala 1. native plant, the bright pink Hawaiian raspberry. 2. pink color. [*He hōkele 'ākala 'o ka Royal Hawaiian.* The Royal Hawaiian is a **pink** hotel.]

akamai 1. smartness, cleverness, skill. 2. smart, clever, skilled. [*Nani ke akamai o nā kūpuna!* Our ancestors were very **skilled!**] [*Malia paha e lilo ana ka makana i ka moho akamai.* Maybe the prize will become the **clever** contestant's.]

'ākau 1. right (direction). [*'O wai kēnā ma ka 'ao'ao 'ākau ou ma ke ki'i?* Who's that on your **right** side in the picture?] 2. north. [*Aia 'o Hawai'i ma ka Pākīpika 'ākau.* Hawai'i is in the **north** Pacific.]

ake 1. liver. (*akemāmā* = lungs) 2. to yearn for, want, desire, wish. [*Ake nui nō ka lāhui Hawai'i e 'ōlelo Hawai'i.* The Hawaiian nationality really **wants** to speak Hawaiian.]

ākea 1. width, breadth. 2. broad, wide, spacious, public. [*He kumulā'au ākea ka 'ōhai.* The monkeypod is a **wide** tree.]

'ākea 1. starboard. 2. outer hull of double hulled canoe (*wa'a kaulua*).

akeakamai 1. science, philosophy. 2. scientist, philosopher, lover of wisdom. [*He mau akeakamai ko kākou mau kūpuna.* Our ancestors were **lovers of wisdom**.]

'ake'ake'a 1. obstruction. 2. interfere, block.

akemāmā lungs.

'ākepa bird; one of the wide variety of Hawaiian honeycreepers, currently endangered.

'aki to nibble, nip, snap. [*'Aki ka manini i ka limu. Manini* fish **nibble** seaweed.]

'ako 1. to pluck a flower. [*A he pua 'oe, ua 'ako 'ia.* You are a flower that has been **plucked**. (song, "Pāpālina Lahilahi," composer unknown)] 2. to trim or cut, as hair.

'ākoakoa to gather together, assemble. [*Ma ka papekema i 'ākoakoa ai ka 'ohana.* It was at the baptism that the family **gathered**.]

'āko'ako'a coral head.

aku 1. bonito fish, prized for delicious flavor. [*'Oiai 'o kēia ka lā hope o ka makahiki, e kū'ai mai kāua i ke aku a e ho'omākaukau i ka i'a maka.* Since this is the last day of the year, let's (you and me) buy **aku** and prepare sashimi (raw fish).] 2. [directional, away from speaker] word added after verb to clarify direction of action, sometimes essential to meaning: *lawe aku* = to take; *lawe mai* = to bring; *kū'ai aku* = to sell; *kū'ai mai* = to buy. [*E hele aku 'oukou!* (You all) go **away**!]

akua 1. god. [*'O Kūkā'ilimoku ko Kamehameha akua kaua.* Kūkā'ilimoku was Kamehameha's war **god**.] 2. spirit, ghost, supernatural being. [*Mai maka'u i nā akua lapu!* Don't be afraid of **ghosts**!] 3. image, idol. [*Nui nā ki'i akua hou ma ka Pu'uhonua 'o Hōnaunau.* There are lots of new **images** at the Hōnaunau City of Refuge.]

ala 1. path, trail, road. (*alahele* = trail, pathway; *alaloa* = freeway; *alanui* = street, road) 2. to wake up, rise up. (*ho'āla* = to wake someone) [*E ala mai! E ho'āla kāua iā Papa!* **Wake** up! Let's **wake up** Daddy!]

'ala scent, smell (*fig.* esteemed). [*Moani ke 'ala o ka laua'e.* The **scent** of the *laua'e* fern is borne on the breeze.] Note: exception to *ke/ka* rule: *ke 'ala*.

alahele trail, pathway.

alahele

ālai 1. obstruction, block, hindrance. 2. to obstruct, block. [*ālai 'ia a'ela e Nounou,* **blocked** by Nounou (chant, "Kūnihi ka Mauna")]

a laila and then, next. [*Ho'i ka wilikī i ke ke'ena. A laila, inu kope 'o ia ala.* The engineer returns to the office. **And then**, she (over there) drinks coffee.]

alaka'i 1. leader, guide. (*alaka'i mele* = song leader) 2. to lead, guide. [*Ke alaka'i nei ke kāpena i nā koa ma ka paikau.* The captain is **leading** the soldiers in the military parade.]

'alalā 1. scream, yell. 2. Hawaiian crow, currently near extinction. 3. to scream, yell. ('Alalākeiki = channel between Maui and Kaho'olawe)

'alalā

alaloa freeway, highway.

'alamihi common black crab.

'alaneo clear, unclouded sky, calm, serene.

'alani orange fruit, orange color.

'alani Pākē tangerine.

alanui street, road.
[*Noho koʻu ʻAnakala
a me koʻu ʻAnakē ma
ke **alanui** ʻo Pāhoa
ma Kaimukī.* My
Uncle and Aunt live
on Pāhoa **Street** in
Kaimukī.]

alanui

ʻālapa 1. athlete. [*He
ʻālapa kaulana ʻo Sid Fernandez.* Sid
Fernandez is a famous **athlete**.] 2. athletic,
active.

alapiʻi staircase, ladder. [*Ua piʻi aʻe nā mōʻī
Kalākaua i ke **alapiʻi** koa.* The Kalākaua
monarchs ascended the *koa* **staircase**.]
(*alapiʻi mele* = musical scale)

ʻalawa to glance quickly (thus to see instinc-
tively or insightfully).

ale to swallow. [*Ua **ale** ke kanaka maʻi i ka
huaale.* The patient **swallowed** the pill.]

ʻale ocean swell, wave. [*ka ʻiwa hehi **ʻale**
(ʻōlelo noʻeau),* the *ʻiwa* bird who steps on
the crests of the **ocean swells**]

ʻaleʻale stirring, rippling. (Waiʻaleʻale = rippling fresh water)

ʻalekohola alcohol. (syn. *lama* = rum, in
Hawaiian used to represent all types of
alcohol) [*ʻAʻole au e inu **lama**.* I will not
drink **alcohol**. (temperance song, 1800s)]

alelo tongue. [*Mai kīkoʻo ʻolua i ko ʻolua mau
alelo!* Don't you two stick out your
tongues!]

ʻalemanaka calendar. [*Kūʻai aku nā ʻAhahui
Kiwila Hawaiʻi i ka **ʻalemanaka** mahina
Hawaiʻi kahiko.* The Hawaiian Civic Clubs
sell the old Hawaiian
moon **calendar**.]

aliʻi 1. chief, ruler. 2.
royal, noble. [*He mau
hale **aliʻi** ko
Honolulu.* Honolulu
has **royal** palaces.]

aliʻi

ʻālina scar. [*He **ʻālina**
lōʻihi ko kona ʻōpū.*
His stomach has a long **scar**.]

alo 1. front of body, face; presence. [*he **alo** a
he **alo**,* **face** to **face**] 2. *(fig.)* reference to
wife.

aloaliʻi royal court (*lit.* in the presence of
royal chiefs). [*Hiki ke ʻike ʻia kekahi
aloaliʻi ma ka hoʻokūkū hula ʻo Merrie
Monarch.* A **royal court** can be seen at the
Merrie Monarch hula contest.]

aloha 1. love, greetings. [***Aloha** nō au i kou
maka.* I **love** your eyes. (song, "Aloha Nō
Au I Kou Maka," by Leleiōhoku)] 2. regret,
sympathy, compassion, grace. 3. farewell.
4. to love. 5. beloved. [*e Hawaiʻi **aloha** ē,*
oh **beloved** Hawaiʻi (song, "Hawaiʻi
Aloha")] 6. too bad, how sad. [*Ua hala ko
lākou makuahine? **Aloha**!* Their (three or
more) mother died? **How sad**!] variations:
aloha nō, aloha ʻino Note: *Aloha* has many
other meanings. (*aloha ʻāina* = patriotism
[*lit.* love for the land]) (*Aloha nō au iā ʻoe*
= I love you) (*Aloha a hui hou kāua!* =
Goodbye until you and I meet again!)

ʻalohi 1. brilliance, splendor, brightness. [*ke
ʻalohi o ka pō Māhealani,* the **brightness**
of the night of the full moon] 2. bright,
shiny.

alu to cooperate, work together. [*E **alu** like
mai kākou, e nā ʻōiwi o Hawaiʻi.* Let's
work together, natives of Hawaiʻi. (song,
"Alu Like," by H. Apoliona)]

ʻalu to bend, stoop, sag, slacken. (*kī hōʻalu* =
slack key, Hawaiian style of guitar playing)

alualu to run, chase after, run for political
office. [***Alualu** ʻo Fasi i ke keʻena kiaʻāina.*
Fasi **runs** for governor.]

ʻaluʻalu loose, baggy. (*keiki ʻaluʻalu* = prema-
ture baby)

ama outrigger float. [*E hāpai i ke **ama**!* Lift
up the **outrigger float**!]

ʻAmelika America. (ʻAmelika ʻĀkau = North
America) (ʻAmelika Hema = South
America) (ʻAmelika Hui Pūʻia = United
States of America)

ʻami 1. joint or hinge. 2. hula step with hip
rotation.

ana 1. measurement, design, pattern, model.
[*Nani kēia **ana** kapa kuiki.* This quilt **pattern** is pretty.] (*anapuni* = circumference)
(*anawaena* = diameter) 2. cave. [*Kiʻekiʻe ka
puka o ke **ana** ʻo Kāne ana.* The entrance
to Kāne ana **cave** is tall.] 3. to measure,

survey, evaluate. (Kalanianaʻole = the immeasurable chief [one whose rank is so high it can not be measured]) (*anawela* = thermometer) [*Ke piʻi aʻe nei ka wela ma ke* **anawela**? *Ke kahe nei koʻu hou.* Is the temperature rising on the **thermometer**? My sweat is pouring off.]

ana ʻāina 1. surveyor. 2. to survey land. [*Ua* **ana ʻāina** *lākou i ke alahao.* They **surveyed** the train track.]

ʻanae mullet fish. (*ʻamaʻama* = immature mullet)

ʻānai 1. friction. 2. to rub, scrub, grind, polish. [*E* **ʻānai** *i ka pōhaku a nemonemo.* **Rub** the stone until it is smooth.]

anaina audience, crowd. [*Ua hoʻōho ke* **anaina**. The **audience** cheered.]

ʻanakala uncle (used to respectfully address any older man as well as family members).

ʻanakē aunt (used to respectfully address any older woman as well as family members).

anana fathom, measurement of six feet (a traditional unit of measurement: the distance between the tips of the longest fingers of a man extending arms out to the sides). [*ʻEkolu* **anana** *ka hohonu o ke kai ma ʻaneʻi.* The sea is three **fathoms** deep here.] Note: other traditional measurements: *ʻiwilei* (measurement from collarbone to tip of middle finger extended), *haʻilima* (distance from elbow to end of finger), *kīkoʻo* (measurement from end of thumb to end of index finger), *muku* (like *anana*, but the measurement of one arm extends to the elbow only)

ʻaneʻane nearly, almost. [**ʻAneʻane** *make loa ka ʻalalā.* The Hawaiian crow is **almost** extinct.]

ʻaneʻi here (location). [*Aia kāna mau puke ma* **ʻaneʻi**? Are his books over **here**?] (*ma ʻō a ma ʻaneʻi* = everywhere [*lit.* there and here]) [*Kūʻai hele lāua ma ʻō a ma ʻaneʻi.* They (two) shop **everywhere**.]

ʻānela (from English) angel. [*ʻAʻole au he* **ʻānela**, *he kanaka wau.* (*ʻōlelo noʻeau*) I'm not an **angel**, I'm a human being (therefore I make mistakes).]

ʻane make loa endangered (*lit.* nearly extinct). [**ʻAne make loa** *ke kāhuli.* The *kāhuli* tree snail is **endangered**.]

aniani 1. glass (material). (*makaaniani* = eyeglasses) (*pilimaka* = contact lenses) 2. mirror. (*aniani kū* = standing mirror) 3. transparent, obvious.

ano awe, reverence, peacefulness. (*hōʻano* = holy, to sanctify, revere)

ʻano 1. type, kind. [*He pakalana ke* **ʻano** *o kēnā pua.* That **type** of flower (by you) is a *pakalana*.] Note: *He aha ke ʻano o* is used to ask for type or brand name. [**He aha ke ʻano o** *kēlā waʻa? He waʻa kaukahi kēlā.* **What kind of** canoe is that? That's a single hull canoe.] [**He aha ke ʻano o** *kona kalaka? He Chevy kona kalaka.* **What kind of** truck does he have? His truck is a Chevy.] 2. personality, mood. [*He aha kou* **ʻano**? What's wrong with your **personality**? 3. used before adj. to mean "sort of." [*Pehea ke kula?* **ʻAno** *maikaʻi ke kula.* How's school? School's **okay (sort of good)**.]

ʻanoʻano seed. [*E ʻōkupu aʻe ana kēia* **ʻanoʻano** *hēʻī?* Will this papaya **seed** sprout?]

ʻano ʻē odd, strange, unusual. [**ʻAno ʻē** *ka hana a kēlā malihini.* That newcomer's behavior is **odd**.]

ʻano hana method, technique. [*He aha ke* **ʻano hana** *a ka mākaʻikiu kaulana?* What is the **method** of the famous detective?]

anu 1. cold, coldness. 2. a cold (illness). [*He* **anu** *ko kā ʻolua moʻopuna wahine?* Does your (two) granddaughter have a **cold**?]

anuanu cold. [**Anuanu** *ʻo uka.* The uplands are **cold**.]

ānuenue rainbow. [*Piʻo ke* **ānuenue**. The **rainbow** arches overhead.] (*ānuenue kau pō* = night rainbow)

ānuenue

anuhea fragrance of the mountain forests, cool and sweet.

ʻānunu 1. greed. 2. greedy. [*palapala* **ʻānunu** *me ka pākaha,* **greedy** document with extortion (song, "Kaulana Nā Pua," by E. Prendergast)] (syn. *ʻānulu, nunu*)

'ānu'u step. [*Ua 'ōkupe ka 'elemakule i ka* **'ānu'u** *hope o ke alapi'i.* The old man stumbled on the last **step** of the staircase.]

ao 1. light, daylight. [*a* **ao** *ka pō,* all night] 2. wisdom, enlighten- ment. 3. dawn. 4. cloud. 5. world, earth. [*Ko kēia* **ao***, ko kēlā* **ao***.* Those of this **world**, those of that **world**. (Doxology)] (*ao holo'oko'a* = universe) 5. to dawn. [*Ua wana'ao/Ua kaiao.* Day has **dawned**.] 6. to regain consciousness.

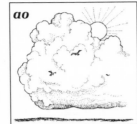
ao

a'o to learn (*a'o mai*), to teach (*a'o aku*). [*Ua* **a'o 'ia mai** *mākou ē, he mea nui ka mali- hini.* We have **learned** that a visitor is an important person. (greeting chant taught in Pūnana Leo school)]

'aoa to bark, howl. [*Ke* **'aoa** *nei nā 'īlio hae?* Are the fierce dogs **barking**?]

'ao'ao 1. side. [*E aloha aku 'oukou i ka luna 'auhau ma ka* **'ao'ao** *'ākau o Kilinahe.* You all greet the tax collector on the right **side** of Kilinahe.] 2. page. [*Aia ka ha'awina ma ka* **'ao'ao** *'umikūmāiwa.* The lesson is on **page** nineteen.] 3. hemi- sphere. [*Aia 'o Aotearoa ma ka* **'ao'ao** *hema o ka honua.* New Zealand is in the southern **hemisphere** of the world.]

'a'ohe none, to have none, to be none. [**'A'ohe** *āna hana.* She **doesn't have** a job.]

'a'ole no, not. [**'A'ole** *nahenahe ko ke kāpena leo.* The captain's voice is **not** soft and sweet.]

'apa to delay, waste time, keep others wait- ing. (*ka mili'apa* = slowpoke) [*Na wai i 'imi i* **ka mili'apa** *i ka pi'i kuahiwi?* Who was it that looked for the **slowpoke** on the hike?]

'āpala (from English) apple. [*'Ono māua i ka pai* **'āpala** *me ka 'aikalima.* We (she/he and I) have a craving for **apple** pie and ice cream.]

'āpana piece, section. [*I* **'āpana** *pai pika nāna, ke 'olu'olu.* Bring him a **piece** of pizza, please.]

'apapane a native bird of the honeycreeper family with black and red feathers that were used for featherwork.

'Apelila (from English) April.

apo 1. circle, hoop, bracelet, ring, circuit. (*apo hele* = orbit of stars, planets) [*He* **apo hele** *lō'ihi ko 'Iao?* Does Jupiter have a long **orbit**?] 2. to clasp, embrace, reach around, hug.

'apo to grab, catch, hug; *fig.* to perceive, understand. [*Ua* **'apo** *koke 'o ia nei i ko'u mana'o.* This one here (she/he) quickly **caught** my meaning.]

'apo'apo 1. fit, palpitation, attack. 2. to have an attack, fit.

apolima bracelet. [*Pipi'i ke* **apolima** *kula Hawai'i.* A Hawaiian gold **bracelet** is expensive.]

apolima

'āpono to approve, con- sent, ratify, to pass a bill. [*E* **'āpono** *ana 'o Alu Like i kā lāua palapala noi kālā.* Alu Like will **approve** their (two) grant application.]

'āpuka 1. fraud, embezzlement, embezzler, deceit. [*Ua lilo kāu kālā i ke kanaka* **'āpuka***?* Did your money become the **embezzler**'s?] 2. to cheat, defraud, deceive.

au 1. period of time, era, age, passage of time. (*i kēia au hou* = in this modern era [these days]) (*i ke au kahiko* = in ancient days) 2. ocean current, tide, movement. [*He* **au** *ikaika ko Makapu'u.* Makapu'u has a strong **current**.] 3. to flow, float, move. 4. I, me (*wau* = variant spelling, pronuncia- tion)

āu your (1), yours (*ke kāwele* **āu***, kāu kāwele* = your (1) towel

a'u 1. marlin, swordfish. 2. my, mine. [*ke kopa holoi lole* **a'u***,* **my** laundry detergent]

'au 1. handle, stem, stalk, long bone of arm, leg. [*Auī! Wela nō ke* **'au** *o kēia ipuhao!* Ouch! The **handle** of this pan is really hot!] Note: exception to *ke/ka* rule: *ke 'au.* 2. to swim, travel by sea, usually to a spe- cific destination. [*Ke* **'au** *nei ke kelamoku* *i ko Palani mokupe'a.* The sailor is **swimming** to Palani's sailboat.]

'au'a to hold back, refuse to part with. [*E 'au'a 'ia e kama i kona moku.* **Refuse**, child, **to part with** your land. (opening line of ancient chant, "'Au'a 'ia," advising Hawaiians to hold on to their heritage)]

'auamo 1. pole across shoulder used to carry burdens, using nets suspended from each end. 2. to carry burden.

'auana to wander from place to place, ramble, drift. (*hula 'auana* = modern style hula, probably so called because *hula kahiko*, ancient hula, has stricter rules)

auane'i by and by, later on. [*E kāwele 'oe i kou lauoho o ma'i* **auane'i**. Dry your hair off or else you'll be sick **later on**.]

'au'au to take a bath or swim. [***'Au'au** anei nā keiki ma mua o ka 'aina ahiahi?* Do the children **take a bath** before dinner?] (*'au'au kai* = to swim in the ocean; sometimes used to distinguish swimming from taking a bath)

auē too bad, gosh, oh dear, wow (used for a wide variety of situations for problems of minor and major importance; many variations, such as *auē nō ho'i ē!* [oh, for goodness sake!]) (gives extra emphasis). [*Inu 'olua a 'ona ma ka hopenapule?* **Auē nō ho'i** *'olua ē!* You (two) drink until drunk on the weekend? **Oh for goodness sake** you folks!]

'auhau taxes, tariff, levy, charge. [*'O nehinei ka lā uku* **'auhau**. *'Ano 'ūlōlohi 'oukou!* Yesterday was the day to pay **taxes**. You all are a little late!]

'auhea where (often used as a poetic way of calling the attention of the person/s being addressed; frequent opening line of songs) [***'Auhea** wale 'oe, e ku'u pua?* **Where** are you, my beloved flower? (*fig.* pay attention, beloved) (song, "Pua Lilia," by A. Alohikea)]

'auhuhu bush used for fish poison.

auhuli to overturn, overthrow; to till.

auī exclamation of pain.

'aui to turn aside, deviate, decline.

'auinalā afternoon (approx. 2 - 6 p.m.; *lit.* the declining of the sun).

'auinalā

'Aukake (from English) August.

'auli'i dainty, trim, cute, neat. [***Auli'i** ko kāna kaikamahine pā'ū hula.* His daughter's hula skirt is **neat**.]

'auloa long limbed.

'aumakua family guardian spirit embodied in animal form, such as *manō* (shark), *pueo* (owl), *mo'o* (lizard), *puhi* (eel). (pl. *'aumākua*) *'Aumākua* are usually considered to be restricted to a specific type or individual animal, also to a specific place frequented by the family. [*'O ka 'io kou* **'aumakua**? Is the Hawaiian hawk your **guardian spirit**?]

'aumoana 1. sailor. 2. to travel on the open sea.

aumoe midnight, late night. [*Hia'ā au i ke* **aumoe**. I'm an insomniac at **midnight**.]

'aumoku fleet of ships. (*'auwa'a* = canoe fleet)

'āuna flock, large group. (*he 'āuna manō* = a school of sharks)

aupuni government, kingdom, nation. [*No ka mea, nou ke* **aupuni**, For thine is the **kingdom** (line from "Ka pule a ka Haku," the Lord's prayer)] (*ke aupuni pekelala* = the federal government) (*aupuni moku 'āina* = the state government) (*aupuni a ka lehulehu* = democracy) (*aupuni mō'ī* = monarchy)

'auwae chin. [*He 'umi'umi ko ko Kāna Kaloka* **'auwae**. Santa Claus's **chin** has a beard.] (*'auwae pu'u* = discouraged)

'auwai canal, ditch, sewer (commonly refers to ditch used to divert water from stream to irrigate taro patch). [*Kahe mau ka wai i nā* **auwai** *kahiko o ka papa lo'i 'o Kānewai.* Does water continue to flow in the old **ditches** of the taro patch flats called Kānewai?]

awa harbor, channel through reef, port. [*ke* **awa** *lau o Pu'uloa*, the many-channeled **harbor** of Pu'uloa (Pearl Harbor)]

'awa plant whose root is chewed or mashed into a narcotic drink important in ceremonies and used throughout Polynesia. Since it numbs the mouth, *'awa* is used as a medicine for toothache.

'awa'awa 1. bitter, sour taste (*fig.* unpleasant, harsh or disagreeable). [*I mua e o'u mau pōki'i a inu i ka wai **'awa'awa**, 'a'ohe hope e ho'i ai.* Go forward my younger brothers and drink the **bitter** waters (of battle), there is no way to retreat. (Kamehameha's words to his warriors at the battle of 'Iao on Maui)] 2. bitterness, sourness (*fig.* anguish, tragedy).

awakea noon time, midday. (*aloha awakea* = noon greetings, said generally between 10 a.m. and 2 p.m.)

awakea

'awapuhi wild ginger, a "pest plant" that takes over and destroys native plant habitats; also, its sweetly scented flower much prized for leis. [*ku'u lei **'awapuhi** melemele,* my yellow **ginger** *lei*]

'awapuhi

awāwa valley. [*Uluwehi ke **awāwa** 'o Moanalua.* Moanalua **Valley** is lush with greenery.]

'awe'awe 1. tentacles of octopus. [*'Ewalu **'awe'awe** o ka he'e.* The octopus has eight **tentacles**.] 2. runners of vine.

'awelika (from English) average. [*'Ehia kālā ka **'awelika** o kāna uku kaulele?* How much money is the **average** of his overtime pay?]

'āweoweo a red fish with big eyes. (*alauwā* = young *'āweoweo*)

'āwīwī 1. quick, fast. 2. quickly. [*Holo **'āwīwī** ke kūkini o ke au kahiko.* The king's runners of the ancient days ran **quickly**.] (syn. *wikiwiki*)

e 1. particle used to address someone/something, usually not translated into English. [*E Hawai'i, e ku'u one hānau ē,* **(oh)** Hawai'i, my birth sands (song, "Hawai'i Aloha," by L. Lyons)] 2. particle used in front of infinitive form of a verb [*Komo 'o Mike Hawai'i i Gold's Gym* **e** *ho'oikaika kino i kēlā lā kēia lā.* Miss Hawai'i enters Gold's Gym **to** exercise every day.] 3. particle used in passive sentence to indicate who performed the action. [*Ua huki 'ia ko ke keiki kolohe pepeiao* **e** *kona 'anakē.* The naughty child's ear was pulled **by** her Aunty.] 4. particle; first word of a command, directly before a verb, usually not translated into English. [*E honi aku iā Tūtū, e ka pēpē.* Kiss grandpa/grandma, baby.]

ē 1. particle used at the end of a formal address, usually not translated into English. [*E ke ali'i hanohano ē,* **o** distinguished chief] 2. particle used to add emphasis as in the exclamation *auē nō ho'i ē!* (oh, for goodness sake!).

'ē 1. strange, foreign. [*nā 'āina* **'ē**, **foreign** lands] 2. before, previously. [*Ua lohe* **'ē** *mākou i ka nūhou.* We (us all, not you) have **already** heard the news.] 3. yes (informal speech). [*Auē! Lepo kēia limu, 'eā?* **'ē 'ē 'ē**. Gosh! This seaweed is dirty, right? **Yah, yah, yah**.]

ea 1. sovereignty, rule. [*Imi nā kānaka maoli i ke* **ea**. The native people of Hawai'i seek **sovereignty**.] 2. life force, breath, gas, vapors. [*Ua mau ke* **ea** *o ka 'āina i ka pono.* State motto, usually translated "The **life** of the land is perpetuated in righteousness" (however, other interpretations are possible).] 3. plastic. [*Nui nā 'eke* **ea** *ma KTA.* KTA has lots of **plastic** bags.]

'ea 1. hawksbill turtle, one type of sea turtle found in Hawai'i, formerly prized for its shell. 2. general term for infections, infectious diseases. [*He ma'i* **'ea** *ke anu.* A cold is an **infectious disease**.] 3. melody of song. [*Nani ke* **'ea** *o "Makalapua."* The **melody** of "Makalapua" is pretty.] 4. isn't that so?/right? added to the end of a sentence. [*Momona kēia kokoleka,* **'ea**? This chocolate is sweet-tasting, **isn't that so?**] 5. spray.

'eā 1. song refrain, "tra la la." [*Nani wale nā hala* **'eā 'eā** *o Naue i ke kai* **'eā 'eā**. So beautiful are the *hala* **tra la la** of Naue by the sea **tra la la**. (song, "Nā Hala o Naue," by J. Kahinu)]

e'e to board plane, boat; to climb, mount. (*hikie'e* = low sofa [*lit.* can climb on]) (*kai e'e* = tidal wave)

'e'ehia 1. awe, reverence, fear. 2. awe-inspiring, solemn, overcome with terror or reverence. [**'E'ehia** *ka hū 'ana o ka pele ma ka pō.* The spouting of lava in the dark is **awe-inspiring**.]

'e'epa 1. extraordinary, peculiar, abnormal. 2. a name for legendary people with unusual powers, such as Nā Mū.

'eha 1. pain, hurt. [*He* **'eha** *koni ko ko'u iwi 'ao'ao pohole.* My bruised rib has a throbbing **pain**.] 2. sore, painful. [**'Eha** *kou wāwae moku, 'eā?* Your cut foot is **sore**, yah?]

'ehā four, a sacred number. In ancient Hawai'i, the counting system was based on 4's. Terms used today to indicate great

numbers are derived from this traditional way of counting: *kāuna* = four; *ka'au* = forty; *lau* = four hundred; *mano* = four thousand; *kini* = forty thousand, many; *lehu* = four hundred thousand, very many.

'ēheu wing. [*Ma lalo kou 'ēheu ko mākou maluhia a mau loa aku nō.* Beneath your **wings** be our peace forever more. ("Queen's Prayer," by Lili'uokalani)]

'ehia 1. question word asking "how many?" [**'Ehia** *kenikeni a nā mo'opuna e ho'olilo ai ma ke kāniwala?* **How many** dimes (change) do the grandchildren have to spend at the carnival?]

ehu 1. dust. [*Nui ka* **ehu** *ma Kaho'olawe.* There's lots of **dust** on Kaho'olawe.] 2. spray. 3. pollen.

'ehu 1. dust. 2. spray. 3. pollen. 4. dark red hair seen in some Hawaiians; also any color hair other than black; note: only *'ehu* (not *ehu*) is used for this meaning.

eia (idiom) here is (person, thing). [**Eia** *kāu mau makana.* **Here are** your prizes (presents).] [**Eia** *ka pane a ke aloha.* **Here is** love's answer. (song, "E Wai'anae," by R. Ngum)] (here, in this place = *'ane'i*) (ant. *aia*, there is, there in that place) (*Eia nei* = "dearie," used to politely address someone whose name you don't know) (*Eia a'e...* = Here comes...) (*eia hou* = furthermore)

'eiwa nine. (syn. *iwa*) (*kanaiwakūmāiwa* = 99 [ten times 9 plus 9])

'eka (from English) acre. [**'Ehia** *mau* **'eka** *ma kēia kīhāpai?* How many **acres** are there in this field?]

'eke bag. [*Piha kēia mau* **'eke** *i ka 'ōpala i kiloi 'ia aku mai nā ka'a aku i ke kapa alanui.* These **bags** are full of garbage that was thrown out of cars onto the sides of the streets.]

'eke kālā wallet, purse.
'eke kua backpack.
'ekolu three. [**'Ekolu** *a lāua hānaiāhuhu.* They (two) have **three** pets.]
'eku to root, as a pig.

'eke kālā

'ele'ele 1. black color. 2. dark.

'elele delegate, messenger. [*He* **'elele** *'o Kūhiō i ka 'Aha'ōlelo lāhui.* Kūhiō was a **delegate** to Congress.]

'elelū cockroach. [*He mū lepo ka* **'elelū**. *The* **cockroach** is a dirty bug.]

'elemakule (plural: *'elemākule*) old man.

'ēlemu rear end, buttocks.

'elepaio native bird (*fig.* gossip).

'elepani (from English) elephant.

'eleu lively, nimble, energetic, alert. [**'Eleu** *maoli nō kā Mililani 'īlio pēpē.* Mililani's puppy is really **lively**.]

'elepaio

'eleweka (from English) elevator.

'eli to dig. [*Ke* **'eli** *nei ka mahi'ai i ka māla 'ai.* The farmer is **digging** in the vegetable garden.]

'elima five.

'elua two.

emi 1. inexpensive, cheap. 2. to lessen, reduce. [**Emi** *nā lau 'ai ma ka mākeke mahi'ai.* Vegetables are **inexpensive** at the farmer's market.] (*kū'ai emi* = sale) (*ho'ēmi kino* = diet, to diet)

'emo delay, wait.

'emo 'ole suddenly, instantly, without delay. [**'Emo 'ole**, *ua kani ke kelepona.* **Suddenly**, the telephone rang.]

'ena'ena red hot, glowing.

'enuhe caterpillar, an *'aumakua* for some Hawaiians.

eo 1. to be defeated by something/someone. This meaning requires *i/iā* + victor following subject, signifying by whom one will be defeated. [*E* **eo** *ana 'o Kāna Lui* **iā** *'Iolani i ka pōpeku.* St. Louis will be **defeated by** 'Iolani in the football game.] 2. to win. [*Ua* **eo** *kā lāua kimi.* Their (two) team won.] (*Lanakila* is most often used for "victory, to win.")

eō 1. to answer, to call. 2. response when name is called, "present." "I'm here." [*E Pāpā?* **Eō**. *Daddy? Yes,* **I'm here**.]

'eono six. (syn *ono*) (*kanakolukūmāono* = 36 [10 x 3 plus 6])

'epane (from English) apron, coverall.

'eu naughty, playful, mischievous.

'eu'eu exciting, rousing, animating. (*hō'eu'eu* = to incite, encourage)

'ewa 1. crooked, out of shape. 2. a traditional direction used instead of "west" on O'ahu as one of four directions: *ma uka* (toward mountains), *ma kai* (toward sea), *'ewa* (west), Diamond Head (east); based on the name of a town on O'ahu).

'ewalu eight. (*nā kai 'ewalu* = the eight seas [for the eight channels between the eight main islands, thus a poetic reference to all Hawai'i])

ēwe 1. birthplace, rootlet, those related by lineage. 2. afterbirth. [*Ma lalo o ke kumu niu e kau ai mākou i ke **ēwe**.* Under the coconut tree is where we should place the **afterbirth**. (The traditional custom of placing a newborn's afterbirth in a sacred place is still followed in some families.)]

hā 1. breath, life force, spiritual power (exchange of breath and *hā* is traditional greeting called *honi*). 2. four (syn. *ʻehā*). 3. stalk of plant.

haʻahaʻa 1. humility, minimum. 2. low, humble, unpretentious. [*ʻO au me ka **haʻahaʻa**. **Humbly** yours. (a common salutation in letters)] (*ke kula haʻahaʻa* = elementary school)

haʻaheo 1. pride, vanity. [*E mau ana ka **haʻaheo**. The **pride** will endure. (song, "E Mau Ana Ka Haʻaheo," by H. Apoliona)] 2. haughty, proud. [***Haʻaheo** māua ʻo Pāpā i kā ʻoukou mau māka maikaʻi. Dad and I are **proud** of your (three or more) good grades.]

haʻalele to leave, resign, abandon.

haʻalulu 1. to shake, quiver, tremble. 2. nervous, shaky. [***Haʻalulu** ka ʻōlapa ma mua o ka hōʻike hula. The dancer is **nervous** before the hula show.]

haʻanui to boast (syn. *kaena*).

hāʻawe 1. burden, backpack. 2. to carry a burden on the back. [*Mai **hāʻawe** i kēnā ʻauamo, e ka hoa!* Don't **carry** that burden, friend! (Don't take on that responsibility.)]

hāʻawi to give, grant, offer. [*E **hāʻawi** kāua i kāna makana iā ia.* Let's you and me **give** him his present.] (*hāʻawi pio* = give up) [*Mai **hāʻawi** pio!* Don't **give up**!] (*hāʻawi wale/hāʻawi lokomaikaʻi* = to give freely)

haʻawina lesson, assignment, monetary award or allotment, contribution, dream (many meanings). [*He mau **haʻawina** kāu ma kāu mau papa like ʻole?* Do you have **assignments** in all your different classes?]

hae 1. flag. (*Kuʻu hae aloha* = my beloved flag [Hawaiian flag quilts sewn in protest against the overthrow of the monarchy often had this motto]) 2. to bark, growl (dog), chirp noisily (mynah bird). 3. to tear (related to *hahae*, to tear). 4. wild, fierce, savage, furious.

hae

haehae to tear to bits.

haele to go, come; used instead of *hele* in poetic language, especially in reference to large numbers of people going or coming.

hāʻena red hot, burning red. (syn. *ʻena, ʻenaʻena* [*fig.* anger, rage]) [*ʻEnaʻena ʻo **Hāʻena** i ka ʻehukai.* (*ʻōlelo noʻeau*) **Hāʻena** is red hot due to the sea spray. (a play on words celebrating the place named Hāʻena; also connotes danger)]

hāhā 1. *kahuna hāhā*, a type of medical practitioner who diagnosed illness by feeling the body. 2. to grope, feel with the hands. [***Hāhā** ka makapō i ke pihi ʻeleweka. The blind person **feels** the elevator button.]

hahae to tear, strip, as *hala* leaves.

hahai to follow, pursue, chase. [*Huli a **hahai** mai iaʻu.* Turn and **follow** me. (hymn, "Kanaka Waiwai," by J. Almeida)]

hai to sacrifice. (*mōhai* = sacrificial offering; *hai kanaka* = human sacrifice)

haʻi 1. to break. 2. to say, tell. [***Haʻi** ʻo Ke Aolama i ka nūhou. Ke Aolama (Hawaiian language news program on radio) **tells** the news.] (*ho'oha'i* = confess, confession)

hāiki restriction, limitation. 2. narrow, pinched. [**Hāiki** *kēia lumi.* This room is **narrow**.] [*He mana'o* **hāiki** *ko ka po'e na'aupō.* Ignorant people are **narrow-minded**.]

haili 1. fond memory. (*haili aloha* = beloved memory) 2. spirit, ghost. (*haili moe* = premonition) [*Kōkua ka* **haili moe** *i ka ho'okele.* **Premonitions** help a navigator.]

ha'ilima distance from elbow to end of finger (*lit.* break arm).

hailona divination.

ha'ina 1. statement, answer, solution. 2. song refrain.

hainakā (from English) handkerchief. (*hainakā pepa* = facial tissue)

hāinu to give drink.

ha'i 'ōlelo 1. speech, sermon. 2. speaker. 3. to preach.

haipule 1. church service. [*Aia kekahi hana* **haipule** *ma Mauna 'Ala no ka ho'omaka 'ana i ka mahina 'ōlelo Hawai'i.* There's a **church service** at Mauna 'Ala for the beginning of Hawaiian Language month.] 2. to worship (pre-missionary: *ho'omana*). 3. religious, devout, pious.

haka 1. platform, shelf, perch. 2. hole, open space. 3. medium, psychic. 4. (from English) heart shape. (*pua haka* = anthurium flower)

haka

hakahaka 1. empty space, vacancy. (*pani hakahaka* = substitute) 2. vacant. (*e ho'opihapiha i nā hakahaka* = fill in the blanks)

hakakā 1. fight, quarrel. 2. to fight, quarrel. [*'Oiai kā kākou mau kāne e* **hakakā** *nei, e kāko'o kākou wāhine kekahi i kekahi.* Although our husbands are **fighting** now, let's us women support each other.]

hakakau shelf. [*'Ehia* **hakakau** *o ka waihona lole kahiko?* How many **shelves** does the old closet have?]

hakakē crowded, entangled, overlapping. [**Hakakē** *nā lālā o ke kumuhau.* The branches of the *hau* tree are **overlapping**.]

hakanū silent, sullen, struck dumb. [**Hakanū** *ke anaina i kā Kaipo oli.* The audience was **struck dumb** by Kaipo's chant.]

hākeakea pale, whitish.

haki 1. to break (syn. *ha'i*). [*Ua* **haki** *'ia ko ka wa'a pe'a kia e ka makani e hao mai ana.* The sailing canoe's mast was **broken** by the wind that was blasting.] 2. broken, cut off. (*haki wale* = fragile, easily broken) (*hakina* = fraction)

hākilo to stare at, observe closely.

hakina fraction.

hākōkō 1. wrestling. 2. wrestler. [*Kaulana 'o Akebono i ka* **hākōkō** *Kepanī i kapa 'ia 'o sumo.* Akebono is famous in Japanese **wrestling**, which is called "sumo."]

haku 1. boss, overseer, lord. (*haku 'āina, haku hale* = landlord) 2. to create, compose music or literature. [*Na Lili'uokalani i* **haku** *iā "Aloha 'oe."* It was Lili'uokalani who **composed** "Aloha 'oe."] (*haku mele* = poet, composer) (*haku puke* = author) 3. to braid, arrange. (*lei haku* = type of *lei* in which several types of plant material are braided together)

hala 1. sin, fault. 2. pandanus tree, whose leaves are woven into hats, bags, etc., known as *lauhala* (leaf of the *hala*). 3. to sin. 4. to pass by, to pass away (euphemism for *make*). [*Ua* **hala** *ē ka Pu'ulena.* (*'ōlelo no'eau*) It's too late (*lit.* the Pu'ulena wind has already **passed by**).] 5. passed away, dead. [*'Ane'ane e* **hala** *kā kona hoanoho hānaiāhuhu.* His neighbor's pet is almost **dead**.]

hala

hāla'i calm, peaceful.

hala kahiki pineapple (*lit.* foreign *hala*, because the fruit of the *hala* resembles pineapple).

hālau 1. meeting house. 2. hula school or troupe. Note: In ancient Hawai'i, *hālau* were open-sided sheds used to store canoes and as a workplace for canoe carving. They evidently became gathering places where hula and other group activities took place. 3. large, numerous.

hālāwai 1. meeting. 2. horizon. (syn. *kūkulu, ʻalihilani*) [*mai ka hoʻokuʻi a ka* **hālāwai**, from the zenith to the **horizon** (line from an *ʻaumakua* chant recorded by David Malo)]

hale any building, house (see types listed below). (*hale ʻaina* = restaurant; *hale aliʻi* = palace; Hale Aliʻi ʻo ʻIolani = ʻIolani Palace; *hale hōʻikeʻike* = museum; *hale hoʻokolokolo* = courthouse; *hale ipu kukui* = lighthouse; *hale ka ʻa* = garage; *hale keaka* = theater; *hale kiʻi ʻoniʻoni* = movie theater; *hale kilo lani, hale kilo hōkū* = astronomical observatory; *hale kinai ahi* = fire station; *hale kū ʻai* = store; *hale kula* = school house; *hale māka ʻi* = police station; *hale pa ʻahao* = jail, prison; *hale pe ʻa* = tent; *hale o Papa* = women's *heiau*; *hale pule* = church; *hale waihona puke* = library)

hale aliʻi

halelū psalm (Bible).

hāleu toilet paper. (syn. *pepa hāleu, hēleu*)

hali ʻa 1. fond remembrance, especially of loved one. [*he* **haliʻa**, *he hāʻupu e hali ʻia mai*, a **remembrance**, a memory that is borne this way (song, "Pūpū o Niʻihau," by M. Kanahele)] 2. to recollect, to recall.

halihali to transport. (*ka ʻa halihali ʻōpala* = garbage truck) (*mea halihali ʻōpala* = garbage men)

hāli ʻi 1. a covering, spread. 2. to spread out as tablecloth or blanket.

hālike alike, similar. (*hoʻohālike* = to compare) [*Mai* **hoʻohālike** *mai ʻoe ia ʻu me kāu ipo mua*. Don't **compare** me with your former sweetheart.]

Hāloa 1. name of first taro, older brother of first human with same name. [*Na* **Hāloa** *mākou Hawaiʻi*. We Hawaiians come from

Hāloa. (Since Hāloa was the name of the first taro as well as the first man, taro is considered to be the respected elder sibling to humans.)] 2. far-reaching, long.

hāmale (from English) 1. hammer. 2. to hammer.

hāmama opened. (*hāmama ka puka* = the door is opened) (*ka pu ʻuwai hāmama* = open-hearted, kind and loving)

hāmau 1. silence. 2. silent. [*E* **hāmau**! Be **silent**! (harsher command than *kulikuli* or *pa ʻa ka waha*)]

hamohamo to rub, pat, pet. [**Hamohamo** *ʻo Manu i kāna lāpaki*. Manu **pets** her rabbit.] (*ʻaila hamohamo* = massage oil)

hana 1. work, job, activity. 2. bay (syn. *hono*) 3. to work, do an activity, make something. [*He aha kāu* **hana**? What are you **doing**?] (*hana hoʻohanohano* = ceremony, ritual; *hana hoʻohauʻoli* = hobby; *hana hoʻohiwahiwa* = celebration to honor someone; *hana hou* = do it again, say it again; *hana ʻino* = to abuse, injure, cruel, wicked; *hana keaka* = skit, theatrical play; *hana lepo* = dirty work, excrement, to excrete [euphemism for *kūkae*]; *hana lima* = hand made, manual; *hana mana* = miracle, supernatural; *hana noʻeau* = art, crafts; *ka hana a ke aloha* = lovemaking; *limahana* = laborer; *pau hana* = work is finished [happy hour])

hana

hānai 1. foster child. 2. to raise, rear, feed. [*Na wai kā i* **hānai** *iā ia*? Who **raised** her for heaven's sake?] 3. adopted. (*hānaiāhuhu* = pet, to care for as a pet)

hanakuli 1. noise. [*Nui ka* **hanakuli** *ma ka ʻaha mele*. There's lots of **noise** at the concert.] 2. noisy.

hanana incident, occurrence. [*Ma ka* **hanana** *ʻelua, ua piholo ka wa ʻa*. On the second **occurrence**, the canoe swamped.]

hānau to give birth. (*lā hānau* = birthday) [*ʻO ka lā hea kona* **lā hānau**? *ʻO ka lā iwakāluakūmālua o ʻAukake kona* **lā**

hānau. Which day is her **birthday**? The 22nd of August is her **birthday**.] (*Hauʻoli Lā Hānau* = Happy Birthday)

hānau ʻia to be born. [*Ua **hānau ʻia** ko koʻu hoaaloha kupuna kāne ma Niʻihau*. My friend's grandfather was **born** on Niʻihau.]

hanauna generation. [*ʻO ka **hanauna** i koho e hoʻōla hou i kā kākou ʻōlelo makuahine, ʻo koʻu **hanauna** ia*. The **generation** that chose to revive our mother tongue, that's my **generation**.]

hanawai 1. to irrigate. 2. to menstruate.

hāneʻe to collapse, slide, cave in. [*Ua **hāneʻe** ka uapo i ke ōlaʻi*. The bridge **collapsed** in the earthquake.]

hanini to spill, overflow. [***Hanini** ka waiū i kāu kīʻaha, e ke kaikamahine*. The milk in your glass **spilled**, girl.]

hānō asthma.

hanohano 1. dignity. 2. honored, noble, glorious. (*hoʻohanohano* = to honor)

hanu breath, to breathe, smell, inhale. (*hanu pilo* = bad breath) (*hanu i loko* = inhale) (*hanu i waho* = exhale)

hānupa 1. choppy sea. 2. surging, swollen.

hao 1. iron, general term for metal. 2. to blast, strike with force as wind or rain. [***Hao** mai ka makani*. The wind is **blowing fiercely**.]

haʻo to long for, miss. [***Haʻo** kā Kauʻinohea ipo iā ia*. Kauʻinohea's sweetheart **misses** her.] [***Haʻo** au iā ʻoe*. I **miss** you.]

haole Caucasian, previously used to denote non-Hawaiians of any race.

hapa 1. part, portion. 2. of mixed blood. [*He **hapa** Hawaiʻi kā lāua moʻopuna*. Their (two) grandchild is **part** Hawaiian.] (*hapahā* = one fourth) [*He **hapahā** koko Pākē kou*? Are you a **quarter** Chinese?] (*hapakolu* = one third) (*hapalua* = one half) [*ʻO ka **hapalua** hola ʻehiku kēia*. It's **half** past seven.] (*hapa loa* = small portion)

hāpai 1. to carry, lift, raise. [***Hāpai** hao ʻo Keanu*. Keanu **lifts** weights.] 2. pregnant.

hapaiki minority. [*ʻAʻohe koko Hawaiʻi o ka hapanui o ko Hawaiʻi poʻe. He **hapaiki** wale nō nā ʻōiwi*. The majority of Hawaiʻi's people don't have Hawaiian blood. The native people are a **minority**.]

hapanui majority.

hāpapa 1. to extend out, grope, experience, feel. 2. reef, coral flat, rock stratum. [*ma ʻō aku o ka **hāpapa**, beyond the **reef**] (syn. *laupapa, papapa*)

hāpuʻu native fern tree.

hau 1. tree with lightweight wood used for canoe *ama*, bark for cordage, sap and flowers for medicine. 2. ice. 3. dew (syn. *kēhau*). (*hau kea* = snow) (*haukalima* = ice cream)

hau

haukapila (from English) hospital. (syn. *hale maʻi*)

hāʻukeʻuke purple sea urchin, considered a delicacy, also used for medicine.

haukohi shave ice.

haukohi

haulani 1. to plunge, as a canoe; to surge, as the sea. 2. restless, constantly moving.

hāʻule 1. loss, failure, defeat. 2. to fall, drop, to lose, fail, to die. [*Ke **hāʻule** kekahi mānaleo, hāʻule pū kekahi ʻike Hawaiʻi*. Whenever a native speaker **passes away**, some Hawaiian knowledge is lost.] (*kau hāʻule lau* = fall semester)

haumāna student.

haumia 1. uncleanliness, filth. 2. obscene. (*hoʻohaumia* = to pollute) [*Mai **hoʻohaumia** i ke kai!* Don't **pollute** the sea!]

hauna 1. foul smelling, stinky. 2. bad odor, especially rotting fish. (*hohono* = body odor; stinky smell) [***Hauna** ka ʻōpala, akā **hohono** ko ka pēpē kaiapa*. The garbage **smells rotten**, but the baby's diaper **smells stinky**.]

haunaele riot, brawl.

hauʻoli 1. happiness, joy. 2. happy, glad, joyful. (*Hauʻoli Lā Hoʻomanaʻo* = Happy Anniversary)

haupia coconut pudding.

hāʻupu to remember, recollect, recall. [*He* ***hāʻupu****, he manaʻo koʻu iā ʻoe.* I **remember** you. (song, "Pūpū o Niʻihau," by M. Kanahele)

Hawaiʻi 1. name of island chain and largest island in archipelago (from *"Hawa iki,"* little Hawa; Hawa iki is a legendary homeland of Polynesians; its exact location is unknown). 2. Hawaiian. [*ʻAʻole ka pīkake he pua* ***Hawaiʻi*** *maoli.* The *pīkake* isn't a native **Hawaiian** flower.]

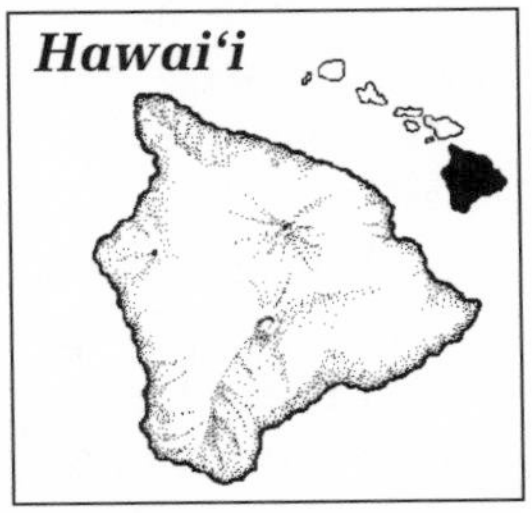
Hawaiʻi

hāwanawana 1. to whisper. 2. whispering. [*ke kai* ***hāwanawana****,* the **whispering** sea]

hāwāwā unskilled, awkward, clumsy. (syn. *hemahema*). [***Hāwāwā*** *ka hoʻopaʻa ʻana ke hoʻomaka ʻoe.* Beating time for dancers is **clumsy** when you begin.]

hāweo glowing.

he a, an. [***He*** *manu laha ʻole ka ʻio.* The Hawaiian hawk is **a** rare bird.] To pluralize, add *mau* after *he.* [***He mau*** *manakō Hayden kēnā mau huaʻai.* Those fruits (by you) are Hayden mango**es**.]

hē grave. [*Ma ka pā ilina Pākē ma Mānoa i ʻeli ʻia ko Gongon* ***hē****.* Grandpa's **grave** was dug in the Chinese cemetery in Mānoa.]

hea 1. to call, to name. [***Hea*** *aku mākou, eō mai ʻoe.* We **call out**, answer us. (a common line in last verse of name chants, requesting a response from the person/god honored)] 2. which. [*Ma ka ʻaoʻao* ***hea*** *ʻoe i heluhelu ai i ke kaʻao?* **Which** page did you read the story on?] 3. where. [*Aia i* ***hea*** *ko ko ʻoukou makua kāne keʻena?* **Where** is your (three or more) father's office?]

heahea 1. a type of welcoming chant. 2. to call out frequently and hospitably, to welcome.

heʻe 1. octopus. 2. to slide, slip, surf, flee, drip. (*ʻauheʻe* = to flee in battle)

heʻe nalu 1. surfing. 2. to surf. (*heʻe nalu makani* = wind surfing)

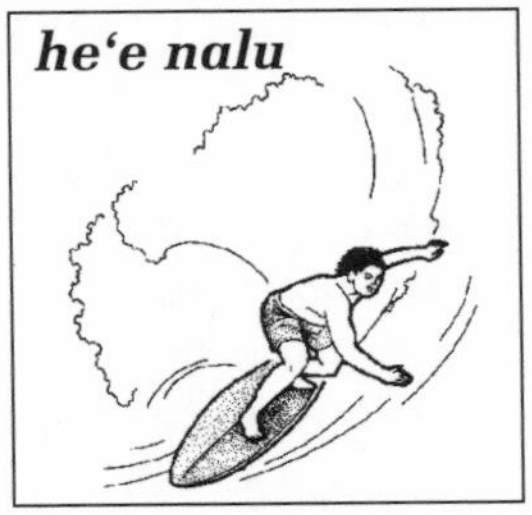
heʻe nalu

heʻe wale 1. miscarriage. 2. to miscarry.

heha lazy, indolent. [***Heha*** *Waipiʻo i ka noe.* Waipiʻo is **laid back** in the mist. (song, "Heha Waipiʻo," by S. Liʻa)]

heheʻe 1. landslide. (syn. *hiolo*) 2. to melt, dissolve, liquefy.

hehena insane, possessed, raving mad. [*He kanaka* ***hehena*** *ke kāpena?* Is the captain a **possessed** person?]

hehi 1. to step on, stamp, trample. [*Hoʻomanaʻo ʻoukou i ka inoa o ke kanaka mua loa i* ***hehi*** *i ka papa mahina?* Do you all remember the name of the first person who **stepped** on the surface of the moon?] (syn. *keʻehi*) (*hehi wāwae* = to pedal) 2. to break a *kapu*.

hei 1. net, snare, stratagem, ruse. 2. string figures. 3. to make string figures. [***Hei*** *ʻo Tui i kēlā lā kēia lā.* Tui **makes string figures** each and every day.]

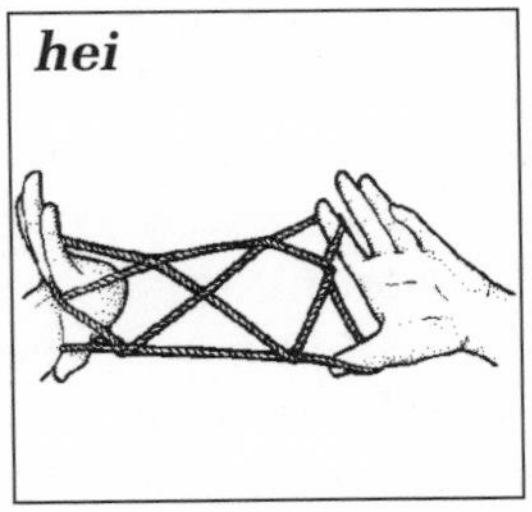
hei

hēʻī papaya.

heiau sacred site of traditional Hawaiian religion, with different types, many of which still exist on each island.

heihei 1. competitive race, such as canoe, foot, horse race. [*Na wai i lanakila i ka* ***heihei*** *holo wāwae?* Who won the foot **race**?] 2. to race. (*hoʻoheihei* = to entrap, to enchant, to mend net)

hekau anchor.

heke best, greatest. [*Molokaʻi nō ka* ***heke****.* (*ʻōlelo noʻeau*) Molokaʻi indeed is the **greatest**.] (*ipu heke* = hula implement made up of two gourds joined together; *heke* is the top gourd)

hekili thunder (*fig.* passion, rage). [*ʻŌlapa ka uila, kuʻi ka hekili.* Lightning flashes, thunder booms. (familiar line in chants)]

hele to come (*hele mai*), to go (*hele aku*), to move. (*hele wāwae* = to walk) (*hoʻohele i ka ʻilio* = to walk the dog) (*hele loa* = to go with no hope of return) (*hele wale* = to go without purpose)

helehelena features, face. [*Lahilahi kona* **helehelena**. Her **features** are smooth and delicate.]

heleleʻi 1. to fall (rain, teeth, hair, tears). [*Ke* **heleleʻi** *nei ka ua ma uka?* Is rain **falling** now up in the mountains?] 2. falling rain, tears, etc. (*hoʻoheleleʻi* = to scatter, sow)

helikopa (from English) helicopter. [*Nui ko ka* **helikopa** *hanakuli ma ka wao nahele.* There's lots of **helicopter** noise in the wilderness.]

helu 1. number. 2. to count, compute. (*helu ʻai* = score, point [games], to keep score). [*He aha ka* **helu ʻai** *i kēia manawa?* What's the **score** now?] (*heluna* = sum, total amount) [*ʻEhia kālā ka* **heluna**? How much money is the **total amount**?]

heluhelu to read.

hema left, south. [*E huli* **hema** *ma ka huina alanui.* Turn **left** at the intersection.] [*Ulu ke kope ma Kona* **Hema**. Coffee grows in **South** Kona.]

hemahema awkward, clumsy, unskilled. [**Hemahema** *ka lele ʻana o ka naiʻa pēpē.* The baby dolphin's leaping is **awkward**.]

hemo loose, unfastened. [*E heleleʻi ana paha ko kā ʻIwalani kaikamahine niho* **hemo** *i kēia pō.* ʻIwalani's daughter's **loose** tooth may fall out tonight.]

hemolele 1. perfection, virtue, goodness. 2. perfect, holy, pristine. [*Kauaʻi* **hemolele** *i ka mālie* (*ʻōlelo noʻeau*), Kauaʻi **pristine** in calmness]

henehene 1. to laugh at, ridicule. (*hoʻohenehene* = to tease, laugh at) 2. teasing, giggling, mocking. [**Henehene** *kou ʻaka, kou leʻaleʻa paha.* Your laugh is **teasing**, you're having fun. (song, "He Mea Maʻa Mau Ia," by J. Almeida)]

henoheno lovable.

hewa 1. mistake, fault, sin, guilt. 2. wrong, sinful, guilty. [*Pololei a i ʻole* **hewa** *kāna i pane ai?* Is what he answered right or **wrong**?] (*hoʻohewa* = to complain, find fault)

hī 1. diarrhea. 2. hiss, flow.

hia delight, desire.

hiaʻā 1. insomnia, insomniac. [**Hiaʻā** *nā ʻelemākule.* The old men are **insomniacs**.] 2. sleepless.

hiaʻai pleased with, delighted. [**Hiaʻai** *nā ʻōpio i ko lākou launa ʻana me nā keiki ma ka Pūnana Leo.* Young people are **delighted** when they get together with the children at Pūnana Leo (Hawaiian Immersion preschools).]

hialoa well trained, skilled.

hiamoe sleep. (*hiamoe iki* = nap) (*hoʻohiamoe* = to put to sleep) [*Ma mua o ko ka mākua* **hoʻohiamoe** *ʻana i kāna pēpē, heluhelu lāua i ka puke.* Before the parent **puts** his baby **to sleep**, they (two) read books.]

hiapo first-born child.

hiehie attractive, distinguished. [*kūlana* **hiehie** *ma ka hanohano*, **attractive** and honored position (song, "Nā Pua Lei ʻIlima," by K. Zuttermeister)]

hihi to spread, entangle, intertwine. (*hoʻohihi* = to be enchanted by someone, "smitten") (*lāʻauhihi* = vine)

hihia 1. entanglement, difficulty. [*Loaʻa ka* **hihia** *me ka hukihuki ma waena o Laʻakea a me kēlā kaikuaʻana ona.* There is **difficulty** and disagreement between Laʻakea and that older brother of his.] 2. entangled in problems.

hīhīmanu stingray.

hiʻi to carry in the arms, as a child.

hiʻipoi to tend, feed, cherish. [*E* **hiʻipoi** *i ka poʻohala.* **Cherish** the family traditions.]

hīhīmanu

hiki 1. can, to be able to. [**Hiki** *iā ia ke ʻōlelo Hawaiʻi?* **Can** he speak Hawaiian?] 2. to reach a destination. [*E* **hiki** *ana anei ka waʻa peʻa i Nāwiliwili ma mua o ka nāpoʻo ʻana o ka lā?* Will the sailing canoe **reach** Nāwiliwili before sunset?] (*hiki nō* = okay, can) (*hiki wale* = easy) (*a hiki i* = until, to, toward) [*E holo* *wāwae ana kāua mai Kalāheo **a hiki i** Keālia.* We (you and I) are going to run from Kalāheo **to** Keālia.]

hikie'e a large, low couch (*lit.* can climb up on).

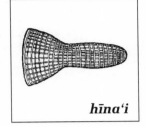
hikie'e

hikina east. [*mai ka **hikina** a i ke komohana,* from **East** to West]

hiki 'ole impossible.

hikiwawe quickly, early, promptly. [*Ua hō'ea **hikiwawe** nā 'ōhua i ke kahua mokulele.* The passengers arrived **early** at the airport.]

hilahila shy, ashamed, embarrassed.

hili to braid, plait, string, whip, hit with a stick. [*Ke ho'omaka nei kēlā kāne ala e **hili** i ko kona lio huelo.* That man over there is starting to **braid** his horse's tail.] [*E **hili** 'olua i ka 'elelū!* (You two) **hit** the cockroach **with a stick!**]

hilina'i to trust, believe, rely on, lean on. [***Hilina'i** au iā 'oe.* I **trust** you.]

hilo 1. first night of Hawaiian moon calendar, new moon. 2. to twist, braid.

hīmeni (from English) 1. hymn, song. 2. to sing. [*Ma kēia Lāpule a'e ana nā hoahānau e **hīmeni** ai i ka **hīmeni** i kapa 'ia 'o Iesu nō ke Kahu hipa.* It's next Sunday that the congregation will **sing** the **hymn** that is called "Iesu Nō ke Kahu hipa."]

hina 1. to fall over, topple. 2. fall over, prostrate.

Hina goddess of the moon, of things feminine, known throughout the Pacific. As wife to Kū, Hina represents forest plants that grow low to the ground (Kū represents those plants that grow upright). Those who gather forest plants traditionally leave offerings for and request permission of Kū and Hina. [*'O **Hina** ka wahine noho mahina.* **Hina** is the woman who lives in the moon.]

hinahina 1. gray color. 2. native beach plant used for leis. 3. silver-

hinahina

sword plant (syn. *'āhinahina*).

hīna'i basket or container used to store food, fish traps (*pōhīna'i* = basketball)

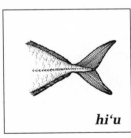
hīna'i

hine splendid, gaudy.

hini delicate, weak.

hinu grease, oil.

hinuhinu bright, shiny. (syn. *'alohi, 'ōlino, hulali*) (*ho'ohinuhinu* = to shine, polish) [*Ke **ho'ohinuhinu** nei ka 'ōlapa i nā pūpū kūpe'e.* The dancer is **polishing** the *kūpe'e* shells.]

hiō 1. to lean, slant. [*Ua **hiō** aku ka mea pā'ani pōpa'ilima a 'ane'ane hina iho.* The volleyball player **leaned** over until he almost toppled over.] 2. leaning, slanting, diagonal.

hi'ohi'ona features of face or landscape. [*Kama'āina 'o Kihalani i nā **hi'ohi'ona** 'āina o Kekaha.* Kihalani is familiar with the **features** of the landscape of Kekaha.]

hipa (from English) sheep. [*Ua hānai **hipa** lākou ma Ni'ihau.* They raised **sheep** on Ni'ihau.] (*kahu hipa* = shepherd)

hīpu'u knot. [*E nāki'i i ka **hīpu'u** i ka lopi.* Tie a **knot** in the thread.]

hi'u tail of fish. (*wahine hi'u i'a* = mermaid) [*Pū ka **hi'u**.* The **tail** sounds (to break wind).]

hiwa black color of prized offerings to gods. [*'O ka pua'a **hiwa** ka mōhai kūpono.* A **black** pig is the appropriate sacrifice.]

hi'u

hiwahiwa precious, beloved, favorite. [*Ke keiki **hiwahiwa** a ke akua.* The precious son of God (Christmas hymn, "Mele Kalikimaka Iā Kākou," composer unknown).]

hoa friend, companion. Note: *ke hoa,* exception to *ke/ka* rule.

ho'ā to turn on electrical appliance, light fire. [*E **ho'ā** mua 'oe i ka lolouila. Auē, ua 'ā* *ka lolouila!* First, **turn on** the computer. Oops, the computer is on!]

hoaaloha friend. [*'O kou* **hoaaloha** *hou kēia? 'Ae, 'o Keonaona ko'u* **hoaaloha** *hou.* Is this your new **friend**? Yes, Keonaona is my new **friend**.] (*hoa hana* = colleague, fellow worker; *hoa hānau* = cousin or member of church congregation; *hoa kula* = schoolmate, classmate; *hoa noho* = roommate, neighbor; *hoa paio* = enemy, combatant)

ho'āhewa to criticize, blame, disapprove. [*Mai* **ho'āhewa** *'oe i kāu mo'opuna wahine. E paka iā ia.* Don't **blame** your granddaughter. Constructively criticize her.] (syn. *'imi hala, ho'ohalahala*)

ho'āhu to save money. [*Inā 'oe e* **ho'āhu** *i kāu kālā, he uku pane'e kāu?* If you could **save money**, would you get interest?]

hō'ai'ē 1. credit, loan, charge account. 2. to borrow, lend.

hō'ailona symbol, sign. [*He mau* **hō'ailona** *ho'okū ka'a ko ke alanui.* The street has some stop **signs**.]

ho'āla to wake someone up. (*uaki ho'āla* = alarm clock)

hō'ala to perfume.

ho'ānu'unu'u to undulate (sway up and down).

ho'ā'o 1. experiment. 2. to try, experiment.

hō'au'au to bathe someone. [*Ke* **hō'au'au** *nei ka makuahine hou i kāna pēpē.* The new mother is **bathing** her baby.]

hoe 1. paddle, oar. 2. to paddle. (*hoe uli* = steering paddle) (*hoe wa'a* = to paddle, paddler)

hō'ea to arrive someplace.

hō'eha to do harm, hurt someone or something.

ho'ēmi to reduce.

hō'eu'eu to stir up, excite, encourage. [*Ke* **hō'eu'eu** *nei ke kāpena moku kolo i nā*

hō'ailona

hoe

mea lu'u kai. The tugboat captain is **encouraging** the divers.]

hōhē 1. coward, cowardice. 2. cowardly.

hohoa round tapa beater.

hohono 1. body odor, bad smell. 2. stinky-smelling (refers to body odors only; other offensive smells are *hauna*).

hohonu deep, profound. [**Hohonu** *ka mana'o o nā mele kahiko.* The meaning of ancient chants is **profound**.] (*ke kai hohonu* = the deep ocean)

hohoa

ho'i 1. chant used as *hālau hula* leaves the stage. 2. to return, go back, to come back (*ho'i mai*). [**Ho'i mai** *ke aloha me nā ali'i.* Love **goes back** with the chiefs. (ancient chant, "Ho'i Ke Aloha i Ni'ihau")]

hoihoi interesting. [**Hoihoi** *nō ka hana ku'i 'ai ke nānā aku.* Pounding poi is a really **interesting**-looking, entertaining activity.]

ho'iho'i to return something to someone. [*Pono māua e* **ho'iho'i** *i kā Tūtū 'umeke.* We two (she/he and I) have to **return** Tūtū's calabash.] (Lā Ho'iho'i Ea = Restoration Day, July 31, a traditional holiday celebrating Admiral Thomas's restoration of Hawaiian sovereignty in 1843)

hō'ike 1. show, demonstration, exam. [*Aia ka* **hō'ike** *hula 'o Kodak ma Kapi'olani Pāka ma kēlā pule kēia pule.* The Kodak hula **show** is at Kapi'olani Park every week.] (*hale hō'ike'ike* = museum) 2. to show, demonstrate, reveal.

hō'ike'ike 1. display, exhibit. 2. circus.

hō'ili'ili to collect, gather. [*'O ka* **hō'ili'ili** *po'oleka kāna hana ho'ohau'oli.* Collecting stamps is his hobby.]

hoka 1. to "lose out." 2. disappointed. [*'A'ole 'oukou i hele i ka 'aha mele 'o Ho'omau?* **Hoka!** You folks didn't go to the Ho'omau concert? You **lost out**.]

hōkele (from English) hotel. [*Kaulana ka* **hōkele** *'ākala 'o ka Royal Hawaiian.* The pink **hotel** the Royal Hawaiian is well known.]

hoki mule.

hōkio 1. small gourd whistle. 2. to whistle.

hoku a night of the full moon in the Hawaiian moon calendar. [*ʻAuhea ʻoe, mahina ʻo* **Hoku***?* Where are you, **Hoku** moon? (song, "Mahina o Hoku," by L. Awa and A. Namakelua)]

hōkū star.

hōkūhele planet (syn. *hōkū ʻaeʻa; hōkū lewa*). [*Hiki iā mākou ke ʻike i ka* **hōkūhele** *ʻo Venuse ma ke ahiahi.* We all (not you) can see the **planet** Venus in the evening.]

hōkū

Hōkūleʻa Arcturus, guiding star for navigators to Hawaiʻi and name of the double-hulled voyaging canoe that began the rediscovery of Hawaiian wayfaring (*lit.* star of gladness/clear star).

hōkūlele shooting star.

Hōkūpaʻa North Star (*lit.* star that doesn't move).

hōkū puhi paka comet.

hola time of day, hour, o'clock. [*ʻO ka* **hola** *ʻehia kēia? ʻO ka* **hola** *ʻeiwa kēia.* What **time** is it? It's nine **o'clock**.]

holo to run, sail, travel, ride, swim. [**Holo** *ke koholā ma ke kai ʻo Pailolo ma ka hoʻoilo.* Humpback whales **swim** in the Pailolo channel in the wet season.]

holoholo to ride around for fun, "cruise."

holoholona animal (*lit.* that which runs).

holoi to wash, erase, clean. [*Mai* **holoi** *i kou maka. E* **holoi** *i kou mau lima!* Don't **wash** your face. **Wash** your hands!] (*kopa holoi lauoho* = shampoo)

holokai to sail.

holo lio to ride a horse.

holomua to make progress, improve, go forward. [*Ke* **holomua** *nei ka lāhui.* The Hawaiian nation is **making progress**.]

holoʻokoʻa 1. entire, whole, all. [*E ʻai ʻia ana ka iʻa manini* **holoʻokoʻa***.* The **entire** *manini* fish will be eaten. 2. entirely.

holopeki to trot, to jog.

holopono to succeed. [**Holopono** *nā kula kaiapuni.* The Hawaiian immersion schools **succeed**.]

holo wāwae to run (*lit.* to travel by foot).

holu 1. to sway (palms), to ripple (water, waves). 2. bumpy (ride).

hōlua ancient royal sport of sledding down grassy slopes, also name of the sled.

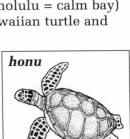
hōlua

hone 1. honey. 2. sweet and soft sounds. [*kou leo* **hone**, your **sweet** voice]

honi 1. traditional greeting in which people touched noses and exchanged breath. 2. to kiss, to smell. [*E* **honi** *kāua wikiwiki.* Let's **kiss** quickly. (song, "E Honi Kāua Wikiwiki," by C. E. King)]

hono bay. (syn. *hana*) (Honolulu = calm bay)

honu general name for Hawaiian turtle and specifically green sea turtle, not the *ʻea*, or tortoiseshell turtle.

honua earth, world. (syn. *ao*) [*Nani kēia* **honua** *holoʻokoʻa.* This entire **earth** is beautiful.]

honu

hoʻo prefix often added to verbs or adjectives to change meaning of root word, adding the thought of making it happen. For example, *kipa* = to visit; *hoʻokipa* = to welcome guests, extend hospitality. *Launa* = friendly, sociable, to socialize; *hoʻolauna* = to introduce people. *Maʻa* = used to, skilled at; *hoʻomaʻamaʻa* = to practice. Note: *Hoʻo* changes to *hō* before an *ʻokina* and a vowel: *ʻeha* (sore, painful) becomes *hōʻeha* (to hurt, harm); however, if there is no *ʻokina* before the vowel, the *kahakō* is added over the vowel: *ala* (to wake up, arise) becomes *hoʻāla* (to wake someone else up). A few words with the prefix *hoʻo* are listed below. To find other words beginning with *hoʻo*, look under the alphabetical entry for the root word, for example, under *maikaʻi* for *hoʻomaikaʻi*.

ho'oha'i 1. confession. 2. to confess. 3. flirt. 4. to cause to break. 4. to bend, sway.

ho'ohalahala to criticize.

ho'ohālike 1. example. 2. to compare.

ho'ohau'oli to have fun.

ho'ohenehene to tease.

ho'oheno 1. to cherish, love. 2. expression of affection. [*He* **ho'oheno** *ke 'ike aku ke kai moana nui lā.* It's an **expression of affection** to be seen, the broad ocean. (song, "Ka Uluwehi O Ke Kai," by E. Kanaka'ole)] 3. affectionate, cherished.

ho'ohiki to promise, to swear an oath. [*Ke* **ho'ohiki** *nei au e mālama i ka honua.* I **promise** to take care of the Earth.]

ho'ōho to exclaim, shout. [**Ho'ōho** *ka lehulehu i ka pā'ani pōhīna'i.* The public **shouts** at basketball games.]

ho'oholo to decide. [*Ke* **ho'oholo** *nei ke kōmike.* The committee is **deciding** now.]

ho'ohui to mix, combine, join, add. [*Mai* **ho'ohui** *i ke kakalina me ka 'aila o pilikia auane'i.* Don't **mix** gasoline and oil or (you'll have) trouble later on.]

ho'ohui 'āina annexation. [*'A'ole i 'ae nā 'ōiwi i ka* **ho'ohui āina**. The native people did not agree to the **annexation**.]

ho'ohuoi to suspect, surmise.

ho'oili 1. inheritance. 2. to land on shore, to load freight, to transfer. 3. to bequeath, leave in will, inherit. 4. to fall upon, as blessing or curse. [*Ua* **ho'oili** *mai kēia 'oihana ko'iko'i.* This important career **fell upon** my shoulders.]

ho'oilina heritage, inheritance, heir. [*He* **ho'oilina** *ko 'oukou, he* **ho'oilina** *ha'aheo.* You all have an **inheritance**, a proud **heritage**. (song, "Ha'aheo," by P. Vaughn)] (*ho'oilina mō'ī* = heir to the throne)

ho'oilo wet season, rainy months, one of two yearly seasons. (*moe kau a ho'oilo* = to have passed away [*lit.* to lie down during the hot and wet seasons])

hō'oio (also **'oio**) 1. to show off. 2. conceited.

ho'okae 'ili racial prejudice.

ho'okahi one of something. (*ho'okahi kālā* = one dollar)

ho'okāhuli aupuni to overthrow the government.

ho'okalakupua magic.

ho'okamani hypocrite.

ho'okano 1. show off. 2. conceited.

ho'okele steersman (*fig.* leader of any enterprise, especially business).

ho'okele

ho'okō to fulfill command, carry out duty. [*Ua* **ho'okō** *ka 'ōhua i ko kona haku mau kauoha.* The servant **carried out** his employer's orders.]

ho'oku'i 1. to hit, pound, collide (*fig.* to hurt feelings). [*Ua* **ho'oku'i** *ke kalaka kinai ahi i ke kalaka halihali 'ōpala.* The fire truck **hit** the garbage truck.] 2. zenith, highest vertical part of sky. [*E nā 'aumākua mai ka* **ho'oku'i** *a ka hālāwai.* Oh the guardian spirits from the **zenith** to the horizon. (line from a chant for *'aumākua* recorded by David Malo)]

ho'okūkū contest, competition. [*He* **ho'okūkū** *oli ko ka* **ho'okūkū** *hula i kapa 'ia 'o Prince Lot?* Does the hula **competition** called Prince Lot Hula Festival have a chanting **contest**?]

ho'okupu offering. [*Nui nā* **ho'okupu** *i waiho 'ia ma ka lua pele 'o Halema'uma'u.* Many **offerings** were left at Halema'uma'u crater (Pele's "home").]

ho'okupu

ho'olā'au 1. to insist, urge persistently. 2. continuously.

ho'olaha to spread abroad, publish, advertise. (*ho'olaha mana'o* = propaganda)

ho'olale to hurry, rush, hasten, incite. [*No ke aha 'oe e* **ho'olale** *mai?* Why are you **rushing** here? (song, "Hōkio," by K. Pukui and M. Lam)]

ho'olulu 1. to be calm. 2. to wait for transportation.

ho'omaha to rest, vacation. (*wā ho'omaha* = vacation) [*I hea ana 'olua e* **ho'omaha** *ai i* ka **wā ho'omaha** Kalikimaka? Where are you (two) going to **vacation** during Christmas **vacation**?]

ho'omaha loa retirement.

ho'omāke'aka 1. to make a joke. 2 funny. (*mea ho'omāke'aka* = joker, clown)

ho'omalimali to flatter. [**Ho'omalimali** *ke kālepa i ke kanaka waiwai.* The merchant **flatters** the rich person.]

ho'onāukiuki to cause irritation, provoke, annoy.

ho'ouna to send. [*Pono 'oe e kū'ai i nā kāleka po'oleka e* **ho'ouna** *aku i kou mau hoaaloha.* You have to buy postcards to **send** to your friends.]

hope 1. last. 2. after, behind. (*Hope Pelekikena* = Vice-President) (*hope loa* = very last) [*'O kēia kona lā* **hope loa** *ma kāna hana.* This is his **very last** day at his job.] (ant. *mua loa* = very first)

hopena result, consequence, ending. [*E 'ike ana 'oe i ka* **hopena** *ma hope!* You'll experience the **consequences** (of your actions) later on!]

hopenapule weekend.

hopohopo 1. anxiety, uncertainty. 2. to worry. 3. anxious, fearful, nervous. [**Hopohopo** *kāu kime ma mua o ka pā'ani pōhili?* Is your team **nervous** before the baseball game?]

hopu to catch, arrest, seize. [*Ua* **hopu** *ka māka'ikiu i ka mea pōā hale.* The detective **caught** the one who robs houses (burglar).]

hopuna 'ōlelo sentence. [*Mai kākau i ka hua 'ōlelo wale nō! E kākau iho i ka* **hopuna 'ōlelo** *holo'oko'a.* Don't just write the word! Write down the entire **sentence**.] (syn. *māmala 'ōlelo*)

hou 1. perspiration. [*Kahe ka* **hou** *o ka lae.* I'm sweating (*lit.* the **sweat** of the brow flows).] 2. to push, shove. 3. new, fresh. 4. again. (*hana hou* = do it again) (*a hui hou* = till we meet again)

hū 1. spinning top. 2. to overflow, to spout up (liquids, lava). [*Ke* **hū** *a'e mai ka pele mai Hualālai mai, maka'ala 'o Kona a me Kekaha.* When lava **spouts up** from

Hualālai, Kona and Kekaha are alert and watchful.] 3. to grunt, or hum.

hua egg, fruit, offspring. (*hua ale* = pill) (*hua helu* = number) (*hua moa* = egg) (*hua 'ōlelo* = word) (*hua palapala* = letter of alphabet) (*hua waina* = grape) (*hua li'ili'i* = berry)

hu'a bubble, suds, foam.

hua 'ai fruit.

huahua'i to boil, bubble up, gush forth (liquids, lava). 2. sexual orgasm.

huaka'i trip, voyage, parade. (*huaka'i pō* = night marchers [spirits said to roam at night]) (*huaka'i hele* = continuous travel) (*ka'i huaka'i* = parade)

hue gourd, water container.

hu'e to remove, uncover, expose, open oven. [*Iā lākou i* **hu'e** *ai i ka imu, ua māpu mai ke 'ala o ka pua'a mo'a.* When they **uncovered** the *imu*, the scent of cooked pig was borne on the wind.]

huehue acne, pimples.

huelo tail of an animal. [*He* **huelo** *mānoanoa ko kēnā pōpoki.* That cat by you has a thick **tail**.]

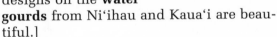
huewai

huewai water container, water gourd. [*Nani ke kīnohinohi ma* **nā huewai** *mai Ni'ihau a me Kaua'i mai.* The designs on the **water gourds** from Ni'ihau and Kaua'i are beautiful.]

huhū 1. anger, wrath. 2. angry. (*huhū wale* = peevish, cantankerous)

hui 1. society, club, partnership, cluster of fruit such as bananas. [*'O Ānuenue ko mākou* **hui** *wa'a.* Ānuenue is our canoe **club**.] 2. to join, meet. (*hui pū* = to unite, mix, combine) (*hui malū* = secret club, fraternity)

huī hello.

huihui 1. constellation. [*'O Nāhiku* (*lit.* the seven) *a me Nā Koa* (*lit.* the soldiers) **nā huihui** *a'u i 'ike mua ai.* The Big Dipper and Orion are the **constellations** I've seen before. 2. cluster, collection.

hu'ihu'i cool, chilly, numbing. [*Ua* **hu'ihu'i** *nā koloaka i nā poke hau āna i ho'okomo ai i nā kī'aha.* The sodas are **chilled** due to the ice cubes he put into the drinking glasses.]

huikala to forgive.

huikau confused, mixed up, confusing. [**Huikau** *nā ilāmuku o ka hui holo lio ma ke ka'i huaka'i.* The marshals of the riding units were **confused** in the parade.]

huila wheel. (*noho huila* = wheelchair)

huina 1. sum, total. 2. geometric shape (with attached number). (*huinakolu* = triangle; *huinahā loa* = rectangle; *huinahā like* = square; *huinalima* = pentagon; *huina alanui* = intersection) (*huina loa'a* = profit)

huinakolu

huki 1. to pull. 2. fit of any kind, convulsion, stroke. [*Ua loa'a ka 'elemakule i ka* **huki**? Did the old man have a **stroke**?]

hukihuki 1. quarrel, disagreement. 2. to pull frequently, to jerk. 3. to disagree, quarrel. [**Hukihuki** *mau nā kaikaina ona.* His younger brothers are always **quarreling**.]

hula

hula Hawaiian dance, dancer or chant used to dance.

hulahula dance of non-Hawaiian origin.

hulali shining. [*A he nani lā ke* **hulali** *nei a he nani maoli nō.* It's a true beauty that is **shining** forth. (song, "Royal Hawaiian Hotel," by H. Robins)]

huli 1. taro top, used to replant. 2. to turn, change. 3. to seek, search for, investigate. (*hulikua* = to turn one's back, refuse to help) (*huli hele* = to search everywhere)

hulō (from English) hurrah! [*Ho'ōho ka lehulehu* "**Hulō! Hulō!** The crowd shouted "**Hurrah! Hurrah!**"]

hulu 1. feather. (*hulu manu* = bird feather) (*humuhumu hulu manu* = featherwork)

2. esteemed (especially older relative), choice. (*nā hulu kūpuna* = the esteemed ancestors)

huluhulu 1. body hair, fur. 2. hairy.

hume to tie on *malo.*

humuhumu to sew, stitch. [**Humuhumu** *nā limahana i ko lākou mau lole makalike.* The laborers **sew** their uniforms.]

humuhumunukunukuāpua'a humuhumu fish with snout like a pig (the state fish of Hawai'i), a *kinolau* (body form) of Kamapua'a.

huna 1. grain, minute particle, crumb. 2. hidden, secret.

hūnā to hide, conceal. (*ho'ohūnā* = to hide, conceal something) [*Ua* **ho'ohūnā** *'ia paha ka leka maiā ia mai?* Was the letter from him perhaps **hidden**?] (*pe'e* = to hide oneself)

hune 1. poor, destitute. 2. fine, tiny.

hunehune minute, very fine. (*hune one* = fine-grained sand)

hūnōnakāne son-in-law.

hūnōnawahine daughter-in-law. [*He* **hūnōnawahine** *lokomaika'i ko ko'u makuahūnōaiwahine.* My mother-in-law has a generous-hearted **daughter-in-law**.] (*makuahūnōaikāne* = father-in-law)

hūpē mucus from nose. [*hūpē kole* (*lit.* running nasal discharge): considered to be an insult]

hūpō stupid, ignorant.

i 1. in, on, at, to. [*Komo hewa ka luna ho'oponopono i ka 'āina ho'opulapula.* The administrator trespassed **on** Hawaiian Homes land.] 2. object marker for indirect or direct object (*iā* is used before pronouns and personal names). [*Kipa aku 'o ia* **iā** *Kamuela, kona hoakula ma Lāna'i ma ka Pō'ahā.* He visits Kamuela (Samuel), his classmate on Lāna'i, on Thursdays.] 3. within descriptive sentence, marks cause of condition. [*Wela ke one i ka lā.* The sand is hot **due to** the sun.] 4. first word of phrase used to indicate when an activity occurred (note that there are several other ways to translate "when"). [**I** *ko ke kauka 'apo'apo 'ana , ua kāhea aku ka mea ma'i "E kōkua mai!"* **When** the doctor was having a fit, the patient called out "help!"]

'ī to say (used frequently in the Hawaiian Bible). [*Ua* **'ī** *akula ke akua iā Moke…*God **said** to Moses….]

ia 1. that (replaces *kēlā*). [*He kuapā ko 'Ualapu'e, Moloka'i. He mau pāpa'i ko ia kuapā.* 'Ualape'e, Moloka'i has a fish pond. **That** fish pond has crabs.] 2. it (sometimes *ia mea*, that thing). [*He peni hou kā Mamo. He peni 'ula'ula ia.* Mamo has a new pen. **It's** a red pen.] 3. she/he (usually *'o ia*) [*Lelele a'e ka pailaka a kīko'oko'o ho'i ia i kona mau wāwae.* The pilot jumps up and down and **she** also stretches her legs.]

iā used in place of *i* as object marker before proper nouns and pronouns. [*Ha'o 'olua* **iā** *Keolalani, 'a'ole anei? Kama'āina māua* **iā** *ia.* You (two) miss Keolalani, isn't that so? We (she and I) know him.]

'ia passive tense marker (follows directly after verb). [*Ua haku* **'ia** *ka mele e ko Hawai'i mō'ī hope loa.* The song **was** compos**ed** by Hawai'i's last monarch.]

i'a 1. fish or any marine creature, including seaweed. 2. Milky Way. [*Ua huli ka* **I'a**. It's past midnight (lit. the **Milky Way** has turned).] (*i'a maka* = raw fish, sashimi) (*i'a 'ula'ula* = goldfish)

'iako outrigger boom attaching *ama* float to canoe.

Ianuali (from English) January.

'Iao Jupiter or morning star. (*kaiao* = the dawn)

Iāpana Japan. [*'Ōlelo Kepanī ko* **Iāpana**. **Japan**'s people speak Japanese.]

ia'u to me, at me (objective case). [*E ho'olohe mai* **ia'u**. Listen **to me**.]

'ie 1. vine that grows around trees, a symbol for Laka. (syn. *'ie'ie*) 2. aerial rootlet of this vine, used to weave baskets, helmets, images. 3. basket, container. (*'ie 'ōpala* = wastebasket) (syn. *kini 'ōpala*) (*'ie lawe* = fish trap)

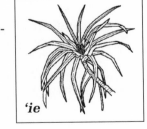

'ie

i'e kuku tapa beater.

'iewe 1. placenta. 2. afterbirth. 3. those descended from a common ancestor. (syn. *ēwe*) [*Ke kanu 'ia nei ko kāna hiapo* **'iewe** *ma lalo o ke kumuniu e ia.* His first-born child's **afterbirth** is being buried under the coconut tree by him.]

ihe spear, dart. [*'O nā* **ihe** *ka mea i 'ō'ō 'ia i ke ali'i.* **Spears** were the things thrown at the chief.] (*ihe paheʻe* = short spear; *ihe pakelo* = lance)

ʻīhepa imbecile, mental incompetent. (syn. *lōlō, hepa*)

ihi to strip, peel bark or fruit.

ihe

ʻihiʻihi sacred, majestic. [**ʻĪhiʻihi ʻo Kamāmalu.** Kamāmalu was **majestic.**] Note: There were two royal ladies named Kamāmalu. This example is a reference to a favorite wife of Liholiho (Kamehameha II) who was known for her large size (over six feet tall) and regal bearing. She accompanied her husband to England where they both contracted measles and died within a few weeks. (*ʻihi lani* = chiefly splendor)

iho 1. directional down (added after verb). [*Ke inu **iho** nei ke kanaka makewai i ka wai hua ʻai ʻalani.* The thirsty person is drinking **down** orange juice.] 2. axle of wheel, axis of earth, core of fruit. 3. to descend.

ihoiho 1. candle, torch. 2. core of tree.

ihu nose, snout, beak, bill. (*ihu waʻa/manu ihu* = bow of canoe)

ʻiʻi 1. tremolo, vibration of chanting voice. [*Kaulana kēia wahine oli i ko kona **ʻiʻi** ikaika.* This female chanter is well known for her strong **tremolo.**] 2. small, stunted, dwarf.

ʻīʻī sour, rancid, moldy.

ʻiʻika 1. to wince, shrivel, contract. 2. wincing with pain. [*ʻOiai he piwa kona, **ʻiʻika** kona maka.* Since he has a fever, his face **winces with pain.**]

ʻiʻini 1. yearning, desire. [*ʻO ia kuʻu **ʻiʻini** puʻuwai.* He is my heart's **desire.**] 2. to desire, crave.

ʻiʻiwi native bird, honeycreeper with red feathers used for capes; a symbol of Hawaiʻi island (whose color is red) and of native Hawaiians (perhaps

ʻiʻiwi

because of the word's similarity to *ʻōiwi*, meaning native).

ikaika 1. strength, force, energy. 2. strong, powerful. (*hoʻoikaika* = to put out great effort) (*hoʻoikika kino* = to exercise, strengthen the body)

Ikalia 1. Italy. 2. Italian.

ʻike 1. sight, knowledge. 2. to see, recognize, know, understand, experience, feel, know sexually. [*Ua **ʻike** ʻia ke anu o Mauna Kea.* The cold of Mauna Kea was **experienced.**] (*ʻike kumu* = basic or fundamental knowledge; *ʻike loa* = to know well; *ʻike maka* = eyewitness, to experience personally; *ʻike pāpālua* = second sight, especially psychic knowledge; *ʻike pono* = to see clearly, certain knowledge)

ʻikena 1. view, sight, scenic point. 2. knowledge, vision.

iki small, little. [*He mea **iki**.* You're welcome (*lit.* it's a **small** thing; one response to "*mahalo*").] (*ke kamaiki* = the small child)

ikiiki (syn. *ikīki*) 1. very humid, hot weather. 2. hot and sticky, humid. [*ʻOiai he pō **ikiiki** ia, ua lele mai nā makika.* Since it was a **humid** night, mosquitoes flew around.]

Ikiiki name of month in Hawaiian moon calendar (during May and June, when hot, humid weather can occur).

ʻīkoi 1. core of some fruit such as breadfruit or apple. 2. float on fishnet.

ʻikuwā 1. clamor, din. 2. to make a loud noise. 3. noisy, loud.

ʻIkuwā name of month of Hawaiian moon calendar (during rainy season of October and November, when storms abound with thunder, high surf).

ila birthmark.

i laila there (used only after the specific place has been named). [*Ua kipa aku māua ʻo kaʻu wahine i Hāʻena a ua nanea **i laila**.* My wife and I visited Hāʻena and relaxed **there.**]

i lalo on bottom, under. (*e noho i lalo* = sit down)

ilāmuku marshall, sheriff.

ili 1. to turn over, to run over with car. 2. stranded. 3. aground (as a ship). [*Ua **ili** ka* *moku 'o Kīlauea ma ka 'āpapa.* The ship Kīlauea ran **aground** on the reef.] (*ili ke aka* = to cast a shadow) 4. to inherit, inheritance. (*ili 'āina* = inheritance of land)

'ili 1. skin, scalp (human), bark of tree, peel of fruit, hide of animal, surface of sea. (*'ili pāpa'a* = sunburned skin) [*He* **'ili pāpa'a** *ko ka malihini.* The newcomer has **sunburned skin.**] (*'ili puakea* = light skin, Caucasian) (*'ili holoholona* = leather) (*ka 'ilikai* = the surface of the sea, horizontal) 2. land division within an *ahupua'a.* 3. strap of any kind, reins, belt. (*'ili kuapo* = seat belt)

'iliahi sandalwood.

'ilihune 1. poverty (*lit.* tiny skin), the poor. [*'A'ohe mea 'ai a 'a'ole nui ke kālā a ka po'e 'ilihune.* The **poor** have no food and little money.] 2. poor.

'ili'ili 1. pebble, stones used for hula. 2. house foundation. (*hō'ili'ili* = to gather, collect)

'Ilikini American Indian.

'ilima native plant used for *lei*, herbal medicine, symbol for island of O'ahu. [*Ola i ka pua o ka 'ilima.* (*'ōlelo no'eau*) Live due to the *'ilima* flower. (wise saying indicating the extensive use of the *'ilima* as an herbal medicine)]

'ilima

ilina grave, tombstone. (*pā ilina* = cemetery)

'īlio dog. (*'īlio hae* = fierce dog, wolf, jackal)

'iliwai 1. surface of freshwater stream, pond. 2. carpenter's level.

ilo 1. maggot. 2. young shoot. 3. to germinate, sprout. (*ho'oilo* = to cause germination, rainy season)

'īloli 1. emotional disturbance, longings, cravings, and other unpleasant side effects of pregnancy. 2. spotted, daubed with color, speckled.

i luna on top, above. (*e kū i luna* = stand up)

'imi to look for, hunt, search. (*'imi a loa'a* = search for until found; *'imi hala* = to find fault with, blame; *'imi hana* = to seek work, to stir up trouble; *'imi 'ike* = to seek knowledge; *'imi kālā* = to seek money, to earn a living; *'imi loa* = distant traveler [*fig.* great knowledge], to seek far; *'imi na'auao* = to seek knowledge, education; *'imi 'ōlelo* = to slander, lie, cause trouble by gossiping; *'imi pono* = endeavor)

'imo to wink, twinkle. (*e 'imo kou maka* = wink your eye) (*hōkū 'imo'imo* = twinkling star)

imu underground oven. (syn. *umu*) (Kaimukī = oven for baking *tī*; the *tī* root was baked, yielding a delicious sweet)

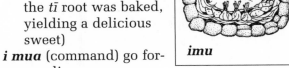
imu

i mua (command) go forward!

inā if. [*Inā 'olua i inu i ka wai, 'a'ole 'olua makewai.* If you two had drunk water, you wouldn't be thirsty (now).]

ināhea when (used only in questions referring to past actions). [*Ināhea i pae ai ka mokulele?* **When** did the plane land?]

inaina 1. anger, hatred. 2. to hate.

'inamona relish made with *kukui* nut.

'īnana animated, stirring with life.

'īnea 1. suffering, hardship, distress. 2. to suffer. [*Nui ka 'īnea o ko kāu wahine makua kāne i ka ma'i pu'uwai, 'a'ole anei?* Your wife's father really **suffered** with heart disease, isn't that so?]

i nehinei yesterday. [*I nehinei i puka ai kāna keiki mai ka Pūnana Leo mai.* It was yesterday that her child graduated from Pūnana Leo (Hawaiian language preschool).]

'Īnia (from English) 1. India. 2. East Indian.

'īniha (from English) inch.

'īnika 1. (from English) ink. 2. spinach.

'iniki 1. to pinch, nip. 2. sharp, piercing (wind, love pangs). [*E* **'iniki** *niki mālie.* Pinch gently. (traditional song, "'Iniki Mālie")]

'inikua (from English) insurance. (*'inikua ola* = life insurance; *'inikua pau ahi* = fire insurance; *palapala 'inikua* = insurance policy)

'ino 1. storm, harm, evil. [*E pale aku i ka* **'ino**. Keep away hurt and **harm**. (common line in prayers)] 2. to harm, hurt. 3. stormy, bad, wicked, sinful. (*he lā* **'ino** = a stormy day, a bad day) 4. spoiled, contaminated, poor quality. 5. an intensifier as in *nui* **'ino**, a great many.

inoa name. (*inoa kapakapa* = nickname) (*inoa 'ohana* = family name, last name) [*'O wai kou* **inoa** *'ohana?* What's your **last name**?] (*inoa pō* = a name received in a dream)

inu to drink. (*inu lama* = to drink alcohol) (*mea inu* = beverage, drink)

'io Hawaiian hawk, found only on Hawai'i island, a symbol of royal rank due to its high flight. (*'Iolani* = heavenly hawk, name of several monarchs and the royal palace in Honolulu)

'i'o 1. flesh, meat, muscle. (*'i'o hipa* = mutton; *'i'o pua'a* = pork; *'i'o pipi* = beef; *'i'o pale niho* = gums) 2. true, genuine, real. (*mana'o'i'o* = faith [*lit.* true thought])

'iole rat, rodent, mouse. (*'iole pua'a* = guinea pig)

'i'o pale niho gums.

ipo sweetheart, lover. [*'O wai ko kāu* **ipo** *inoa?* What's your **sweetheart**'s name?] (*ho'oipoipo* = to make love)

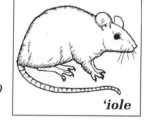
'iole

ipu 1. gourd, in old Hawai'i, an all-purpose container used for food and water. 2. hula implement. (*ipu 'ai maka* = watermelon) (*ipu 'au'au* = wash basin; syn. *ipu holoi*) (*ipuhao* = pan, pot [*lit.* iron container]; *ipu heke* = gourd drum, two gourds attached together; *ipu kī* = teapot; *ipu kī'o'e* = dipper; *ipu kukui* = lamp, lighthouse; *ipu kuni 'ala* = incense burner; *ipu pāwehe* = gourd calabash decorated with tapa designs, found primarily on Ni'ihau and Kaua'i; *ipu wai* = water container)

ipu

'iu lofty, sacred. (*'iulani* = the heavenly uplands, the heavenly sacred one, a distant land of the gods. Ka'iulani is the name of the last heir to the Hawaiian throne, Lili'uokalani's niece. A renowned beauty, she died a few years after the overthrow, apparently brokenhearted at the United States's refusal to restore the monarchy.)

'iu'iu majestic, lofty, very high.

Iulai (from English) July.

Iune (from English) June.

iwa nine. (syn. *'eiwa, 'aiwa*)

'iwa frigate bird (*fig.* thief, since this seabird is known for stealing fish from other birds)

'iwa'iwa maidenhair fern.

iwakālua twenty.

iwi 1. bone. 2. shell of 'opihi, shellfish. 3. midrib of coconut or *tī* leaf. (*iwi ā* = jawbone; *iwi 'ao'ao* = rib; *iwi hilo* = thigh bone, femur; *iwi kanaka* = human bone, skeleton; *iwi kuamo'o* = spine, backbone, close relative of chief who served as his personal attendant; *iwilei* = collarbone, measurement from collarbone to tip of middle finger extended; *iwi 'ō* = wishbone; *iwi po'o* = skull, head bone)

'iwa

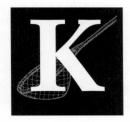

ka the. Note: *Ka* is used with most Hawaiian words; *ke* is used before words that begin with k, e, a, and o. [*'A'ala* **ka** *pua pīkake.* **The** *pīkake* flower is fragrant.] [*He mea nui* **ke** *ea i kānaka maoli.* Sovereignty is **the** important thing to the native people of Hawai'i.]

kā 1. beater for knee drum, usually made of dried *tī* leaves. [*ke* **kā** *pahu niu,* the knee drum **beater**] 2. to strike, dash, hurl. 3. to bail water from a canoe. [**Kā** *nā liu.* **Bail** out the bilges.] 4. exclamation expressing surprise, frustration, disgust (usually pronounced "tsā!"). 5. particle indicating possession. [**kā** *kāu kāne kālā,* your husband's money] [*He kālā* **kā** *kāu kāne.* Your husband **has** money.] [**kā** *lākou mau puke makemakika,* **their** (3) math books] [*He puke makemakika* **kā** *lākou.* They **have** math books.] (Kahi'ukā = the striking tail [name of shark at Pearl Harbor, brother of Ka'ahupāhau, the female *ali'i* shark of Hawai'i])

ka'a 1. car, vehicle. (*ke ka'aahi* = train, railroad; *ke ka'a ho'olima* = taxi, rental car; *ke ka'a lawe ma'i* = ambulance; *ke ka'a lio* = carriage; *ke ka'a 'ōhua* = bus) 2. to roll, twist, revolve. 3. rocking, twisting, tumbling. [*ka 'uala* **ka'a,** the **tumbling** sweet potato]

ka'ahele to make a tour, travel around. (syn. *ka'apuni*)

kā'ai sennit container for chief's bones. [*Na wai i lawe aku i nā* **kā'ai**? Who took the *kā'ai*?]

ka'akua 1. extreme dizziness. 2. to lean back in pain, roll over backwards.

kā'alo to pass by. (syn. *mā'alo*)

ka'ama'i chronic illness. [*'O ka mimi kō ke* **ka'ama'i** *ma'amau o nā Hawai'i.* Diabetes is the most common **chronic illness** of Hawaiians.]

ka'ana to divide, share. [*E* **ka'ana** *like kākou i nā i'a.* Let's **divide** up the fish.]

ka'ao tale, legend, myth (considered to be made up, as opposed to *mo'olelo,* which are considered to be true stories). [*pīpī holo* **ka'ao** (*lit.* sprinkled the **tale** runs on); traditional phrase to indicate end of a story]

ka'apuni to make a tour, go around, surround. [**ka'apuni** *o Maui e 'ike i nā wai 'ehā,* **going around** Maui to see the four waters (the four well-known places whose names start with *wai,* indicating freshwater streams there: Waikapu, Wailuku, Waiehu, Waihe'e) (song, "Nā Wai Kaulana," by A. Namakelua)]

ka'au forty (part of traditional counting system, based on fours: 4, 40, 400, etc.).

ka'awale separate, separated, not in use, free. [*Ua* **ka'awale** *ka pa'a male.* The married couple are **separated**.] (*ho'oka'awale* = to separate) (*manawa ka'awale* = free time)

kae contraction of "*ka mea e*," the one who should, will. [*'O Nainoa* **kae** *alaka'i i nā ho'okele.* Nainoa is **the one who should** lead the navigators.]

kae treated with contempt, scorn. (*ho'okae* = to despise, treat with contempt, scorn) (*ho'okae 'ili* = racial prejudice) [*Loa'a ka* **ho'okae 'ili** *ma Hawai'i nei?* Is there **racial prejudice** here in Hawai'i?]

ka'e 1. brink, border, curb. 2. to sulk, fuss, swear. 3. sullen, cross.

kā'e'a'e'a expert, hero, champion.

kā'e'e 1. hand net. 2. to scoop with a hand net. 3. to strain food. [*Kā'e'e 'o Keola i ka hua 'ai na ka pēpē.* Keola **strains** the fruit for the baby.]

kā'e'e

kā'eke'eke hula implement, pieces of bamboo held vertically and pounded on the floor; different lengths of bamboo produce higher or lower pitch.

ka'ele empty and hollow, as a bowl or a canoe (syn. *'olohaka* [unlike *ka'ele, 'olohaka* implies emptiness due to deficiency]).

kā'elo soaked.

Kā'elo name of month during wet season of December and January in traditional Hawaiian calendar.

kaena to boast, brag. [*Kaena ke kā'e'a'e'a i kāna hana mokomoko.* The champion **boasts** about his wrestling.]

kā'eo full, referring to calabash (*fig.* full of knowledge). [*ka 'umeke kā'eo ('ōlelo no'eau),* the **full** calabash (a knowledgeable person)]

kaha 1. grade, mark, punctuation. (*kahaapo* = parentheses, brackets) 2. to mark, draw, scratch, slice open fish or animal. [*E kaha 'oe i ka i'a.* **Slice open** the fish.] (*kahanalu* = body surfing, to body surf)

kāhāhā 1. exclamation of surprise, wonder. 2. surprising, astonishing. 3. to be surprised. [*Kāhāhā nā luāhine i ka lohe 'ana i ka 'ōpio i oli le'a ai.* The old ladies were **surprised** when they heard the youth joyfully chanting.]

kahakaha 1. marking, lines, stripes. 2. striped. [*He i'a kahakaha kāna.* She has a **striped** fish.]

kahakai beach. [*E uhaele kākou i kahakai.* Let's all (lots of people) go to the **beach**.] Note: Unlike English nouns, Hawaiian nouns require "noun

kahakai

announcers," such as demonstratives (this, that, the) or possessive pronouns (their, my, our). *Kahakai* is one of a handful of words that do not follow this rule: *ke kahakai* is used only before the name of the beach. [*Laukanaka ke kahakai 'o Hanauma.* The **beach** named Hanauama is crowded with people.]

kaha ki'i 1. artist. 2. to draw or paint pictures. (*kaha ki'i hale* = architect)

kahakō long mark over vowel to indicate elongation of sound. (*pohō* = waste time, no use doing something; *poho* = palm of hand, pouch)

kahakū to trespass, go where one pleases.

kahamaha to interrupt. (syn. *mau'a'e*) [*Mai kahamaha mai iā mākou.* Don't **interrupt** us.]

kahaone sandy beach.

kahape'a to make a cross or X.

kāha'u to lessen, diminish, as a storm or an illness. [*Ke kāha'u nei ka 'eha konikoni o kona wāwae moku.* The throbbing pain of his cut foot is **diminishing**.]

kahawai stream, river.

kahe to flow (liquids). [*Kahe ka wai ma ke kahawai.* Water **flows** in the stream.] (*kahe ka hou* = to sweat, perspire) [*Kahe ka hou o ko nā limahana lae i ke kanu 'ana iho i nā kumuniu.* The laborers **sweat** when they plant the coconut trees.]

kahawai

kāhea to call out, cry out, greet, name. [*Ua kāhea aku kūpuna i nā malihini "Mai, mai e 'ai."* The elders **called out** to newcomers, "Come, come and eat."]

kāhehi to stumble, misstep.

kāheka tidepool. [*Nui nā pe'ape'a ma ke kāheka.* There are a lot of starfish in the **tidepool**.]

kāhela 1. wide expanse of land or sea. [*He kāhela ka 'ikena mai Pukalani aku.* The view from Pukalani is a **vast expanse of land**.] 2. hula step and beat of gourd. 3. prone, flat, to lie spread out.

kahelelani small shell of various colors, often used in Ni'ihau shell *lei*, named for an ancient chief of Ni'ihau.

kahi 1. place (contraction of *ka + wahi*). ['*O Miloli'i* **kahi** *i pi'i ai ke kai e'e ma ka lā 'elima o Pepeluali.* Miloli'i is the **place** where the tidal wave rose up on February 5th.] 2. one (the number). (syn. *'ekahi, 'akahi*) (*kahi, lua, kolu* = one, two, three) 3. to cut, comb, shave, scrape sides of poi bowl. (*kahi 'umi'umi* = barber, to shave beard)

kahiau to give generously without thought of return.

Kahiki 1. ancestral Polynesian homeland toward the East. [*Pele mai* **Kahiki** *mai,* Pele from the ancestral homeland (Pele is a latecomer to Hawai'i)] 2. any foreign country, place outside of Hawai'i.

kahiko old, ancient. [*i ke au* **kahiko**, in **ancient** days]

kāhiko 1. finery, adornment. [*Wailele hune nā pali, kou* **kāhiko** *nō ia.* Waterfalls spray the cliffs, it indeed is your **adornment**. (song, "Moloka'i Waltz," by M. Kane)] 2. decorated, adorned.

kahikolu trinity. ['*O ke* **kahikolu** *ka makua, ke keiki a me ka 'uhane hemolele.* The **trinity** is the father, son and holy ghost.]

kāhili feather standard, a symbol of an ali'i, carried in processions in front of a royal entourage. ['*O ke* **kāhili** *'ele'ele ka hō'ailona no Kalaniana'ole.* The

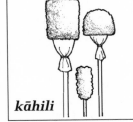

kāhili

black **feather standard** is a symbol for Kalaniana'ole.]

kāhoahoa to appeal, intercede. [*Ke* **kāhoahoa** *nei ko Moloka'i i ke aupuni e hō'ole i ka hui Kepanī e lawe aku i ka wai.* Moloka'i's people are **appealing** to the government to prevent Japanese businesses from taking water.]

kāholo 1. hula step. 2. to hurry, speed. 3. swift, hasty.

Kaho'olawe island formerly used as a bombing target by the U.S. military. It was returned to the state of Hawai'i in 1994.

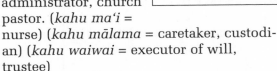

Kaho'olawe

kahu guardian, keeper, administrator, church pastor. (*kahu ma'i* = nurse) (*kahu mālama* = caretaker, custodian) (*kahu waiwai* = executor of will, trustee)

kahua 1. foundation, base, location, site. 2. any broad, flat field. (*kahua hānai pipi* = ranch; *kahua holoholona* = zoo; *kahua ho'omoana* = campground; *kahua kula* = school campus; *kahua mokulele* = airport; *kahua pā'ani* = stadium, playing field; *kahua waihona 'ōpala* = garbage dump)

kahu hipa shepherd ['*O Iesu ko'u* **kahu hipa**, *'a'ole o'u mea e nele ai.* (Halelū 23) The Lord is my **shepherd**, I shall not want. (Psalm 23)]

kāhuli 1. native Hawaiian tree snail (currently close to extinction, but once collected for its brilliantly colored shells). [**Kāhuli** *aku,* **kāhuli** *mai.* Turn under, turn up. (The tree snail frequently turns under leaves.) (traditional song, "Kāhuli Aku Kāhuli Mai," music by J. Kamanā)] 2. to change. 3. to capsize, overthrow. (*ho'okāhuli aupuni* = to overthrow the government)

kahuna expert in any craft or field of knowledge, priest (many different kinds, including *kahuna lā'au lapa'au*, herbal medicine doctor; *kahuna kālai wa'a*, canoe carver).

kahunapule minister, priest.

kai 1. sea, sea water, current, tide. (*kai holo* = current; *kai huki* = undertow; other phrases for the rising and receding of the tide include *kai malo'o* = low tide; *kai piha* = high tide; *kai ho'i* = ebbing tide; *kai ulu* = full tide, rising

kai

sea) [*Aia ke* **kai malo'o** *ma ka hola 'ekolu.* **Low tide** is at 3 o'clock.] 2. sauce, gravy, dressing. 3. contraction of *ka mea i,* "the one who." [*'O McGuire* **kai** *huaka'i pū i 'Enelani me ke kuini Kapi'olani.* McGuire is **the one who** journeyed to England with the queen Kapi'olani.]

ka'i 1. a type of hula chant used for entrance onto the stage. 2. to lead, direct, walk in procession. (*ka'i huaka'i* = parade, procession, to walk in a parade)

kaiaka 1. water fluid, thinned down. 2. (from English) kayak .

kaiao 1. dawn. (syn. *wana'ao, pukana lā* [sunrise]) 2. to enlighten.

kaiapa (from English) diaper. [*Pulu ko ka pēpē* **kaiapa.** The baby's **diaper** is wet.]

kaiapuni Hawai'i Hawaiian immersion program.

kaiaulu community, neighborhood. [*Mālie wale ko Nā'ālehu* **kaiaulu.** Nā'ālehu's **community** is calm and peaceful.] (*kula nui kaiaulu* = community college)

kai e'e tidal wave (*lit.* mounting seas).

kaikaina younger sister of female, younger brother of male. [*'O kēlā mea he'e nalu ko Malu* **kaikaina**? Is that surfer Malu's **younger brother**?]

kaikamahine girl, daughter (pl. *kaikamāhine*). (*kaikamahine 'ohana* = niece) [*Auē ke akahai o kāna mau* **kaikamāhine 'ohana!** Gosh how gentle his **nieces** are!]

kaiko'eke brother-in-law of male, sister-in-law of female. (*kaiko'eke kāne* = brother-in-law of female) (*kaiko'eke wahine* = sister-in-law of male)

ka'ikōkō bedridden, extremely old. [*E ola a kolopupū a* **ka'ikōkō.** Live until you crawl around and **have to be carried in a net**. (a familiar line in chants and prayers asking for long life)]

kaikua'ana older sister of female, older brother of male. [*'O wai ko kou kupuna wahine* **kaikua'ana**?

kaikua'ana

What is your grandmother's **older sister**'s name?]

kaikuahine 1. sister of a male. 2. female cousin of a male.

kaikunāne 1. brother of a female. [*'A'ohe ona* **kaikunāne.** She doesn't have a **brother**.] 2. male cousin of a female.

kaila (from English) 1. style. 2. stylish, in fashion. [*Hō ka nani!* **Kaila** *kou lole!* How pretty! Your clothes are **stylish**!]

kā'ili 1. to snatch, grab, take by force. (*Kūkā'ilimoku* = Kū, snatcher of land divisions, Kamehameha I's war god.) 2. to gasp for breath.

ka'ina sequence, order, succession. [*He* **ka'ina** *ko kāu hana ho'oma'ema'e hale?* Do you clean house in any particular **order**?]

ka'inapu up and down motion, tossing of ship or prancing of horse. [**Ka'inapu** *ko kēlā wahine holo lio lio 'eleu i ke ka'i huaka'i.* The woman rider's lively horse is **prancing** in the parade.]

kainō, kainoa expresses the idea "I assumed, but I was wrong." [**Kainō** *paha ua pa'a kou mana'o i 'ane'i.* **I believed mistakenly** that your thoughts were fixed on me. (song, "Alekoki," by L. Alohikea)]

kaiolohia calm sea (*fig.* peace of mind). [*'O ke* **kaiolohia** *ka pahuhopu.* **Peace of mind** is the goal.]

kaka to rinse, clean. [*Ma hope o ka wehe 'ana i ka pahapaha a me ka 'ōpū, e* **kaka** *i ka i'a.* After removing the gills and the stomach, **rinse** off the fish.]

kaka'a to roll, turn over, revolve (wheels, gears in machine). [**Kaka'a** *nā kia a holo ka mīkini.* The gears **revolve** and the machine runs.]

kakahiaka

kakahiaka morning, approximately 6 to 10 a.m. (*kakahiaka nui* = early morning, between 12 p.m. and 6 a.m.)

kaka'ikahi few, scarce. [**Kaka'ikahi** *nā mānaleo Hawai'i.* Hawaiian native speakers are **scarce**.]

kakalina gasoline.

kakani 1. to chatter, talk continuously. 2. noisy, squeaking, crunchy. [*Kakani ka 'ai 'ana i ka 'ōpelu i palai 'ia.* Eating fried 'ōpelu sounds **crunchy**.]

kākā'ōlelo traditional style of oratory, orator.

kākau 1. to write. (*kākau 'ōlelo* = secretary) (*kākau nūpepa* = reporter) 2. tattoo. (syn. *kākau 'ili*) [*He kākau 'ili ko ke kāne Kāmoa ma ke kīkala.* The Samoan man has a **tattoo** on his hips.] 3. to tattoo.

kākau inoa to register, sign up (sometimes shortened to *kau inoa*). [*Kū laina nā haumāna e kākau inoa i nā papa like 'ole.* The students stand in line to **register** for all kinds of classes.]

kakekake 1. to jerk, fidget, interfere. 2. to shuffle cards.

kāki'i to strike at, aim at. [*Ua kāki'i ke kupu'eu i kona hoa paio i ka lā'au pālau.* The hero **aimed** his war club at his enemy.]

kākini 1. dozen. 2. stocking.

kāki'o mange, impetigo.

kāko'o 1. support, aid. 2. to support, aid, assist. [*Kāko'o kona 'ohana i ke kupuna kāne i hele a huikau a 'auana aku.* His family **supports** the grandfather who became confused and wandered away.]

kākou we all, us all (three or more). Note: *Kākou* includes everyone present, as in the greeting "*aloha kākou*" (hello to all of us); *mākou* also means we, us (three or more), but excludes the person addressed.

kala 1. (from English) crayon, color. (syn. *waiho'olu'u*) 2. to color. [*E kala i kēnā ki'i.* **Color** in that (near you) picture.] 3. to loosen, free, forgive, excuse. (*E kala mai ia'u* = I'm sorry, excuse me) 4. rough in texture, like a shark's skin.

kālā money, dollars. [*'Ehia āu kālā? He iwakālua a'u kālā.* How much **money** do you have? I have twenty **dollars**.]

kālā'au hula implement and type of hula using sticks that are hit against each other or those of another dancer.

kālai to carve, cut, hew. (*kālai ki'i* = image carver) (*kālai wa'a* = canoe carver)

kālai 'āina 1. politics. 2. political (based on traditional practice of giving all lands to new ruler to allocate to his supporters and ranking chiefs [*lit.* carving up the land]).

kalaiwa (from English) to drive. [*Ua kalaiwa mamao ko'u hoaaloha i ke alanui mālualua.* My friend **drove** far down the bumpy road.]

kalaka (from English) truck.

kalakala rough, harsh, rude. (syn. *kīko'olā*) [*He hana kalakala ka maha'oi.* Being overly aggressive is **rude** behavior.] (*pepa kalakala* = sandpaper)

kalakoa (from English) calico, variegated in color.

kalakupua magic.

kalana county. [*He luna kā Lehua kāne no ke kalana o Maui.* Lehua's husband is a supervisor for Maui **county**.]

kālani gallon.

kalauna (from English) clown. (syn. *mea ho'omāke'aka*)

kalauna

kalaunu (from English) crown. [*Eia kou lei kalaunu.* Here is your royal **crown**. (song, "E Nihi Ka Hele," by D. Kalākaua)]

kāleka (from English) card, postcard. (*kāleka Kalikimaka* = Christmas card)

kālele 1. support. 2. to trust, depend on. 3. stress.

kalena taut, stretched.

kālena (from English) talent. [*He kālena ko Ka'upena no ke oli 'ana.* Ka'upena has a **talent** for chanting.]

kālepa trader, salesman, merchant. [*Kū'ai aku ke kālepa i ke ka'a.* The **salesman** sells cars.]

Kaleponi (from English) California. [*Kipa aku i Kaleponi he 'āina anu.* Visit **California**, a cold land. (song, "E Nihi Ka Hele," by D. Kalākaua)]

kālewa 1. to float in the wind. 2. to peddle goods. [*Kālewa 'o Nālani i ka 'ohe hano ihu i ka mākeke.* Nālani **peddles** nose flutes at the open air market.]

kali to wait, hesitate. (syn. *alia*) [*E* **kali** *iki!* Wait a little!]

Kalikimaka (from English) Christmas. (Hau'oli Lā Kalikimaka = Happy Christmas)

kalima (from English) cream. (*kalima hamo* = ointment) (*'aikalima/haukalima* = ice cream)

kalipa (from English) slipper.

kalo taro, main food of ancient Hawai'i and a symbol of the Hawaiian's family connection to nature and the earth.

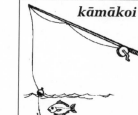
kalo

kāloke (from English) carrot.

kālua to cook in underground oven, *imu*. [*Ke* **kālua** *'ia nei ka pelehū me ka pua'a.* The turkey is being **cooked** in the underground oven with the pig.]

kama child. [*E* **kama** *i ka huli au,* Oh **child** in the changing times (ancient chant "'Au'a 'Ia," urging Hawaiians to hold on to their heritage and land)] (*kama lele* = orphan) (*kama kahi* = only child)

kāma'a shoe. [*'A'ole mākou komo i ke* **kāma'a** *i loko o ka hale. E wehe 'oukou i ko 'oukou mau* **kāma'a** *ma waho.* We (three, not you) don't wear **shoes** in the house. Take off your (all) **shoes** outside.]

kama'āina 1. native born, local person. 2. familiar, acquainted with. [*Kama'āina paha 'oe i ka 'ao'ao Ko'olau o ka mokupuni nui?* Are you perhaps **acquainted with** the windward side of the Big Island?]

kamaehu firmness of resolution.

kamaha'o wonderful, astonishing, surprising. [*Pō la'i e, Pō* **kamaha'o.** Peaceful night, **Wonderful** night. (translation of song "Silent Night" by Stephen and Mary Desha)]

kamahele 1. main branch. 2. strong, far-reaching.

kāma'i to prostitute. (syn. *ho'okamakama* = prostitution, prostitute)

kamaiki child. (*lit.* little child).

kama'ilio to talk, converse.

kāmaka sodomy. (*ho'okāmaka* = homosexuality)

kāmākoi to fish with pole.

kamali'i children (implies children of *ali'i*). (*kamali'i wahine* = princess) (*kamali'i kāne* = prince)

kamanā carpenter.

kamani 1. native tree with fragrant blossoms. 2. smooth, polished. (*ho'okamani* = hypocrite; to act as a hypocrite)

kāmau to keep on, persevere. (*kāmau kī'aha* = to lift glass, share a drink)

kamawae difficult to please, finicky. [*Kamawae kona 'ai 'ana.* He's a **finicky** eater.]

Kāmoa 1. Samoa. 2. Samoan.

kamu (from English) chewing gum.

kana numerical prefix equivalent to 10 x, used for all numbers from 30 - 99. (*kanakolu* = 30 [*kana* = ten times, *kolu* = 3 (from *'ekolu*), or 10 x 3]; *kanahā* = 40; *kanalima* = 50; *kanahikukūmāhiku* = 77)

kāna 1. (*cap.*) saint. (Kāna Kaloka = St. Nick, Santa Claus). 2. his/her or he has/she has. [*He pā mea 'ai* **kāna** *mai Masu's mai.* **She/he has** a plate lunch from Masu's.] (*kāna hana* = his/her work)

kanaka human being, person. (pl. *kānaka*)(*kanaka maoli* = native Hawaiian; syn. *'ōiwi, kupa*) (*kanaka makua* = adult, mature person) (*kanaka nui* or *maka nui* = VIP)

kanakē (from English) candy.

kanalima fifty.

Kanaloa god of the sea.

kānalua 1. to doubt, distrust. 2. doubtful, uncertain, undecided. [*'Ano* **kānalua** *ke kauka inā e ola ana ke kanaka ma'i.* The doctor is rather **doubtful** that the sick person will live.]

kānana 1. sieve, strainer. 2. to strain, as *'awa*.

kanapī (from English) centipede.

kānāwai 1. law, code, statute, rule. 2. to obey a law, to learn from experience. [*Ua* **kānāwai** *kānaka maoli i kūʻē i ke aupuni.* The native people who opposed the government **learned from experience**.] 3. legal.

kāne male, husband, man. (*kāne wahine make* = widower) (*wahine kāne make* = widow)

Kāne name of major god of old, a creator god symbolized in fresh water as *Kāne i ka wai ola,* Kāne of the waters of life.

kani 1. sound of any kind. 2. to sound, cry out, roar. [**Kani** *ka pila!* Let the instrument **sound** (play music!).] (*hoʻokani pila* = to play an instrument)

kaniʻahē to giggle, laugh softly.

kanikau lamentation, chant of mourning.

kanikē 1. tolling sound of bell, clock. 2. to toll bell, clock. (*kanikō* = long drawn-out peal of a bell)

kaniʻuhū 1. sorrow, grief. [*Nui ko ke kāne wahine make* **kaniʻuhū** *i ka lohe ʻana i ke kanikau.* The widower's **sorrow** was intense when he heard the mourning chant.] 2. to sigh, moan. (syn. *ʻuhū, ʻū*)

kanu to plant, bury. [*Hoʻomau kona ʻohana i ka loina kahiko i ke* **kanu** *ʻana i kekahi kumuniu me ka piko o ka pēpē.* Her family continues the ancient custom of **planting** a coconut tree with the umbilical cord of the baby.] (*mea kanu* = plant)

kanuwika (from English) sandwich.

kao 1. dart, spear (fishing), skyrocket. 2. goat. 3. to throw javelin, dart. (*ahikao* = fireworks)

kao

kaomi 1. to push, press. [*E* **kaomi** *i ke pihi.* **Press** the button.] 2. to suppress thought, emotion; restrain. [*Hoʻāʻo ke kanaka maoli e* **kaomi** *i kona huhū i ka hana kaulike ʻole.* The native Hawaiian tries to **restrain** her anger at the injustice.]

kaona 1. hidden meaning in Hawaiian poetry. 2. (from English) town, downtown. [*Ua*

kipa aku ke kuaʻāina i ke **kaona***.* The country person visited the **town**.]

kapa 1. tapa, Hawaiian cloth made from the bark of trees such as *wauke, māmaki.* 2. clothing made of this cloth, often scented and elaborately dyed and decorated. 3. edge, border. [*Ua kū aʻe ka pueo ma* **kapa** *alanui.* The owl appeared on the **edge** of the street.] (*kapa ʻia* = to give a name, to be called or named) [*E* **kapa** *ʻia ana kona inoa ʻo Kawehi.* Her **name will be called** Kawehi.]

kapa

kāpae to set aside, skip, delete, "pass" in card game. [*ʻOiai lākou e* **kāpae** *ana i ka pāʻani hua ʻōlelo, e pāʻani pū kāua ma hope.* Although they are **skipping** the word game, let's you and me play later.]

kapakahi lopsided, crooked. [*Kūlanalana ka ʻōpio i ka piʻi ʻana aʻe i ke alapiʻi* **kapakahi***.* The young person totters when he climbs up the **crooked** staircase.]

kapakē to splash, as raindrops in water. (syn. *pakī*) [**Kapakē** *nā pakapaka ua.* The raindrops **splash**.]

kāpala 1. printing, stamping as decorating tapa cloth. 2. to blot, stain, print tapa with carved bamboo stamp (*ʻohe kāpala*).

kapalili trembling, throbbing with emotion. (*kapalili ka puʻuwai* = the throbbing heart) Note: Emotional agitation is compared to the fluttering of the *kalo* leaf in the wind.

kapalulu roaring, crackling, whirring sounds. (*manu kapalulu* = quail)

kapa moe blanket of ancient Hawaiʻi consisting of five pieces of tapa, the top piece decorated and sometimes dyed.

kāpekepeke 1. to walk unsteadily. 2. insecure. (*fig.* uncertain, doubtful) (*pili kāpekepeke* = uncertain relationship)

kāpena (from English) captain. [*ʻO Kāwika Kapahulehua ke* **kāpena** *mua o ka Hōkūleʻa.* Kāwika Kapahulehua was the first **captain** of the Hōkūleʻa.]

kāpī to sprinkle with salt.

kāpi'i curly, person with curly hair (*fig.* warrior, attendant to a chief). (syn. *pi'ipi'i*)

kapikala (from English) capital, capitol.

kāpili to build, put together, mend, repair, unite. [*Hiki ke **kāpili** hou 'ia nā 'āpana hune o ke pola i hā'ule a nahā?* Can the fine pieces of the bowl that fell and cracked be **mended**?]

kapu 1. taboo, prohibition, sacredness. [*Ua noa ke **kapu**.* The **prohibition** has been lifted.] 2. forbidden, sacred, consecrated. [*Kapu ka heiau.* The sacred site is **consecrated**.]

kapuahi fireplace, stove. (*kapuahi ea* = gas stove; *kapuahi uila* = electric stove)

kapua'i foot (measurement). [*'Ewalu **kapua'i** ka lō'ihi o ka moena lauhala.* The length of the *lauhala* mat is eight **feet**.] (*kapua'i kuea* = square foot)

kapu'au'au bathtub.

kapukapu 1. dignity, regal appearance. 2. dignified, regal. [*Kapukapu nā maka o Hāli'ilua lā, lana mālie.* **Regal** are the eyes of Hāli'ilua, floating calmly. (traditional song, "Hāli'ilua Lā")]

kāpulu careless, slovenly, gross, disgusting. (Note: *Mōkākī* also means messy and disheveled; however; it doesn't imply carelessness as *kāpulu* does.)

kau 1. season, time. (*kauwela* = summer; *kau hā'ule lau* = fall, autumn; *kau kupu lau* = spring; *kau ho'oilo* = rainy season, winter) (*no nā kau a kau* = forever and always) 2. to place, put, perch. 3. a chant of sacrifice to a deity. 4. to board ship, vehicle. [*Ke kau nei nā kelamoku ma luna o ka mokuahi.* The sailors are **boarding** the ship.] (*kau ma luna o* = to board transportation) (*kau kānāwai* = legislator)

kāu you (1) have, yours. [*He aha **kāu** hana?* What are **you** doing? What is your job?] [*He hana **kāu**?* Do **you have** a job?] Note: *Kou* has the same meaning, but is used to indicate possession of things one cannot control (chiefs and gods, land, lineage, emotions, name), transportation or things one can wear or enter into (clothes, buildings).

ka'u my, I have. [*ka'u papa heluhelu,* **my** reading class] [*Heluhelu au i ka'u puke i ke ahiahi.* I read **my** book in the evening.] Note: *Ko'u* has the same meaning, but is used to indicate possession of things one cannot control (chiefs and gods, land, lineage, emotions, name), transportation or things one can wear or enter into (clothes, buildings).

kaua war, battle. (Kalākaua = the day of battle) (*kaua kūloko* = civil war)

kāua we, us (two) (speaker and person spoken to only). When answering the telephone, say "aloha kāua." Note: *Māua* also means we (two), but excludes the person being addressed.

kauā 1. in ancient days, outcast or slave class. 2. servant. [*He kauā ko kona kupuna wahine kaikua'ana no Lili'uokalani.* His grandmother's older sister was a **servant** for Lili'uokalani.]

Kaua'i island famous for the natural beauty of the Nā Pali coast and Waimea Canyon.

Kaua'i

kaualakō to drag something. (syn. *kauō*)

kauhale home, in ancient Hawai'i a cluster of houses, each used for a separate purpose.

kauhale

kauhua 1. desire. 2. pregnancy.

kauila native tree with hard wood used for weapons, sorcery.

kauka doctor. (*kauka niho* = dentist) (*kauka holoholona* = veterinarian)

kaukahi to stand alone.

kauka'i to depend on. [*Kauka'i ka ho'okele 'oihana ma kāna kākau 'ōlelo.* The CEO **depends on** his secretary.]

kaukani thousand. [*'Elua haneli **kaukani** kānaka hapa Hawai'i.* (There are) two hundred **thousand** part-Hawaiians.]

kaukau 1. chant of mourning. 2. lower chiefly rank.

kaula rope, cord, string. (*kaula hao* = chain) (*pā kaula hao* = chain link fence) (*kaula ʻili* = lasso)

kaula

kāula prophet, *kahuna* able to predict the future.

kaulaʻi 1. to dry in sun (clothes, fish). 2. dried in sun (clothes, fish). [*ʻOno ka heʻe* **kaulaʻi**. **Dried** octopus is delicious.]

kaulana 1. famous, well known. 2. to become famous. [*E* **kaulana** *ana ka waʻa kaulua ʻo Hawaiʻiloa?* Will the double-hulled canoe Hawaiʻiloa **become famous**?] 3. resting place, setting of sun.

kaulele to take flight. (*ahikaulele* = rocket)

kaulike 1. equality, justice. 2. equal, just, fair.

kaulike ʻole 1. injustice. 2. unequal, unjust, unfair. [**Kaulike ʻole** *ka uku a ka wahine.* Women's pay is **unequal**.]

kaulua 1. double-hulled canoe. 2. pair.

kaumaha 1. weight, heaviness. 2. heavy. [**Kaumaha** *kēia pahu.* This box is **heavy**.] 3. sad, depressed. [*Ke maʻi kou kupuna kāne,* **kaumaha** *hoʻi ʻo ia?* When your grandfather is ill, is he also **depressed**?]

kaumaha

kāuna number four in ancient counting, four of something. (*lau* = four hundred; *mano* = four thousand; *kini* = forty thousand; *lehu* = four hundred thousand; all are used figuratively to indicate many, very numerous)

kaunaʻoa native vine, orange in color, *lei* of Lānaʻi.

kauoha 1. command, order, testament. [*Ua hoʻokō ka ʻōhua i ke* **kauoha** *a ke aliʻi.* The servant fulfilled the chief's **command**.] (Kauoha Hou = New Testament; Kauoha Kahiko = Old Testament) 2. to

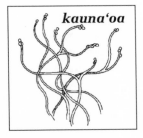

kaunaʻoa

order, command.

kaupale boundary, barrier.

kaupalena 1. limit, deadline. [*ʻO ka lā ʻehā o Iune ke* **kaupalena** *no ke kālewa ʻana aku i nā laulau.* The fourth of June is the **deadline** for peddling the *laulau*.] (*kaupalena hānau* = birth control) 2. to limit, set a deadline, mark a border.

kaupoku ceiling, roof.

kauwela summer.

kāwele 1. towel, napkin. 2. kind of chant and hula step. 3. to wipe, dry. [*Na lāua e* **kāwele** *i nā pā.* They two are the ones who should **wipe** the dishes.]

kāwili to mix food, stir, blend. [*E* **kāwili** *i ke kōpaʻa me ka palaoa.* **Mix** the sugar with the flour.]

ke 1. the (used before words beginning with k, e, a, o). [*Hanohano* **ke** *kahunapule.* **The** minister is distinguished.]

kea white, clear. (Mauna Kea = White Mountain [because it sometimes has snow])

keʻa cross, crucifix. (*fig.* to hinder, obstruct)

keaka theater. (*hana keaka* = theatrical play, skit)

keʻe crooked, bent. (syn. *kīkeʻekeʻe*) (*hoʻokeʻe* = to make a turn) (*keʻekeʻe* = zigzag)

keʻehi 1. to stamp, step, tread. (syn. *hehi*) 2. stirrup.

keʻena 1. office, room. (*keʻena hale* = apartment) (*keʻena kauka niho* = dentist's office)

keha 1. pride, dignity. 2. proud, dignified, majestic. (*kehakeha* = majestic, dignified)

kēhau dew, mist, dew drop.

kēia this (this person or thing). [*He haumāna ʻōlelo Hawaiʻi* **kēia**. **This** is a Hawaiian language student.] (*i kēia mua aku* = in the future)

keiki child, boy. (*keiki papakema* = godchild) (*keiki ʻohana* = nephew) (syn. *keiki hanauna*)

keiki kāne son, boy.

kekahi a, one, another. [*Hākeakea* **kekahi** *kalo. Uliuli* **kekahi** *kalo.* **One** of the taro is pale. **Another** taro is dark.] Note: If used before *mau*, means some, several: *kekahi* *kini* means a can, one of the cans, another can; *kekahi mau kini* means some cans, several cans. (*i kekahi manawa* = sometimes) [*Pāʻani kenika* **kekahi** *mau haku ʻāina* **i kekahi manawa.** **Some** of the landlords play tennis **sometimes.**]

kekele degree of various kinds, including latitude, music, academic, temperature. [*ʻEhia* **kekele** *ka wela o kēia lā?* What's the **temperature** today?] (*kekele loea* = master's degree) (*kekele kauka* = Ph.D.) [*Ua puka aku nei ka wilikī. Ua loaʻa ke* **kekele** *iā ia.* The engineer just graduated. She received her **degree.**]

Kēkēmapa (from English) December.

keko monkey, ape. [*He mau* **keko** *nā keiki liʻiliʻi ma ke kahua pāʻani.* The little children are **monkeys** on the playground.]

kekona second (time). [*ʻEhia mau* **kekona** *o ka hola?* How many **seconds** does an hour have?]

kela 1. excelling. 2. to excel, reach high above. (*hoʻokela* = to surpass, outdo, excel) (*hoʻokelakela* = to flaunt, show off, overbearing, conceited)

kēlā that (far away from speaker, person spoken to). [*ʻO ko Ikaika waʻa peʻa* **kēlā?** Is **that** Ikaika's sailing canoe?] (*kēlā mea kēia mea* = each and every one, everything)

kelakela majestic.

kelakona (from English) dragon.

kelalole tailor.

kelamoku sailor.

kele watery, swampy, greasy, fat. (*waokele* = rain forest) (*hoʻokele* = to navigate, navigator [*fig.* to conduct business])

keleawe general name for metals, brass, copper, tin.

kelekalapa (from English) telegraph.

kelepona (from English) telephone.

kena quenched (thirst). [*ʻAʻole i* **kena** *kona makewai i ka inu koloaka.* Her thirst wasn't **quenched** from drinking soda.] (*hoʻokena* = to quench thirst)

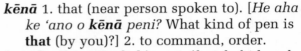

kelepona

kēnā 1. that (near person spoken to). [*He aha ke ʻano o* **kēnā** *peni?* What kind of pen is **that** (by you)?] 2. to command, order.

keneka (from English) cent. (*hoʻokahi keneka* = one cent)

kenekoa (from English) senator.

kenekulia (from English) century. (*i kēlā kenekulia aku nei* = in the last century)

kenikeni (from English) pocket change, dime or ten cents. Note: *Keneka* (cents) and *kenikeni* (ten) are both used to indicate pocket change or loose coins. *Koena* (*lit.* left over) is used for change from a purchase.

keʻokeʻo 1. white, clear. 2. muslin.

keonimana (from English) gentleman. [*He* **keonimana** *kona ʻano.* His character is that of a **gentleman.**]

kepa notched wedge used to repair calabashes.

Kepakemapa (from English) September.

kepakepa a style of chant in which rapid speech is used.

Kepanī (from English) Japanese. (*ka ʻōlelo Kepanī* = Japanese language) (*Iāpana* = Japan)

Kepania (from English) 1. Spain. 2. Spanish.

kēpau resin, gum, paste. (*ʻulu kēpau* = breadfruit paste)

kepolō (from English) devil. [*E komo ana paha ʻolua i nā ʻaʻahu* **kepolō** *no ka pō Heleuī?* Are you two maybe going to put on **devil** costumes for Halloween night?]

keu remaining, excessive, spare, more, most, too much. [*He* **keu** *ʻoe a ke kolohe!* You are the **most** mischievous!]

kewe 1. convex, concave, crescent. [*Kewe ka mahina ma ka pō Hilo.* The moon is **crescent** on the night of Hilo.] 2. crane, boom. [*He* **kewe** *nui ko ka uapo.* The wharf has a big **crane.**]

kī 1. *tī* plant. 2. key. 3. tea. [*I* **kī** *a i ʻole i kope nāu?* Would you like **tea** or coffee?] 4. to shoot gun. 5. to spout up, spurt out.

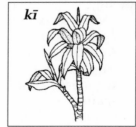

kī

kia 1. pillar, post, prop, mast of ship. (*kiakahi* = person of fixed purpose, alone, supreme, unique) (*moku kiakahi* = one-masted sailboat, sloop) 2. (from English) deer. 3. (from English) gear of machine.

kia'āina governor (*lit.* prop of the land).

kī'aha cup, mug, pitcher, drinking glass.

kī'aha

kia'i 1. guard, watchman, caretaker. 2. to guard, watch. (*kia'i kai* = coast guard)

kia'i kino bodyguard.

kia'i ola lifeguard.

kia'i pō night watchman.

kia manu 1. bird catcher. 2. to catch bird with sticky sap or gum from breadfruit, *pāpalakēpau* and other trees.

kī'amo 1. stopper, plug. 2. sanitary napkin.

kīau to gallop, walk lightly and swiftly.

kiawe 1. tree with wood used to smoke meat. 2. to stream, as rain, to sway.

ki'ei to peek, peer through door, crevice.

ki'eki'e 1. height, tallness. 2. high, lofty. (*kula ki'eki'e* = high school)

kiele gardenia. [*'A'ala nō ke **kiele**. The **gardenia** is very fragrant.*]

kīhā 1. to belch, burp. 2. to rise and pitch, as a canoe in heavy seas. [*Kīhā nā wa'a i ke kōā 'o Kaiwi. The canoes **rise and pitch** in the Kaiwi Channel (channel between Moloka'i and O'ahu, crossed each year in what many consider the world's greatest canoe race).*]

kīhāpai 1. field, farm, garden, small land division. [*He 'āina momona ko māua **kīhāpai**. Our (his and my) **farm** is fertile.*] 2. parish of a church, department of a business.

kīhau 1. frugal. 2. sparingly. [*'Ai **kīhau** 'o ia nei me he manu lā. This one eats **sparingly**, like a bird.*]

kihe 1. sneeze. 2. to sneeze. [*Kihe a maoli ola. **Sneeze** and live. (blessing after someone sneezes, like *Gesundheit*; often shortened to *ola*)*]

kīhei shawl, cloak, cape.

kīhei pili bed covering made of two sheets sewn together.

kīhele to "cruise" around town, go here and there.

kīhene bundle of *ti* leaves used to carry flowers, etc. [*wāhine **kīhene** pua,* the women with **bundles** of flowers (song, "Makalapua," by Konia/Holt)]

kihi outside corner of house, tip, extremity.

kihikihi 1. curves, zigzag. 2. a fish with yellow and black bands.

kī hō'alu (*lit.* slackened key) slack key style of guitar playing, so called because strings are slackened in tuning.

ki'i 1. picture, photo, statue, image, doll. (*ki'i akua* = idol, image of god) (*ki'i ho'ohenehene* = caricature) (*ki'i ho'oweli* = scarecrow) (*ki'i 'oni'oni* = movie, moving picture) (*ki'i pōhaku* = petroglyph) (*ki'i pēpē* = doll) 2. to go and get, fetch. [*E **ki'i** i nā kikiki ma mua o ka hola 'ehā. **Get** the tickets before 4 o'clock.*]

ki'i

kīkā (from English) cigar, cigar flower, guitar. [*Ho'okani 'o Lokelani i ke **kīkā**. Lokelani plays the **guitar**.*]

kīkaha to soar, glide as bird, to detour, deviate. [*Kīkaha ka 'iwa, he lā mālie. ('ōlelo no'eau) The frigate **soars**, it's a calm day.*]

kīkaha

kīkala hip, hip bone.

kīke'eke'e curving, zigzag, crooked (road or path). [*Kīke'eke'e ke alanui i Haleakalā. The road to Haleakalā is **crooked**.*]

kīkēkē to rap, knock. [*I ke kulu aumoe i **kīkēkē** ai kekahi kanaka ma ka puka o ka hale. It was at midnight that someone **knocked** on the door.*]

kīkepa woman's garment, worn under one arm, over opposite shoulder.

kīkī 1. to shoot. (*kīkī wai* = to hose, shoot water with hose) 2. spouting up, shooting as lava, water. (Waikīkī = spouting fresh water [previously known for the many freshwater springs in the area and for the development of extensive taro patches and fishponds])

kīki'i to lean back, tilt, extend.

kikiki (from English) 1. to cheat. 2. ticket (syn. *likiki*).

kiko 1. dot, spot, punctuation mark, freckle. 2. dotted, freckled. (*kiko ho'ōho* = exclamation mark; *kiko ho'omaha* = comma; *kiko nīnau* = question mark; *kiko pau* = period)

kikokiko 1. to type, peck. 2. spotted, freckled.

kīko'o 1. measurement from end of thumb to end of index finger. 2. to extend, stretch, stick out. [*Mai kīko'o i ke alelo!* Don't **stick out** your tongue!] 3. to pay out funds. (*pila kīko'o* = check [*lit.* bill extending credit])

kīko'olā sarcastic, rude, impertinent.

kikowaena center of circle, headquarters.

kikowaena kū'ai shopping center, mall. [*Pono paha 'oe e nānā i nā lole kaila hou ma ke kikowaena kū'ai*. You should perhaps look at the new-style clothes at the **shopping center**.]

kilakila 1. tall, strong, poised, majestic. 2. majestically. [*Kū kilakila 'o Haleakalā, kuahiwi nani o Maui*. Haleakalā, beautiful mountain of Maui, stands **majestically**. (song, "Kilakila 'o Haleakalā," by A. Namakelua)]

kilihune fine, light rain, wind-blown spray.

kili'opu contented, absorbed in pleasant activity like lovemaking. [*Ua kili'opu māua i ka nahele*. We had a **pleasant** time in the forest. (song, "Ku'uipo I Ka He'e Pu'u One," composer unknown)]

kilo stargazer, reader of omens, astrologer. (*kilo hōkū* = astronomer) (*kilo moana* = oceanography, oceanographer) (*kilo 'uhane* = spiritualism, spiritualist)

kilohana top, decorated sheet of traditional tapa bed covering (*fig.* the best, top quality).

kiloi to throw away. [*Mai poina e kiloi aku i ka 'ōpala!* Don't forget to **throw away** the garbage!]

kilu ancient game in which romantic favors were granted to the winner.

kime (also **kimi**) (from English) team. [*Lanakila mau ke kime ikaika i nā pā'ani pōpeku*. The strong **team** always wins the football games.]

kimeki (from English) cement. [*Ho'ohana 'ia nā palaka kimeki ma ke kahua hale*. **Cement** blocks are used for house foundations.]

kīmō to smash to pieces, break into bits.

kīmopō to assassinate, waylay in the dark (*fig.* any underhanded act).

Kina (from English) 1. China. 2. Chinese. (syn. Pākē)

kīnā 1. blemish, blotch, defect. 2. crop loss due to natural disaster. [*Ke kupu a'e kekahi kīnā, he pōpilikia no ke aupuni 'ilihune*. When **crop loss** occurs, it's a calamity for poverty-stricken governments.]

kinai to quench fire. (*kalaka kinai ahi* = fire truck) (*kinai ahi* = firefighter) [*'O ke kinai ahi kae pinana i ke alapi'i a loa'a ka pōpoki ma luna o ke kumu'ulu*. The **firefighter** is the one who could climb the ladder to get the cat on top of the breadfruit tree.]

kalaka kinai ahi

kini 1. forty thousand. 2. multitude, many. 3. (from English) tin, can, gin (alcohol). [*'O kēnā kini kupa kāna 'aina awakea*. That **can** of soup (by you) is his lunch.] (*kini 'ōpala* = garbage can)

kinikini 1. marbles 2. very many.

kinipōpō ball used in sports, recently shortened to *pō* in names of games. (*pōhili* = baseball; *pōpa'ilima* = volleyball; *pōhīna'i* = basketball; *pōpeku* = soccer, football)

kino 1. body, form, shape. (*kino aka* = spirit of a living person; *kino wailua* = corpse, spirit of a dead person) (*kinolau* = body form [*lit.* many bodies]; supernatural beings such as Māui and Pele could change shape at will; the *kukui* leaf, *humuhumunukunukuāpuaʻa* fish, *ʻamaʻu* fern, and pig are some of Kamapuaʻa's *kinolau*) 2. physical self.

kinohi genesis, beginning. (*mai kinohi mai* = from the beginning)

kīnohi decorated, ornamented.

kīoe small surfboard.

kīʻoʻe 1. ladle, dip, cup. 2. to ladle, scoop. [*E* **kīʻoʻe** *i ka pipi kū.* **Ladle** out the beef stew.]

kīʻohuʻohu misty, misty place. (syn. *noe*) [**Kīʻohuʻohu** *pinepine ʻo Lānaʻi City i ke kakahiaka.* Lānaʻi City is frequently **misty** in the morning.]

kiʻo wai puddle. (syn. *loko wai*)

kipa to visit. [*E* **kipa** *aku ana ko Kanani mau malihini i ka Hale Aliʻi ʻo Hānaiakamalama.* Kanani's houseguests are going to **visit** Queen Emma's summer palace.] (*hoʻokipa* = to greet, welcome, entertain) (*ka hale hoʻokipa malihini* = the house which welcomes guests [line in many songs])

kipaku to send away, expel, discharge. [*E* **kipaku** *ʻia ana lākou ʻehā mai ka pūʻali koa aku.* The four of them will be **discharged** from the military.]

kīpapa pavement, to pave (ancient stories tell of Kīpapa Gulch, Oʻahu, being named for the numerous bodies stacked up in battles there).

kīpē bribe, bribery. [*Ua loaʻa ke* **kīpē** *i ke kālai ʻāina?* Did the politician get the **bribe**?]

kipi 1. rebellion, rebel. [*He* **kipi** *kaulana ʻo Wilikoki.* Wilcox is a well-known rebel. (Robert Wilcox is renowned for his role in a short-lived rebellion in 1895 that sought to restore the monarchy, although his flamboyantly princely manner may have obscured the credit due to other leaders such as Bertelman and Widemann.)] 2. to revolt, rebel. 3. rebellious.

kipikua pick-axe.

kipona mixed, mingled colors or texture. (*lei kipona* = a style of Niʻihau shell *lei* or flower *lei* with different shells or colors)

kī pū to shoot or fire a gun. [*Mai* **kī pū**! Don't **shoot**!]

kīpuka 1. clearing in a lava flow where original vegetation grows. 2. lasso. (syn. *kaula ʻili*) (*kīpuka ʻili* = lariat, lasso) 3. short shoulder cape.

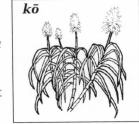

kīpuka

kīpulu fertilizer, mulch.

kiu to spy, observe secretly. (*mākaʻikiu* = detective)

kiwi 1. horn of animal, curved object. 2. bent, curved (*lio lae kiwi* = unicorn)

kīwila (from English) civil, civic, civilian. [*kūʻai hewa i ka pono* **kīwila** *aʻo ke kanaka,* wrongful selling of the **civil** rights of the people (song, "Kaulana Nā Pua," by E. Prendergast)]

kō 1. sugarcane. 2. to fulfill, come to pass, to become pregnant. 3. towed, dragged, long, as vowels with *kahakō* mark. (*kōpaʻa* = sugar) (*mahikō* = sugar plantation) (*hoʻokō* = to carry out orders, fulfill commands)

kō

koa 1. soldier, warrior. 2. native tree with beautiful hard wood prized for furniture, bowls, canoes (*fig.* long lived, like the *koa* tree). 3. brave, courageous.

kōā (sometimes spelled *kōwā*) 1. space between objects. 2. channel. [*ʻO ʻAlenuihāhā kekahi* **kōā** *makaʻu.* ʻAlenuihāhā is one of the dangerous **channels**.] 3. separated.

koʻa 1. coral, coral head. 2. fishing shrine, fishing grounds.

koʻa

koaʻe tropic bird, bird with long tail living in cliffs. *Koaʻe ʻula* has a red tail; *koaʻe keʻokeʻo* has a white tail.

kō'ala to broil meat.

koali 1. morning glory, some varieties used in medicines. 2. to swing. (*lele koali* = to jump rope, swing)

koana space, spacing between rows of stitching on quilt, width of *lauhala* leaf in weaving.

koe 1. remainder, surplus, leftovers. 2. to remain, exclude. 3. not yet, almost. (*koena* = remainder, leftovers, change from paying) [*Eia ke* **koena**. Here's the **change**.] (*koe wale* = except for) [*Maika'i ke kula,* **koe wale** *kēia, nui ka ha'awina*. School is good, **except for** this, there's lots of homework.]

ko'e worm of any type.

kō'eha'eha 1. heat, sultriness (*fig.* mental or physical discomfort, distress). 2. uncomfortably hot. [**Kō'eha'eha** *'o 'Ewa nei i ke kauwela*. Here in 'Ewa it's **uncomfortably hot** in summer.]

ko'eko'e cool, damp, insipid, tasteless.

kōelepālau dessert made with sweet potatoes and coconut milk.

kohana barren, naked, alone. (syn. *'ōlohelohe*) (*kū kohana* = to stand alone)

kohe 1. vagina. 2. crease, groove.

kōheoheo 1. to fall through air. 2. poisonous. [**Kōheoheo** *ka lā'au make*. Insecticides are **poisonous**.]

kōhi 1. to gather. 2. to restrain, hold back. 3. fatty, rich food.

koho 1. guess, choice, selection. 2. to guess, choose. (*koho mua* = first choice, first guess, hypothesis) (*koho pāloka* = election, to elect [*lit.* choose ballot])

koholā whale, humpback. (*palaoa* = sperm whale)

kohu 1. resemblance, appearance, likeness. 2. alike, similar. 3. attractive, pleasing, in good taste. (*kohu like* = similar, alike) (*kohu 'ole* = inappropriate, improper) (*kohu mea* = it seems as if) [**Kohu mea**, *he 'opihi kēia kaikamahine*. **It seems as if** this little girl is an *'opihi* (always clinging).] (*ho'okohu* = to take a fancy to, have a crush on, to appoint, authorize, presumption, pretense) [*'O Samuel Wilder King ke kia'āina i* **ho'okohu** *'ia*. Samuel Wilder King was the governor who was **appointed**.]

koi 1. requirement. 2. fishing pole. 3. to urge, implore, require, insist on. [*E* **koi** *ana nā alaka'i hula iā 'oukou e ho'oma'ama'a*. The hula leaders are going to **require** you folks to practice.]

ko'i adze, axe. [*Ke kua iho nei 'o Kaipo lāua 'o Makoa i ke kumukoa i ke* **ko'i**? *Kāhāhā!* Kaipo and Makoa are cutting down the koa tree with an **adze**? Astonishing!]

ko'i

ko'iawe light rain, rain shower. [*he* **ko'iawe** *ka huila wai*, water wheel's **shower** (song, "Huila Wai," by Lili'uokalani)]

koihonua genealogical chant for *ali'i* family.

ko'iko'i 1. stress, weight, responsibility. (*ho'oko'iko'i* = to emphasize in speech, to burden) 2. urgent, prominent, important, harsh, severe. [*He mea* **ko'iko'i** *ka ho'iho'i 'ana mai i nā iwi o kūpuna i lawe aku 'ia*. Returning the bones of ancestors that were taken away is an **urgent** matter.]

koi pohō 1. suit for damages. [*Na ka hui 'oihana kahiko e uku i ka ho'opa'i ma ke* **koi pohō**? Will the old corporation pay the fine in the **suit for damages**?] 2. to sue for damages.

kōkala thorns of *lauhala*, pineapple.

kō kānāwai law enforcement. [*'O ke* **kō kānāwai** *kā kāu mo'opuna wahine 'oihana*? Is **law enforcement** your granddaughter's career?]

koke 1. quick. 2. near, quickly, soon, immediately. [*E pahū* **koke** *ana kēnā pāluna*. That balloon (by you) will **quickly** explode.]

koki'o native hibiscus with red flowers, state plant. (*koki'o ke'oke'o* = hibiscus with white flowers)

koko blood. [*He pili* **koko** *ko 'olua*? Are you two related by **blood**?]

kōkō carrying net, used for hanging calabashes.

kokoke nearby, close, almost. [***Kokoke e mākaukau nā pāʻū lāʻī no ka hōʻike hula.** The *tī* leaf skirts are **almost** ready for the hula exhibition.*]

kokoleka chocolate, cocoa. [*Ma mua o ka hoʻi a hiamoe ʻana, e inu i ke* **kokoleka**. Before going to sleep, drink **cocoa**.]

kōkoʻo partnership, partner; a number added to *kōkoʻo* specifies the number of partners. *Kōkoʻohia* is used to ask how many partners or companions are involved. [*He* **kōkoʻohia** *o kēia hui kauka? He* **kōkoʻohiku** *kēia.* How many **partners** does this medical association have? This is a **seven-doctor partnership**.] (*kōkoʻolua* = companion, associate)

kōkua

kōkua 1. help, assistance. 2. helper. 3. to help, assist. [*Hiki anei paha iā ʻolua ke* **kōkua** *mai iā ia?* Can you two perhaps **help** him?]

kolamu (from English) column.

kōlea 1. bird, plover. 2. step-parent [*ko Kaipo makua kāne kōlea,* Kaipo's **stepfather**] 3. Korea. 4. Korean.

kōlea

kolepa (from English) 1. golf. [*Auē ka nui o nā kahua pāʻani* **kolepa** *ma Oʻahu nei!* Gosh, there are lots of **golf** courses here on Oʻahu!] 2. to play golf.

koli to whittle, pare, sharpen. [***Koli** mau ka paniolo i ka lāʻau.* The cowboy always **whittles** wood.]

kōliʻuliʻu dim, distant object or sound, obscure.

kolo to creep, crawl. [*He mau ʻelelū ko ka hale popopo e* **kolo** *nei ma ka papahele.* The rotting house has some cockroaches **crawling** on the floor.]

koloa Hawaiian duck.

koloaka (from English) soda.

kolohe 1. rascal, mischief-maker, misbehavior (also means comic, crook, vandal, lecher, many other meanings). [*ʻO ka hana* **kolohe** *a kāna kaikamahine ʻohana ke kumu āna e nuku mau ai iā ia.* His niece's **misbehavior** is the reason why he would always scold her.] 2. to misbehave, cheat. 3. mischievous, naughty, unethical, fraudulent. Note: *Kolohe* covers a wide range of behavior from mischievous to criminal.

kolokolo to track down. (*hoʻokolokolo* = trial, to investigate, try in court)

kolonahe gentle, mild, softly blowing.

kolopua fragrant, filled with the scent of flowers. [***Kolopua** ke ea ma ka pō ikīki.* The air is **fragrant with the smell of flowers** on humid nights.]

kolopupū old, infirm. [*E ola a* **kolopupū** *a haumakaʻiole.* Live until **old**, with eyes like a rat's. (familiar line in chants and prayers requesting long life)]

kōmike (from English) committee.

komikina (from English) commissioner.

komo 1. to enter, go into, wear, put on. [*E* **komo** *mai. Nou ka hale.* **Come inside**, the house is yours. (traditional greeting in a society where hospitality is very important)] 2. to join a class. 3. to feel emotion. [*Ua* **komo** *ka huhū i loko ona.* She **felt** anger.] (*hoʻokomo* = to insert, put into, deposit, to dress someone) [*Ke* **hoʻokomo** *nei ke kuke i ka haupia i ka pahu hau.* The cook is **putting** the *haupia* (coconut pudding) into the icebox (refrigerator).] [***Hoʻokomo** ke kupuna kāne i kāna moʻopuna i ka lole.* The grandfather **dresses** his grandchild.] (*komo lima* = ring)

komohana west (where sun "enters" sea).

komohewa to trespass. (*komo ʻino* = to invade, enter wrongly; *komo wale* = trespass, intrude)

kona 1. leeward side of each island, less rainy than *koʻolau,* or windward side. 2. his, her. (syn. *kāna*).

kōnane 1. bright moonlight. [*ka pā* **kōnane** *a ka mahina,* the moon's **bright moonlight** (common line in songs)] 2. ancient game like checkers. 3. to shine (moon).

koneko (from English) doughnut.

koni to throb, tingle, flutter. [**Koni** *au i ka wai huʻihuʻi*. My heart **tingles** for the cool waters. (song, "Koni Au i ka Wai," by Kalākaua)] (*konikoni* = to beat, throb with passion or pain)

kono 1. invitation. [*Loaʻa mai ke **kono** mai Keawaiki*. An **invitation** has been received from Keawaiki. (song, "Keawaiki," by H. D. Beamer)] 2. to invite.

konohiki overseer, headman of *ahupuaʻa*.

koʻo brace, support, prop.

koʻokoʻo cane, staff, rod, support. [*E ola a kani **koʻokoʻo***. Live until the **cane** sounds. (familiar line in traditional prayers asking for long life)]

koʻokoʻolau native shrub used for medicinal tea.

koʻolau windward side of each island, rainy side (*fig.* difficulties). (ant. *kona*) [*Aia ʻo Hilo ma ka ʻaoʻao **koʻolau** o ka mokupuni nui*. Hilo is on the **windward side** of the Big Island.]

kopa (from English) soap.

kope (from English) 1. coffee, copy, rake. 2. to make a copy, to rake. (*kopekope* = to rake)

kou 1. your (1), you have. [*Nani **kou** mau maka!* **Your** eyes are pretty!] [*He mau maka nani **kou**.* **You have** pretty eyes.] (syn. *kāu*) 2. old name for Honolulu area. Note: *O*-class possessive pronouns are used before nouns referring to things one is born with, such as chiefs and gods, land, family, heritage; they can also include buildings or transportation, and clothes.)

koʻu 1. my, mine, I have. [*ʻO Hāmākua **koʻu** moku*. Hāmākua is **my** land division (where I'm from).] [*He ʻāina **koʻu**.* **I have** land.] (syn. *kaʻu*) 2. to conceive; male potency.

kū 1. to stand, stop, appear, arrive. [*Kū aʻe ʻo Hiʻiaka ma ka lua pele*. Hiʻiaka **appeared** in the crater.] 2. resembling, having the appearance or character of a parent. [*Kū ʻo ia i kona makuahine i kona lauoho*. Her hair is just like her mother's. (Her hair closely **resembles** her mother's.)] (*kū ʻole i ke kānāwai* = illegal) (*hoʻokū* = to stop car or machine) (*kū hou* = to rise again, to res-

urrect) (*kū ʻiʻo* = fact, truth)

Kū 1. name of important god of ancient Hawaiʻi, often associated with war, human sacrifice, but also a god of the forest, canoe building and other activities. 2. name of days of month in Hawaiian moon calendar, days sacred to god Kū.

kua 1. back, burden. (*huli kua* = to turn one's back, thus insulting someone) 2. to chop, cut. 3. tapa anvil.

kuaʻāina 1. country (vs. city). 2. person from country, rustic.

kuaʻana shortened form of *kaikuaʻana*, older sibling, term of address for older sibling.

kuaʻeho tumor.

kuahaua proclamation, declaration.

kuahine (often pronounced with "t" sound, *tuahine*) shortened form of *kaikuahine*, sister of male. [*Ua hele mai au no **tuahine**. I have come to fetch my **sister**. (traditional song, "ʻŌpae ē")]

kuahiwi mountain. [*ʻO Mauna Kea ke **kuahiwi** lōʻihi loa o ka honua*. Mauna Kea is the tallest **mountain** on earth.]

kuahu altar in *hālau hula* where various plants are placed to honor Laka and other gods. [*ʻO ka ʻieʻie, ka lama a me ka palaʻā nā mea kanu i kau ai ma luna o ke **kuahu**. ʻIeʻie, lama and palaʻā are plants placed on the **hula altar**.]

kūʻai to buy, sell. [*Hiki paha ke **kūʻai** ʻia aku kou mau apolima kula, ʻaʻole paha? ʻAʻole hiki!* Can your gold bracelets be **sold** or not? No, they can't!] (directionals *mai* and *aku* are often added to clarify meaning) (*kūʻai aku* = to sell) (*kūʻai mai* = to buy) (*hale kūʻai* = store)

kūʻai emi sale.

kūakā loud sound, boom.

kuakea faded, bleached, pale, unhealthy looking.

kualā dorsal fin. [*He **kualā** ko ka naiʻa*. Dolphins have **dorsal fins**.]

kualono ridge, region near top of mountain.

kuamoʻo backbone, spine, road.

kūamuamu to curse, blaspheme.

kuapā wall of fish pond. (*loko kuapā* = fish pond made by building a wall on a reef)

kuapa'a 1. servant, slave, hard labor. 2. oppressed, enslaved.

kuapapa 1. heap, pile. 2. peace, quiet, tranquility.

kuapo 1. belt. 2. to put on a belt. 3. to swap, exchange. (*kuapo 'ili* = seat belt) [*E komo i kou* **kuapo 'ili**. Put on your **seat belt**.]

kuapu'u hunchback.

kū'au handle, stem, stick. [*ka wai* **kū'au** *hoe o Kalalau,* (*'ōlelo no'eau*) the water that drips down the shaft of the paddle at Kalalau. (wise saying celebrating Kalalau Valley on Kaua'i)]

kū'auhau 1. genealogy. 2. to recite genealogy. (syn. *mo'okū'auhau*)

kuawa guava.

kū'ē 1. opposition, opposite. 2. to oppose, resist. [*Ua* **kū'ē** *'o Kauka Aluli a me ka PKO i ka pōkā pahū 'ana i ka mokupuni 'o Kaho'olawe.* Dr. Aluli and the PKO (Protect Kaho'olawe 'Ohana) **opposed** the bombing of the island of Kaho'olawe.]

kuehu to shake, stir up dust. [*ka makani* **kuehu** *lepo o Ka'ū,* (*'ōlelo no'eau*) the **dust-stirring** wind of Ka'ū.]

kueka (from English) sweater.

ku'eku'e elbow, wrist bone, joint, knuckle. (*ku'eku'e lima* = wrist; *ku'eku'e maka* = eyebrow; *ku'eku'e wāwae* = ankle, heel; *ku'e* = to push with the elbows)

kuene waiter, waitress, flight attendant.

kuewa vagabond, wanderer, friendless one, exile.

kuha 1. saliva, spit. 2. to spit.

kūha'o independent, standing alone (*fig.* extraordinary).

kūhele to get up and go.

kūhewa sudden attack, stroke. (*pilikia kūhewa* = emergency, sudden trouble)

kuhi 1. to point, gesture. 2. to suppose, guess. [**Kuhi** *ka lima, hele ka maka.* (*'ōlelo no'eau*) Where the hands **point**, the eyes follow. (hula rule)]

kuhihewa to err in judgment, to suppose wrongly, to think mistakenly. [*A he* **kuhihewa** *ko'u lā aia i ka poli.* **I thought (mistakenly)** she was here in my embrace. (traditional song, "He'eia")] (*inā 'a'ole au i kuhihewa* = if I am not mistaken)

kuhikuhi to show, teach, give orders. (*'ōlelo kuhikuhi* = directions, instructions) (*papa kuhikuhi* = index, prescription)

kuhikuhipu'uone seer, expert on location of house, temple, etc.

kuhina cabinet minister, regent, ambassador. (*kuhina nui* = prime minister) (*kuhina waiwai* = minister of finances)

kūhohonu complex, complicated, deep thought.

kui 1. pin, needle, screw, nail. (*kui kaiapa* = diaper pin; *kuikala* = screwdriver; *kui lauoho* = hairpin; *kui 'onou* = thumbtack) 2. to string on a thread or cord such as flowers for *lei*, fish. (*kui lima* = to join hands, go arm in arm) (*kuipapa* = method of *lei* making by sewing flowers onto flat strip of *lauhala* or other material)

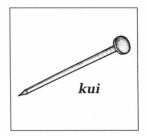

kui

ku'i 1. to pound, punch, strike, join, unite, stitch. (*ku'i 'ai* = to pound poi; *ku'i kā* = to pound smooth; *ho'oku'i* = to hit, pound, collide [*fig.* to hurt feelings]) 2. a type of hula. 3. to spread news. [**Ku'i** *ka lono i Pelekane.* The news **spread** to England. (chant for Kalākaua, "Kāwika")] 4. artificial. (*niho ku'i* = false teeth)

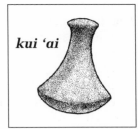

kui 'ai

ku'ikahi 1. treaty, covenant. [*He mau* **ku'ikahi** *ko Kauikeaouli me nā 'āina 'ē.* Kauikeaouli (Kamehameha III) had **treaties** with foreign countries.] 2. unified, united.

kūikawā temporary, for the time being, special, free and independent, such as independent counsel. [**Kūikawā** *kona ho'ohana 'ana i ke ko'oko'o kālele.* His using a crutch is **temporary**.]

kū'ike 1. cash. 2. to know beforehand, in advance. (*uku kū'ike* = cash payment) *kuiki* (from English) 1. quilt (syn. *kapakuiki*). 2. to quilt. [*Nāna, na Meali'i i* **kuiki** *i kāna* **kapa kuiki**? Was it she, was it Meali'i who **quilted** his **quilt**?]

ku'iku'i 1. boxing. 2. to box.

ku'ina 1. blow, punch, peal of thunder. 2. joint, joining, seam. [*'A'ole hiki ke 'ike 'ia ke* **ku'ina** *ma ke kapa.* **Seams** can't be seen on tapa cloth.]

kuka (from English) coat. (*kuka ua* = raincoat; *kui lā'ī* = raincoat of old days, made of dried *tī* leaf tied to *olonā* netting))

kūka'a 1. bolt, roll of cloth or *lauhala*. 2. to roll up as tapa or cloth.

kūkae 1. excrement. 2. to excrete. (*kūkaehao* = rust) (*kūkaelio* = mushroom) (*kūkaeloli* = mildew)

kūkahekahe 1. pleasant conversation. 2. to spend time in pleasant conversation.

kūkā kama'ilio interview, conference.

kūkākūkā 1. discussion, consultation. [*Na ke kahunapule e alaka'i ana i ke* **kūkākūkā** *ma ka hālāwai.* It is the minister who will lead the **discussion** at the meeting.] 2. to discuss, consult.

kūkala to proclaim publicly. (*kūkala hewa* = false alarm; *kūkala nūhou* = to broadcast news)

kūkālā 1. auction. 2. to auction. [*E* **kūkālā** *'ia ana kēlā mau waiwai ho'oilina.* Those estates will be **auctioned** off.]

kūkapu 1. chastity. 2. chaste.

kuke 1. cook. 2. to cook.

kūkini 1. runner, swift messenger. 2. to run swiftly.

kuko 1. strong desire. 2. to lust. 3. lusty. [**Kuko** *ke kanaka u'i.* The handsome man is **lusty**. (song, "Ka Pua o ka Makahala," by V.I. Rodrigues and L. Aarona)]

kūkonukonu excessive, deep, profound, complicated. [**Kūkonukonu** *ko kēia mo'olelo 'aumoana mana'o.* The meaning of this voyaging story is **profound**.]

kuku

kuku to beat, as tapa.

kukū 1. thorn, burr. 2. thorny, prickly. 3. pierced by a thorn.

kūkū 1. tūtū, grandpa, grandma (from *kupuna*). 2. gourd beat. (*ho'okūkū* = contest, competition) (*ho'okūkū hīmeni* = song contest) (*ho'okūkū hula* = hula competition)

kuku'e clubfoot; one with a deformed leg or foot.

kukui 1. tree, symbol of Moloka'i. 2. light, torch (*kukui* nuts were lit to provide light at night). (*kukui hele pō* = lantern) (*kukui pa'a lima* = flashlight) (*hale ipu kukui* = lighthouse)

kukui

kuku'i 'ōlelo storyteller.

kūkulu 1. horizon, border. (*kūkulu o Kahiki* = Eastern horizon, portals through which sun rises in direction of ancient Polynesian homeland Kahiki [*lit.* the east, the arrival]) 2. post, pillar. 3. to build a house, set up a tent. [*Pipi'i ke* **kūkulu** *hale 'ana ma Honolulu nei.* **Building a house** here in Honolulu is expensive.] 4. to tie a horse, to park.

kukuna ray of sun, spoke of wheel, spike of sea urchin. [*Ua 'ike mua 'oe i nā* **kukuna** *o ka lā ma ka hikina ma kaiao?* Have you seen the **rays of the sun** in the east at dawn?]

kukupa'u to do with great enthusiasm, with might and main. [**Kukupa'u** *nā 'ōpio i ka wa'u niu.* The young people grate coconut **with great enthusiasm**.]

kula 1. plain, open country, pasture. (*kula iwi* = birth place [*lit.* plain of bones], a place one has close ties to since generations of ancestral bones are buried there). 2. school. (*kula ha'aha'a* = elementary school; *kula ki'eki'e* = high school; *kula nui* = university; *kula pō* = night school; *kula waena* = intermediate school) 3. gold. (*kula pepeiao* = earring) (syn. *mea ho'onani pepeiao*) (*kula waiwai* = source of income, livelihood)

kula'i to push over, knock down, shove to one side, dash to pieces.

kulāiwi native land, homeland.

kulana 1. to tilt, reel. 2. unsteady (*fig.* insecure, hesitant).

kūlana 1. rank, position, reputation. (*kūlana helu 'ekahi* = first place, first prize) [*Ua lilo ke* **kūlana helu 'ekolu** *i ka ho'okūkū hula keiki i kā Lahela hālau.* The **third place** in the children's hula contest went to Lahela's *hālau.*] 2. site, place. 3. outstanding, prominent.

kūlanakauhale town, city. [*'O Wailuku kekahi* **kūlanakauhale** *kahiko.* Wailuku is an old **town**.]

kūlanakauhale

Kūlanihāko'i legendary lake in the sky considered to overflow when it rains, sometimes used symbolically in chants of mourning.

kūlapa 1. to frolic, jump, skip. [*Kūlapa nā kao keiki.* The baby goats **skip** around.] 2. earth piled at the edge of a taro patch or furrow.

kuleana 1. right, authority, responsibility. [*He* **kuleana** *ko ka 'ōiwi Hawai'i.* The Hawaiian native people have **rights and responsibilities**.] 2. property, title, ownership. 3. cause, justification. 4. small land division.

kuli 1. knee. (*kukuli* = to kneel) 2. deafness, deaf person. 3. deaf. (*kuli ka pepeiao* = deaf the ear [can't hear]) (*kuli hiamoe* = to doze)

kūlia to try, to strive. [*E* **kūlia** *i ka nu'u.* **Strive** for the highest. (Kapi'olani's motto)]

kūlike alike, conforming.

kulikuli 1. noise, din. [*Kulikuli!* Be quiet (you are making **noise**).] 2. noisy.

kūlina (from English) corn. (*kūlina pohāpohā* = popcorn; *kūlina wali* = cornmeal)

kūloko local, domestic. (*kaua kūloko* = civil war) (*ka nūhou kūloko* = local news)

kūlolo dessert made of baked, grated taro and coconut milk.

kūlou to bow the head, bend down.

kulu 1. drip, leak, flow of tears. [*Ua* **kulu** *nā waimaka ma ka ho'olewa.* Tears **flowed** at the funeral.] 2. to drip, trickle, leak. (*kulu aumoe* = midnight, late night)

kuluma 1. customary, usual. 2. acquainted with, intimate. (*ma'i kuluma* = chronic illness) (syn. *ka'a ma'i*)

kūmaka eyewitness (syn. *'ike maka*).

kūmakahiki annual, yearly.

kumakaia 1. traitor. 2. to betray. 3. traitorous.

kūmakani windbreak.

kūmaumau continuous, regular.

kumu 1. basis, foundation, bottom. [*He* **kumu** *kahua ko kou hale?* Does your house have a **foundation**?] (*ho'okumu* = to establish, found, create) [*Ua* **ho'okumu** *nā mikionele i ke kula 'o Lahainaluna.* Missionaries **established** Lahainaluna school.] (*ho'okumu honua* = creation of the world) (*kumulipo* = origin, source of darkness [name of creation chant]) 2. trunk of tree, handle. (*kumuniu* = coconut tree) 3. pattern, manual. 4. origin, source, beginning, teacher. (Sometimes *kumu a'o* is used to specify teacher.) (*kumu hula* = hula teacher) 5. reason, cause. [*He aha ke* **kumu** *no kou uē 'ana, e ka pēpē?* What is the **reason** for your crying, baby?] (*kumuhana* = subject, topic)

kumu a'o

(*kumu kū'ai* = price, cost) (*kumu mana'o* = theory) (*kumu ho'opuka uila* = electrical outlet) (*kumu lā'au* = tree)

kūmū type of fish, slang for sweetheart.

kumu kānāwai constitution (legal document).

kūmūmū dull, blunt (knife, scissors). [*Kūmūmū kēnā 'ūpā kahiko, akā 'o 'oi nō kēia 'ūpā hou.* That old scissors (by you) is **dull**, but this new scissors is really sharp.]

kūna'au to bear a grudge.

kūna'e to stand firmly against opposition.

kūnāhihi numb, shocked, dazed.

kūnānā puzzled, surprised, bewildered. [*Mai* **kūnānā** *me ke kōkua 'ole!* Don't just stand **bewildered** without helping.]

kunāne shortened form of *kaikunāne*, brother of female.

kūnewa to pass, of time, to age.

kuni to burn, blaze, brand.

kūnihi 1. ridge of cliff, feather helmet or hair. 2. steep, precarious. [*Kūnihi ka mauna i ka laʻi ē.* The mountain is **steep** in the calmness. (first line of *mele kāhea*, chant requesting permission to enter)]

kunu 1. cough. 2. to cough. [*Ke loaʻa ʻoe i ke anu,* **kunu** *mau ʻoe?* When you have a cold, do you always **cough**?]

kūō to cry loudly with joy, pain; howl.

kūʻokoʻa 1. independence, liberty, freedom. 2. independent, free.

kūola alive and safe (after being in danger).

kūʻono 1. inside corner of a house. 2. bay, gulf.

kūʻonoʻono well off, comfortably situated. [*Kūʻonoʻono ka nohona o nā kānaka waiwai.* The life-style of the wealthy is **comfortable**.]

kupa citizen, native, well acquainted. [*Ua noho au a* **kupa** *i kou alo.* I have become **well acquainted** with you. (song, "Ua Noho Au a Kupa," by J. Almeida)] (*nā kupa o ka ʻāina* = the natives of the land)

kūpaʻa 1. loyalty, allegiance. 2. firm, steadfast. 3. firmly. [**kūpaʻa** *ma hope o ka ʻāina,* standing **firmly** behind the land (song, "Kaulana Nā Pua," by E. Prendergast)]

kūpaʻakai to eat poi or sweet potato with salt, symbol of Hawaiian ideal of hospitality, always offering whatever food is available. [*Me ia nō e* **kūpaʻakai** *ai.* It is with him (the visitor) that we should **eat**, extending hospitality. (chant, "Mele Hoʻokipa")]

kupaianaha surprising, strange, wonderful. [*ʻO* **Kupaianaha** *ka inoa o ka lua pele hou ma Puna.* **Kupaianaha** is the name of the new crater (vent) in Puna.]

kūpaka to kick, smash, writhe, twist.

kūpaku resuscitation.

kūpale 1. defense. 2. to defend, ward off. [*ʻO ka lua kona* **kūpale***.* Her **defense** is Hawaiian martial arts.]

kūpalu to stuff with food.

kūpaoa strong, penetrating fragrance. (syn. *paoa*) [**Kūpaoa** *ke onaona o ka puakenikeni.* The scent of the *puakenikeni* flower is **strong**.]

kupapaʻu corpse, dead body. (syn. *kino wailua*)

kūpau entirely finished.

kūpeʻe 1. varicolored shellfish. 2. anklet, bracelet, handcuffs.

kūpinaʻi 1. to echo, reverberate. 2. mourn, lament.

kūpipi crowded, as with people or stars.

kūpono 1. honest, proper, fair, just. [*Ua* **kūpono** *kāna hāʻawi ʻana aku i ka pila kīkoʻo iā Lokalia.* Her giving the check to Lokalia was **fair**.] 2. qualified, suitable, fit. [*He moho* **kūpono** *kāna wahine no ke keʻena o kiaʻāina.* His wife is a **suitable** candidate for the office of governor.]

kūpouli dazed, stricken with emotion.

kupu growth, sprout, upstart. (*ke kau kupulau* = spring semester) (*hoʻokupu* = offering) (*He aha ka mea i kupu aʻe ai?* = What happened?)

kupua supernatural being. [*ʻO Māui ke* **kupua** *kaulana loa o ka Pākīpika.* Māui is the best known **supernatural being** of the Pacific.] (*pōhaku kupua* = stones considered to have spiritual force or healing powers)

kupuna grandparent, ancestor (pl. *kūpuna*). (*kupuna kāne* = grandfather; *kupuna wahine* = grandmother; *kupuna kuakahi* = great-grandparent; *mai nā kūpuna mai* = from the ancestors)

kupuna kāne

kuʻu 1. to release, let go, abandon. [*Ua* **kuʻu** *aku ke kia manu i ka manu āna e hoʻopaʻa ana.* The bird catcher **released** the bird he was holding.] (*hoʻokuʻu* = to discharge, release, liberate) 2. my, mine (possessive). Unlike *koʻu* or *kaʻu*, which also mean "my" or "mine," **kuʻu** is used to express emotional closeness and implies "my beloved," as in *ku'u home*, "my beloved home," or *ku'u ipo*, "my beloved sweetheart."

kū'ula stone god used to attract fish, altar near sea for worship of the fish god.

ku'una 1. slope of hill. 2. traditional, hereditary. (*ma'i ku'una* = inherited disease) 3. relieved, relaxed.

ku'upau 1. to go to the limit, try one's hardest. 2. to release all restraints, inhibitions.

lā 1. sun, day. [*Wela ka lā*. The **sun** is hot.] (*lā hana* = workday) (*lā uku* = payday) (*lā puka* = rising sun) (*lā kau* = setting sun [syn. *lā welo, napo'o ka lā*]) (*i kēia lā* = today) [*I kēia lā, ua 'ike 'o Leilehua i ke kualā manō*. **Today**, Leilehua saw the dorsal fin of a shark.] (*lā 'ae'oia* = good old days, past time of youth, beauty) 2. sail, fin.

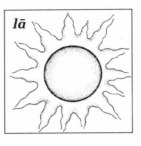

lā

la'a sacred, holy. (*la'a kea* = sacred light, sacred knowledge)

la'amia calabash tree, fruit used to make *'ulī'ulī* (hula implement).

lā'au 1. plant, tree, wood. (*kumulā'au* = tree) (*lā'au 'ala* = fragrant wood, sandalwood [harvest for China trade in early 19th century caused great suffering]) (*lā'au 'ai* = chopsticks) (*lā'au ana* = yardstick, ruler, survey rod) (*lā'au Kalikimaka* = Christmas tree) 2. medicine (herbs were used for medicine). (*lā'au hamo* = salve, ointment) (*lā'au kāhea* = healing through prayer) 3. strength, stiffness. 4. blow of a club. (*lā'au pālau* = war club) 5. medical. (*lā'au hihi* = vine) (*Lā'au Kū Kahi/Lā'au Kū Lua* = days of the lunar month sacred to Kū)

lā'au 'ai

lā'au 'ino drugs. [*Kōheoheo kekahi lā'au 'ino*. Some **drugs** are poisonous.]

lā'au lapa'au herbal medicine. [*'O ka lā'au lapa'au kekahi ho'oilina waiwai*. **Herbal medicine** is a valued heritage.]

lā'au make poison, insecticide. [*E kīkī 'ia ana ka lā'au make i nā nāhelehele*. **Insecticide** will be sprayed on the weeds.]

lae 1. forehead. 2. point of land jutting out into ocean; peninsula. [*'O Kalae ka lae nui o Hawai'i nei*. Kalae is the big **peninsula** here in Hawai'i.] (*lae o'o* = expert [syn. *lae 'ula, mahao'o*])

laha widespread, widely known, broadcast, spread out. [*Ua laha ka nūhou e pili ana i ka wī ma Somalia*. The news about the famine in Somalia is **widely known**.] (*ho'olaha* = to spread abroad, publish, advertise) (*ho'olaha mana'o* = propaganda)

lā hānau birthday. (*Hau'oli Lā Hānau* = Happy Birthday)

laha 'ole rare, unique, uncommon. [*He mea laha 'ole 'o Ke Aolama*. Ke Aolama (Hawaiian language radio news) is an **uncommon** thing.]

lā hānau

lahi thin, frail, delicate.

lahilahi delicate, dainty. [*Aloha au iā 'oe lā, kou pāpālina lahilahi*. I love you, your **dainty** cheeks. (song, "Pāpālina Lahilahi," composer unknown)]

laho scrotum. (*laholena* = lazy, indolent)

laholio 1. rubber, rubber band. 2. elastic, rubbery.

lā ho'omana'o (also **lā piha makahiki**) day of remembrance, anniversary.

lāhui nationality, race, nation. [*He keu ke*

akahai o ka **lāhui** *Hawai'i.* The gentle nature of the Hawaiian **race** is outstanding.]

la'i 1. calmness, stillness, quiet of nature. 2. calm, peaceful, silent. (Pō La'i ē = Silent Night)

laiki (from English) rice.

laikini (from English) license. [*Ua ho'opiha au i ka palapala noi i* **laikini** *kalaiwa ka'a hou.* I filled out the application for a new driving **license**. (*laikini kī pū* = firearms license)

laiki

laila over there (location is known). [*Ua kipa aku māua 'o ka'u kāne i Ho'okipa Pāka a ua nānā i nā mea he'e nalu makani ma* **laila**. My husband and I visited Ho'okipa Park and saw the windsurfers **over there**.] (*no laila* = therefore) (*a laila* = and then, next)

laka 1. (from English) lock. 2. (from English) to lock. [*Ua pa'a ka puka i ka* **laka** *'ia.* The door was **locked** shut.] 3. tame, domesticated, gentle. [*Ua* **laka** *kā Puakea manu aloha.* Puakea's parrot is **tame**.]

Laka 1. name of hula goddess. [*E* **Laka** *ē, e nauē kāua i uka, i ka nahele.* Oh **Laka**, let's move to the uplands, to the forest. (familiar line in hula chants)]

lakeke (from English) jacket.

laki (from English) lucky. (*pakalaki* = bad luck, unlucky)

lako 1. provisions, supplies. 2. well supplied, prosperous. (*lako ke'ena* = office supplies) (syn. *pono ke'ena*)

lākou they all (three or more), them.

lala diagonal, slanting, oblique. (syn. *hiō*)

lālā 1. branch, limb. 2. member of a club, group. [*He* **lālā** *'o Manu o ka hui hīmeni 'o Ho'okena.* Manu is a **member** of the singing group Ho'okena.] (*ho'olālā* = to plan) [**Ho'olālā** *ka 'ahahui e ho'omoana ma Kualoa.* The organization **plans** to camp at Kualoa.]

lālama 1. to pilfer, meddle. 2. daring, fearless. (*lālama ka lima* = don't meddle, don't goof around [*lit.* the hand meddles])

lālani 1. row, rank, line. 2. line of poetry. (syn. *laina*) [*Nāna e oli i ka* **lālani** *mua.* She is the one who should chant the first **line**.] (*hele lālani* = march in line) (*kū laina* = stand in line)

lalau 1. mistake, blunder. 2. to err, wander, go astray. [**Lalau** *wale nā 'ōpio lapuwale.* The young good-for-nothings **go astray**.]

lālau to seize, reach out for, take hold of. [*Ua* **lālau** *ka 'elemakule i ke apolima kula.* The old man **seized** the gold bracelet.]

lalawe thrilling, overwhelming, overcome with emotion. [*Ke* **lalawe** *nei ku'u nui kino.* My entire body is **overcome with emotion**. (song, "Ahi Wela," by M. Doirin and L. Beckley)]

lale to hurry, hasten, urge on. (*ho'olale* = to hurry, hasten, incite)

lalo 1. depth. 2. down, under, low. [*Aia kāu nūpepa ma* **lalo** *o kou noho.* Your newspaper is **under** your chair.] 3. a leeward, southerly direction. [*E holo kai kākou i* **lalo**. Let's sail downwind, **leeward**.]

lama 1. native plant with yellow wood used as symbol of light and knowledge, used in hula altar. 2. symbol of enlightenment. 3. torch, light, lamp. (*lama kuhikuhi* = beacon, signal light)

lamakū large torch.

lamalama 1. torch fishing at night. 2 to go torch fishing. 3. bright-looking, vivacious, animated.

lana 1. to float. [*Ua* **lana** *mālie ka 'iwa ma ka 'ale.* The frigate bird **floated** calmly on the ocean swell.] 2. floating, buoyant. 3. lowest platform of oracle tower. (*ho'olana* = to launch a project, canoe [*fig.* to cheer up]) [*Āhea ana e* **ho'olana** *'ia ai ka wa'a kaulua hou?* When will the new double-hulled canoe be **launched**?] (*mana'olana* = hope, to hope)

lanaau to drift with the current, wander aimlessly.

lānai porch, patio.

Lānaʻi island that is part of Maui County; in ancient days, Lānaʻi was believed to be inhabited by evil spirits who were chased away by Kaululāʻau.

Lānaʻi

lanakila 1. victory, triumph. 2. to win, triumph, overcome. [*ʻO wai ke kime i **lanakila**?* Which team **won**?]

lananuʻumamao oracle tower of *heiau* with three levels or platforms for different purposes. (*lana* = lowest platform; *nuʻu* = middle platform; *mamao* = highest platform, most sacred)

lani 1. sky, heaven. 2. high chief, majesty. 3. heavenly, spiritual. (*ka makua lani* = heavenly father)

lanipō dense, dark (luxuriant growth of vegetation, rain).

lā nui holiday, various types. (Lā Heleuī = Halloween; Lā Hoʻomaikaʻi = Thanksgiving; Lā Kalikimaka = Christmas; Lā Pakoa = Easter)

lapa 1. ridge, steep ravine. 2. overactive, cavorting like young animal. (*lapa ahi* = blaze, flame) (*lapalapa* = many ridges, to bubble, boil) (*lapa kai* = restless sea)

lapaʻau medical practice. (*lāʻau lapaʻau* = herbal medicine) [*Holomua nā kumu **lāʻau lapaʻau** Hawaiʻi.* Hawaiian **herbal medicine** teachers are making progress.]

lapalapa 1. many ridges. 2. to bubble, boil, cavort.

lapauila 1. lightning flash. 2. to flash, as lightning.

lapu 1. ghost, apparition. 2. to haunt. 3. haunted. (*kiliki o lapu* = trick or treat)

Lāpule Sunday (*lit.* day of prayer).

lapuwale 1. vanity, foolishness. 2. good-for-nothing person, wastrel, scoundrel. 3. worthless. [***Lapuwale** ka hopohopo.* Worrying is **worthless**.]

latitu (also *lakikū*) latitude (geographic). [*He ʻumikūmāiwa kekele ka **latitu** ʻo Hawaiʻi nei.* Hawaiʻi's **latitude** is 19 degrees.]

lau 1. leaf. [*Holunape ka **lau** o ka niu.* The

leaf of the coconut is swaying.] 2. four hundred. 3. numerous, many. (Kīlauea = numerous spoutings up of gases [place name of volcano area])

lauaʻe 1. fern with fragrant leaf with scent reminiscent of *maile*. 2. beloved.

lauahi to destroy by fire, lava. [*Ua **lauahi** ʻia ka hale pule Kalawina ma Kalapana.* The Protestant church at Kalapana was **destroyed by lava**.]

laua'e

lauʻai edible leaves, salad, vegetables.

lauākea 1. commoner. 2. common. [***Lauākea** ke kani manu ma nā kumu ʻōhiʻa.* Bird calls are **common** in ʻōhiʻa trees.]

lauhala 1. leaf of *hala* tree 2. baskets, hats, mats or other items woven from this leaf.

lauhalalana vagabond, drifter (*lit.* floating *hala* leaf).

laukanaka 1. to populate. 2. densely populated, many people, crowded (with the public). [***Laukanaka** mau ʻoe i ka lehulehu.* You are always **crowded** with the public. (song, "Haleʻiwa Pāka," by A. Namakelua)] (*hoʻolaukanaka* = to have many people around, to dispel loneliness with people) [*Loaʻa mai ke kono mai Keawaiki, e kipa, e nanea a e **hoʻolaukanaka**.* An invitation has been received from Keawaiki (Francis Brown's home) to visit, to relax and to **dispel loneliness with people**. (song, "Keawaiki," by Helen Desha Beamer)]

lau kapalili fluttering leaf, part of name of first taro plant, Hāloanakalaukapalili.

laulā broad, wide, general. [*ʻO ke olakino ke kumuhana **laulā**.* The **broad** topic is health.] (*maʻi laulā* = epidemic, contagious disease) (*manaʻo laulā* = broadminded, general theme or idea)

laulau 1. wrapping, wrapped package. 2. a bundle of food wrapped in *tī* leaves and steamed, a favorite dish at parties and *lūʻau*. Usual ingredients in *laulau* are pieces of pork, fish, taro leaves.

laule'a 1. peace, happiness, friendship. 2. happy, glad, genial. (*ho'olaule'a* = festival, celebration, to hold a celebration, to restore peace, friendship)

lau li'i a small leaf, a variety of *maile* found especially on Kaua'i.

laulima cooperation (*lit.* many hands), working together. [*Ua mākaukau koke ka hana haipule i ka* **laulima** *a ka 'ekalesia.* The church service was quickly prepared due to the **cooperation** of the congregation.]

launa 1. to socialize, have fun. 2. friendly, sociable. (*launa palapala* = correspondence, to correspond) (*ho'olauna* = to introduce people) [*E* **ho'olauna** *ana ko'u hoaaloha ia'u me ke Kenekoa.* My friend will **introduce** me to the Senator.]

launa 'ole beyond compare, unique. [*He leo nahenahe* **launa 'ole** *ko ka pu'ukani.* The singer has an **incomparable** sweetness of voice.]

lau niu coconut leaf.

lauoho hair of head. (*huluhulu* = body hair)

laupapa reef. (syn. *'āpapa, pāpapa*)

lauwili circuitous, unstable, fickle, two-faced. [*Hō ke 'ano* **lauwili** *o nā moho koho pāloka!* Darn the **two-faced** character of political candidates!]

lawa 1. enough, ample, satisfied. 2. possessed of enough, therefore, wise, capable. (*ua lawa* = that's enough [call used sometimes at end of hula or song])

lawai'a 1. fisherman. 2. to fish.

lawakua 1. to bind or tie fast (*fig.* to be a dear friend). 2. strong back, bulging with muscles.

lāwalu cooking technique, barbecuing fish wrapped in *tī* leaves on coals).

lawe 1. to take (*lawe aku*). 2. to bring (*lawe mai*). (*lawe leka* = postman) (*lawe ola* = manslaughter, to take a life) (*lawe pio* = conquest, to capture, take prisoner) (*lawe wale* = extortion, to take without right) (*ho'olawe* = subtract, deduct) [*Ua* **ho'olawe** *'ia aku 'elua kaukani kālā mai kāu mau 'auhau e uku ai.* Two thousand dollars were **deducted** from the taxes you have to pay.]

lawea to drift apart, to depart.

lawehala 1. sin, sinner. 2. delinquent, evil. (*lawehala 'ōpiopio* = juvenile delinquent) (*ho'olawehala* = accusation, to accuse) [**Ho'olawehala** *ka ilāmuku i ke kālepa lā'au 'ino.* The sheriff **accuses** the drug seller.]

lawehana 1. to do labor, work. 2. industrious. [*He po'e* **lawehana** *nā Pilipino ma Hawai'i.* The Filipinos in Hawai'i are an **industrious** people.]

lawelawe 1. to serve, attend to, wait on tables. (*lawelawe 'ana* = service) [*Maiau ko ke kuene* **lawelawe 'ana** *mai.* The waitress's **service** is skilled.]

lawelawelima 1. to pitch in, lend a hand. (*lawelawelima 'ana* = pitching in, lending a hand) [*Ho'opau koke ke kūkulu hale ma ka 'āina ho'opulapula i ka* **lawelawelima 'ana**. Housebuilding on Hawaiian Homes lands is quickly finished due to **pitching in**.]

le'a 1. joy, happiness. 2. sexual gratification, orgasm. 3. delightful, happy, completely successful.

le'ale'a fun.

lehe lip. (*lehe luhe* = pouting lip)

lehelehe 1. lips 2. labia of vagina.

lehia 1. expert. [*He* **lehia** *'o Pua i ke kuku kapa.* Pua is an **expert** at beating tapa.] 2. skilled. (syn. *loea*)

leho general term for cowry shell, used in octopus lures.

lehu 1. ashes. 2. four hundred thousand. 3. numerous, very many. 4. ash colored.

lehua tree and blossom of the *'ōhi'a lehua*, symbol of Hawai'i island.

lehulehu multitude, crowd, the public. [*Nui a* **lehulehu** *nā pua mamo i 'ākoakoa mai e ho'olohe i ka pāna puhi 'ohe 'o ka Royal Hawaiian Band.* Numerous indeed were the **multitudes** of Hawaiians who gathered to hear the Royal Hawaiian Band.]

lei 1. garland, necklace. 2. yoke, wreath. 3. to wear as *lei* (*fig.* a beloved child, per-

lei

son). Kinds of *lei* include *lei pua* (flower *lei*), *lei pūpū* (shell *lei*), *lei ʻanoʻano* (seed *lei*), *lei ʻāʻī* (neck *lei*), *lei hulu* (feather *lei*). Familiar styles of *lei*-making include *haku* (several

lei hulu

types of flowers/foliage are braided), *wili* (flowers/foliage are bound with twine to *tī* leaf or other backing), *hili* (one type of foliage or flower is braided), *kui* (single flowers are strung on a thread). (*lei poʻo* = head *lei*) (*hoʻolei* = to wear as *lei*, to fling, toss, throw and retrieve) [**Hoʻolei** ka paniolo i ke kaula ʻili. The cowboy **throws** the lariat.] (*hoʻoleilei* = to juggle)

lei poʻo

lēʻia abundance. (Mokulēʻia = land district full of abundance) [*Ka moena pāwehe o* **Mokulēʻia**. (*ʻōlelo noʻeau*) The patterned carpet of the **abundant land**.]

leina 1. places on each island where spirits gathered then leaped together into the underworld, Milu. (syn. *leina ka ʻuhane*) 2. leap, bound.

leinakia (from English) reindeer.

lei niho palaoa whale tooth, ivory pendant from whale's tooth, symbol of high rank.

leiomano weapon with single shark's tooth.

leka letter, mail. (*hale leka* = post office;

lei niho palaoa

kāleka = postcard, card [syn. *pepa poʻoleka, kāleka poʻoleka*]; *lawe leka* = postman; *pahu leka* = mail box; *poʻoleka* = stamp; *wahī leka* = envelope)

lekapī (from English) recipe.

leki (from English) cellophane tape, tape. [*E wahī i ka makana i ka pepa me ka* **leki**. Wrap the present with paper and **tape**.]

lekiō (from English) radio.

lēkō watercress.

lekuke (from English) lettuce.

lele 1. a jump, leap, attack. 2. a hula step. 3. sacrificial altar of *heiau*. 4. to fly, jump, leap. [*E* **lele** *i Kalalau*. (*ʻōlelo noʻeau*) **Fly off** to Kalalau. (equivalent in meaning to "Go jump in a lake.")] Note: *Lele* has many other meanings. (*lele kawa* = to leap into the ocean feet first without splashing, a game in ancient days) (*lele koali* = to jump rope, swing) (*lele koke* = to leap suddenly [fig. short-tempered]) (*lele lupe* = to rise and fall like a canoe in rough seas [*fig.* rise and fall of emotions]) (*lelepau* = to trust completely) (*lele wai* = to cleanse, purify with water, to purge) (*lele wale* = phrase at end of ancient prayer, to speed prayer on) (*hoʻolele* = to fly plane, kite) [*Ua* **hoʻolele** *ko kākou mau kūpuna i nā lupe ʻano poepoe*. Our ancestors **flew** kites that were sort of round.] (*hoʻolele lupe* = to fly a kite)

leleʻē to jump to conclusions, speak prematurely.

lelele to jump about, hop around, to beat swiftly (heart).

leleponi to die suddenly, as in accident, by stroke.

lelepono to jump carefully (*fig.* to live a happy life, to rise rapidly to success, to do business justly).

lemi (from English) lemon, lime.

leo voice, tone, command, advice. (*leo mana* = voice of authority) (*leo mele* = tune of song, notes of scale) (*leo nui* = loud voice, to speak loudly) (*leo ʻole* = agreeable, uncomplaining) (*leo paʻa* = deaf mute, unable to speak)

lepa flag, tapa cloth on stick used to mark boundaries, as of *kapu* areas.

lepahū to lose courage, give up. [*Mai* **lepahū** *a lilo i hōhē!* Don't **give up** and become a coward!]

lepe 1. hem or fringe of any garment. 2. rooster comb, turkey wattles. [**lepe** *ʻulaʻula*, **lepe** *a ka moa*, red **comb** of the rooster (sexual reference). (song, "Lepe ʻUlaʻula," by Kaimanahila)] (*lepelepe o Hina* = monarch or Kamehameha butterfly) (*lepe lua* = turncoat)

lepo 1. dirt, earth, filth. 2. excrement, used as euphemism for *kūkae*. 3. dirty, soiled. [*Ma hope of ka holoi 'ana, ma'ema'e paha kou mau lole **lepo** loa?* After washing, will your very **dirty** clothes be clean?] (*moe lepo* = bum, shiftless person)

lewa 1. sky, atmosphere, upper heavens. The ancient Hawaiians had separate names for different biogeographic zones of the Earth. They also named different sections of the sky and

lewa

sea. *Lewa lani* refers to the highest section of the sky, while *lewa nu'u* is the section just below that. [*E nā akua o ka **lewa lani**, o ka **lewa nu'u**,* Oh gods of the **highest stratum**, of the **upper heavens** (familiar line in ancient chants and prayers)] 2. to float, dangle, swing. (*lewa ho'omakua* = space just above Earth's surface, lower atmosphere) (*lewa lilo loa* = outer space) (*ho'olewa* = funeral, to lift up and carry) [*Aia ka **ho'olewa** ma ka Lāpule.* The **funeral** is on Sunday.]

lī 1. chill. (*lī lua* = extremely chilly) 2. shoelace. 3. to have chills, feel horrified. 4. hang, gird.

lewalewa dangling.

li'a 1. strong desire, yearning. 2. to yearn for. [*'O 'oe ka'u mea e **li'a** mau ai.* You are the one I always **yearn for**. (a common line in love songs)]

līhau 1. gentle rain. 2. moist, fresh.

lihi 1. edge, border, boundary. (*ka lihikai* = the edge of the sea) 2. rain. 3. small quantity or amount. [*He 'ike **lihi** ko kēlā haumāna.* That student has a **small amount** of knowledge.]

lihilihi 1. eyelashes. [*Lō'ihi ko kē keiki kāne mau **lihilihi** maka.* That (by you) boy's **eyelashes** are long.] 2. flower petal. 3. lace. 4. crochet.

liholiho very hot, glowing, fiery.

li'ili'i small, little. (*ka wā li'ili'i* = childhood)

like like, alike, similar, equal. [*Ua **like** nō a like au me ku'u one hānau.* I am just **like** my birthplace. (song, "Moloka'i Nui a Hina," by M. Kāne)]

like 'ole various, different. (*nā 'ano 'oihana like 'ole* = various kinds of careers, businesses) (*nā 'ano nananana like 'ole* = all different kinds of spiders)

likiki ticket, receipt. (syn. *kikiki*) [*Ua nalowale ka'u **likiki** mai ka panakō mai!* My **receipt** from the bank disappeared!]

liko 1. leaf bud (*fig.* a child or youth). 2. to bud, put forth leaves. (*liko lehua* = bud of *lehua*, new leaf buds of *lehua*, used in Hawaiian herbal medicine) (*likoliko* = fresh, young, oily)

lili 1. jealousy. 2. highly sensitive to criticism. (*ho'olili* = to provoke jealousy, jealous)

līlia (from English) lily. [*'A'ala ku'u pua **līlia**.* My **lily** flower is fragrant. (song, "Pua Līlia," by A. Alohikea)] (*līlia lana wai* = water lily)

liliha nauseating, nauseated, of fatty, rich foods (*fig.* revolted, heartsick).

liliko'i passion flower and fruit.

lilinoe fine mist.

Lilinoe goddess of the mists.

lili'u scorching, smarting, burning (of eyes). Note: Lili'uokalani was given her royal name because of the burning, painful eyes suffered by the Kuhina Nui (regent) Kīna'u, a maternal relative, at the time of her birth. Although Lili'uokalani was her royal name, the queen is reported to have preferred her childhood name, Lydia.)

lilo 1. to be lost, gone. [*Ua **lilo** ka hale leka i ka makani pāhili.* The post office was **lost** in the hurricane.] 2. to become, turn into. [*E **lilo** ana kā ke kumu kaikamahine i luna awa.* The teacher's daughter will **become** a harbor master.] 3. to be engrossed, absorbed in an activity. [***Lilo** 'o Mikala i ka pā'ani hei.* Mikala's **absorbed** in playing string figures.] (*lilo loa* = permanently lost, completely engrossed) 4. far, distant. (*ma uka lilo* = far upland)

(*hoʻolilo kālā* = spendthrift, to spend money)

lima 1. arm, hand, sleeve, finger. 2. five. (*kanalima* = fifty) (*lima ʻākau* = right hand) (*lima hema* = left hand) (*lima ikaika* = to handle roughly, a strong arm or hand, power) (*lima koko* = assassin, murderer, shedder of blood) (*lima kuhi* = index finger) (*lima kuhikuhi* = hands of clock) (*lima ulu* = green thumb)

limahana laborer, employee, labor.

limalima to pilfer, to hire. (*hoʻolimalima* = lease, rental, to lease, rent) (*hale hoʻolimalima* = rental house) (*kaʻa hoʻolimalima* = taxi, rental car)

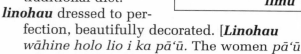
limu

limu general name for seaweed, an item in traditional diet.

linohau dressed to perfection, beautifully decorated. [*Linohau wāhine holo lio i ka pāʻū.* The women *pāʻū* riders are **dressed to perfection**.]

linohau

lio 1. horse. [*Kīau nā lio ma ke kahua hānai pipi.* **Horses** gallop at the ranch.] 2. tight, taut. (*lio lāʻau* = merry-go-round, wooden "horse" for quilting)

lipine (from English) ribbon, tape (reel-to-reel or other kinds of tape). [*ʻEkolu* **lipine** *o ko Tūtū pāpale.* Tūtū's hat has three **ribbons**.]

lipo 1. dark blue-black. [*ʻO ka* **lipo** *o ka lā, ʻo ka* **lipo** *o ka pō,* **Dark blue-black** of the day, **dark blue-black** of the night (line from *Kumulipo,* creation chant)] 2. dim, distant.

liu 1. bilge. 2. to leak.

liʻu slow, tardy, taking a long time.

liʻulā twilight, mirage.

liuliu prepared.

liʻuliʻu to spend much time (*ʻaʻole i liʻuliʻu* = not long afterward)

loa 1. distance, length, height. [*ʻEhia mau mile ka* **loa** *o ka heihei paikikala?* How many miles is the **distance** of the bike race?] 2. very, very much, most, excessive.

loaʻa 1. to find, get, obtain, receive. [**Loaʻa** *kāna kālā i kā kēia luahine moʻopuna kāne?* Does this old lady's grandson **get** her money?] (*loaʻa ke ahipele?* = got a match?) 2. wealth, property, earnings. Note: *Loaʻa* has many other meanings.

loea 1. skill, ingenuity, cleverness. 2. expert, skillful, clever. [*ʻO Kauʻi Zuttermeister ka* **loea** *hula hope loa.* Kauʻi Zuttermeister was the last of four master hula teachers honored with the title of "*loea.*"]

lohe 1. to hear, mind, obey. 2. obedient. (*lohe pepeiao* = hearsay) (*lohe pono* = listen carefully, attentive) (*hoʻolohe* = to listen) [*E nānā aku i ke kumu, e* **hoʻolohe** *mai.* Look to the teacher and **listen**. (song, "Alu Like," by H. Apoliona)]

lohelohe to eavesdrop, listen carefully.

lohi slow, late, mentally retarded. [*Komo* **lohi** *ka haumāna i kāna papa.* The student comes to class **late**.] (*ʻūlōlohi* = late; *lohiʻau* = retarded, backward, slow; *hoʻolohi* = to delay; *lohina* = a delay)

loi to look over critically, to criticize.

loʻi irrigated terrace for growing taro, later used for rice. [*He papa* **loʻi** *a he mau ʻauwai ko ke kula nui.* The university has a field of **taro patches** and water ditches.]

loʻi

lōʻihi 1. length, height. 2. tall, long (time or physical dimension). [*Lōʻihi loa nā hōkele hou.* The new hotels are really **tall**.]

loiloi to evaluate, judge. (*luna loiloi* = judge in speech, hula, or song contest) [*He* **luna loiloi** *ʻo ʻAnakē Pat ma ka Merrie Monarch.* Aunty Pat is a **judge** at Merrie Monarch.]

loina custom, tradition. (syn. *kuluma*) [*He* **loina** *ka ʻaha waimaka ma ko lākou ʻohana.* The gathering one year after a death is a **tradition** in their family.]

loio (from English) lawyer. [*Makemake nō ʻo Mike Hawaiʻi e lilo i* **loio**. Miss Hawaiʻi really wants to become a **lawyer**.]

lōkahi unity, agreement, accord, harmony. [*Inā* **lōkahi** *ka ʻohana, ʻaʻohe mea e ālai aʻe ai*. If the family is united in **harmony**, there is nothing to create obstacles.] (*manaʻo lōkahi* = unanimous)

loke (from English) 1. rose. 2. rosy.

lokelani pink rose, symbol of Maui island.

lokelau green rose. [*no ka pua* **lokelau** *ke aloha,* love for the **green rose** (song, "Green Rose Hula," by J. Almeida)]

lokelani

loko 1. interior, pond, lake, character, entrails. [*Nani ʻo* **loko** *o ka hale pule pena ʻia*. The **interior** of the painted church is beautiful.] 2. internal. 3. inside. [*Aia kā Kawelu kāwele i* **loko** *o ko Wailani kalaka*. Kawelu's towel is **inside** Wailani's truck.] (*loko iʻa* = fishpond; syn. *loko kuapā* [fishpond with walls built on top of a reef]) (*loko wai* = freshwater lake, fountain)

loko iʻa

loko ʻino 1. unkindness. 2. evil, merciless, heartless. [*E pale aku i ka* **loko ʻino**. Defend against **unkindness**. (prayer for protection)]

lokomaikaʻi generosity, kindness, goodwill. [*Nui ko Nākila* **lokomaikaʻi** *i kona kākoʻo iā "Ka Leo Hawaiʻi."* Nākila is very **generous** in his support of "Ka Leo Hawaiʻi" (Hawaiian language radio program).]

loku downpour of rain, blowing of wind (*fig.* deep sorrow, pain, emotion, to cry). [*ka ua* **loku** *a ʻo Hanalei,* (*ʻōlelo noʻeau*) the **pouring rain** of Hanalei (Reverence for nature and delight in names are combined in poetic descriptions of places, often including the names of the winds and rain of that place, such as the heavy rains of Hanalei, Kauaʻi.)]

lola 1. rolling pin, cassette tape. [*Ua loaʻa iā ia ka* **lola** *hou a kākou e hoʻolohe ai?* Does he have the new **cassette** that we're supposed to listen to?] 2. to roll. 3. droopy, sluggish.

lole 1. cloth, clothes, dress. 2. to reverse, unfold, handle, turn over. (*lole ʻauʻau* = swimming clothes) (*lole holoi* = dirty laundry; syn. *lole lepo*) (*lole wāwae* = pants, shorts) (*hoʻololi lole* = to change clothes) [*E* **hoʻololi lole** *ʻoukou, e nā keiki*. **Change** clothes, children.]

lolelua variable, two-faced, fickle. [*He* **lolelua** *ke ʻano o ka meia*. The mayor's character is **two-faced**.]

loli 1. to change, alert. [*Ua* **loli** *ka waihoʻoluʻu o ka pua hau*. The color of the *hau* flower **changed**.] 2. sea slug. 3. speckled, dotted, changed. (*hoʻololi* = to change, take a new form)

lōliʻi relaxed, at ease, carefree.

lolo brains, bone marrow. (*lolo kaʻa* = dizziness)

lōlō paralyzed, numb (*fig.* stupid, dumb). (*pakalōlō* = marijuana [*lit.* cigarette that makes you paralyzed and stupid])

loloa 1. length. 2. long.

lolouila computer (*lit.* electric brain). (syn. *kamepiula*) [*Lohi kā ka mea kūʻai hale* **lolouila**. The realtor's **computer** is slow.]

lolokū midday.

lomi to rub, press, squeeze.

lomilomi 1. masseuse, masseur, one who massages. 2. to massage.

lono news report, remembrance. (*lono papa* = news spread far and wide) (*hoʻolono* = to listen, hear, obey)

Lono one of the four main gods of ancient days. Lono i ka makahiki presided over the harvest season, when war was forbidden.

lōpā 1. peasant, farmer. 2. shiftless.

lopi (from English) thread.

lou 1. hook, long pole for picking fruit. 2. to hook, fasten with a hook. [*Ke* **lou** *nei ka mahiʻai i ka pea a me ka hēʻī*. The farmer is **hooking** avocados and papayas.]

loulu native fan palm used to weave mats, hats.

lū to scatter, sow seed, spend recklessly.

lua 1. hole, pit, grave, toilet, outhouse. (*lua pele* = volcanic crater) (*lua 'uhane* = tear duct, where soul exits and reenters body during sleep) 2. ancient martial arts. 3. two, twice, double.

lua pele

luaahi victim. [*Na wai e kāko'o i ka* **luaahi** *ma ka hana 'ino?* Who will support the **victim** of abuse?]

luahine old woman.

lua'i to vomit, throw up. [*Poluea 'oe i ke holokai? Mai* **lua'i!** Are you nauseated from sailing? Don't **throw up!**] (*lua'i kū* = disgusting; *lua'i pō* = outcasts)

luahine

luaiele to lead dissipated life, not taking care of health. [*Inā* **luaiele** *ka 'ōpio, pilikia auane'i.* If the youth **doesn't take care of his health**, he will have trouble later on.]

luakini a large kind of *heiau* (temple, church.) Note: Perhaps because *luakini* were large *heiau*, the term is often used to indicate any place of worship, including churches and temples of various religions, and no longer refers exclusively to the human sacrifice *heiau* that was introduced into ancient society by Pā'ao in about 1200.

luana to enjoy yourself, relax, socialize.

lua 'ole incomparable, unequaled, unmatched. [*He nani* **lua 'ole** *ko ke mele Hawai'i.* Hawaiian poetry has **incomparable** beauty.]

lua puhi blow hole.

lū'au young taro leaves, used in many food items at a *pā'ina* or party, therefore, by extension, party with traditional Hawaiian food.

luhe to droop, hang down.

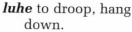
lū'au

lūhe'e 1. fishing lure for octopus with cowry shell and stone for weight. 2. to fish with this type of lure.

luhi weary, tired. (*luhi hewa* = tired from activity that ends without results) (*ho'oluhi* = to bother, disturb, burden)

lūhe'e

luku 1. destruction. 2. to destroy. [*Ma Wai***luku** *i lanakila ai ko ka na'i aupuni mau koa.* It was at Wailuku (*lit.* waters of **destruction**) that the conqueror's soldiers were victorious.]

luli 1. to shake head, to wag tail. 2. to totter, sway to and fro, pitch about, as a ship.

luliluli shaky, unsteady. [***Luliluli*** *ke keiki ma ka noho lio.* The child is **unsteady** in the saddle.]

lulu 1. calm, peace, shelter. [***Lulu*** *ke awa kū moku 'o Māmala.* Honolulu harbor (Māmala) is **calm**.] 2. to lie at anchor in calm water. (Honolulu = calm bay)

lūlū 1. to shake, scatter, sow seeds. 2. to make donation. (*lūlū hua* = sower, to sow seeds) (*lūlū lima* = to shake hands) [*E* **lūlū lima**, *e ku'u wahi 'īlio!* **Shake hands**, my sweet doggie!]

luma'i to capsize (*fig.* to destroy).

lumi (from English) room. (*lumi 'au'au* = bathroom [*syn. lumi ho'opau pilikia*]; *lumi ho'okipa* = living room; *lumi kuke* = kitchen; *lumi moe* = bedroom)

luna 1. above, on top of, high up. [*Aia ka manu i* **luna** *o ke kumukōpiko.* The bird is **on top of** the *kōpiko* tree.] 2. foreman, boss, overseer, manager. [*He* **luna** *kona kupuna kāne ma ka mahikō.* His grandfather was an **overseer** on the sugar plantation.] (*luna 'auhau* = tax collector; *luna aupuni* = government official; *luna awa* = harbor master; *luna helu kālā* = bank teller; *luna ho'oponopono* = editor; *luna 'ike hala* = conscience [*syn. lunawaemana'o*]; *luna kānāwai* = law judge; *luna maka'āinana* = representative in legislature)

lupe kite. (*hoʻolele lupe* = to fly a kite) [*Ma Kapiʻolani Pāka e **hoʻolele lupe** ai ka lehulehu.* It's at Kapiʻolani Park that the public **flies kites**.]

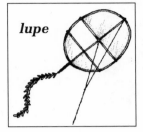

luʻu to dive, plunge into water. (*hoʻoluʻu* = to dip, immerse, dye cloth)

luʻuluʻu burdened with weight, trouble, grief; painful, sorrowful. [*Ua **luʻuluʻu** ke kāne wahine make i ke kaumaha.* The widower was **burdened with grief**.]

ma in, on, at, by, to. [*Aia kā Leilani mau pā lolouila* **ma** *luna o ka loloula.* Leilani's computer diskettes are **on** top of the computer.] (*ma ka Pō'akolu* = on Wednesday)

mā 1. to fade away. (*mā wale* = to fade quickly) 2. faded, wilted, stained, discolored. 3. used after person or place name to indicate several people, places. [*Waipahe 'o Ku'ulei* **mā**. Ku'ulei folks (Ku'ulei **and at least one other person**) are courteous.] [*Wela 'o Makena* **mā**. Makena **and those places** are hot.]

ma'a used to, accustomed to, experienced, familiar. [*Ma'a 'o Mahina mā i ka hīmeni 'ana ma mua o ke anaina.* Mahina folks are **used to** singing in front of an audience.] (*ho'oma'ama'a* = to practice, become used to)

ma'alahi 1. simplicity, contentment. 2. easy, simple. [*'A'ole* **ma'alahi** *ka hō'ike waenakau.* The midterm exam wasn't **easy**.]

ma'alea 1. craftiness, cunning, deceit. 2. crafty, cunning. [*He hana ma'alea kā ka mea pā'ani pepa.* The card player did a **cunning** thing.]

ma'alili 1. cooled down (food). [*E 'ai kāua o* **ma'alili** *ka 'i'o.* Let's eat or else the meat will be **cooled down**.] 2. abated, cooled down passion.

mā'alo to pass along, pass by. [*Ke kipa aku 'o 'Anakē iā Lilia,* **mā'alo** *'o ia i ka mākeke i'a 'o Tamashiro.* Whenever Aunty visits Lilia, she **passes by** Tamashiro fish market.] (syn. *kā'alo*)

ma'amau usual, customary, common. [*'O ka poi a me ka poke kāna mea 'ai* **ma'amau**. Poi and poke are her **usual** food.]

ma'awe thread, wisp, faint footprint. (*ma'awe ala* = faint path (*fig.* departure of soul after death)

mae 1. to fade (clothes), to wilt (flowers), wither. 2. to waste away in illness.

mā'e'ele numb, horrified. [*He hu'i* **mā'e'ele** *ko'u nui kino.* My entire body is **numb** (with shock). (song, "Lā 'Elima," by the family of Diana Aki)]

ma'ema'e clean, pure, chaste, attractive. [*He po'e* **ma'ema'e** *ka lāhui Hawai'i.* The Hawaiian people are a **clean** people (personal cleanliness is important).] [**Ma'ema'e** *kou mau lima?* Are your hands **clean**?]

māewa swinging, fluttering, unstable.

ma'ewa reproachful, scornful. (*ho'oma'ewa* = to reproach, sneer at, mimic, ridicule) [*Mai* **ho'oma'ewa** *iā ha'i!* Don't **ridicule** others!] Note: *Ha'i* can be used as a noun meaning "someone else, other people."

maha 1. temple, forehead. 2. to rest, repose, vacation. [*Ke pi'i mākou i Lē'ahi,* **maha** *iki mākou ma ka 'ānu'u hope loa.* Whenever we (us three, not you) climb Lē'ahi (Diamond Head), we **rest** a little on the last step. (*ho'omaha* = to vacation, take a rest) (*ho'omaha loa* = to retire, retirement)

mahalo 1. gratitude, thanks. 2. respect, admiration, praise. [*Nui ko'u* **mahalo** *i nā ali'i wahine o Hawai'i kahiko.* I have a great **respect** for the chiefly women of ancient Hawai'i.]

mahamaha 1. fish gills. 2. to show love, affection. (*ka pili mahamaha* = affectionate relationship)

mahana warmth. (syn. *mehana*)

maha ʻoi bold, overly aggressive (an offensive trait to Hawaiians).

māhele 1. portion, part, share, division. (*māhele kālā* = dividend) (*māhele kino* = body organ, body part) (*hoʻomāhele* = to divide up, distribute) [*E **hoʻomāhele** i nā manakō a ʻoukou i ʻako ai.* **Divide up** the mangoes that you folks picked.] 2. to translate, interpret.

mahi 1. plantation, farm. 2. to cultivate, farm. [***Mahi** kona kupuna wahine i kona māla ʻai.* Her grandmother **cultivates** her vegetable garden.] (*mahikō* = sugar plantation) (*mahi pua* = horticulture)

mahiʻai 1. farmer, farm. [*He **mahiʻai** lēkō ko Sumida mā.* Sumida folks have a watercress **farm**.] 2. to farm.

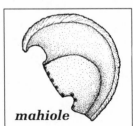

mahiʻai

māhiehie 1. delightful, charming, pleasant. 2. delightfully. [*Ulu **māhiehie** nā pua ma ka māla.* Flowers grow **delightfully** in the garden.]

mahiki 1. a seesaw, to seesaw. 2. to peel, pry off. 3. to jump, leap, move up and down. 4. to exorcise spirits.

mahikina lā crack of dawn.

mahikō sugar plantation.

mahina moon, moonlit, month. [*He **mahina** wela ʻo ʻAukake.* August is a hot **month**.] (*mahina hapalua mua* = waxing moon; *mahina hapalua hope* = waning moon; *mahina hou* = new moon; *mahina piha* = full moon [syn. Māhealani, night of full moon in Hawaiian moon calendar])

mahina

mahiole feather helmet. [*He **mahiole** a he ʻahuʻula ka lole o ke aliʻi.* A **feather helmet** and a feather cape were the clothes of the chief.]

mahiole

māhoe twins. (*Māhoe Hope* = month of Hawaiian calendar, approximately mid-September to mid-October) (*Māhoe Mua* = month of Hawaiian calendar, approximately mid-August to mid-September)

mahole to bruise, skin, scrape, hurt feelings.

māhu 1. steam, vapor. 2. to steam, exude vapor. [*I ka māhu ʻia ʻana o ka laulau, ua moʻa ka ʻiʻo puaʻa.* When the *laulau* was **steamed**, the pork was cooked.]

mahū 1. weak, flat, as stale beer. 2. insipid.

māhū 1. homosexual of either sex. (syn. *hoʻokāmaka, aikāne* [male homosexuality])

māhua to increase, grow. [*Ke **māhua** nei nā ʻōpio e hiki ke ʻōlelo Hawaiʻi.* The number of youths who can speak Hawaiian is **increasing**.] (*hoʻomāhua* = to increase, multiply, grow).

mahuʻi to guess, suppose, expect, imagine. (*ʻike mahuʻi* = to catch a glimpse of) (*lohe mahuʻi* = to hear a hint of, without detail)

mahuka to flee, escape, elope. [*E **mahuka** aku ana nā pio kaua.* The war prisoners will **escape**.]

mai 1. particle indicating movement or action in direction of the person speaking. [*E hele **mai**.* Come **here**.] 2. command "don't" when followed immediately by a verb. [***Mai** hana pēlā!* **Don't** do that!] 3. from (*mai* place *mai/aku*). [*Ua heihei nā waʻa peʻa **mai** Oʻahu **aku** a hiki i Kauaʻi.* The sailing canoes raced **from** Oʻahu to Kauaʻi.] Note: Either *mai* or *aku* is used after the place of origin. If *mai* is used, it indicates that the travel was from the place of origin toward the place where the speaker is. If *aku* is used, it indicates that the travel was from the place of origin away from the place where the speaker is. Both *mai* before place of origin and *mai/aku* after it are necessary to translate as "from."

maʻi 1. illness, disease. [*Hoʻomanawanui ka mea **maʻi**.* The patient endures **illness**. 2. genitals. 3. menstrual period. 4. ill, sick. (*maʻi ʻaʻai* = cancer; *maʻi ahulau* = epidemic; *maʻi hana ei* = AIDS, sexually transmitted diseases; *maʻi huki* = convulsion; *ma'i kau* = chronic disease; *ma'i koko pi'i* = high blood pressure; *ma'i lele* = contagious disease; *ma'i mimikō* = diabetes; *ma'i pu'uwai* = heart disease; *ma'i wahine* = female illness, menstrual period; *mea ma'i* = sick person, patient; *mele ma'i* = chant/hula celebrating reproductive ability of chiefs, symbolic of giving life to the Hawaiian nation)

maiā from (refers to a person; used before a name or pronoun; *maiā* <u>person</u> *mai/aku*) [*Ua loa'a iā māua kekahi leka maiā Lahela mai. Maiā wai mai kāu leka?* We (us two, not you) received a letter **from** Lahela. Who is your letter **from**?]

mai'a general term for banana.

maiau 1. neat and careful in work, correct and careful in speech. 2. carefully, skilled, expertly, ingenious. [*Kālai maiau 'o Kana'e i ka pahu niu.* Kana'e **expertly** carves the coconut drum.]

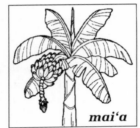

mai'a

māihi to peel, strip bark. (*māihi ola* = to escape by the skin of your teeth, barely escape)

ma'ihi dwarf.

maika ancient game similar to bowling.

maika'i 1. good, fine, well. [*Maika'i kā kēia mau haumāna mau kumu.* These students' teachers are **fine**.] 2. good-looking, beautiful. [*He kāne maika'i 'o ia ala ke nānā aku.* He (over there) is a **good-looking** man.] (*ho'omaika'i* = congratulations, to congratulate)

mā'ila 1. light-brown skin, as some part-Hawaiians have. 2. clear (as the sea on sunny days, as when the depths are visible).

maile native shrub whose leaves are stripped for fragrant *lei*.

māino 1. cruelty, misery, harm. 2. cruel, miserable, hurt. (*ho'omāino*

maile

= to treat cruelly, abuse, persecute) (*hana māinoino i nā holoholona* = cruelty to animals)

mā'ino'ino 1. graffiti. [*E holoi i kāu hana mā'ino'ino ma ka paia!* Wash your **graffiti** off the wall!] 2. to deface, mar, spoil, ruin. (*ho'omā'ino'ino* = to defame, slander)

maka 1. eye, face, sight, view, mesh of net, beloved person. [*He 'upena maka nui kēnā.* That (by you) is a big-**meshed** net.] (*maka'ā* = wide, staring eyes) (*maka 'ē* = to look askance) (*makaaniani* = eyeglasses; *makaaniani pale lā* = sunglasses) [*Ma mua o ko 'oukou hehi 'ana i ke one, e komo i ka makaaniani pale lā a me ka 'aila hamo pale lā!* Before you all step onto the sand, put on **sunglasses** and sunscreen!] 2. raw, ripe, fresh. (*ka i'a maka* = raw fish) (*maka mua* = first time, beginning, commencement) [*'O ka maka mua kēia o kou hula 'ana?* Is this the very **first time** you've danced the hula?] (*maka hilahila* = bashful, shy) (*maka hiamoe* = sleepy, drowsy) (*ho'omaka* = to start) [*Ma ka hola 'ehia e ho'omaka ai ka hālāwai?* What time does the meeting **start**?]

makaaniani

māka (from English) 1. mark, target, grade. 2. to mark.

maka'āinana commoner, citizen. (*luna maka'āinana* = legislative representative)

maka'ala alert, vigilant, watchful, careful. [*E maka'ala!* **Look out!** (syn. *E akahele!*)]

maka'alā blind but with eyes that look normal.

mākaha fierce, savage, ferocious.

mākāhā sluice gate of fishpond. [*I mea aha ka mākāhā? I mea e komo ai ka i'a i loko o ka loko i'a.* What's a **sluice gate** for? It's to let fish enter the fishpond.]

makahehi admiration, desire for. 2. to admire. [*E makahehi 'ia ana nā 'ōiwi 'ōlelo Hawai'i.* The native people who speak Hawaiian will be **admired**.]

makahiki 1. year, ancient festival lasting several months during rainy season, when war was forbidden. 2. annually. (*makahiki hou* = new year) (*makahiki lā keu* = leap year) (*i kēia makahiki a'e* = next year) (*i kēlā makahiki aku nei* = last year) [*I kēlā **makahiki aku nei**, ua kū'ai aku māua 'o Pahikaua i ko māua kahua hānai pipi ma Kohala.* **Last year**, Pahikaua and I sold our (two) ranch in Kohala.]

makahiki

ma kai toward the sea, downhill direction.

māka'i police officer, guard. [*He **māka'i** maka'ala ko kēia kahu ma'i kupuna wahine.* This nurse's grandmother is a watchful **police officer**.]

ma kai

mākaia traitor, treachery, revenge, vengeance. [*He **mākaia** ke kumuhana o nā ki'i 'oni'oni Samurai.* **Vengeance** is a theme of Samurai movies.]

māka'ika'i 1. tourist. 2. to visit, sightsee, stroll around. [*Nui ka po'e **māka'ika'i** Kepanī ma Honolulu.* There are lots of Japanese **tourists** in Honolulu.]

maka 'ike to see clearly, more than most, especially supernatural things, to have gift of second sight.

māka'ikiu detective.

makakēhau heart's desire (*lit.* dewy-eyed)

makakilo 1. to watch with great attention. 2. observant, watchful eyes.

makalapua 1. many blossoms. 2. to blossom forth. 3. handsome, beautiful. [*'o **makalapua** ulu māhiehie,* **many blossoms** growing delightfully (song, "Makalapua," by Konia/E. Holt)]

maka launa friendly.

maka lena unfriendly.

makali'i tiny, very small.

Makali'i 1. name of month in Hawaiian calendar. 2. Pleiades. [*i ke au o **Makali'i** ka pō,* at the time when the **Pleiades** appear in the night sky (line from *Kumulipo*, creation chant)]

makalike uniform. [*He **makalike** kaila ko ke kuene.* The waiter has a stylish **uniform**.]

makaloa sedge from which fine mats were woven, especially on Ni'ihau.

makamae priceless, of great value. [*'O ko kākou ho'oilina hīmeni he mea **makamae**.* Our heritage of song is a **precious** treasure.]

makamaka intimate friend, host (*fig.* anything very helpful). [*Ho'okahi nō **makamaka**, 'o ke aloha.* There is only one **helpful** thing, that is love. (line from "E Nihi Ka Hele," by D. Kalākaua)]

makana gift, present, scholarship, prize. (*makana kūlana 'ekahi* = first prize)

makani wind, breeze, ghost, spirit. (*makani pāhili* = hurricane) [*He **makani pāhili** 'ino nō 'o 'Iniki.* 'Iniki was a very bad **hurricane**.]

makapehu suffering from hunger, hungry person, swollen (*lit.* swollen eyes). [***Makapehu** nā keiki ma Somalia.* Children in Somalia **suffer from hunger**.]

makapō blindness, blind person. (*maka pa'a* = person blind in one eye)

makau fishhook. [*'O Mānaiakalani ka **makau** mana a Māui.* Mānaiakalani is Māui's powerful **fishhook**.]

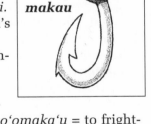

makau

maka'u 1. fear, risk, danger. 2. frightened, dangerous. (*maka'u wale* = coward, cowardice; *syn.* hōhē) (*ho'omaka'u* = to frighten) [*Mai **ho'omaka'u** i kāu keiki!* Don't **frighten** your child!]

mākaukau 1. proficiency, competence, preparation. 2. able, competent, capable, qualified. (*ho'omākaukau* = to prepare, get ready)

mākaukau 'ole incompetent, unskilled, unprepared.

makauli'i thrifty, economical, miserly, avaricious.

makawalu numerous, much, many (*lit.* eight eyes). [*Makawalu nā hōkū lele ma ka mahina 'o 'Aukake.* There are **numerous** shooting stars in the month of August.]

makawela hatred, anger.

make 1. death, peril, misfortune. 2. to die, to faint. (*ho'omake* = to put to death, kill) 3. killed, defeated, dead. (*make loa* = extinct) ['*Ane'ane* **make loa** *ka 'alalā.* The *'alalā* (Hawaiian crow) is almost **extinct**.] (*make pōloli* = to starve to death) (*make 'ole* = immortal)

makehewa 1. vain attempt. 2. in vain, useless. [*Makehewa kā Mikana ho'ā'o.* Mikana's experiment was **useless**.]

mākeke outdoor market. [*Pa'apū nā mākeke mahi'ai.* The farmers' **markets** are crowded.]

makemake to desire, want, wish. [*He aha kou* **makemake**? What do you **want**?] Note: often shortened to *mamake* in colloquial speech.

makemakika (from English) math.

mākēneki (from English) magnet.

makepono profitable. [*He 'oihana* **makepono** *ka halihali 'ana i nā pono hale.* Transporting furniture is a **profitable** business.]

makewai 1. thirst. 2. thirsty. [*I ko Mika lāua 'o Leinani holopeki 'ana ma ka pāka,* **makewai**, *akā ke inu wai lāua, ua kena.* When Mika and Leinani jog at the park, they are **thirsty**, but when they drink water, (their thirst is) quenched.]

mākia 1. motto, purpose, aim. ['*O* "'*Onipa'a*" *ko Lili'uokalani* **mākia**. Lili'uokalani's **motto** was "Steadfast."] 2. pin, nail, spike. 3. to strive for, concentrate on, to nail, bolt.

makika (from English) mosquito.

makoa fearless, courageous. (*ho'omakoa* = to act bravely)

mākoi fishing pole. [*Mai 'a'e i ka* **mākoi**. Don't step over the **fishing pole**.] 2. to fish with a pole.

mākole red-eyed, inflamed. [*Mākole ko ka lawai'a maka i ka lā.* The fisherman's eye is **inflamed** due to the sun.]

mākonā hard-hearted, mean, nasty. [*Mākonā kā ka'u kāne luna.* My husband's supervisor is **hard-hearted**.]

mākou us, we (not including the person being spoken to). [*Ke holoi nei* **mākou** *i ko ka lehulehu mau ka'a i mea e 'imi kālā ai no ke kalapu.* **We** are washing the public's cars as a thing that would raise money for the club.]

makua parent, relative of parents' generation. (pl. *mākua*) (*mākuakua* = aged, old) (*makua kōlea* = stepparent) (*makua papekema* = godparents [*lit.* baptism parents]) (*ho'omakua* = to grow into maturity)

makuahine mother, aunt. (*makuahine kōlea* = stepmother)

makuahūnōaikāne father-in law. (*hūnōnakāne* = son-in-law)

makuahūnōaiwahine mother-in-law. (*hūnōnawahine* = daughter-in-law)

makua kāne father, uncle. (*makua kāne kōlea* = stepfather)

makua kāne

māla garden, cultivated field. (*māla 'ai* = vegetable garden) (*māla a'o* = kindergarten) (*māla pua* = flower garden)

māla'e cloudless. [*Māla'e ka lewa i ke kauwela.* The sky is **cloudless** in summer.]

Malaki (from English) March.

malama month, light, moon. (syn. *mahina*)

mālama 1. care, preservation, loyalty, custodian, caretaker. 2. to care for, preserve, take care of. [*E* **mālama** *i ka honua!* **Take care of** the earth!] (*mālama ola* = to support financially, means of livelihood, social security; *helu mālama ola* = social security number)

mālamalama clarity of thinking or explanation, shining, clear. (*ho'omālamalama* = to cause light, to enlighten, inform) [*E* **ho'omālamalama** *i ka malama,* **to cause light** to shine in the moon (line from the beginning of the *Kumulipo*, best known of the Hawaiian creation chants)]

mālānai undisturbed, serene. [*Mālānai ka ho'omoana ma ke kahakai 'o Kīholo.* Camping at the beach at Kīholo is **serene**.]

male (from English) 1. marriage, wedding. 2. to marry. [*Ua* **male** *'ia lāua ma waho.* They were **married** outdoors.] (*pa'a male* = married couple) (*'oki male* = divorce)

pa'a male

mali to flatter, soothe, persuade, cajole. (*ho'omalimali* = to flatter, soothe, quiet)

mālie 1. calmness, quietness. 2. calm, quiet, still, gentle. [*He nohona* **mālie** *ko ke kua'āina.* The country person has a **calm** lifestyle.]

malihini 1. stranger, newcomer, guest, foreigner. 2. unfamiliar, strange, foreign. [*Ho'okipa mau nā hālau hula o kēia pae 'āina i nā hula hālau* **malihini** *mai nā 'āina 'ē mai.* The hula schools of this island chain always welcome guest hula schools from **foreign** lands.]

malino calm, quiet (sea), peaceful (spirit), smooth, unwrinkled. [*ke kai* **malino** *a'o Kona,* (*'ōlelo no'eau*) the **calm** sea of Kona. Specific natural phenomena, such as wind, rain, and clouds, were often noted in poetic references to a place; here the calmness of the ocean at Kona, which was a favorite residence of chiefs, may also represent the calm weather and abundance of the land.]

maliu to heed, give attention to. [*Eia ala e* **maliu** *mai.* **Pay attention**. (song, "Ku'u Ipo i ka He'e Pu'e One," by Likelike)]

malo male loincloth. (*hume i ka malo* = to put on loincloth)

mālo'elo'e tired, stiff. [*E* **mālo'elo'e** *ana ko Keali'i mau po'ohiwi ma hope o kona huki 'ana i ka lū'au kalo ma ka lo'i.* Keali'i's shoulders will be **stiff** after he pulls the taro leaves in the taro patch.]

malohi drowsy.

mālolo general name for flying fish.

malo'o dry, dried up, evaporated. [*He 'āina* **malo'o** *'o Makena.* Makena is **dry** land.] (*hīmeni malo'o* = a capella singing, without accompaniment) (*kai malo'o* = low tide)

malu 1. shade, shelter, protection, government, control, strength. [*Ma lalo o ka* **malu** *o ke aupuni, he mau pono kīwila ko ke kanaka.* Under the protection of the **government**, citizens have civil rights.] 2. shaded, peaceful, quiet. (*ho'omalu* = probation, to protect, restrict, quarantine, govern)

malū secretly, clandestinely, illegally. [*Ua hui* **malū** *nā kipi.* The rebels met **secretly**.] (*ho'opae malū* = to smuggle)

Māluaki'iwai sea breeze with showers, famous in hula.

mālualua 1. rough terrain. 2. bumpy, pitted road.

maluhia 1. peace, quiet, security, safety. [*E* **maluhia** *ka honua!* Let there be **peace** on earth!] 2. peaceful, restful, solemnity, awe during ceremony.

māluhiluhi tired.

māmā fast, quick, lightweight. [**Māmā** *ko ka pōpoki po'i 'ana ma luna o ka manu.* The cat's pouncing on the bird is **quick**.]

māmaki native tree used for tapa, medicine.

māmala fragment, splinter, chip, stroke of war club. (Māmalahoe = law of splintered paddle [proclaimed by Kamehameha I to guarantee safety of all travelers])

māmala 'ōlelo sentence (*lit.* speech fragment). (syn. *hopuna 'ōlelo*)

māmalu 1. protection, defense. 2. umbrella. [*Auē nō ho'i ē! 'A'ohe āu* **māmalu** *a pulu ho'i i ka ua Tuahine!* Oh wow! You didn't have an **umbrella** and got soaked in the Tuahine rain (of Mānoa)!]

mamao far, distant, remote. (*kū mamao* = aloof)

mamo bird, black Hawaiian honeycreeper, now extinct, whose yellow feathers were prized for cloaks and *lei*. 2. descendant, posterity. [*He* **mamo** *Hawai'i au na ko'u mau kūpuna.* I am a Hawaiian **descendant** of my ancestors.]

mana 1. spiritual power, divine power, authority. [*He* **mana** *ko ke kia'āina.* The governor has **authority**.] (*mana ho'okolokolo* = jurisdiction, power of passing judgment) (*mana makua* =

parental authority) 2. branch, limb, variations, versions of story. [*Nui nā* **mana** *o nā ka'ao manō.* There are lots of **versions** of shark tales.] (*ho'omana* = religious sect, to worship [pre-missionary], empower, authorize)

māna food chewed by adult for child, trait acquired from those who raise child.

mānā desert.

mānai 1. *lei* needle. 2. to string *lei*.

manakā boring, dull, monotonous, uninteresting.

manakō (from English) mango.

manakuke (from English) mongoose.

mānaleo native speaker.

mānalo 1. drinkable, as water. (*waimānalo* = drinkable water) 2. to appease. [**Mānalo** *ka 'ohana i ke kupuna kāne kuakahi pōniuniu.* The family **appeases** the confused great-grandfather.] 3. safe from harm, danger.

manamana lima finger. (*manamana lima komo* = ring finger; *manamana lima kuhi* = index finger; *manamana lima nui* = thumb; *manamana wāwae* = toe)

mana'o 1. thought, idea, belief, meaning, theory. [*He aha ka* **mana'o** *o "pi'o"?* What's the **meaning** of "*pi'o*"?] (*mana'o hāiki* = narrow mind, intolerant; *mana'o ho'omanamana* = superstition; *mana'o ikaika* = zeal; *mana'o kuhihewa* = delusion; *mana'o laulā* = tolerant, broad-minded, general idea; *mana'o nui* = important idea or meaning; *mana'o pa'a* = conviction, determination, firm intention; *mana'o ulu wale* = whim, fancy, impulse, imagination) (*ho'omana'o* = to remember, recall, remind) (*kia ho'omana'o* = monument, statue, memorial) 2. to think. (syn. *no'ono'o*) (*mana'o wale* = to suppose, presume)

mana'o'i'o faith, confidence, to have faith, confidence.

mana'olana 1. hope, expectation. [*Ka mana'o'i'o, ka* **mana'olana***, a me ke aloha.* Faith, **Hope** and Charity.] 2. to hope. [**Mana'olana** *nā mākua e ho'okumu i mau kula kaiapuni hou ma nā wahi like 'ole o nā mokupuni.* Parents **hope** to establish several new immersion schools at various sites on the islands.]

manawa time, turn, season, date. (*holo ka manawa* = time passes by) (*i kekahi manawa* = sometimes) (*manawa ka'awale* = free time) (*manawa kūpono* = appropriate time, opportunity) (*no ka manawa* = temporary; syn. *kūikawā*) (*'o kou manawa kēia* = it's your turn)

manawale'a 1. charity, donation. 2. to give freely. 3. benevolent. [**Manawale'a** *ko ke kauka maka kōkua 'ana aku i ka po'e 'ilihune.* The eye doctor's helping poor people is a **benevolent** act.]

manawanui 1. patience, fortitude. 2. to have patience, fortitude. (*e ho'omanawanui* = be patient, put up with the situation)

manene shuddery sensation of fear, revulsion. [*'Oiai ko'u kaikunāne e lele kawa ana, pi'i ko'u* **manene**. While my brother was playing *lele kawa*, I felt that **shuddery feeling**. (*Lele kawa* was a sport of ancient days in which contestants jumped into the ocean from a cliff, feet first. The one who created the smallest splash won.)]

mane'o 1. itch. 2. itchy, sexually stimulated, "horny." [*Hiki paha iā 'oe ke wa'u i ko'u kua? Ua* **mane'o**! Can you perhaps scratch my back? It's **itchy**! (*ho'omane'o* = to tickle)

māneoneo barren.

mānewanewa 1. grief, sorrow, mourning, exaggerated expression of grief, such as tattooing tongue, knocking out teeth (sometimes done in old Hawai'i upon the death of a high chief). 2. unkind, to treat unkindly.

manini 1. small reef fish with stripes. 2. stingy. (syn. *pī*) [**Manini** *ko kēlā luna ho'oponopono 'ano.* That editor has a **stingy** personality.]

mano 1. four thousand. 2. thick, many, numerous. (*ho'omano* = to increase, do repeatedly, persistently)

mano̅ shark. [*pau Pele, pau* **mano̅**, (*'o̅lelo no'eau*) oath "to do or die" (*lit.* destroyed by lava, destroyed by shark)]

mano̅

manoa numerous, many.

ma̅noa thick, solid, great depth. Ma̅noa valley on O'ahu is known for the large number of people who lived there in ancient days.

ma̅noanoa 1. depth, thickness. 2. thick, solid, vast. 3. coarse, dull-witted, stupid.

ma̅nowai dam, stream (*fig.* heart and circulatory system).

manu bird (*fig.* person). (*manu hulu* = wealthy person, *lit.* feathered bird) [*He mau* **manu hulu** *na̅ kahu waiwai o ka panako̅.* The bank trustees are **wealthy people**.] (*manu aloha* = parrot; *manu ku̅* = dove; *manu mele* = canary)

manu

manuahi free, no charge. [**Manuahi** *ka likiki mokulele.* The airplane ticket is **free**.] (*ka̅ne manuahi* = common-law husband) (*wahine manuahi* = common-law wife)

manuea 1. type of seaweed. 2. careless, blundering, slipshod.

mao clear (sky after rain). [*Ma uka nei o Honouliuli, helele'i ka ua ma ka po̅ aka̅* **mao** *ke kaiao.* Here in the uplands of Honouliuli, rain falls at night but dawn is **clear**.]

ma'o 1. native cotton. 2. green.

ma̅'oki'oki streaked, cut into pieces. [*Ke kai* **ma̅'oki'oki** *a'o Kona,* (*'o̅lelo no'eau*) the **streaked** ocean of Kona]

maoli native, indigenous, true, real. [*'O ka 'apapane a me ka 'o̅ma'o kekahi mau manu* **maoli**. The *'apapane* and the *'o̅ma'o* are some of the **indigenous** birds.] (*ke kanaka maoli* = native Hawaiian)

ma̅'ona (often pronounced *ma̅'ana*) satisfied after eating, full stomach. [*'Ai a* **ma̅'ona**, *inu a kena.* (*'o̅lelo no'eau*) Eat until **full**, drink until (your thirst is) quenched.]

maopopo to understand, recognize clearly, know. (*'a'ole maopopo ia'u* = I don't know, I don't understand) [**Maopopo** *ke̅ia mo'olelo ia̅ ia? E kala mai! 'A'ole* **maopopo ia̅ ia.** Does she/he **understand** this story? I'm sorry! **She doesn't understand**.] (*ho'omaopopo* = to make clear, tell clearly) (*maopopo 'ole* = unintelligible)

ma̅pele a type of *heiau* for worship of Lono. Note: Unlike at *luakini heiau*, no human sacrifices were made at *ma̅pele*.

ma̅pu 1. windborne fragrance, bubbling, wafted. (syn. *ma̅puana*) 2. surging, as emotions.

ma̅puna bubbling spring, froth of rough sea (*fig.* surging emotions). (*ma̅puna hoe* = dip of paddle) [*E komo 'oe i ka̅u* **ma̅puna hoe.** (*'o̅lelo no'eau*) Pitch in and help (*lit.* put in your **dip of the paddle**).] (*ma̅puna leo* = whispered words of love)

mau 1. to continue, persevere. 2. always, unceasing, perpetual. [**Mau** *no̅ ke aloha.* Love is **unceasing**.] (*a mau loa aku* = forever) 3. pluralizer. [*He* **mau** *lei pua onaona ka̅ la̅ua.* They (two) have **some** sweet-smelling flower lei**s** (they made).] (*ho'omau* = to keep on, persist, continue) [*E* **ho'omau** *i ka 'imi na'auao.* **Keep on** seeking knowledge/wisdom.]

ma'u̅ damp, moist, wet, cool, refreshing. [*He mau'u* **ma'u̅** *ko ka pa̅ hale i ke̅ia kakahiaka.* The yard has **wet** grass this morning.] [*He* **ma'u̅**, **ma'u̅**, **ma'u̅** *i ka pu'u ke moni.* It's **moist, cool, refreshing** in the throat when you swallow. (song, "Niu Haohao," by B. Mossman)]

ma̅ua we (2, not including person spoken to). [*'Elima a* **ma̅ua** *mo'opuna.* **We** (she/he and I) have five grandchildren.]

mau'a'e to intrude, transgress, interrupt. [**Mau'a'e** *na̅ ka̅naka ku̅'e̅ i ka̅ ka moho ha'i 'o̅lelo.* The people opposing her **interrupt** the candidate's speech.]

mauhala 1. grudge, resentment. 2. unforgiving.

Maui second-largest island in the archipelago; Maui County includes the islands of Maui, Lānaʻi, Molokaʻi and Kahoʻolawe.

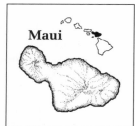
Maui

Māui trickster hero of Polynesia. [*ʻO Māui ke kupuʻeu kaulana o ka Pākīpika.* **Māui** is the famous hero of the Pacific.]

ma uka toward the mountains, uphill direction, inland (if one is on the ocean, *ma uka* means on shore).

ma uka

maʻule 1. to faint. 2. faint-hearted, dispirited.

mauleho callused. (*hoʻomauleho* = to cause calluses, to overwork, oppress)

mauli life, heart, spirit, ghost. (*mauli ola* = breath of life) (*kihe a mauli ola* = "sneeze and live," a blessing said after someone sneezes; often shortened to *ola*)

maumau frequent.

mauna mountain, mountainous region. (syn. *kuahiwi*)

māuna waste, mistreatment.

māunauna extravagant, wasteful. [*ʻAʻole ka nohona māunauna he hana mālama i ko kākou ʻāina.* A **wasteful** lifestyle is not something that protects our land.]

maunu bait.

mauʻu grass. (*hoʻomauʻu* = to give nothing of value)

māwae 1. cleft, fissure in rocks. 2. to separate, sort, select, to cleanse from defilement.

me with. [*Hana ʻo Mokihana me ia a me aʻu.* Mokihana works **with** him and **with** me.]

mea general word for thing or person. (*mea ʻai* = food; *mea ʻai māmā* = snack; *mea inu* = beverage, drink; *mea ʻono* = dessert, cake, pastries) (*mea halihali ʻōpala* = garbage man; *mea hali ukana* = porter; *mea hana noʻeau* = craftsman; *mea hoʻokani pila* = musician; *mea hoʻokipa* = receptionist; *mea kaha kiʻi* = artist; *mea ʻohi kālā* = cashier; *mea pāʻani* = player) (*mea hao* = hardware, metal; *mea hoʻohana* = tool, implement; *mea hoʻolohe* = hearing aid) (*mea hou* = news, new) [*He aha ka* **mea hou**? What's **new**?] (*mea kanu* = plant) (*mea kaua* = weapon) (*mea kolo* = insect) (*mea makamae* = treasure) (*mea nui* = important thing, person) (*mea oli* = chanter) (*he mea iki* = "you're welcome" [response to *mahalo, lit.* it's a small thing]) (*hoʻomeamea* = to pretend, disguise) [**Hoʻomeamea** *wale ka ʻōpio ē he laikini kalaiwa kaʻa kāna.* The young person just **pretends** that he has a driver's license.]

mea oli

mea ʻole inconsequential, insignificant. [**Mea ʻole** *ka luli i ka lana mālie.* Swaying is **nothing** to disturb our calm enjoyment. (song, "Holo Waʻapā, by L. Machado)]

meʻe hero, heroine. (syn. *kupuʻeu*) [*ʻO koʻu hulu kupuna wahine kuʻu* **meʻe**. My honored grandmother is my beloved **heroine**.]

mehameha 1. loneliness, solitariness. 2. silent, lonely.

mehana 1. warmth. 2. warm. (*aloha pumehana* = warm greetings)

meheu track, footprint. (*hoʻomeheu* = to trace, track down) [*ʻO ka* **hoʻomeheu** *i ko ʻoukou mau kūpuna kā ʻoukou hana?* Is **tracing** your ancestors what you all are doing?]

Mei (from English) May.

meia (from English) mayor.

mekala (from English) medal, metal.

mekanika (from English) mechanic.

mele music, song, chant. (*mele aupuni* = national anthem) (*mele hoʻonānā keiki* = lullaby; syn. *mele hoʻohiamoe keiki*) (*mele inoa* = name chant) (*mele kāhea* = chant calling out to request permission to enter house, *hālau* [hula school])

melemele yellow. (*lenalena* = orange-yellow)

meli (from English) bee, honey.

melia plumeria.

melu decomposed.

menehune legendary small people, possibly an early migratory group.

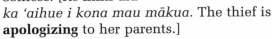

melia

mihi 1. repentance. 2. to repent, apologize, confess. [*Ke* **mihi** *ala ka 'aihue i kona mau mākua*. The thief is **apologizing** to her parents.]

mika (from English) Mister.

mike (from English) Mrs., Miss.

miki quick, active, nimble, prompt.

miki'ala alert, prompt.

miki'ao 1. fingernail, toenail. 2. claw.

mīkini (from English) machine. [*He* **mīkini** *miki ka lolouila*. The computer is a quick **machine**.]

mikioi dainty and neat in doing everything, made with skill.

mikionele missionary.

miko salted, seasoned with salt. [**Miko** *ka pipi kaula me ka he'e kaula'i*. The beef jerky and dried octopus are **salted**.]

mīkole to eat in small bits, persevere.

mile (from English) mileage, mile.

mili 1. to handle, fondle, caress, beloved. 2. slow, inefficient at work. (*mili ka'a* = to do repeatedly, caress over and over)

mili'apa slow, slowpoke.

mililani to praise, exalt, to treat as a favorite.

milimili toy, plaything, favorite, beloved, darling. [*A he* **milimili** *'oe, a he hiwahiwa na'u a he lei 'oe no ko'u kino*. You are a favorite for me and you are a garland for my body. (song, "Ka Makani Kā'ili Aloha," by M. Kāne)]

milo 1. tree used for medicine and dyes. 2. curl. 3. abortion. 4. to curl, twist.

milu 1. underworld which spirits jump into after death.

Milu ruler of the underworld.

mimi 1. urine. 2. to urinate. [*Pono 'oe e* **mimi**, *e ka pēpē?* Do you have to **urinate**, baby?

(*mimikō* = diabetes)

minamina 1. to regret, be sorry, deplore. [**Minamina** *nā Hawai'i i ka 'ike kahiko i lilo loa*. Hawaiians **regret** that ancient knowledge has been swept away.] 2. to prize greatly. 3. thrifty, economical, covetous.

mino 1. dimple, depression. 2. dimpled, creased.

mino'aka smile.

minomino wrinkle, as with age.

mino'aka

minuke (from English) minute (time). [*'Ehia* **minuke** *i koe a mo'a ka mea 'ono?* How many **minutes** left until the dessert is cooked?]

miomio 1. precise, neat, clear-cut. 2. to dive into water without splashing.

moa 1. chicken. 2. primitive plant with medicinal uses.

mo'a cooked, done. [*Ua* **mo'a** *ka 'i'o moa*. The chicken is **cooked**.] (*mo'a kolekole* = rare cooked [meat])

Moa'e trade wind. [*Pā mai ka makani* **Moa'e** *i ka hapanui o ka makahiki*. The **trade winds** blow most of the year.]

mōakāka clear, plain, intelligible. [**Mōakāka** *ko ke alaka'i wehewehe 'ana*. The leader's explanation was **clear**.]

moana ocean, open sea. (*ho'omoana* = to camp) [*Ma ke kauwela,* **ho'omoana** *kona 'ohana ma kahakai*. In the summer, his family **camps** at the beach.]

moani 1. light breeze with fragrance, wafted fragrance. 2. to blow perfume. [*ke 'ala e* **moani** *nei*, the gentle **fragrance** that wafts sweetly on the breeze. (song, "Moanike'ala," by Nawahi/Beamer)]

moe 1. bed, dream. 2. to lie down, sleep. [*E* **moe** *iho ana kāu 'īlio ma luna o ka moe*. Your dog is going to **lie down** on the bed.] 3. horizontal, prone. (*moe hewa* = nightmare, to have nightmare, sleep restlessly) (*moe like* = parallel) (*moe luliluli* = cradle) (*moe 'uhane* = dream, to dream)

moena couch, bed, mat. (*moena pāwehe* = fine mat woven in patterns, especially from Kaua‘i and Ni‘ihau, sometimes with *makaloa* sedge)

moena

mōhai sacrifice.

mōhala 1. to blossom, develop (open flower or youth). [*Ke mōhala nei ka pua.* The flower is **opening** now (the child is developing).] 2. evolved, developed. (*ho‘omōhala* = to develop, evolve, development) [*He mau hana ho‘omōhala ha‘awina kā nā kumu kula.* The school teachers have some curriculum **development** activities.]

moho candidate, representative. [*He moho ‘o Kaleleonālani no ka mō‘ī Hawai‘i.* Kaleleonālani was a **candidate** for sovereign of Hawai‘i.]

mō‘ī monarch, sovereign. (*mō‘ī kāne* = king) (*mō‘ī wahine* = queen) (*aupuni mō‘ī* = monarchy, kingdom)

mō‘ī

mō‘ike 1. dream interpreter. 2. to interpret dreams.

mōkākī 1. mess, chaos, disorder. 2. littered, disordered. (*ho‘omōkākī* = to litter, cause disorder) [*Mai ho‘omōkākī i nā kahakai!* Don't **litter** the beaches!]

mokihana tree found only on Kaua‘i, a symbol of that island; It bears fragrant berries. A *mokihana lei* is much prized for its rarity and its lasting fragrance.]

mokihana

mokokaikala (from English) motorcycle.

mokomoko 1. hand-to-hand combat of any kind. 2. to box, fight.

moku 1. island, district. [*aloha ku‘u moku ‘o Kaho‘olawe,* love for my **island** Kaho‘olawe (song, "Mele No Kaho‘olawe," by H. Mitchell)] 2. fragment, cut. 3. to be cut, severed, amputated.

mokuahi steamship, cruise ship. (*mokukolu* = tugboat) (*moku pe‘a* = sailboat)

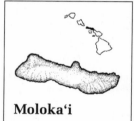
moku ahi

moku ‘āina state. [*‘Ehia mokupuni o kēia moku ‘āina?* How many islands does this **state** have?]

mokulele airplane.

mokulu‘u submarine.

mokupuni island.

mole 1. taproot, main root. 2. smooth, round, bald.

mōlehulehu twilight, dusk. [*Ua ‘ike ‘ia ka hōkū welowelo ma ka mōlehulehu.* The comet was seen at **dusk**.]

moloā lazy, indolent. [*‘A‘ole moloā nā mo‘ohelu ma ka panakō. Pa‘ahana lākou.* The tellers at the bank aren't **lazy**. They're busy.]

Moloka‘i island between O‘ahu and Maui.

momi pearl. [*Waiwai loa ko kona makuahine lei momi.* His mother's **pearl** necklace is very valuable.]

Moloka‘i

momona 1. fertile, rich (soil), fruitful, fat. 2. sweet-tasting, rich-tasting. [*Momona ka ‘i‘o pua‘a ma ka lū‘au.* The pork at the lū‘au is **rich-tasting**.]

momona

moni to swallow, gulp down, absorb. (*moni ka hā‘ae* = swallow spittle, salivate at sight of food, attractive person)

mo‘o 1. lizard, reptile, gecko. 2. succession, series. (*mo‘o ali‘i* = genealogy of chiefs) (*mo‘o lono* = priests of lineage of Lono)

mo‘ohelu budget, counting, list of expenditures, teller.

mo‘okū‘auhau genealogy.

mo'olelo story, history, tradition (*lit.* succession of talk).

mo'opuna grandchild. (*mo'opuna kuakahi* = great-grandchild)

mo'opuna kāne grandson.

mo'opuna wahine granddaughter.

mū 1. insects. 2. legendary people. 3. silent.

mua 1. man's eating house. 2. before, ahead, forward. (*i mua* = go forward) [*I mua a loa'a ka lei o ka lanakila.* **Go forward** until the *lei* of victory is attained. (chant, "Ke au Hawai'i")] (*kā i mua* = initiation ceremony for young boy to men's eating house).

mu'emu'e bitter, sour taste, bitter tasting. (syn. *'awa'awa*) [*Mu'emu'e ka lā'au lapa'au i ka noni.* Herbal medicine made with *noni* is **bitter tasting**.)

muku 1. cut short, amputated, at an end. 2. measurement from fingertip of one hand to elbow of other hand when both arms are extended to the side.

muli 1. after, afterward, behind, following behind. (*muli loa* = youngest born in family) [*'O Nā'ala kā kēia kauka wahine muli loa?* Is Nā'ala this woman doctor's **youngest child**?] (*ma muli o* = through, by means of) [*Ma muli o ko kāna hui 'oihana kāko'o, ua holopono ka 'aha mele 'imi kālā.* **Through** the support of her business, the money-raising concert was a success.]

muliwai mouth of river, estuary. [*Aia i ka muliwai ku'u home nani.* There at the **mouth of the river** is my beautiful home. (song, "Ka Muliwai," by D. Pokipala)]

mūmū 1. to rinse out mouth with water. 2. dull, blunt. [*'Oiai e huki 'ia ana kou niho na'auao, mai poina e mūmū i ka wai pa'akai.* Since your wisdom tooth will be pulled out, don't forget to **rinse your mouth** with salt water.]

mumuhu buzzing, humming sound of insects, flies.

mumule speechless, silent, sullen.

mumulu to swarm, as bees, mosquitoes, flies.

mu'o 1. leaf bud. 2. to bud like a tree or bush. [*Ua mu'o a lau a ulu.* (The plant) **budded** and leafed and grew. (common line in creation chants)]

mu'umu'u 1. loose gown. [*'Ane'ane e 'ōkupe 'o Nāpua i kona mu'umu'u lō'ihi.* Nāpua almost tripped on her long, **loose gown**.] 2. amputee. 3. cut off, amputated.

mu'umu'u

na 1. for, by, belong to. [*Na kēlā makuahine kēiā pēpē uē.* This crying baby **belongs to** that mother.] [*He makana kēia **na** ko kāna ipo hoaaloha.* This is a present **for** her sweetheart's friend.]

nā 1. calm, pacified, assuaged. [*Ua **nā** ka pēpē uē.* The crying baby was **pacified**.] (*ho'onā* = to relieve pain, soothe, quiet) [*Hiki ke **ho'onā** 'ia ko'u po'o 'eha, e ke kahu ma'i?* Can my headache pain be **relieved**, nurse?] 2. plural for "the." (*ka hua moa* = the egg; *nā hua moa* = the eggs)

na'au 1. intestines, bowels. 2. mind, center of emotions, or "heart." [*'Eha kou **na'au** i ka 'eha a ke aloha, 'a'ole anei?* Your **heart** is sore due to the pain of love, isn't that so?] (*na'au 'ino* = malicious, malevolent; syn. *loko 'ino*) (*na'au kūhili* = blundering, careless, thoughtless)

na'auao learned, educated, enlightened. (*ho'ona'auao* = to educate, instruct)

na'au'auā 1. intense grief, great anguish. 2. to mourn. 3. grieving. [*Lohe 'o Ka'iulani i nā leo **na'au'auā** o ko Hawai'i.* Ka'iulani heard the **grieving** voices of Hawai'i's people.]

na'aukake sausage.

na'aupō ignorant, unenlightened, uneducated.

nae 1. shortness of breath. 2. fine mesh (of fishing net). [*He 'upena **nae**, 'a'ohe i'a hei 'ole.* (*'ōlelo no'eau*) It's a **fine mesh** net, there is no fish that isn't caught (*fig.* a good-looking person attractive to everyone).] 3. fragrant.

na'e 1. easterly, eastern, windward. [*'Aia 'o Hālawa ma **na'e** o Moloka'i.* Hālawa is on the **eastern** side of Moloka'i.] 2. but, furthermore, yet, however (often used in phrase *akā nō na'e*). [*Nāwaliwali kona kino; **akā nō na'e**, ikaika kona mana'o.* His body is weak; **however**, his mind is strong.]

naele 1. rock, crevice. 2. full of holes, crevices. 3. stretched out of shape.

nahā 1. cracked, broken. 2. loss of virginity. (*ho'onahā* = to smash, crack, split)

nahae 1. to tear. 2. torn, rent (*fig.* torn with emotion).

nahele forest, grove, wilderness. [*Me ka ua hāli'i i ka **nahele**.* And the rain spread through the **forest**. (song, "Wehiwehi 'Oe," by S. Kalama)]

nāhelehele weeds, undergrowth.

nahenahe soft, sweet voice or music. [*Nahenahe ko Ka'ahuanu Lake mā hīmeni 'ana.* Ka'ahuanu Lake folks' singing is **soft and sweet**.]

Nāhiku Big Dipper constellation (*lit.* the seven).

nāhili blundering, confused, perplexed. (*ho'onāhili* = to cause to blunder, procrastinate, waste time through blundering)

nahoa 1. bold, defiant, daring. 2. intense headache. (*po'o nahoa* = fractured skull)

nahu 1. to bite, to sting like driving rain. 2. pain of childbirth. [*Nahu anei kēia 'ano naonao?* Does this type of ant **bite**?]

na'i 1. to conquer, strive, obtain. (*ka na'i aupuni* = the conqueror) 2. to endeavor to understand.

nai'a porpoise, dolphin.

naio a native tree scented like sandalwood, called false sandalwood.

naka to quiver, shake like Jell-o, with fear or cold, crack open (earth)

nai'a

nakeke rattling, rustling.

nāki'i to tie.

nākolo rumbling, roaring (of surf or thunder), reverberating.

naku'e 1. elbowing, up and down motion. 2. to elbow.

nāku'i 1. to rumble, roar. 2. thrilled.

nakulu 1. echo, clatter. 2. to circulate (gossip, rumor). 3. dripping (liquid), rumbling of stomach.

nalala dinosaur.

nalo 1. housefly. [*Hili 'o Lei i ka **nalo** i loko o ka lumi kuke.* Lei hits **flies** in the kitchen. (song, "Nalo," by J. Lum Ho)] 2. lost, vanished, forgotten, concealed.

nalo

nalomeli honeybee.

nalowale 1. to disappear. [*Ua **nalowale** kā ka mea 'ohi kālā 'eke kālā.* The cashier's wallet **disappeared**.] 2. lost, gone. Note: One doesn't "lose" an item in Hawaiian; it simply "disappears" without reference to who lost it.

nalu 1. wave, surf. [*Po'i koke ka **nalu** ma Pōka'ī.* The **waves** break fast at Pōka'ī.] (*nalu miki* = receding wave) 2. to ponder, mull over, speculate. [***Nalu** ke akeakamai e pili ana no ka UFO.* The scientist **speculates** about UFOs.] (*'ale* = ocean swell which, unlike waves, doesn't break)

nalukai 1. weather-worn. 2. old person who has weathered the storms of life.

nalunalu rough seas with high waves.

namu 1. gibberish, unintelligible mumbling. 2. to speak any foreign language, especially English. [*Mai **namu** haole!* Don't **speak English!**]

namunamu to grumble, complain. [***Namunamu** mai nā limahana āu.* Your employees **complain**.]

nana to come to life, spread.

Nana name of month in Hawaiian calendar during season of new growth, approximately mid-March to mid-April.

nāna It is she/he who, She/he is the one who… [***Nāna** e hōlua, na kāna wahine e he'e nalu.* **He is the one who** goes sledding, his wife is the one who goes surfing.]

nānā to look at, watch, observe, see, care for, inspect. (*nānā pono* = to note carefully, pay particular attention to)

nānahu charcoal.

nanahuki 1. to pull away from. 2. contrary, disdainful.

nānākuli to look at, but not respond when spoken to. (*lit.* deaf looking).

nānā maka to look without helping.

nananana spider. (syn. *lanalana*) [*Nahu nā **nananana** ma nā naupaka i nā mū.* The **spiders** on the *naupaka* plants bite insects.]

nānā 'ole to disregard, pay no attention to.

nanau 1. to pay no attention to, as former friends. 2. unfriendly, estranged.

nane 1. riddle, puzzle, parable. [*Nanea nā 'ōlelo **nane**. **Riddles** are fascinating.] 2. to riddle.

nanea enjoyable, fascinating, relaxed, at leisure. [*he **nanea** mai ho'i kau* (idiomatic phrase adding emphasis), so **relaxed** (song, "Holoholo Ka'a," by C. Kinney)]

nani 1. beauty, glory, splendor. 2. beautiful, glorious, splendid, plentiful. [*Nani ka hana no'eau o ke au kahiko.* The crafts of the old time were **splendid**.] [*ka **nani** a'o Waiakea,* the **beauty** of Waiakea (song, "Hilo Ē" by M. Heanu)] (*ho'onani* = to glorify, praise, to beautify) [*Ho'onani ka makua mau.* **Glorify** the everlasting father. (opening phrase of the Hawaiian doxology)]

nao 1. ripple, grain, groove. 2. to thrust hands into opening, as in fishing. 3. rippled, grooved.

naonao ants. [*Na nā* **naonao** *e hāpai a'e nei i nā huna laiki.* It is the **ants** that are carrying the pieces of rice.]

napa 1. delay, procrastination. 2. uneven, crooked. 3. springy, elastic.

nape 1. to rise and fall as the chest does in breathing. [*Nape nā nalu kai.* The ocean waves **rise and fall**.] 2. bending and swaying, as coconut fronds do.

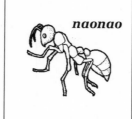
naonao

napele 1. soft, overripe like fruit. 2. bruised, wounded in spirit.

napo'o 1. cavity, hollow, depression. 2. to sink down, set of sun. (*ka napo'o 'ana o ka lā* = sunset) [*Ma Ala Moana mākou i nānā ai i* **ka napo'o 'ana o ka lā**. It was at Ala Moana that we watched the **sunset**.]

napo'o

nau to chew, munch. (**naunau** = to munch one's words, speak indistinctly)

nāu yours, belonging to you. [*Nāu kēia lāpaki?* Is this rabbit **yours**?] [*Nāu e hele, na'u e noho.* (*'ōlelo no'eau*) **You are the one who** will go, I am the one who will stay.]

na'u mine, belonging to me. [*Na'u kēnā pepa.* That paper next to you is **mine**.]

naue to move, shake, tremble. [*E naue kākou!* Let's **move** it! Let's go.] [*Ku'i ka hekili,* **naue** *ka honua.* Lightning flashes, the earth **shakes**. (common line in chants, sometimes used to symbolize birth pains)]

nāukiuki impatient, irritable, cross. (*ho'onāukiuki* = to cause irritation, provoke, annoy) [*Inā* **ho'onāukiuki** *'oe i kou kaikua'ana, e 'ike ana 'oe i ka hopena.* If you **provoke** your older brother (sister) you will see what happens.]

nāulu 1. sudden shower of rain. 2. to rain suddenly, as a rain squall. 3. showery, irritated by being teased or nagged. [*Nāulu 'o ia i kona kaikaina.* He is **irritated** at his younger brother's nagging.] (*he ua nāulu* = sudden rain shower)

naunau to munch one's words, speak indistinctly.

naupaka native plant found at the beach, in the mountains.

nāwaliwali 1. weakness, feebleness. 2. weak, feeble, infirm.

nē to fret, nag for something. [*'A'ohe mea* **nē** *'ole.* (*'ōlelo no'eau*) There is nothing that isn't **fretted about** (a cranky child or old person).]

ne'e to move a little, step along, squirm. (*ne'e i hope* = to move back, retreat; *ne'e i mua* = to advance, go forward, progress) (*ne'ene'e* = to snuggle) (*ho'one'e* = to move goods, household furniture) [*Pono ko'u hoahānau e* **ho'one'e** *hale ma ka hopenapule.* My cousin has to **move house** on the weekend.]

ne'epapa to move as a whole, work in unison. [*Ne'epapa nā helu ma luna o ka 'āina.* The rays (of the sun) are **moving** over the land. (chant, "Mele Noi Na'auao")]

nehe to rustle, as pebbles in sea. [*me ke kai* **nehe** *i ka 'ili'ili,* with the sea **rustling** the pebbles (song, "Ku'u ipo I Ka He'e Pu'e One," probably by Likelike)]

nehinei yesterday. [*'O* **nehinei** *ka lā āna i kelepona aku ai i ka ipo hou āna.* **Yesterday** was the day he phoned his new sweetheart.]

nei 1. indistinct sound. 2. to rumble, like the movement of the earth in an earthquake. 3. here. [*Ua* **nei** *ka honua.* The earth **moved, rumbled**.] (Hawai'i *nei* = here in Hawai'i)

nele lacking, destitute, needy, poor. [*Nele ka po'e 'ilihune i ke kāko'o a me ka ho'ona'auao.* **Poor** people lack support and education.]

nema criticizing, critical.

nemanema to belittle, criticize. [*Nemanema ke 'ano o kekahi kanaka.* Some people's nature is to be **critical**.]

nemonemo smooth, smoothly polished.

nēnē 1. Hawaiian goose. [*'Ano laka nā* **nēnē** *i ho'oku'u 'ia.* The **Hawaiian geese** that have been released are sort of tame.] 2. to chirp, croak, whimper (like a sleeping baby). 3. to cherish.

nēnē

neo 1. empty, bare, desolated. 2. nothing. (*ho'oneo* = devastate)

nepunepu plump, full and round in flesh, bulging. [***Nepunepu** ko ka wahine hāpai 'ōpū.* The pregnant lady's stomach is **bulging**.]

newa war club, cudgel, stone inserted in end of war club.

newe plump, as a pregnant woman; billowy, as a cloud.

newa

nia 1. smooth, round, bald. (*po'o nia* = bald head) 2. calm sea.

ni'a 1. malicious gossip or accusation. 2. slanderous.

niau to move smoothly, swiftly, silently. [*Holo* **niau** *nā wa'a pe'a.* Sailing canoes **move swiftly**.]

nī'au coconut leaf midrib. (*pūlumi nī'au* = broom made of coconut midrib) [*Na ke kahu hale e pūlumi nei i ke kū'ono i ka* **pūlumi nī'au**. It is the caretaker who is sweeping the corner with the **coconut midrib broom**.]

niau

nī'aupi'o highest *ali'i* rank, such as that of Nāhi'ena'ena and her brother Kauikeaouli (Kamehameha III); these chiefs were considered to be living gods.

nīele too inquisitive, nosy.

nihi 1. edge, brink, rim, border. 2. stealthily, quietly. 3. to creep silently, stealthily. [*Kaulana wale ka ua a'o Hanalei, ke* **nihi** *a'e nei i nā pali.* The rain of Hanalei is very well known, it's **creeping** along the cliffs. (song, "Ka Ua Loku," by A. Alohikea)]

nihinihi fastidious, overly dainty, strict.

niho tooth, teeth. (*niho 'elepani* = ivory, elephant tooth; *niho hu'i* = toothache; *niho ku'i* = false teeth; *niho 'ole* = toothless; *niho palaoa* = whale tooth, whale tooth pendant, symbol of royalty; *niho peku* = new tooth; *niho pu'u* = buck teeth)

Nihoa 1. island between Kaua'i and Midway. 2. toothed, notched, jagged. 3. firmly embedded, as stones in a fence.

nihoniho serrated, jagged.

ni'i salt-encrusted.

Ni'ihau privately owned island to the southwest of Kaua'i where Hawaiian is the primary language.

Ni'ihau

nīnau 1. question. 2. to question, interrogate. (*noi* = to ask a favor)

ninini to pour liquid.

niniu 1. dizziness. 2. dizzy.

nīoi pepper. (*kai nīoi* = chili pepper water)

niolopua handsome. (*niolo* = upright, stately)

Niolopua god of sleep.

nipo 1. to yearn for, be in love with. 2. drowsy, sleepy.

niu 1. coconut. [*i ka 'olu o ka* **niu**, *i ka poli o ke onaona,* cool **coconut** grove and in its meat only sweetness. (song, "Old Plantation," by Montano/Nape)] 2. spinning, dizzy.

niuhi man-eating shark.

no for, of, from. [*He inoa* **no** *ka lani Liholiho.* This is a name chant **for** the chief Liholiho.]

nō an intensifying particle, with various English translations, including very, indeed, truly, really, and so on. [*Pōloli* **nō** *nā pōpoki keiki.* The kittens are **very** hungry.]

niu

noa freed from *kapu*. (*'āmama ua **noa**!* = it's **free**, the prayer flies off! [ending of traditional prayers]) [*Ua kapu kēlā wahi akā i kēia manawa ua **noa**. That place was forbidden but now it's **free from restriction**.]

noe 1. mist, spray of rain, fog. 2. misty. (syn. *uhiwai*).

no'eau skilled, clever, skilled with the hands. (*'ōlelo no'eau* = wise saying of traditional wisdom)

noenoe 1. foggy, misty. 2. foggy feeling due to drinking too much. [*Ke **noenoe** mai nei.* It's getting **misty** (that drunken feeling is coming on). (line in songs)]

nohea 1. fine appearance. 2. handsome, good looking. [***Nohea** ka'u kāne!* My husband is **handsome**!]

noho 1. seat, chair, bench. 2. to stay or live someplace. [*Aia i hea 'oe e **noho** nei? Ke **noho** nei au i Hakipu'u.* Where are you **living**? I'm **living** in Hakipu'u (*ahupua'a* near Kualoa, O'ahu.)] (*noho ali'i* = throne, reign) [*I ka **noho ali'i** o Liholiho, ua 'a'e 'ia ka 'aikapu.* In the **reign** of Liholiho, the eating *kapu* was broken.] (*noho huila* = wheelchair) (*noho lio* = saddle) (*noho loa* = to remain long, permanently) (*noho pono* = behaving well) (*ho'onohonoho* = to edit, file, classify) (*ho'onohonoho helu* = calculate) [*Hiki paha iā 'olua ke **ho'onohonoho helu** i ka heluna o ka uku no ke kālai 'ana i ka noho paipai koa?* Can you two perhaps **calculate** the total of the cost for carving (making) the *koa* rocking chair?]

noho

noho lio

nohona dwelling, residence, life-style. [*Nui nā kapu o ka **nohona** kahiko.* The ancient **life-style** had lots of rules (taboos).]

noi 1. favor, request. [*He **noi** ka'u iā 'oe.* I have a **favor** to ask of you.] 2. to ask favor, request. [*Ke **noi** nei ka 'ōpio i kona mau mākua e 'ae mai iā ia e kalaiwa i ke ka'a.* The young person is **asking** his parents to allow him to drive the car.]

noi'i to seek knowledge, research, investigate. [***Noi'i** mau 'o Ka'imiloa i ka 'ike no ka ho'oulu pōhue.* Ka'imiloa is always **investigating** how to grow gourds.]

noio Hawaiian sea bird, tern.

no ka mea because. [*No ke aha 'oukou i ho'ohenehene ai i kā 'oukou pōki'i? **No ka mea**, ua nuku mai 'o ia ala iā mākou.* Why did you all tease your baby sister? **Because** she (over there) scolded us.]

noke to persist, continue, persevere, push forward. [*Hoaka e ka lani, **noke noke**, e Pele e Pele ē.* The sky is shining, Pele (fire goddess) is **pushing forward**. (song, "Aia Lā 'o Pele," traditional chant, Loebenstein)]

no ke aha (phrase) why. [***No ke aha** i ha'i mai ai 'o Pi'ilani i kēlā?* **Why** did Pi'ilani tell me that?]

nokule numb. [***Nokule** ko Meleana lima 'ākau i ke kikokiko 'ana ma ka lolouila.* Meleana's right arm is **numb** due to typing on the computer.] (syn. *ma'e'ele*)

no laila therefore, so. [*A **no laila**, e Kahulumealani, he aha ka hopena o kāu noi i ka ho'opi'i 'ana i ka uku?* And **so**, Kahulumealani, what was the result of your request for a raise?] [*He piwa ko kāna hiapo, **no laila**, ua ho'i lākou.* His (her) eldest child has a fever; **therefore**, they (three or more) went home.]

nolupē graceful, bending, swaying, drenched. [***nolupē** i ka ua*, **drenched** in rain]

nome to munch, nibble continuously, as a horse grazes. [***Nome** a'ela 'o Pele iā Puna.* Pele then **munches** on Puna (covering the land with lava). (song, "Aia Lā 'o Pele," by traditional chant, Loebenstein)] (*nome-nome* = to mouth words without speaking)

nona his, hers, indicating object possessed belongs to him or her. [*'O wai ke kanaka **nona** kēia pālule aloha?* Who is the person this aloha shirt **belongs to**?] [*No wai kēia* *hale? Nona ka hale.* Whose house is this? The house is **hers/his**.]

noni important medicinal plant.

nonō 1. snore. 2. to snore. [*Inā nonō kāu kāne, e hoʻāla ʻoe iā ia.* If your husband **snores**, wake him up.] (syn. *nonolo*)

noʻonoʻo 1. thought, reflection, meditation. 2. to think, reflect. [*Ke noʻonoʻo iho au i kuʻu wā kamaliʻi, kupu aʻela nā haili aloha i o nā hulu kūpuna.* Whenever I **think** about my childhood, beloved memories spring up of the precious grandparents.] (syn. *manaʻo*) (*noʻonoʻo ʻole* = thoughtless, without thinking) (*noʻonoʻo ulu wale* = imagination)

nou 1. to throw, hurl, pitch. 2. you (1), yours, for you, belonging to you. [*Nou ka lei onaona.* The sweet-smelling *lei* is for **you**.]

noʻu 1. to eat greedily. 2. short, plump. 3. mine, for me, for you, belonging to you.

nowelo 1. seeking knowledge, searching. 2. to delve, seek for knowledge.

Nowemapa (from English) November.

nōweo bright, shiny.

nū 1. to cough, roar, groan. 2. mentally agitated, grieving. (*hoʻonū* = to moan, hum)

nuʻa 1. thick, piled up, as ocean swells or multitudes of people. 2. thickly. [*Nuʻa ka lehua ʻau i ke kai.* The people swimming in the sea **pile up** thickly. (song, "Kaleleonālani," by Nuʻuanu)] (*nuʻanuʻa* = soft and fleshy)

nuha sulky. [*Nuha kāna keiki kāne i ka nuku ʻia.* His son is **sulky** because of being scolded.]

nuha

nūhou 1. news. [*Ua lohe anei ʻoukou i ka nūhou?* Did you all hear the **news**? Note: *Anei* in a question demands a yes or no answer.] 2. new. [*He aha ka nūhou?* What's **new**?]

nui 1. quantity, size. [*Pehea ka nui o kou lakeke? He waena anei?* What's the **size** of your jacket? Is it a medium?] 2. big, large, great, important. [*He kanaka nui ʻo Jesse Kuhaulua.* Jesse Kuhaulua is a **big** man.]

nuku 1. beak, snout, tip. 2. to scold, grumble.

nukuwai mouth of stream. (syn. *muliwai*)

nūnē to speculate, wonder. [*Nūnē pinepine kākou e pili ana i ke ea.* We all frequently **speculate** about sovereignty.]

nūnū 1. pigeon. 2. cooing.

nunulu to snarl like a dog or warble like a bird; reverberate.

nuʻu 1. height, high place. (Nuʻuanu = cool heights) (Nuʻuhiwa = Marquesas) 2. second platform of oracle tower.

o 1. of, belonging to. [*'O kēia kāne ke kupuna **o** kāna kaiko'eke wahine.* This man is the grandfather **of** his sister-in-law.] 2. or, lest. [*Mai mumule **o** nuku mai 'o 'Anakē.* Don't be sullen **or** Aunty will scold you.]

'o [particle marking subject, identification sentence pattern] [*Nani **'o** Nālei.* Nālei is beautiful.] [**'O** *wai kou inoa?* What's your name?]

'ō 1. fork, spear, pin, anything used to pierce. 2. to spear, pierce, vaccinate. [*'O ke **'ō** 'ana i ka i'a ka mea ho'omaka'u i nā keiki āna.* **Spearing** fish is what makes his children scared.]

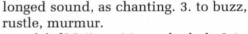

'ō'ā mixed (nationality, colors in *lei*). [*He koko **'ō'ā** ko ka hapanui o ko Hawai'i po'e.* The majority of Hawai'i's people are of **mixed** blood.]

'ōahi 1. rocket. [*E pahū ana paha kēlā **'ōahi**?* Will that **rocket** possibly explode?] 2. clump of burning lava.

O'ahu most populated island, located between Kaua'i and Moloka'i (*lit.* the gathering place).

'oama fish, young stage of *weke*.

oe 1. buzzing, rustling, murmuring sounds of nature, insects. [*ka pūpū kani **oe**,* the shell that **sounds** (Hawaiian tree snail, which was believed to sing)] 2. a pro-longed sound, as chanting. 3. to buzz, rustle, murmur.

'oe you (1). [*Ma'i anei **'oe**, e ka haku?* Are **you** sick, boss?]

'o'e 1. to prod, jab, gore. [**'O'e** *ke kukū o ka wana i ka wāwae o ke kama'āina.* The local person's foot was **jabbed** by the sea urchin's spine.] 2. jagged, spiked.

'oeha'a 1. to waddle, walk awkwardly. [**'Oeha'a** *ko ka 'elemakule hele wāwae 'ana.* The old man **walks awkwardly**.] 2. crooked, distorted, deformed.

oeoe 1. whistle, siren. 2. prolonged (sound) or elongated (object). (*ho'ōeoe* = to pro-long sound, toll bell, yodel high) [*Ua* **ho'ōeoe** *'ia ka pele hale pule ma ka lā nui.* The church bell was **tolled** on the holiday.]

oha 1. spreading vines. 2. greeting. 3. to grow with affection, love, to greet. (*ohaoha/'oha'oha* = affection, greeting)

'ohā taro offshoot growing from root.

'ohāhā flourishing, fully developed, healthy.

'ōhai monkeypod tree.

'ohana family, relatives. (*hui 'ohana* = family reunion) [*E pa'i ki'i ana mākou i kā mākou **'ohana** ma ka **hui 'ohana**.* We (not including person being spoken to) will take pictures of our **family** at the **family reunion**.]

'ohana

ohaoha (also **'oha'oha**) affection, greeting (from *oha*, delight). [*He **ohaoha** kūpono ke oli kāhea.* A calling chant is an appropriate **greeting**.]

'ohe all kinds of bamboo. ('ohe hano ihu = nose flute) ('ohe kāpala = carved bamboo piece used for printing *kapa*, to print *kapa*) ('ohe nānā = spyglass, telescope) ('ohe ho'onui 'ike = microscope)

'ohe kāpala

'ōhea drowsy after big meal (*fig.* weak, ineffective).

'ōhelo native shrub with reddish berries, a symbol of Pele. ('ōhelo papa = strawberry)

'ōhelo

'ohi to collect money, to gather harvest. [*Aia 'o Wini e* **'ohi** *limu nei ma Kuli'ou'ou.* Wini is **gathering** seaweed at Kuli'ou'ou.] (syn. *hō'ili*)

'ōhi'a lehua native tree common in mountain areas, with red blossom, symbol of Pele and island of Hawai'i. ('ōhi'a mamo = same tree with yellow blossoms, symbol for native Hawaiians ['ōhi'a blossoms range from white to orange]) ('ōhi'a 'ai = mountain apple) ('ōhi'a lomi = tomato)

'ōhi'a lehua

'ōhiki 1. sand crab. 2. to probe, pry, pick out, pick teeth, nose. [***'Ōhiki** nā kauka niho i ko lākou mau niho pono'ī.* The dentists **pick** their own teeth.]

'ōhinu 1. roast, grease. 2. shiny, greasy. [***'Ōhinu** ka 'i'o pua'a.* Pork is **greasy**.]

oho 1. hair of head, leaves of plant. 2. to call out, cry out. (ho'ōho = to cheer)

ohohia 1. enthusiasm. 2. enthusiastic, delighted. [***Ohohia** nā alaka'i hula.* The hula leaders are **enthusiastic**.]

'ohu 1. mist, fog, vapor. 2. adorned with mist or *lei* (often reduplicated). [***'Ohu'ohu** 'o Haleakalā.* Haleakalā is adorned with **mist**.]

'ōhua 1. retainers, servants, passenger. 2. young fish such as *hīnālea, manini.* (ka'a 'ōhua = bus)

'ōhule 1. bald person, bald. 2. defeated without getting any score.

'ōhumu 1. plot, conspiracy. 2. to grumble, complain, conspire. [*Ua* **'ōhumu** *pū nā pūkaua e ho'ouka iā Kīwala'ō.* The war leaders **plotted** to attack Kīwala'ō.]

oi to move, turn away in contempt.

'oi 1. sharpness. 2. sharp, pointed, superior, best. [*Maui nō ka* **'oi**. Maui indeed is the **best**.] [*Ke aloha kai* **'oi** *a'e.* Love is the **best** of all the rest. (song, "'Ekolu Mea Nui," by R. Nāwāhine)] ('oi aku = greater than [used for comparison]) [***Oi aku** ka uluwehi o Waimanu ma mua o Kalihi.* The verdant beauty of Waimanu is **greater than** Kalihi's.]

'o ia she, he. [*'Ano ma'i kāu kāne a 'a'aka* **'o ia**. Your husband is kind of sick and **he**'s grouchy.] Note: *Ia* is the correct form for the objective case. [*Kōkua ke kelamoku iā* **ia**. The sailor helps **her**.] *Ia* is also used for "it" or "that." [*He mea hūnā* **ia**. It's a secret.]

oiai 1. while. [***Oiai** 'o ia e ho'oikaika kino ana, ua pōā 'ia kona ka'a.* **While** he was exercising, his car was burglarized.] 2. although. 3. meanwhile, during.

'oia'i'o 1. truth. 2. truly, firmly. (hō'oia'i'o = to verify, confirm; syn. hō'oia) [*Inā 'imi 'o Nani i kona laikini kalaiwa mokukaikala, pono 'o ia e* **hō'oia'i'o** *i kona lā hānau.* If Nani is seeking her motorcycle operator's license, she has to **verify** her birthdate.]

'o ia mau nō (idiomatic phrase) same as always (response to *Pehea 'oe?* How are you?).

'oihana occupation, trade, profession, job, business, career. ('oihana ho'ona'auao = educational system, education department) ('oihana kālā = finance) ('oihana kiu = secret service) (ka hui 'oihana = business, corporation)

'ō'ili 1. emotions, heart. 2. to appear, come into view. ('ō'ili lua = prominent, conspicuous) ('ō'ili wale = to appear for no reason) 'oio (also **hō'oio**) 1. to show off. 2. conceited.

'oi'oi 1. a superior person. 2. full of sharp points, thorns. 3. superior.

'ōiwi native person. (syn. *kanaka maoli, kupa*)

oka 1. dregs, crumbs, sediment, small bits. 2. (from English) to order goods from catalog or food, etc.

'ōka'a 1. to revolve, spin, to roll as mat, top. ['*Ōka'a ka honua a puni ka lā.* The earth **revolves** around the sun.] 2. syn. for *pōka'a*, rolled bundle, as in '*ōka'a lauhala*, roll of pandanus leaves.

'ōkaikai rough (like the ocean), angry, bad tempered.

'Okakopa (from English) October.

'ōkalakala 1. goose bumps, chicken skin, creepy sensation. 2. coarse, rough (texture like sandpaper or rude behavior).

oki to stop, finish. [*Uoki!* **Stop** that!]

'oki to cut, sever, separate. ('*oki 'ino* = to mutilate; '*oki male* = divorce, to divorce; '*oki mau'u* = to cut grass; '*oki'oki* = to cut into pieces; '*oki poepoe* = to circumcise, circumcision; '*oki pu'u* = forest clearing)

'okika (from English) orchid.

'oko'a 1. different, entire. ['*Oko'a ka 'ōlelo a nā kānaka Ni'ihau.* The speech of Ni'ihau people is **different**.] 2. wholly. (*kū'oko'a* = independence, freedom, liberty, independent, free) (*kula kū'oko'a* = private school) (*holo'oko'a* = entire) [*E hana ana ko'u makua kāne ma ka hopenapule holo'oko'a.* My father will work the **entire** weekend.] (*hō'oko'a* = to separate, distinguish)

'ōkole anus, buttocks. Note: *'Ēlemu* is the more polite term for rear end, buttocks.

'ōkolehao liquor from *tī* plant root.

'ōkoleoioi to turn your back on someone who has angered you, to scorn.

'ōku'eku'e knuckles.

'ōkuma rough, coarse, pimply. ['*Ōkuma kona maka i ka huehue.* His face is **rough** due to pimples.]

'ōkupe to stumble, go astray morally. [*'A'ole e 'ōkupe ana ka po'e 'onipa'a.* Steadfast people will not **go astray**.]

'ōku'u 1. to crouch down, squat down. 2. Hawaiian slang, equivalent to "kick back," or relax. [*Ma ka wā ho'omaha 'o ia e 'ōku'u wale ai ma ka hale.* It is during vacation that she/he should really "kick back" at home.] 3. to settle, as a mist.

ola 1. life, health, well being, livelihood, salvation. 2. alive, living, healthy, cured (of illness). [*He pēpē ola kā kēlā makuahine.* That mother has a **healthy** baby.] [*Ua ola ko 'Enoka kunu.* 'Enoka's cough was **cured**.] 3. to live, thrive, heal. (*ola honua* = earthly life) (*ola hou* = to revive, resuscitate, resurrected) (*ola kino* = health) (*ola mau* = immortal) (*ho'ola* = salvation, to save, heal, cure, spare, give life to) [*E ho'ōla lāhui.* **Give life to** the Hawaiian race. (Kalākaua's motto)]

ōla'i 1. earthquake. ['*Ōlapa ka uila, ku'i ka hekili, nei ke ōla'i.* Lightning flashes, thunder roars, the **earthquake** rumbles. (common lines in birth and name chants)] 2. to rumble or quake, as in an earthquake.

'Ōlala to bask in the sun. ['*Ōlala kēlā wahi pōpoki keiki āu i ka lā.* That dear little kitten of yours **basks in the sun**.]

'ōlapa 1. dancer. 2. native tree. 3. to flash (lightning). 4. to dance hula.

'ole 1. zero, nothing. (*mea 'ole* = nothing) [*He mea 'ole kēia.* It's **nothing** (you're welcome).] 2. without, lacking, not. (*niho 'ole* = without teeth) ('*ole wale* = not at all; '*ole loa* = not at all, not in the least) [*He mea hoihoi 'ole loa ke kolepa ia'u.* Golf is **not in the least** interesting to me.] (*hō'ole* = refusal, denial, negative, to deny, contradict, refuse) [*Hō'ole nā mākua i kā lākou mau keiki e pā'ani i nā kahua pā'ani i ka pō.* Parents **forbid** their children to play in the playgrounds after dark.]

'Ole nights of Hawaiian month, considered unlucky or unproductive.

'ōlelo 1. language, speech, word. 2. to speak, say, tell. ('*ōlelo a'o* = counsel, advice, instruction) ('*ōlelo haole* = English; syn. '*ōlelo* Pelekane) ('*ōlelo Hawai'i* = Hawaiian language) ('*ōlelo hō'ike* = affidavit, testimony) ('*ōlelo hō'ino* = curse, defamation, to curse, defame) (*'ōlelo ho'ohiki* = oath, vow, promise; syn. *'ōlelo pa'a*) (*'ōlelo ho'oholo* = jury verdict, judgment, decision) (*'ōlelo ho'omāke'aka* = joke) (*'ōlelo ho'oweliweli* = threat, to threaten) (*'ōlelo hou* = say it again) (*'ōlelo kuhikuhi* = instructions, directions) (*'ōlelo makuahine* = mother tongue) [*O ka* **'ōlelo makuahine** *ka 'ōlelo e mālama ai.* Our **mother tongue** is the **language** we have to preserve.] (*'ōlelo nane* = riddle, parable) (*'ōlelo no'eau* = wise saying, proverb) (*'ōlelo pa'i 'ai* = pidgin English, *lit.* hard taro speech)

'ōlena turmeric, plant used for dye, medicine.

'ōlepe 1. a shell used for hat *lei.* 2. to open and shut, like window blinds. 3. to upset, overturn. 4. to peel off, like shingles in a gale.

oli 1. chant. 2. to chant. [*Oli mau kēia mau 'ōlapa i ke* **oli** *komo.* These dancers always **chant** the entrance **chant.**]

'oli 1. joy, happiness. 2. happy, joyful. 3. to rejoice. [**'Oli** *ē!* **'Oli** *ē!* **Rejoice! Rejoice!** (song, "Hawai'i Aloha," by L. Lyons)]

'ōlinolino 1. brightness. 2. bright, sparkling. Many other words, including *'ālohilohi* and *mālamalama*, have similar meanings.

olo 1. to rub back and forth, saw. 2. to resound, long sound. 3. to grate. (*pahiolo* = saw) (*pahiolo uila* = electric saw)

'olo 1. gourd used for water or *'awa.* 2. double chin, sagging chin. 3. to sag, hang down. 4. pendulous, hanging down.

'olohaka 1. emptiness, desolation. [*Kani ka ipu i ka* **'olohaka** *o loko.* (*'ōlelo no'eau*) The gourd sounds due to the **emptiness** within (an empty-headed person).] 2. empty, hollow.

'olohani 1. to strike, mutiny, riot. 2. to cause a strike or mutiny. (*hō'olohani* = to cause a strike)

'ōlohe 1. bare, naked, bald. 2. destitute, needy. [**'Ōlohe** *nā 'ohana pōloli.* The hungry families are **destitute.**] 3. skilled, especially in *lua* fighting.

'olohewa demented, deranged, delirious.

'ololā broad (used in refrain in *Kumulipo* creation chant to refer to female fertility).

'ololī narrow (used in refrain in *Kumulipo* creation chant to refer to male fertility).

olonā 1. shrub from which strong cordage was made. 2. linen. 3. muscle, ligament. [*'Eha wale kona mau* **olonā** *'ā'ī ma muli o ka ulia ka'a.* Her neck **muscles** were painful due to the car accident.]

'olopū 1. blister. [*Nui kona mau* **'olopū** *a me pohole i nā kāma'a puti hou.* She has lots of **blisters** and bruises due to her new boots.] 2. inflated, puffed out, as a sail.

'olu cool, refreshing, soft, supple.

'olua you two. [*'Ono* **'olua** *i ka i'a maka, e ka wahine a me ke kāne?* Are **you two** craving raw fish, lady and gentleman?]

'oluea ease, mental relaxation.

'olu'olu 1. good natured, kind. 2. comfortable, pleasant. 3. "please." [*E* **'olu'olu**, *e kelepona i ke kauka holoholona no ka mea, ma'i ka'u pua'a.* **Please** phone the vet because my pig is sick.]

'oma stove, oven, baking pan. (*'oma wiki* = microwave)

'oma

'ōma'ima'i chronic illness.

'ōmalumalu cloudy, overcast. [**'Ōmalumalu** *kēia lā.* Today is **cloudy.**]

'ōma'oma'o green color, green plants.

'ōmilo to twist, turn, drill, curl.

omo 1. to suck. 2. sucking. (*mea omo* = drinking straw) [*Pa'a ka* **mea omo** *i kēnā mau poke hau i kāu kī'aha.* The **straw** is stuck in those (by you) ice cubes in your glass.]

'ōmole 1. bottle. [*Ke omo nei kā Mehana pēpē i kāna* **'ōmole** *wai hua 'ai.* Mehana's baby is sucking his juice **bottle.**] 2. bare, smooth, hairless.

'ōmou to fasten, pin on (corsage, jewelry).

'ōmole

ona 1. infatuated, attracted. 2. his/her, of him, of her. [*'Ōmou ke kamali'i wahine i nā mekala i ka lole makalike o ka me'e* **ona.**

The princess pinned the medals on the uniform of the **infatuated** hero./**her** hero.]

'ona 1. (from English) owner. (*'ona miliona* = millionaire) [*He **'ona miliona** ka ho'okele 'oihana o ka panakō?* Is the bank CEO a **millionaire**?] 2. drunk, intoxicated. [*Pākea ka maka o ke kelamoku **'ona**. The **intoxicated** sailor's face is ashen.]

onaona softly fragrant, alluring, attractive, lovely.

'ona'ona intoxicated, dizzy.

one 1. sand. 2. sandy. [*He papahele **one** ko ka hale i kūkulu 'ia ma ka 'ae kai.* The house that was built on the sea shore has a **sandy** floor.] (*one hānau* = lit. birth sands, a poetic name for birthplace) [*'O Kaupō ko Tūtū Lani **one hānau**.* Kaupō is Tūtū Lani's **birthplace**.]

'oni 1. movement, motion. 2. to move, stir, shift, fidget. [*E **'oni** kou kino.* **Move** your body.]

'ōni'o spotted, streaked with colors. [***Ōni'o** ke kapa hou.* The new tapa is **streaked with color**.]

onipa'a steadfast, resolute.

'ono 1. flavor, deliciousness. 2. to crave food, taste. [***'Ono** kou mau hoahānau i ka poke a me ke pola poi.* Your cousins **crave** poke (cubed raw fish mixed with seaweed, onions, and other condiments) and a bowl of poi.] [*Pehea ka **'ono** o ka i'a?* What does the fish **taste** like?] 3. delicious, tasty.

'ōnohi eyeball, center. (*ka **'ōnohi** o ka lā* = the **eyeball** [center] of the sun [*fig.* a favorite person])

o'o mature (fruit, person). [*He kanaka **o'o** ko ke kaikamahine kaikua'ana.* The girl's older sister is a **mature** person.] (*o'o 'ole* = immature)

'o'ō to crow (rooster). [***O'ō** ka moa kuakahi a holo nā menehune 'ekolu.* The first cock **crowed** and the three *menehune* ran away. (traditional song, "Nā Menehune 'Ekolu")]

'ō'ō 1. digging stick. 2. native bird, recently extinct. 3. to pierce, poke, insert. 4. to abort.

'o'ole'a 1. hardness, strength (*fig.* strenuous, rigid, severe, obstinate). 2. rigid, stiff, strong, tough. [***'O'ole'a** ke kino ona.* Her body is **tough**.]

'o'olokū 1. fury, rage. 2. boisterous, stormy.

'o'opa 1. to limp. 2. lame, crippled.

'o'opu goby, general name for a type of native fish found in streams, considered to be a delicacy and known for its ability to climb rocks using a sucker on its belly; includes *'o'opu nākea*, known for its delicious taste.

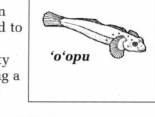

'o'opu

'ōpae general name for shrimp. (*'ōpae 'ula* = red shrimp found in anchialine ponds such as those on the Kona coast, used for bait or food)

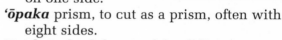

'ōpae

'ōpaha dented, flattened on one side.

'ōpaka prism, to cut as a prism, often with eight sides.

'ōpakapaka fish prized for delicious taste, blue snapper.

'ōpala trash, garbage, litter. (*kalaka halihali 'ōpala* = garbage truck) (*kini 'ōpala* = garbage can) (*ho'ōpala* = to litter, make garbage)

'ōpala

'ope 1. bundle, package. 2. to tie in bundle. (*'ope'ope* = bundles, to fold [clothes])

'ōpe'ape'a Hawaiian bat.

'ope'ope 1. bundles. 2. to fold (clothes).

'opi 1. to fold. 2. creased, wrinkled. [***'Opi** paha nā pālule i ka paiki?* Are the shirts in the satchel **wrinkled**?]

'ōpe'ape'a

'opihi limpet, shellfish considered a great delicacy. (*ku'i 'opihi* = to pick *'opihi*)

ʻōpikipiki anxiety, mental disturbance.

ʻōpio youth, juvenile. [*E hauʻoli e nā **ʻōpio** o Hawaiʻi nei.* Be happy, **youth** of Hawaiʻi. (song, "Hawaiʻi Aloha," by L. Lyons)]

ʻōpiopio young, immature, unripe. [*ʻAno **ʻōpiopio** nā hoʻokele hou.* The new navigators are a little **immature**.]

ʻōpiopio

ōpū 1. clump of fruit, sugarcane, grass. [*ʻO koʻu **ōpū** weuweu lā, nou ia.* My little **clump of grass** (grass house), it is yours. (common line in welcoming chants)] 2. to open, grow.

ʻōpū 1. stomach, bladder. 2. disposition.

ʻōpua puffy clouds on horizon, a bank of clouds (often used symbolically). [*Kona kai **ʻōpua**,* (ʻōlelo noʻeau) Kona of the billowy clouds]

ʻōpulepule moronic, somewhat crazy.

ʻōpuʻu a bud, child. [*Ua kupu a lau a muʻo a **ʻōpuʻu**.* (It, plant) sprouted and leafed and formed **buds**. (line frequently used in creation, name chants)]

ou your, belonging to you. (both *ke ola ou* and *kou ola* = your life)

oʻu mine, belonging to me. (both *ka ʻāina ʻōiwi oʻu* and *koʻu ʻāina ʻōiwi* = my native land)

ʻōʻū 1. endangered native bird of the honeycreeper family. 2. to pinch off, as a bud.

ʻōuli sign, omen, symptom. [*ʻO ke ao pouli ka **ʻōuli** kūpono.* The dark clouds are the appropriate **omen**.]

ʻōwili 1. roll of paper, cloth, skein, coil. 2. to roll up, coil, to fold arms. [*Ua **ʻōwili** ʻia nā lauhala i pōkaʻa.* The *hala* leaves were **rolled up** into a bundle.]

pā 1. fence, wall, enclosure, house lot. (*pā hale* = house lot, yard) (*pā kaula hao* = chain-link fence) 2. dish, plate. (*pā holoi* = dishpan or basin) (*pā halihali* = tray) (*pā pepa* =

pā mea 'ai

paper plate) (*pā mea 'ai* = plate lunch) 3. to shine (sun), to blow (wind). [*E ka makani e, e* **pā** *mai me ke aheahe.* Oh wind, **blow** gently. (song, "Moloka'i Nui a Hina," by M. Kāne)] 4. prefix to number. (*pākahi* = by ones, individually) (*pākolu* = by threes) [*E kama'ilio* **pahā** *ana 'oukou i kēia pō'alima a'e.* You all will converse **by fours** (in groups of four) next Friday.] (*ho'opā* = to touch, influence)

pa'a 1. firm, solid, completed, permanent, stuck. [*Pa'a ka hale holoi lole.* The Laundromat is **completed** (finished being built).] 2. pair. (*pa'a male* = married couple) 3. memorized, learned in subject. (*pa'a mo'olelo* = versed in lore, legends, history) (*pa'a iwi* = skeleton) (*pa'a poepoe* = globe, sphere; syn. *poepoe honua*) (*pa'a lole* = suit of clothes) Note: *Pa'a* has many other meanings. (*ho'opa'a* = hula drummer and chanter, to make fast, firm, to learn, study, hold) [*Le'a ka hula i ka* **ho'opa'a**. (*'ōlelo no'eau*) The hula is fun due to the **chanter** (fig. all details are important).] [*E* **ho'opa'a** *i ko kou kaikaina lima, e ke kaikamahine.* **Hold** your younger sister's hand, girl.] (*ho'opa'a ha'awina* = to do homework)

(*ho'opa'a hau* = to freeze) (*ho'opa'a leo* = to record voice) (*ho'opa'a na'au* = to memorize) (*ho'opa'a wikiō* = to make a video)

pa'ahana busy, industrious, hard working. [*Pa'ahana kāua i kēia hopenapule a'e?* Are we (you and I) **busy** next weekend?] (*mea pa'ahana* = tool) [*He mea pa'ahana waiwai ke kui kala.* The screwdriver is a valuable **tool**.]

pa'ahao 1. prisoner, convict. 2. to be imprisoned. [*Ko'u noho mihi 'ana a pa'ahao 'ia.* I live in sorrow **imprisoned**. (hymn, "Queen's Prayer," by Lili'uokalani)] (*hale pa'ahao* = jail, prison) (*ho'opa'ahao* = to take prisoner)

pa'a'ili solid. (*pa'a'iliono* = cube)

pa'akai salt. (*pela pa'akai* = salt bed, still used on Kaua'i for collecting sea salt)

pela pa'akai

pa'akikī hard, tough, inflexible.

pa'akūkū to clot, jell.

pā'ani 1. game, sport, amusement. 2. to play game, sport. [*Pā'ani ke kime pōhīna'i i 'elima pā'ani o ka pule.* The basketball team **plays** five **games** a week.]

pa'apa'a dispute, argument. (*ho'opa'apa'a* = to argue, dispute) [*Ho'opa'apa'a mau ke keiki maha'oi.* The overly aggressive child always **argues**.]

pa'apa'a'ina to snap, crackle. [*Pa'apa'a'ina ka pele 'a'ā hou ke puapua'i 'ia.* New 'a'ā lava **crackles** when it is spewed out.]

pa'apa'anā to ease pain, to soothe. [*Pa'apa'anā 'o 'Anakē i ko kāna kāne* *kua 'eha i ka lomilomi.* Aunty **soothes** her husband's sore back with *lomilomi.*]

pa'apū crowded, congested with people, stuffy, dense with clouds. (syn. *piha ku'i*) [***Pa'apū** ke kikowaena kū'ai 'o Ala Moana me ka po'e māka'ika'i Kepanī.* Ala Moana Shopping Center is **crowded** with Japanese tourists.]

pae 1. cluster, row, group. (*pae 'āina* = archipelago) (*pae niho* = row of teeth) (*ho'opae* = to build an embankment, row; to land, come ashore) 2. to catch a wave, to disembark. [*'A'ole i **pae** ka wa'a i ka nalu.* The canoe didn't **catch the wave.**]

pā'ē'ē here and there, everywhere but right place. (*kuhi pā'ē'ē* = to misdirect, mislead, give inaccurate information)

pā'ele 1. African American, Negro. [*I kēlā kenekulia aku nei, ua kapa 'ia **nā Pā'ele** mua i Hawai'i he "haole."* In the last century, the first **African Americans** in Hawai'i were called "haole" (foreigner).] 2. black, dark.

paepae 1. pavement, house platform, prop, support. (*paepae puka* = threshold) (*paepae pukaaniani* = window sill) 2. to hold up, support. 3. rows, aligned in a row. [*He **paepae** moku, he lalani moku.* A **row** of islands, a line of islands (familiar line in voyaging chants)]

pa'ewa misshapen, crooked, imperfect, incorrect.

pā'ewa'ewa biased, partial, unfair.

pāha'oha'o mysterious, incomprehensible.

pahe'e 1. to slip, slide. 2. slippery, smooth. [*He pakika, he **pahe'e** ke momoni aku.* It's **smooth** when you swallow. (song, "Niu Haohao," by B. Mossman)]

pahi knife, flint. (*pahi kaua* = sword) (*pahiolo* = saw)

pāhili to blow strongly (wind), to lash (storm). (*makani pāhili* = hurricane) [*He **makani pāhili** 'ino 'o 'Iniki.* 'Iniki was a bad **hurricane.**]

pahi

pahiolo saw. (*pahiolo uila* = electric saw)

pāhoa short dagger, sign of *kapu.*

pāhoehoe 1. smooth, unbroken type of lava (contrast to *'a'ā*). 2. satin. [*He mau uhi pela **pāhoehoe** kā ka wahine nona kēia hōkele.* The woman who owns this hotel has **satin** sheets.]

pahu 1. box, drum, trunk, barrel, stake, pole. [*Hinuhinu wale ka **pahu** kamani.* The *kamani* wood **box** is shiny.] (*pahu heiau* = temple drum) (*pahu hula* = hula drum)

pahu 'ume

(*pahuhope* = goal, goal post) (*pahu kupapa'u* = coffin) (*pahu leka* = mailbox) (*pahu pa'i ki'i* = camera) (*pahu 'ume* = dresser drawer, buffet) 2. to push, shove (*fig.* to hurt feelings of others). (*pahu ku'i* = hypodermic injection, to be injected)

pahū to explode, burst. (*kūlina pahūpahū* = popcorn)

pahu hau ice box (refrigerator).

pahulu 1. nightmare, ghost. 2. worn-out soil. [*Hiki ke mahi 'ia ka 'uala i ka lepo **pahulu**.* Sweet potatoes can be farmed on the **worn-out soil.**] 3. haunted, unlucky.

pai 1. to encourage, urge, stir up. [*Pono kākou e **pai** kekahi i kekahi e 'ōlelo Hawai'i.* We have to **urge** each other to speak Hawaiian.] 2. to praise, lift up.

pa'i 1. to slap, clap, print, stamp. [*Na ke aupuni Hawai'i i **pa'i** i ke kālā a me ke po'oleka.* The Hawaiian kingdom was the one that **printed** money and stamps.] (*pa'i hewa* = typo, misprint) (*pa'i ki'i* = to snap pictures with camera, take photograph) [*Ke **pa'i ki'i** 'ia nei ko'u hoaaloha no kāna kāleka kākī.* My friend is being **photographed** now for her charge card.] (*pa'i puke* = to print book, publish) (*pa'i umauma* = to slap chest, in expressing grief or dancing) 2. tie, equal score. (*pa'i a pa'i* = tied score in game, sports, contest)

paia wall, side of house.

pa'ihi clear (weather), cloudless, neat, well dressed. [***Pa'ihi** kona 'ohana ma ka hale *pule.* His family is **well dressed** at church.]

paikau to march, drill, parade.

paiki suitcase, satchel, bag. [***paiki, pū'olo pa'a i ka lima,*** suitcase, bag held firmly in the hand (song, "Lā 'Elima," composed by the family of Diane 'Aki to commemorate a destructive tidal wave at Miloli'i, a fishing village near South Point, Hawai'i island)]

paiki

paikikala (from English) bicycle.

pā ilina cemetery.

paila (from English) 1. pile, heap. 2. to pile up, heap up. (*kū ka paila!* = What a lot! [*lit.* the pile stands])

pailaka (from English) pilot. [*Ma Līhu'e i pae ai ka* ***pailaka*** *hou.* The new **pilot** landed at Līhu'e.]

pailani 1. to spoil. 2. spoiled. [*'O kā kēlā makua kāne keiki kāne ke keu o nā keiki* ***pailani****!* That father's son is the worst of the **spoiled** boys!]

pailua 1. to cause nausea, vomiting. 2. nauseating, abominable. (*ho'opailua* = gross, disgusting) [*Auē ka* ***ho'opailua*** *o ka wai haumia o ke Ala Wai!* Gosh how **gross** the polluted water of the Ala Wai is!]

pa'imalau Portuguese man-of-war. [*E hamohamo i ke one ma kahi 'eha i ka* ***pa'imalau****.* Rub sand on the spot that's sore due to the **Portuguese man-of-war**.]

pā'ina 1. meal, dinner, party. [*Aia kō lāua* ***pā'ina*** *piha 'umi makahiki o ka male 'ana ma ka hale 'aina o Teshima ma Kona.* Their tenth wedding anniversary **party** is at Teshima's restaurant in Kona.] 2. to eat a meal, to have a party. [*Ua* ***pā'ina*** *'oe i kēia lā?* Have you **eaten** today?] (*pā'ina lā hānau* = birthday party) (*pā'ina male* = wedding feast)

paio to quarrel, argue, fight. (*hoa paio* = opponent, enemy)

paipai 1. to encourage, urge on. 2. to lobby. 3. to rock. (*ho'opaipai* = promotion, agitator, to promote, lobby) (*noho paipai* = rocking chair)

pa'ipa'i 1. applause. 2. to applaud, clap. [*E* ***pa'ipa'i*** *lima!* **Clap** your hands!]

Paipala (from English) Bible. [*'O ke Kauoha Hou ka māhele o ka* ***Paipala*** *a ke kahu e heluhelu nei.* The New Testament is the section of the **Bible** that the minister is reading now.]

paipu (from English) pipe, faucet. [*Nui ke kūkaehao ma nā* ***paipu*** *o ka hale.* There's lots of rust in the **pipes** of the house.]

paka 1. raindrops. (syn. *pakapaka ua*) 2. to strain out dregs. 3. to criticize constructively, teach. [*E* ***paka*** *ana ke kumu i kā kāna mau haumāna mau ha'i 'ōlelo.* The teacher will **constructively criticize** his student's speeches.] 4. tobacco, cigarette. (*puhi paka* = to smoke a cigarette)

pāka (from English) park. [*'A'ole hiki iā ia ke puhi paka me ka holo pū i ka* ***pāka****.* He can't smoke a cigarette and run in the **park** at the same time.]

pākaha 1. robbery, raid. 2. to cheat, plunder, rob.

pakalaki 1. (from English) bad luck. 2. to dole out little by little.

pakalana fragrant *lei* flower, one of many scented flowers brought to Hawai'i by Chinese immigrants.

pākali (from English) battery.

pakalana

pakapaka many, numerous. [***Pakapaka*** *nā pinao na ka loko wai.* There are **many** dragonflies at the pond.]

pākaukau table, desk, counter, booth. [*E hāli'i 'ia ana ka hāli'i pākaukau ma luna o ka* ***pākaukau****.* The tablecloth will be spread out on top of the **table**.]

Pākē 1. China. 2. Chinese. [*'Ono loa nā 'ano mea 'ai* ***Pākē*** *like 'ole.* All kinds of **Chinese** food are really delicious.]

pākeke (from English) bucket, pocket.

pakele to escape. [*Na wai nō 'oe e* ***pakele*** *aku?* Who can **escape** you? (line in songs

describing an attractive person)]
(*ho'opakele* = to rescue, save) [*Ua*
ho'opakele 'ia nā kānaka i hā'ule i loko o
ka lua pele. The people who fell into the
crater were **rescued**.]

pakeneka (from English) percent.

pakī to splash, spatter, squirt. (*ka 'auwai pakī*
= water ditch that barely runs)

pāki'i flattened.

pākīkē rude, sarcastic.

pākōlī musical scale (transliteration of do re
mi).

pakū to burst out.

pākū 1. curtain, screen, veil. [*E huki i ka*
pākū 'au'au a pa'a ke 'au'au 'oe. Pull the
shower **curtain** closed when you take a
shower. 2. shield, defense.

pāku'i 1. to add on, splice, join. [*Ma ka 'uapo*
'o ia e pāku'i ai i ke kaula i ka 'upena. It
is on the wharf that she should **splice** the
rope to the net.] 2. prefix, suffix, affix.

pala 1. smear, daub of excrement used in
insults such as *pala naio, pala kūkae.*
(*palahe'a* = stained, smeared) 2. a native
fern. 3. ripe, mellow. (*palahū* = overripe,
rotten; *palakū* = ripe to perfection)

pala'ai pumpkin, squash. (syn. *pū* = general
term for pumpkin)

pālaha wide, broad, spread out. (*pālahalaha*
= widespread, flat, epidemic) (*hina pālaha*
= to fall sprawling)

palahē 1. fragile, easily torn. 2. overcooked to
point of falling apart.

palahū rotten, overripe.

palai 1. native fern, used as offering to Laka,
the hula goddess; also general name for
ferns. (syn *palapalai*) 2. to turn face away in
embarrassment or confusion. [*Iā ia e komo*
ai i ke ke'ena, palai ke kākau 'ōlelo. When
he enters the office, the secretary **turns**
away in confusion.]

pala'ie children's game
with loop and ball
made from coconut
midribs and tapa.

palaka (from English) 1.
block print cotton
cloth originally worn

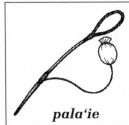

pala'ie

on sugar plantations. 2. block. [*Aia ka hale*
kū'ai hou ma kēia palaka a'e. The new
store is in this next **block**.]

palaki (from English) 1. brush. 2. to brush.
[*Mai poina e palaki i kou mau niho ma*
hope o ka 'ai 'ana. Don't forget to **brush**
your teeth after eating.] (*palaki lauoho* =
hairbrush) (*palaki niho* = toothbrush)

palalē to speak indistinctly or with an accent.

pālama sacred enclosure especially for royal
women.

Palani (from English) 1. Frank, Francis. 2.
French. (*'āina Palani* = France)

palaoa 1. sperm whale, ivory. (*lei niho*
palaoa = whale tooth pendant braided
with human hair, worn by high chiefs) 2.
flour, bread, wheat. [*Malo'o ka pāpa'a*
palaoa ma ke kanuwika āu? Is the slice of
bread in your sandwich stale?]

palapala document of any kind, writing of
any kind, deed, manuscript, policy, etc.
(*palapala 'aelike* = written contract) (*pala-*
pala 'āina = map) (*palapala hānau* = birth
certificate) (*palapala ho'āpono* = passport)
(*palapala ho'oilina* = will, testament; syn.
palapala kauoha) (*palapala ho'okuleana* =
copyright, patent) (*palapala 'inikua* =
insurance policy) (*palapala kū'ai* = deed
or bill of sale) (*palapala male* = marriage
license) (*palapala noi* = application form,
petition)

palapalai fern used by hula dancers; also a
general name for ferns.

palapū wound, flesh injury.

palau 1. engaged, betrothed. [*E lilo ana lāua i*
pa'a palau ma ka Lā Aloha. They two will
become an **engaged** couple on Valentine's
Day.] 2. plow.

pālau 1. to exaggerate, tell tales. 2. war club.

palaualelo lazy, idle person who talks a lot.
[*Auē nā palaualelo ma ke kīwī.* Gosh, the
lazy windbags on TV.]

pale 1. to ward off, thrust aside, fend off.
(*pale ka'a* = car bumper) (*pale makani* =
windshield) (*ho'opale* = to defend; syn.
kūpale) [*'O Nahoa kae ho'opale aku i ke*
kauka i ka 'aha ho'okolokolo. Nahoa is the
one who may **defend** the doctor in court.]

2. to ignore a law or command. [**Pale** *aku 'o Mehana i ka pāpā 'ana i ka puhi paka.* Mehana **ignores** the smoking prohibition.] (*pale ma'i* = underpants) (*pale waiū* = bra)

palekana 1. safety, security. [*Pono ka 'ohana e no'ono'o i ka* **palekana**. The family should think about **safety**.] 2. safe, rescued, convalescent.

paleki (from English) brake. (syn. *peleki*)

palena boundary, limit, border, margin. [*'O Waimea ka* **palena** *o ka moku 'o Ko'olauloa.* Waimea is the **boundary** of the Ko'olauloa land division.] (*kau palena* = to place a limit, set a deadline, limitation, deadline) [*'O ka lā hope o ka mahina ke* **kau palena** *no nā palapala noi 'oihana.* The last day of the month is the **deadline** for the job applications.]

palena 'ole without limits, without boundaries. [*'O ke aloha* **palena 'ole** *ke aloha 'ohana.* Family love is unconditional love, love **without limit**.]

pāleuleu old, worn out (refers to material, clothing, mats). [*Pāleuleu ka lole o kēnā kanaka 'ilihune.* That poor person's clothes are **worn out**.]

pali cliff, precipice, steep hill (*fig.* difficulty, obstacle). [*Pehea oe? Maika'i wau i ke alo* **pali**. How are you? I'm fine in spite of **difficulties**. (Aunty Malia Craver)] (*pali kū* = 1. vertical cliff. 2. beginning of a genealogical line [Malo])

pali

palipali precipitous, full of cliffs and small hills.

pāloka (from English) ballot. (*koho pāloka* = election, to vote) [*Mai poina e* **koho pāloka** *no ke ke'ena o kia'āina.* Don't forget to **vote** for the office of governor.]

palolo glib gossiping.

pālolo clay, mortar.

palu 1. to lick, lap. 2. relish made from fish head, stomach.

pālua 1. dual. 2. by twos. (*makani pālua* = wind blowing in several directions at once)

pālule (from English) shirt. (*pālule aloha* = aloha shirt) [*Waiwai nā* **pālule aloha** *kahiko.* Old **aloha shirts** are valuable.]

pālule aloha

pālulu shield, screen, protection from elements of any kind.

pāluna (from English) balloon.

palupalu soft, fragile, limber, flexible. [*He mau wāwae* **palupalu** *ko ka paniolo.* The cowboy has **flexible** legs.]

pāmalō 1. dry, rainless. 2. expressionless, dull. [*Pāmalō paha ka papa 'epekema, 'a'ole paha?* Is science class **dull** or not?]

pana 1. pulse, heartbeat. 2. beat in music. [*'Āwīwī ka* **pana** *mele o ke mele o ke au hou.* The **beat** of the music of modern times is fast.] Note: *Ka mele* is used to indicate a song, *ke mele* for music in general. 3. bow and arrow. (*pua pana* = arrow)(*wahi pana* = legendary places, celebrated places)

pāna'i reciprocity, reward, revenge.

panakō (from English) bank.

panalā'au colony, dependency. [*He panalā'au 'o Kilipaki ma lalo o Kalākaua.* Kiribati was a **colony** under Kalākaua.]

pānānā compass, pilot.

pana pua archery.

pane 1. answer, reply. 2. to answer, reply, speak. (*pane 'ole* = unresponsive)

pane'e 1. delay, postponement. (*ho'opane'e* = to postpone) [*Pono kāua e* **ho'opane'e** *i kā kāua hālāwai a hiki i kēia mahina a'e.* We (you and I) have to **postpone** our meeting until next month.] (*uku pane'e* = interest on principal in banking, finance) 2. to push, move along. [*Ke* **pane'e** *aku nei ke kalaiwa ka'a i ke ka'a poloke i ke kapa alanui.* The driver is **pushing** the broken car over to the side of the road.]

pani 1. to close, cut, substitute. (*pani hakahaka* = substitute, replacement, to substitute, fill a vacancy, replace) 2. closure of medical treatment with food offering. 3. lid, cover, stopper, door.

panina end, conclusion.

pānini prickly pear cactus.

paniolo 1. cowboy. 2. Spain, Spaniard. 3. Spanish. [*ka **paniolo** pipi me ka pipi 'āhiu,* the **cowboys** with the wild cattle (song, "Hu'i ē," by L. Kekuewa)] Note: This word is derived from *espaniolo* (which means "Spanish"), for the Mexican cowboys brought to Waimea, Hawai'i, to teach Hawaiians how to handle wild cattle.

paniolo

pano dark, as clouds (*fig.* unapproachable, outside the ordinary).

panoa 1. desert. 2. arid, dry. [*He 'āina **panoa** ko Ka'ū.* Ka'ū has a **dry** land (desert).] 3. dry coral bank at low tide.

panopano deep darkness.

paoa 1. strong-smelling, either good or bad smell. 2. unlucky, bad luck.

paoke'e to betray, to slander; traitor.

paona (from English) pound, weight, scale. (*hāpai paona* = lift weights) (*kau paona* = to weigh something)

papa 1. foundation, stratum, flat surface. (*papahele* = floor, level) [*Aia nā pono hale ma ka **papahele** hea?* What **floor** are the home furnishings on?] (*papahele 'ekolu* = third floor) (*papa 'āiana* = ironing board) (*papa 'ele'ele* = blackboard) (*papa hana* = work method, plan, strategy) (*papa he'e nalu* = surfboard) (*papa kuhikuhi* = index, table of contents) (*papa kuhikuhi mea 'ai* = menu) (*papa ku'i 'ai* = poi-pounding board) (*papa lā'au* = board, plank) (*papa ola* = board of health) 2. class, rank. [*E like me kā lākou mau keiki, he **papa** 'ōlelo*

papa he'e nalu

papa ku'i 'ai

Hawai'i kā mākua. Like their children, the parents have a Hawaiian language **class**.] 3. flat, level. 4. in unison, all together. (*ne'epapa* = to move as a whole, in unison)

pāpā to forbid, prohibit. [*Ua **pāpā** 'ia ka puhi paka ma ka mokulele.* Smoking is **prohibited** in airplanes.]

pāpa'a 1. cooked crisp, burned. [*'Ono ka 'ili pua'a **pāpa'a**!* **Burnt** pork skin is delicious!] (*pāpa'a lā* = sunburned) 2. slice of bread. 3. scab of sore.

pāpa'a'ina crackle, snap.

pāpa'i 1. general name for crabs. 2. temporary shelter.

pāpa'i

pāpale hat. [*'O ka **pāpale** lauhala ke 'ano o kā Momi **pāpale** punahele.* lauhala **hats** are Momi's favorite kind of **hat**.]

pāpālina cheeks.

papau deeply engaged in activity, absorbed, engrossed. [***Papau** 'o Palani i ka pā'ani lolouila.* Palani is **absorbed** in the computer game.]

pāpa'u shallow. [***Pāpa'u** ke kai ma ke kāheka.* The ocean water in the tidepool is **shallow**.]

pāpū 1. fort, fortress. 2. plain, clear space. 3. clear, unobstructed, in plain sight.

pau ended, destroyed, finished. [*Ua **pau** ko kāna mo'opuna wahine hale i ke kai e'e.* His granddaughter's house was **destroyed** in the tidal wave.] (*pau hana* = end of work) (*pau 'ole* = unceasing, constant, forever) (*ho'opau* = to finish, cancel, waste) [*Aia a **ho'opau** 'olua i ka ho'oma'ema'e hale, hiki iā 'olua ke puka i waho.* As soon as you two **finish** cleaning house, you can go outside.] (*ho'opau manawa* = waste time) [*Mai **ho'opau manawa**.* Don't **waste time**.] (*nā mea a pau* = everyone, everything) [*Pōmaika'i **nā mea a pau**.* **Everything** is blessed. (hymn, "'Ekolu Mea Nui," by R. Nāwāhine)]

pa'ū damp, moist. (syn. *ma'ū*)

pā'ū 1. woman's skirt, made of tapa cloth in ancient days; these days often refers to a hula skirt (*pā'ū hula*). 2. outer garment worn by female horseback riders to protect fine clothes underneath, first used on Hawai'i island in 1800s.

pau ahi destroyed by fire.

pa'u hana tedious, constant work.

pa'uhia overcome by sleep, overwhelmed by desire, overtaken by evil, calamity.

pauka (from English) powder, paste. (*pauka niho* = toothpaste)

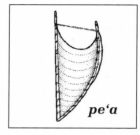

pauka niho

paukū 1. verse of Bible or song, section, piece, paragraph. 2. to make *lei* with sections of different colors.

paulele 1. faith, confidence, trust. [*He paulele ikaika kona i ko ke kahunapule mana'o.* She/he has strong **confidence** in the minister's opinion.] 2. to lean on, rely on.

paumauno'ono'o keepsake, memento, souvenir.

pā'umi to count by tens.

paupauaho (also *pauaho*) out of breath, breathless (*fig.* discouraged, faint-hearted, exhausted, despairing). [*Ma hope o ka hula 'ana i ka hula kahiko,* **paupauaho** *nā 'ōlapa.* After dancing ancient-style hula, the dancers are **out of breath**.]

pawa darkness just before dawn. [*Moku ka pawa o ke ao.* The **darkness** has been broken by the dawn. (common line in chants)]

pāwalu to count by eights.

pāwehe 1. generic name for geometric designs found in mats from Ni'ihau and Kaua'i. 2. to make such designs.

pē 1. crushed, flattened, humble. 2. perfumed, drenched. [*pulu pē i ka ua,* **drenched** in rain (*fig.* sexual reference). (common line in love songs)]

pea (from English) bear, pear (avocado).

pe'a 1. cross. (syn. *ke'a*) 2. sail of canoe. 3. boundary. 4. to menstruate. 5. menstruating. (*hale pe'a* = house where women stayed during menstruation)

pe'ahi 1. fan. 2. to fan, wave. (*pe'ahi lima* = to wave hand, beckon to) [*E* **pe'ahi** *lima aku iā 'Anakala!* **Wave** to Uncle!]

pe'a

pe'ape'a 1. starfish. 2. entangled, crossing.

pe'e to hide oneself. (*ho'ohūnā* = to hide something)

pehea how, what, how about it? [*Pehea ka pa'a 'oki male hou? Hau'oli lāua?* **How** is the newly divorced couple? Are they happy?] (*pehea kou mana'o?* = what's your opinion?) (*pehea lāua?* = how are they [two]?)

pehu 1. to swell (*fig.* conceited). 2. swollen, swelling, distended. (*kai pehu* = swelling sea) (*makapehu* = hungry)

peki (from English) to pace, trudge along, to back up car. (*holopeki* = to trot [horse], jog)

peku 1. kick. 2. to kick. [*Ke* **peku** *'ia nei ka lio e ka mea holo lio.* The horse is being **kicked** by the rider.] (*pōpeku* = football, soccer)

pela (from English) mattress, bale, pail, to spell. (*pela pa'akai* = salt flats, still used on Kaua'i to make salt from sea water)

pēlā like that (what I've just told you). [*Pēlā 'olua e hana ai.* **That**'s how you (two) should do it.] [*Mai hana* **pēlā***!* Don't do **that**!] (*pēlā paha* = maybe) (*a pēlā aku* = etc., and so on)

pelapela filthy, nasty, obscene. (*'ōlelo pelapela* = swearing) [*E kala mai i kā ka'u ipo 'ōlelo pelapela.* I apologize for my sweetheart's **swearing**.]

pele 1. lava, volcano, eruption. [*Hū mai ka pele mai ka lua pele 'o 'Ō'ō.* The **lava** erupts from the 'Ō'ō crater. 2. (from

pele

English) bell. [*Kanikani* **pele***, kanikani* **pele***, kani ma 'ō ma 'ane'i.* Jingle **bells**, jingle **bells**, jingle all over the place.]

Pele name of fire goddess.

Pelekane 1. (from English) Britain, England. (*ka 'ōlelo* Pelekane = English; syn. *ka 'ōlelo haole*)

peleki (from English) 1. brake. 2. to apply brakes.

pelekunu bad smelling, musty. [*No ke aha i kapa 'ia ai ke awāwa nani ma Moloka'i 'o* **Pelekunu***?* Why is the beautiful valley on Moloka'i called **Pelekunu**?]

pelu to fold, turn over, bend. (*ho'opelu* = to tuck, hem, fold over)

pena (from English) 1. paint. 2. to paint. (*pena ki'i* = to paint pictures)

peni (from English) pen, pencil.

penikala (from English) pencil.

pepa (from English) paper, card. (*hainakā pepa* = facial tissue) (*nūpepa* = newspaper) (*pepa hēleu* = toilet paper) (*pepa mānoanoa* = cardboard) (*pepa pipili* = sticker) (*pepa po'oleka* = post card) (*pepa wahī* = wrapping paper) (*pā'ani pepa* = to play cards)

peni

pēpē 1. baby. 2. flat, squatty.

pepehi to beat, strike, kill. [*Mai* **pepehi** *i kāu lio!* Don't **beat** your horse!] (*pepehi a make loa* = beaten until dead, beaten to death)

pepeiao 1. ear. 2. to hear. (*lohe pepeiao* = hearsay)

Pepeluali (from English) February.

pewa tail of fish, shrimp, lobster.

pī 1. stingy, frugal. [*'O ka 'awa'awa ka hopena o ke* **pī***.* Bitterness is the consequence of being **stingy**.] 2. to sprinkle on water with the fingers.

pia arrowroot plant, beer.

pī 'ā pā alphabet. (*hua palapala* = letter of alphabet)

piapia white discharge from eyes after sleeping. (*maka piapia* = eye with discharge [insult: one who doesn't see what one should])

piha 1. full, filled (liquid), complete. 2. full-blooded, one hundred percent pure (nationality). [*He Hawai'i* **piha** *ko Kaipo kupuna kāne.* Kaipo's grandfather is a **full-blooded** Hawaiian.] (*piha ku'i* = jam packed, crowded to limits; syn. *piha'ū*) (*piha makahiki* = yearly anniversary) (*piha pono* = completely full, complete)

pihapiha 1. gills of fish. 2. full, complete. (*ho'opihapiha* = to fill out any form) [*E* **ho'opihapiha** *i ka palapala noi.* **Fill out** the application form.]

pihe din of voices, shouting, lamentation.

pihi 1. scab, scar. 2. button, badge. [*'Akahi nō 'o ia i kaomi i ke* **pihi** *i mea e ho'opio ai i ka mīkini ho'omalo'o lole.* He just pressed the **button** to turn off the clothes dryer.]

pīhoihoi excited, worried, disturbed.

piholo to sink, drown, be swamped (canoe filled with ocean water). [*'Oiai e* **piholo** *ai ka mea he'e nalu, 'a'ole maka'u ke kia'i ola.* While the surfer may **sink**, the lifeguard isn't afraid.]

pi'i 1. to climb up, go up, go inland. 2. to rise up (emotions). (*pi'i ka wela* = anger rises up; to get a fever) (*pi'i ke kai* = lit. the sea rises, poetic phrase indicating that anger rises up) (*pi'i kuahiwi* = to hike) (*ho'opi'i* = lawsuit, court case, to sue) [*E* **ho'opi'i** *ana nā 'ōiwi i ke aupuni.* The natives will **sue** the government.]

pi'ikoi to claim honors or rank not rightfully yours, to rise above your station. [*Mai* **pi'ikoi** *'oe i ke akule la.* Don't **try (to rise beyond your station)** for *akule* fish. (song, "He 'Ono," by B. Mossman)]

pi'ina climb, ascent. [*Kūnihi ka* **pi'ina** *i ka 'ikena i loko o ka lua pele kahiko.* The **climb** up to the view inside the old crater is steep.]

pi'ipi'i 1. curly, wavy. 2. bubbling up. [***Pi'ipi'i*** *ko ko'u kupuna wahine lauoho.* My grandmother's hair is **curly**.]

pī kai to sprinkle with salt water in order to purify.

pīkake (from English) jasmine flower, named for Ka'iulani's peacocks.

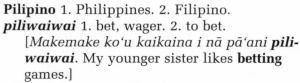

pīkake

Pīkī 1. Fiji. 2. Fijian. 2. PG, Provisional Government.

pikiniki (from English) picnic.

piko 1. navel, umbilical cord (*fig.* genitals). 2. crown of head.

pīkoi core of fruit.

pila 1. any musical instrument. [*Kani ka **pila**! Let **the instrument** sound (play music)!*] 2. (from English) bill. [*Inā 'oe i uku i ka **pila** uila, inā ua hiki ke nānā i ke kīwī. If you had paid the electric **bill**, then you could watch TV.*] (*pila kīko'o* = bank check)

pilau 1. stench. 2. to stink. 3. rotten, spoiled.

pili 1. to stick, join, be close to. (*pili wale* = to cling for no reason) (*ho'opili* = to mimic, imitate, to bring together, stick) [*E **ho'opili** mai ia'u. **Repeat after** me.*] [*Iā ia e **ho'opili** ana i ke ki'i i ka pepa, ua pa'a kona manamana lima. When he was **sticking** the picture to the paper, his finger got stuck.*] 2. to be related. [*He **pili** 'ohana māua 'o Nonohe. Nonohe and I are **related**.*] (*pili mua* = older relative) 3. close relationship. (*pili kāmau* = close friendship)

pilialo beloved wife (*lit.* close to the front of the body).

pilialoha close relationship, beloved companion. (*pili 'ao'ao* = mate, lover)

pilikia 1. trouble of any kind, distress, difficulty, accident. 2. troubled, bothered. [*I ka wā **pilikia** me ka wā hau'oli. In times of **trouble** and in times of happiness.*] (*ho'opilikia* = to cause trouble, harm)

pilikino personal, private.

pilikoko blood relationship.

pilikua 1. beloved husband (*lit.* close to the back of the body). 2. giant.

pilina association, union, meeting.

pilipa'a sticking firmly together, associating constantly.

Pilipino 1. Philippines. 2. Filipino.

piliwaiwai 1. bet, wager. 2. to bet. [*Makemake ko'u kaikaina i nā pā'ani **piliwaiwai**. My younger sister likes **betting** games.*]

pilo 1. swampy, polluted. 2. Hawaiian trees of coffee family. 3. foul odor, bad breath.

pinao dragonfly. [*He nani maoli nō ka **pinao**. **Dragonflies** are truly beautiful.*]

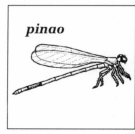

pinao

pine 1. pin, peg, bolt. 2. to pin.

pinepine often, frequent, frequently.

pio 1. captive, prisoner. (*hā'awi pio* = to give up) 2. to peep, chirp (chicks, birds). Note: In the following example, the reduplication imitates a chirping sound. [***Pio pio** mau mā pūnua pōloli. The hungry fledglings **chirp** continuously. 3. extinguished (fire), turned off. (*ho'opio* = to turn off) [*Hiki paha iā ia ke **ho'opio** i ka lolouila? Can she perhaps **turn off** the computer?*]

pi'o 1. arch, arc, curve. [*He mau **pi'o** ko ke kahawai ma ke awāwa 'o Waipi'o. The stream in Waipi'o valley has **curves**.*] 2. an *ali'i* rank, offspring of brother and sister. 3. to arch, bend. 4. curved, bent, arched.

pipi 1. pearl oyster. [*'O ka **pipi** ma Pu'uloa ka i'a hāmau leo. The **pearl oyster** at Pearl Harbor is the silent-voiced fish (you must not talk when getting it, for if it hears your voice, it will hide).*] 2. cattle, beef. (*'i'o pipi* = beef) (*pipi kāne* = bull) (*pipi wahine* = cow)

pīpī 1. sprinkle. [***Pīpī**, holo ka'ao. **Sprinkled** about, the story runs on. (traditional ending to stories, giving the idea that a story will live and change in the retelling)] 2. (from English) to urinate (syn. *mimi*). (*pīpīnoke* = to talk incessantly)

pipi'i expensive. [*He **pipi'i** ho'i kau nā hale ma O'ahu. Houses on O'ahu are truly **expensive**.*]

pipili sticky, tenacious. [***Pipili** nā po'oleka.

Stamps are **sticky**.]

piwa (from English) fever. [*He **piwa** ko ka mea ma'i.* The sick person has a **fever**.]

pō

pō 1. night, darkness, ancient realm from which life originated. 2. weekday. (Pō'akahi = Monday; Pō'alua = Tuesday; Pō'akolu = Wednesday; Pō'ahā = Thursday; Pō'alima = Friday; Pō'aono = Saturday; Lāpule = Sunday) The traditional lunar calendar had names for each night of the lunar month.

pōā 1. robber, thief. [*Ua **pōā** ka 'aihue i ka panakō i nehinei.* The **thief** robbed the bank yesterday.] 2. to rob a person or place. (The verb *pōā* implies plundering a place or location, while *'aihue* implies taking away the thing stolen.)

pō'ai 1. circle, circuit, hoop. 2. to go around, make a circuit, encircle, coil. 3. surrounded, encircled. (*pō'ai hapalua* = semi-circle) (*pō'ai lani* = horizon) (*pō'ai lō'ihi* = ellipse) (*pō'ai puni* = to circumnavigate, go completely around) (*pō'ai waena honua* = equator)

po'e 1. people, group. 2. pluralizer, used in place of *mau*. [*Nui ka **po'e** pōhaku pele ma ko kēlā hale pā.* There are **many** lava rocks in that house's fence.] (*ka po'e kāne* = men) (*ka po'e wahine* = women)

pō'ele'ele 1. darkness. 2. dark.

poepoe 1. globe, sphere. (*ka poepoe honua* = globe of the earth; syn. *pa'a honua*) 2. round, rounded, full (moon). [*He lei **poepoe** ka lei kīkā.* The cigar *lei* is a **round** *lei*.]

pohā 1. non-native edible berry. 2. to burst, crack, break forth. 3. bursting, cracking.

pōhāhā breaking forth. (syn. *hua'i*) (*pōhāhāwai* = bubble)

pōhai 1. circle, group, gathering. 2. to encircle, surround, gather in a circle. [***Pōhai** ke aloha lā i ke kino.* Love **encircles** the body. (song, "Pōhai Ke Aloha," by L. Machado and M. Kealakai)]

pōhaku

pōhaku 1. rock, stone, mineral. 2. rocky, stony. (*pōhaku ku'i 'ai* = poi pounder) (*pōhaku lepo* = adobe, brick) (*pōhaku pele* = any lava rock)

pohala 1. to recover consciousness, revive after fainting, recover from illness. [*Ua mā'ule ka mea pena hale wela a ua **pohala** a'ela.* The hot housepainter fainted and then **revived**.] 2. rest, recreation.

pōheoheo knob, any knob-like object, rounded top of poi pounder.

pohihihi obscure, entangled, mysterious, intricate. [***Pohihihi** ka ho'okumu honua.* The creation of the earth is **obscure**.]

poho 1. hollow or palm of hand, foot, depression. [*Ua 'eha kou **poho** wāwae i kou hehi 'ana ma luna o ke kukū kiawe?* Did the **hollow** of your foot hurt when you stepped on the *kiawe* tree thorn?] 2. powder compact, match box. 3. patch on clothes. 4. chalk. (*poho mea kanu* = flower pot)

pohō 1. loss, damage. 2. out of luck, useless. [***Pohō** ka 'imi 'ana i ke kanaka ku'i 'opihi i lilo i ke kai.* (It is) **useless** to search for the *'opihi* picker who was taken by the ocean.]

poholalo underhanded, deceitful, dishonest. [***Poholalo** paha kā Kamehameha hana iā Keouakū'ahu'ula?* Was what Kamehameha did to Keouakū'ahu'ula **deceitful**?]

pohole 1. sore, bruise. 2. bruised, skinned, scraped. [***Pohole** ko ka hope po'o kumu 'ili i ka pūko'a ma ka'e kāheka.* The vice-principal's skin is **bruised** due to the coral head on the edge of the tidepool.]

pohopoho patched. (*kuiki pohopoho* = patchwork quilt)

pōhue general name for gourd plants.

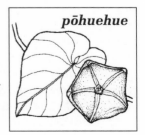

pōhuehue

pōhuehue 1. beach morning glory, used to drive fish into nets. 2. to call up surf by a ritual involving striking the sea with *pōhuehue* vine while chanting a prayer of supplication.

pōhūhū dusty, smoky.

poi food made by pounding cooked taro corm (syn. *ka ʻai*, *lit.* the food, indicating the central importance of the *kalo* plant and *poi* to the Hawaiian culture). (*ka ʻai me ka iʻa* = fish and poi)

poʻi 1. cover, lid, crest of breaking wave. 2. to cover, to break (wave). (*poʻina kai* = place where waves break) 3. to pounce on, catch between the hands. [**Poʻi** *ka pōpoki ma luna o ka ʻiole*. The cat **pounces on** the mouse.]

poina 1. to forget, forgettable. [*Mai* **poina** *e hoʻouna aku i kaʻu mau leka!* Don't **forget** to mail my letters!] 2. forgotten. (*poina wale* = absentminded) (*poina ka noʻonoʻo* = amnesia, forgetful)

poina ʻole unforgettable. [*He lei* **poina** *ʻole ke keiki.* (ʻōlelo noʻeau) A child is an **unforgettable** *lei.*]

pōʻino 1. misfortune, ill luck, affliction, storm, disaster. 2. unfortunate. (*hoʻopōʻino* = to harm, injure, cause damage)

poʻipū 1. attack, onslaught. 2. to cover over entirely with clouds, waves.

pōkā bullet, cannonball, pellet. (*pōkā pahū* = bomb, bombardment, to bomb)

pōkaʻa 1. ball, coil, spool of string, roll of *lauhala* leaves. 2. to wind, roll, coil.

poke 1. section, slice, piece, cubed raw fish served as appetizer. 2. to cut into cubes, sections. (*poke hau* = ice cube)

poki 1. fine stitches, mesh. 2. (*cap.*) general name for supernatural dogs.

pōkiʻi younger brother or sister (term of affection). [*Lahela kuʻu* **pōkiʻi**, Lahela, my beloved younger sister (song, "Lahela Kuʻu Pōkiʻi," by L. L. Conn)]

pōkole short. (*pōkole ka naʻau* = quick-tempered)

pola 1. flap of a *malo*, tail of a kite. 2. platform between hulls of a double canoe.

polapola 1. to get well, recover from illness. [*E* **polapola** *wikiwiki a e hoʻi mai i ka hana!* **Recover** quickly and come back to work!] 2. recovered from illness. (*polapola iki* = a

little better) 3. (*cap.*) Tahiti (from Borabora).

poli bosom, breast. [*Ma kuʻu* **poli** *mai ʻoe e kuʻu ipo aloha.* Here upon my **breast** you are cherished. (song, "Ke Aloha," by L. Collins)]

Poliʻahu goddess of snow on Mauna Kea.

polikua far reaches of ocean or sky that are invisible, beyond the horizon, the "great beyond."

polinahe soft and gentle.

polo thick, plump.

polohina misty, smoky, gray (*fig.* affectionate pity, grief).

polohiwa glistening black.

poloke (from English) broken. [**Poloke** *kou mopeka?* Is your moped **broken**?]

pololei correct, right, accurate, straight. [*E kalaiwa* **pololei** *a hiki i ka huina alanui a e huli hema ma laila.* Drive **straight** ahead up to the intersection and turn left there.] (*hoʻopololei* = to 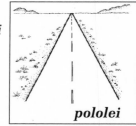 straighten, correct) [*Pono nā haumāna e* **hoʻopololei** *i nā pepa.* The students have to **correct** the papers.]

pōloli 1. hunger. 2. hungry. [**Pōloli** *kā koʻu ʻohana mau hānaiāhuhu.* My family's pets are **hungry**.] (*make pōloli* = starved to death)

pololia jellyfish.

pololo talk without tact.

poluea 1. nausea, seasickness, hangover. 2. nauseated, seasick.

pōmaikaʻi good fortune, blessedness, prosperity. (*hoʻomaikaʻi* = congratulations) (*hoʻopōmaikaʻi* = to bless someone) [*Ua* **hoʻopōmaikaʻi** *ʻia ka pēpē e ke kahunapule.* The baby was **blessed** by the minister.]

poni 1. purple. 2. to anoint, consecrate, crown, inaugurate, ordain. [*Ua* **poni** *ʻo Kalākaua iā ia ponoʻī.* Kalākaua **crowned** himself.] (*poni mōʻī* = coronation, carnation)

pōniuniu dizzy. [*Hō ke kūhohonu o ko kēlā mea ʻakeakamai manaʻo!* **Pōniuniu** *ke poʻo!* Goodness how complicated that scientist's ideas are! My head is **dizzy**!]

pono 1. morality, excellence, goodness, duty, true nature. [*E nānā i ka* **pono**. Look to **excellence**.] (*pono 'ole* = dishonest, improper) (*nā pono kiwila* = civil rights) (*pono kope* = copyright) 2. supplies, gear. (*nā pono hale* = furniture) (*nā pono lawai'a* = fishing supplies) 3. should, must, ought to. [*'O ke keiki Kaiapuni Hawai'i, he haumāna e a'o* **pono** *'ia*. A child of the Hawaiian Immersion program **should** be a student who is well taught.] 4. intensifying particle used after word. 5. preceding verb, to do [verb] carelessly, any old way. [*Mai* **pono** *kākau, e kākau* **pono***!* Don't write **any old way**, write **properly**!]

pono'ī 1. self, own. (Hawai'i Pono'ī = Hawai'i's own [Hawai'i's people]) 2. directly, exactly.

pono 'ole dishonest, improper.

ponopono 1. mental clearing, restoring balance within individual and/or family. (*ho'oponopono* = to fix [machine], to correct) 2. neat, in order.

po'o 1. head. (*po'o 'eha* = headache) (*po'o kanaka* = skull) (*po'omana'o* = headlines, theme, topic) 2. summit. 3. director of organization. (*po'ohala* = to carry on family skills and traditions) (*po'o kumu* = school principal) (*po'o 'ole* = illegitimate) (*po'oleka* = stamp)

po'ohina gray-haired.

po'ohiwi shoulder.

po'okela 1. champion, the best. [*He* **po'okela** *o nā wāhine he'e nalu 'o Rell Sun*. Rell Sun is a **champion** of women surfers.] 2. to excel. 3. superior.

po'olua of uncertain parentage.

po'o pa'akikī stubborn (*lit.* hard head). [*'O 'oe ma ka* **po'o pa'akikī***!* Gee, how **stubborn** can you be!]

pōpilikia misfortune, trouble, calamity, ordeal.

pōpō roundness, ball for sports.

popohe shapely, round. [*Ka pua i* **popohe** *a mōhala i ke aumoe*. The flower that became **round** and blossomed at midnight (*fig.* description of beautiful woman).]

pōpoki cat. (*pōpoki pe'elua* = tabby cat)

pōpoki

pōpolo 1. herb used for medicine, ceremonies. 2. uncomplimentary slang for a black person; *pā'ele* is the more polite term.

popopo 1. rot (wood), decay (teeth). 2. to rot. [**Popopo** *koke ka hale lā'au ma Hawai'i nei*. Wooden houses quickly **rot** here in Hawai'i.] 3. rotten, decayed.

pou post, main post in house, canoe mast.

pouli 1. eclipse, dark night, darkness. 2. dark. (*pouli lā* = eclipse of sun)

poupou short and husky (*fig.* mainstay of family).

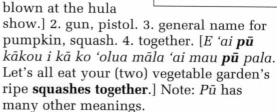

pū

pū 1. conch shell or any wind instrument. [*Ua kani 'ia ka* **pū** *ma ka hō'ike hula*. The **conch shell** was blown at the hula show.] 2. gun, pistol. 3. general name for pumpkin, squash. 4. together. [*E 'ai* **pū** *kākou i kā ko 'olua māla 'ai mau* **pū** *pala*. Let's all eat your (two) vegetable garden's ripe **squashes together**.] Note: *Pū* has many other meanings.

pua 1. flower, blossom. [*ku'u* **pua** *mae 'ole*, my never-fading **flower** (common line in love songs, comparing the beloved to an unfading flower)] 2. child, descendant, fry of fish. [*ku'u* **pua**, *ku'u lei nani mae 'ole, 'eā*, my **child**, my beloved never-fading *lei* (song, "Ku'u Lei Poina 'ole," by E. de Fries)] 3. to flower, blossom. 4. to appear, come forth.

pua'a 1. pig, pork. [*Aia a hu'e 'ia ka imu, a moni ka hā'ae i ke 'ala o ka 'i'o* **pua'a** *kālua*. As soon as the *imu* is uncovered, (we) salivate due to the smell of the baked

pua'a

pig.] 2. banks of fog or clouds over mountain, cloud forms of Kamapua'a.

pua'i to flow out, to bubble, gurgle. [***Pua'i*** *aku ka wai mai ka puna wai.* Water **bubbles** out of the spring.] (syn. *hua'i*)

puakea light color. (*'ili puakea* = white person, light-skinned part-Hawaiian)

pū'ali 1. warrior. (*pū'ali koa* = armed forces, troops) 2. to gird tightly around the waist. 3. grooved, notched. [***Pū'ali*** *ka hau nui i ka hau iki.* (*'ōlelo no'eau*) The large *hau* branch is **grooved** by the small *hau* branch (a little person has conquered a big one).] (*pū'ali'ali* = of varying thickness)

puana 1. refrain of song. [*Ha'ina 'ia mai ana ka* **puana.** Tell again the **refrain.** (line beginning last verse of many songs, indicating song's theme or person honored will be mentioned next)] 2. pronunciation, utterance.

pu'e 1. hill, dune. (*pu'e one* = sandbar, sand dune) (*pu'e 'uala* = sweet potato mound [earth was mounded up to plant sweet potatoes]) 2. to hill up. 3. to rape, force, attack.

puehu 1. scattered, dispersed. [***Puehu*** *ka 'ehu kai i ka makani.* The sea foam is **scattered** by the wind.] 2. peeling (sunburn).

pueo Hawaiian owl, well-known family guardian spirit.

pueo

pūhā 1. abscess, ulcer. 2. to belch, burp (syn. *kūhā*). [*Mai* ***pūhā*** *ma ka pā'ina!* Don't **burp** at the party!] 3. to break, burst.

pūhaka loins, waist.

puhi 1. eel. 2. blowhole. 3. to blow, puff. (*puhi paka* = to smoke a cigarette) (*pana puhi 'ohe* = music band) 4. to burn, set on fire. (*puhi ahi* = arson, to burn, set fire to, cremate) (*puhi pau* = completely burned, blown away)

puhi

pūhi'u 1. to break wind. 2. rude, irreverent.

pūhuluhulu hairy, shaggy.

pū'ili bamboo rattles for dancing.

pū'iwa 1. amazement. 2. surprised, astonished. (*ho'opū'iwa* = to startle, astonish)

puka 1. door, opening, hole. (*pukaaniani* = window) (*puka ihu* = nostril) (*pukapuka* = many holes) 2. to emerge, pass through, rise (sun). [*Ua* ***puka*** *aku kākou i ka wā pōpilikia ma hope o ka makani pāhili.* We all **emerged from** the time of misfortune after the hurricane.] 3. to graduate. [*Ma ke kau kula hea ana 'oukou e* ***puka*** *ai?* What semester will you all **graduate**?] 4. to say, utter. 5. to gain, win profit. Note: *Puka* has many other meanings.

puka a maka the birth of a child affirms a permanent relationship (*lit.* appears to the eye).

pukaaniani window.

pukana 1. outlet, exit. 2. keepsake, souvenir. (*pukana aloha* = souvenir of loved one) (*pukana lā* = sunrise)

pukapuka many holes, porous.

puke (from English) book. (*puke ho'omana'o* = diary, journal) (*puke kuhikuhi* = manual) (*puke wehewehe 'ōlelo* = dictionary)

puke

pūko'a coral head.

pūkolu trio, triplet.

pūku'i 1. to collect, assemble people or things. [*Na Kawena Pukui i* ***pūku'i*** *i nā hua 'ōlelo Hawai'i.* It was Kawena Pukui who **collected** Hawaiian words.] 2. council of gods, chiefs.

pukupuku 1. wrinkles, frowning. 2. to wrinkle, purse lips. (*pukupuku kū'ē maka* = wrinkled brow)

pula particle, speck.

pulakaumaka obsession (*lit.* particle in eye). [*He* ***pulakaumaka*** *ko ke kālai pōhaku.* The rock carver has an **obsession**.]

pūlale to hurry, rush. [*No ke aha lā 'oe e* ***pūlale*** *mai?* Why do you **rush** over here? (song, "Hōkio," by M. Pukui and M. Lam)]

pūlama 1. to cherish, care for. 2. cherished. [*He lei* ***pūlama*** *'ia ke aloha e lei mau ai.*

Love is a **cherished** *lei* to wear always.] 3.
torch.

pulapula seedling, sprout, descendant.
(*hoʻopulapula* = rehabilitation, to rehabili-
tate, procreate, start seedlings, multiply)
(*ʻāina hoʻopulapula* = Hawaiian Homes
lands) [*ʻEhia makahiki a kona ʻohana i
kali ai a loaʻa ka **ʻāina hoʻopulapula** iā
lākou?* How many years did her family
wait until they got **Hawaiian Homes land**?]

pule 1. prayer, blessing, church. (*pule hoʻopōmaikaʻi* = blessing) 2. week. (*hopenapule* = weekend)

pūlehu to barbeque,
cook over coals.

pūlehulehu twilight.

pulelehua butterfly,
moth.

pulelo to float, wave,
rise (as a flag does).
[*E **pulelo** ana ka hae
Hawaiʻi.* The Hawaiian flag will **rise** in triumph.]

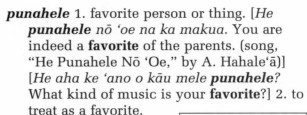
pule

pūliki to embrace, hug.

pūlima 1. wrist, cuff. 2. signature. 3. to clasp
hands. 4. to sign. [*Na ka loiō e **pūlima** i ka
palapala ʻoki male.* It is the lawyer who
should **sign** the divorce document.]

pūloʻuloʻu crossed
sticks topped with a
tapa-covered ball,
indicating a *kapu*
area reserved for
aliʻi.

pulu 1. mulch, coconut
husk, tree fern fiber
(once used to stuff
mattresses, quilts). 2. soaked, moist.

pūloʻuloʻu

pūlumi broom, to sweep.

pulu pē thoroughly soaked, drenched. [***pulu
pē** i ka ua,* **drenched** in the rain (common
line in songs with sexual reference)]

pumehana 1. warmth, affection. 2. warm,
warm hearted. [*Me ke aloha **pumehana**.*
With **warm** greetings. (common salutation)]

puna 1. spring of water. 2. coral, lime, plas-
ter. 3. (from English) spoon. (*puna kī* =
teaspoon) (*puna pākaukau* = tablespoon)

punahele 1. favorite person or thing. [*He
punahele nō ʻoe na ka makua.* You are
indeed a **favorite** of the parents. (song,
"He Punahele Nō ʻOe," by A. Hahaleʻā)]
[*He aha ke ʻano o kāu mele **punahele**?*
What kind of music is your **favorite**?] 2. to
treat as a favorite.

punalua shared spouse.

pūnana nest, hive (*fig.*
home). (Pūnana Leo =
language nest
[Hawaiian immersion
preschool]) (*pūnana
manu* = bird's nest;
pūnua = fledgling,
baby bird) (*pūnana meli* = beehive)

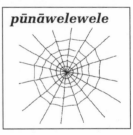
pūnana

pūnāwai spring of water.

pūnāwelewele cobweb, spider's web.

pūneʻe couch.

puni 1. to covet, desire.
(*puni kālā* = merce-
nary, greedy; *puni
waiwai* = covetous,
desirous of others'
wealth) 2. surround-
ed, controlled, over-
come with emotion.
3. deceived, deluded. (*puni wale* =
gullible, easily swayed) (*hoʻopunipuni* =
to lie, tell falsehood)

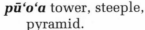

pūnāwelewele

pūnohu to rise (smoke, mist), to spread out
(sail, cloud).

pūnua fledgling, baby
bird (*fig.* young
child). [*Aia ka
pūnua ma lalo o ko
kona makua ʻēheu.*
The **fledgling** is
under her parent's
wing.]

pūnua

pūʻoʻa tower, steeple,
pyramid.

puoho 1. to cry out in
shock. 2. startled. 3.
to explode, as lava
flow.

pūʻolo bundle, bag, container. [*Aia nō a

pūʻolo

nāki'i 'ia nā lei i nā **pū'olo** *lā'ī, mākaukau ka pā'ina.* As soon as the *lei* are tied in the *tī* leaf **bundles**, the party is ready.]

pūpū 1. general name for shell, beads. 2. snack, relish. 3. bunch, bundle (grass, bouquet).

pupuāhulu 1. to hurry 2. in a hurry. [*Mai hele a* **pupuāhulu**! Don't get **in a hurry**!] 3. to make a careless mistake.

pupuka ugly, unsightly, homely (sometimes used when referring to a beautiful baby, so that jealousy isn't aroused).

pūpūkahi united in cooperation. (syn. *lōkahi*)

pupule crazy, reckless, wild.

pupu'u to huddle or curl up limbs in a fetal position (*fig.* the womb).

pu'u 1. any kind of bump, protuberance. 2. hill, mound. 3. any protuberance on the body, such as a pimple, Adam's apple, callus, wart, knuckle. (*pu'upu'u* = kidney, knuckle) 4. heaped, pregnant (*fig.* obstacle, burden, discomfort). (*pu'u kālā* = sum of money) [*'A'ole mākou a'e minamina i ka* **pu'u kālā** *o ke aupuni.* We place no value on the government's **money**. (protest song, "Kaulana Nā Pua," by E. Prendergast)] (*pu'uaahi* = bonfire) (*pu'upa'a* = virgin) (*pu'u pepa* = deck of playing cards) Note: *Pu'u* has many other meanings.

pu'uhonua place of refuge, asylum.

pu'ukani 1. singer. 2. sweet voiced.

pu'ukū treasurer.

Pu'ulena famous cold wind at Kīlauea, Hawai'i. [*Mai kali a pau nā niho, o hala 'ē ka* **Pu'ulena**. Don't wait until all your teeth are gone, or else the **Pu'ulena** wind has passed by (an idiomatic expression for "it's too late"). (song, "Nā 'Ono o Ka 'Āina," probably by A. Kauila)]

pu'uhonua

pu'ulima fist.

pū'ulu 1. group, crowd. 2. to crowd, assemble.

pu'unaue to divide, share.

pu'upu'u 1. knuckles. 2. full of lumps, piled in heaps. (*pu'upu'u lima* = clenched fist, blow of fist) (*pu'upu'u wāwae* = ankle bones)

pu'uwai heart, lungs. (*haka* = heart-shaped) (*ka pu'uwai hāmana* = open-hearted, generous)

U

ū 1. breast, udder. [*‘Olo‘olo ko ka pipi wahine mau **ū**. The cow's **udders** are pendulous.] 2. to drip. 3. moist.

‘ū 1. grief, sorrow. 2. to moan, groan, sigh, grieve. (syn: *kani‘uhū, ‘uhū*) (*noho ‘ū* = grief-stricken [syn. *lu‘ulu‘u*])

ua rain. [*noenoe **ua** kea o Hāna,* white misty **rain** of Hāna (song, "Ua Kea o Hāna," by E. Pu‘ukea)] 2. to rain. 3. rainy. 4. verb tense marker for past tense.

ua

‘uā to shout, cry out.

‘u‘a 1. good-for-nothing person. 2. useless, worn out, unattractive. [**‘U‘a** *wale nō ka pepehi ‘elelū.* Killing cockroaches is **useless**.]

uahi smoke, dust, spray. (*ka uahi a Pele* = a type of taro reserved for ceremonial use [*lit.* Pele's smoke]) (*uauahi* = vog, smog, haze)

uahi

uakea white mist of Hāna, Maui.

uaki (from English) watch, clock. (*uaki ho‘āla* = alarm clock) [*E ho‘opio i kāu **uaki ho‘āla**. Turn off your **alarm clock**.]

uakoko low-lying rainbow. [*ālai ‘ia e ka **uakoko**,* blocked by the **low-lying rainbow** (line from chant)]

‘uala sweet potato. [*Poni ka **‘uala** mai*

‘uala

Okinawa mai. The **sweet potato** from Okinawa is purple.] (*‘uala kahiki* = Irish potato [*lit.* foreign potato])

ualo to cry out for help.

‘uao 1. peacemaker, arbitrator. [*‘O ka mea **‘uao** ka luna kānāwai hapa Hawai‘i.* The part-Hawaiian judge is the **arbitrator**.] 2. to intercede, arbitrate, reconcile.

uapo bridge, pier, wharf. [*ka **uapo** a‘o Māmala, e ‘au a‘e nei ma hope,* the **pier** of Māmala (Honolulu harbor) that is swimming away behind us (song, "He Aloha Nō ‘O Honolulu," by L. Kauwe)]

‘ua‘u sea bird, dark-rumped petrel.

uaua tough, sinewy (*fig.* hard-headed, willful). [**Uaua** *kēia ‘i‘o hipa ma‘alili.* This cooled-down mutton is **tough** (to chew).]

uauahi vog, smog, haze. [*‘Oiai e hū a‘e nei ka pele, uhi ‘ia ‘o Kona i ka **uauahi**.* Since lava is bubbling up now, Kona is covered with **vog**.]

uē 1. mourning. (*uē helu* = type of mourning chant recounting experiences shared with deceased). 2. to cry, weep, lament. (*uē ‘ino* = tantrum; *uē wale* = to cry for no reason, crybaby)

uē

uea (from English) wire. (*uea makika* = mosquito screen on doors, windows)

‘uehe hula step.

‘uha 1. waste, extravagance. 2. wasteful, extravagant. [*‘O ka uku **‘uha** a nā kahu waiwai ka‘u mea e ho‘ohalahala ai.* The **extravagant** salary of the trustees is the thing I would criticize.] (*‘uha ‘ai* = to waste food, squander anything)

'ūhā thigh, lap.

'uhaloa weed whose root and leaves are used as medicine for cold, sore throat; a *kinolau* (body form) of Kamapua'a.

'uhane soul, spirit, ghost. (*ka 'uhane hemolele* = the holy ghost) (*lele ka 'uhane* = the soul leaves [death])

'uhene 1. exclamation in songs. 2. to tease, flirt, talk romantically. [***'Uhene** kēnā ipo āu i nā manawa a pau.* That sweetheart of yours **flirts** all the time.]

uhi 1. cover, lid, veil, covering. 2. to cover, spread, conceal, overwhelm (*fig.* to hide truth, deceive). (*uhi moe* = bedspread; *uhi pela* = bedsheet; *uhi pākaukau* = tablecloth [syn. *hāli'i pākaukau*]) 3. solid tattooing.

uhikino body covering, shield.

'ūhini grasshopper. (*'ūhini lele* = cricket)

uhiwai heavy fog, mist.

ūhī'ūhā sounds heard in flowing lava, like huffing and puffing. [***'Ūhī'ūhā** mai ana 'eā, e Pele e Pele ē.* **Huffing and puffing** along, oh Pele. (traditional chant, "Aia Lā 'o Pele," Loebenstein)]

'ūhini

uhu parrot fish.

'uhū to moan, groan, sigh (usually used with *kani*). (syn: *'ū*) [*Kani**'uhū** ka māka'ikiu ma ka 'ao'ao ho'opale.* The detective on the side of the defendant **groaned**.]

ui 1. question, catechism. 2. to ask, question, appeal. [*He **ui**, he nīnau aku ana au iā 'oe, aia i hea ka wai a Kāne?* A query, a **question** I have for you, Where is the water of Kāne? (line from ancient chant, "Ka Wai a Kāne")]

u'i youthful, handsome, vigorous, beautiful. [*I kona wā **u'i**.* In his/her **youth** (*lit.* time of physical beauty)]

'uī 1. to squeak, squeal. [***'Uī** wale ka lekiō i ka uila a me ka hekili.* The radio **squeals** a lot due to the thunder and lightning.] 2. to squeeze, grind.

uiki 1. (from English) wick of kerosene lamp.

[*I kekahi manawa, pipī ke kukui i ka **uiki**.* Sometimes the light flickers due to the **wick**.] 2. to glimmer, as a light through a hole or crack.

uila lightning, electricity. [***'Ōlapa ka **uila**, ku'i ka hekili.* **Lightning** flashes, thunder booms.] [*Ua 'ā anei ka **uila** ma ke ke'ena hou?* Is the **electricity** on in the new office?] 2. electric. (*lolouila* = computer [*lit.* electric brain]) (syn. *kamepiula*)

uila

uilani restless, irritated by constraint, spirited. [***Uilani** nā pa'ahao i ka laka 'ia i loko.* The prisoners are **irritated** at being locked up inside.]

'u'ina 1. crackling sound. 2. to crack, snap, creak. [***'U'ina**, 'u'ina ē, 'u'ina nā wai a'o nā Molokama.* **Crackling** are the waters of Nā Molokama. (song, "Na Wai A'o Nā Molokama," by A. Alohikea)]

'u'inakolo 1. roar, rustle. 2. to rustle.

uka inland, up toward mountains. (*ho'ouka* = to load cargo, freight, attack in battle)

ukali 1. follower, attendant. [***'O McGuire kekahi o **nā ukali** i ko Kapi'olani lāua 'o Lili'uokalani huaka'i i ko ko Pelekania mō'ī wahine lā Iubile.* McGuire was one of the **attendants** on Kapi'olani and Lili'uokalani's trip to Britain's Queen's Jubilee Day.] 2. to follow, attend, escort.

ukana baggage, luggage, freight, cargo. [*He mau **ukana** kaumaha kā nā po'e waiwai.* Rich people have heavy **baggage**.]

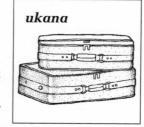
ukana

'ūkēkē stringed instrument of ancient days; held to the mouth, it could be used to convey spoken words as "sweet nothings" to a lover.

'ūkele muddy, oily. (syn. *kele*) [***'Ūkele** nā alahele ma ka 'ao'ao Ko'olau.* The trails on the windward side are **muddy**.]

ukiuki 1. anger, resentment. 2. angry,

annoyed, offended. (*hoʻonāukiuki* = to provoke, annoy)

uku 1. pay, wages, reward, price, tax. 2. to pay, compensate. (*lā uku* = pay day) (*uku hana* = salary) (*uku hoʻopaʻi* = fine, forfeit) (*uku kaulele* = overtime pay) (*uku kūmau* = usual fees, dues, taxes) (*uku lawelawe* = tip) (*uku pānaʻi* = refund, ransom, to refund, redeem) (*uku paneʻe* = interest [savings]) [*ʻAʻole nui ka* **uku paneʻe** *ma nā panakō i kēia mau lā.* The **interest** at the banks isn't very high these days.] 3. revenge.

ʻuku louse, flea. (*ʻuku lio* = bedbug; *ʻuku poʻo* = head lice)

ukuhi to dip out liquids, water, to wean child. [*Aia nō a* **ukuhi** *ʻo ʻUlu i ka wai mai ka pūnāwai mai, e inu kāua i ka wai huʻihuʻi.* As soon as ʻUlu **dips out** the water from the spring, let's you and me drink the chilled water.]

ʻukulele instrument (*lit.* jumping flea).

ukupau labor paid by job, not by time.

ula Hawaiian lobster.

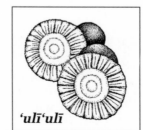
ula

ʻūlāleo 1. voice from spirits. 2. intense appeal to gods.

ulana to weave, knit, braid, plait. [*ʻO ka* **ulana** *lauhala kā koʻu kupuna wahine hana noʻeau.* **Weaving** *lauhala* is my grandmother's craft.]

ʻulaʻula (syn. *ʻula*) 1. red color, blood. 2. ghost. 3. sacred. (*ʻahuʻula* = feather cloak, symbol of royalty) (*ʻili ʻulaʻula* = brown Hawaiian skin)

ule penis. (*uhi ule* = condom)

ʻūlei native shrub with flexible branches used in making fish-traps; also a medicinal plant.

ʻulī to rattle, gurgle. (*ʻulīʻulī* = hula rattle)

ulia accident. [*ʻO ia nei kai ʻike maka i ka*

ʻulīʻulī

ulia *kaʻa ma ka huina alanui kahi i hala ai ka luahine.* She/he (this one here) is the one who witnessed the car **accident** at the intersection where the old lady died.] (*ulia pōpilikia* = emergency; syn. *pilikia kūhewa*)

ʻūlili 1. tattler bird from Alaska, spends winter in Hawaiʻi. 2. whistle, to whistle. 3. hula step, also hula implement used to make whirring sound.

uliuli (syn. *uli*) 1. any dark color, green, brown, blue. [**Uliuli** *ka moana.* The ocean is dark **blue.**] Note: *Polū* (from English) is sometimes used for the color blue; however, many prefer to use *uliuli* for blue. [*e Hawaiʻi nui kuauli,* oh dark-backed big Hawaiʻi (song, "Ka Naʻi Aupuni," composer unknown)] 2. steersman. 3. to steer. (*hoe uli* = steering paddle)

ulu 1. grove, collection, flock. (*ulu lāʻau* = forest) 2. to grow, increase. (*ulu a nui* = to grow up) [*Ua* **ulu a nui** *ko mākou mau kūpuna ma ka mahikō.* Our (us, not you) grandparents **grew up** on the sugar plantation.] (*ulu pono* = thriving, successful) (*ulu wale* = to grow easily, overgrown [vegetation] (*ulu hānau* = contemporary, of same age group) [*He mau* **ulu hānau** *ʻo Kaʻahumanu a me Mānono.* Mānono and Kaʻahumanu were **contemporaries.**] 3. possessed by or inspired by god, spirit. (*hoʻoulu* = to grow plants, inspire)

ʻulu 1. breadfruit, a staple food. [*ʻO ka* **ʻulu** *ka lau kūpono no kā ʻoukou mau kapa kuiki mua loa.* The **breadfruit** is an appropriate design for your (all) very first quilt.] 2. gum used for paste. 3. symbol for growth and being fed, nourished.

ʻulu

ulua fish used in ancient ceremonies as substitute for human sacrifice (*fig.* man, sweetheart).

uluāhewa 1. delusion, craziness, overgrowth. [*He mau* **uluāhewa** *ko ka poʻe hehena.*

Insane people have **delusions**.] 2. to grow wild (vegetation).

uluaō'a 1. confusion, disturbance, mob. (syn. *haunaele*) 2. jungle.

uluhua frustrated, annoyed.

ulu lā'au forest.

ulumāhiehie 1. to make a fine appearance. 2. festive, attractively adorned. [**Ulumāhiehie** *ke kahua no ka hō'ike lā mua o Mei*. The stage for the May Day pageant is **attractively adorned**.]

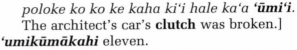

'ulu maika

'ulu maika ancient sport somewhat like bowling. (*'ulu maika haole* = bowling)

uluna pillow, cushion.

uluwehi lush and beautiful (of nature), festively adorned.

uluwehi

umauma breast, chest. (*pa'i umauma* = slapping chest, in mourning or in hula dance)

'ume 1. to draw, pull, attract. 2. attractive, alluring. (*pahu 'ume* = drawer of bureau, desk, etc.) (*'ume makēneki* = pull of magnet)

'umeke bowl, calabash. (*'umeke kā'eo* = full calabash [*fig.* one with deep knowledge]) (*'umeke pala 'ole* = empty calabash [empty mind]) (*'umeke pōhue* = gourd calabash)

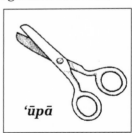

'umeke

'umi 1. ten. 2. to strangle, choke, repress desire. (syn. *'u'umi*) [**U'umi** *i ke aloha me ka waimaka lā.* **Repress** love with tears. (song, "Kaimukī Hula," by A. Richart)] (*'umikūmākahi* = eleven [ten plus one])

'ūmi'i 1. cramp, sharp pain. 2. to clamp, clip, clasp. (*'ūmi'i 'iole* = rat trap, mouse trap) (*'ūmi'i kuapo* = belt buckle) (*mikini 'ūmi'i* = stapler) 3. clutch of car or vehicle. [*Ua poloke ko ko ke kaha ki'i hale ka'a* **'ūmi'i**. The architect's car's **clutch** was broken.]

'umikūmākahi eleven.

'umi'umi beard, mustache. (*kahi 'umi'umi* = to shave) (*pahi 'umi'umi* = razor)

unahi 1. fish scale. 2. to scale fish. [*Iā 'olua e* **unahi** *i'a ai, e ho'ohana i ke puna.* When you (two) **scale** fish, use a spoon.]

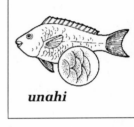

unahi

unauna hermit crab.

une 1. lever. 2. to pry (*fig.* to urge, harass).

unea = nausea. (syn. *poluea*)

'unihipili spirit of dead person, used for sorcery in ancient days.

'ūniki graduation exercises for hula, martial arts.

unu 1. pebble, wedge. 2. to wedge, prop.

'unu to shorten, hoist, jerk upwards.

unuhi 1. translator, interpreter. 2. to take out, withdraw (money). 3. to translate.

uō to howl, to bellow.

'ūpā 1. scissors, any instrument that opens and shuts such as tongs, shears. 2. to open and shut, slam, bang. (*'ūpā makani* = bellows; *'ūpā miki'ao* = fingernail scissors; *'ūpā 'ūmi'i* = pliers)

'upa'i to flap wings, walk with flapping movement.

'ūpalu gentle, mild, soft-spoken, fragile.

ūpē crushed, flattened, humble.

'ūpā

ūpē mucus (*fig.* tears, grief). (syn. *hūpē*)

'upena fishing net, net, web. [*He* **'upena** *kiloi ko ka lawai'a.* The fisherman has a throw **net**.]

'upena

'upī 1. sponge, syringe. [*E ho'oma'ema'e kāua i nā pākaukau i kēia mau* **'upī**! Let's (you and me) clean the tables with these **sponges**!] 2. to squirt, squeeze.

'ūpiki 1. trap, snare, treachery. 2. to snap together as trap. (syn. *'āpiki*) (*'ūpiki lima* = handcuff)

'upu recurring thought, desire, attachment, expectation. [**'Upu** *a'e ka mana'o iā 'oe, e ka ipo.* The **thought** of you keeps coming up, sweetheart.] 2. to desire, long for.

'u'u 1. to strip *maile* (to bring out fragrance). 2. to hoist sail. 3. to masturbate.

'ū'ū to stutter, stammer.

'u'uku tiny, very small. [**'U'uku** *wale nā pua i'a.* Fish fry are truly **tiny**.]

W

wā 1. period of time, epoch, era. [*i ka* **wā** *o Kuali'i,* in the **time** of Kuali'i] (*wā ho'omaha* = vacation) (*wā kamali'i* = childhood) 2. roar, noise. 3. fret of stringed instrument such as *'ukulele.* 4. to make noise, talk a lot. (*'Ikuwā* = month in Hawaiian moon calendar [mid-October] known for stormy weather) (*kai ho'owā* = roaring sea) 5. space between objects or time.

wa'a 1. canoe. (*wa'a 'auhau* = tribute canoe set out to sea during makahiki season) (*wa'a kaulua* = double-hulled canoe such as *Mo'olele*) (*wa'a kaukahi* = single-hulled canoe) 2. trench, furrow.

wa'a kaukahi

wa'apā boat, skiff, rowboat.

wa'awa'a 1. full of gulches. 2. grooved, gullied. 3. muscular. 4. stupid, ignorant.

wae to choose, select, sort. (*wae mana'o* = conscience)

waena 1. middle, center, average. (*waenakonu* = center, middle) (*kikowaena* = center of circle, headquarters) 2. cultivated field, used in place names to indicate an area between mountains and sea. [Kalihi **waena**, **mid**-Kalihi, area near Honolulu Community College]

waha 1. mouth. 2. oral. 3. to talk too much. (*waha he'e* = liar, a lie, to lie, deceitful, lying [syn. *waha wale*]; *waha mana* = voice of authority; *waha nui* = big mouth, to talk too much; *waha 'ōlelo* = spokesperson; *waha pa'a* = argumentative; *waha pilo* = halitosis, foul mouth; *waha pio* = speechless; *waha pu'u* = protruding lips, unintelligible speech, such as of one who has had a stroke)

wahāwahā to treat with contempt, despise, ridicule. (*ho'owahāwahā i ka 'aha* = contempt of court)

wahi place (*ka wahi,* "the place," is often contracted to *kahi*). [*'O Liliha* **kahi** *āna e noho nei.* Liliha is **the place** he is living.] 2. some, a few. 3. to say, according to. [**Wahi** *a ka'u loio,* **according to** my lawyer, my lawyer said] 4. can be used before a noun to indicate one's attitude toward that noun. [*ku'u* **wahi** *'īlio,* my **sweet little** doggie] [*kēlā* **wahi** *'īlio* = that **darned** dog]

wahī 1. wrapper, envelope. (*wahī leka* = envelope for letter) 2. to wrap, cover, bundle up, roll up. [*Ua* **wahī** *'ia ka pēpē i ka lole.* The baby was **wrapped** in the cloth.]

wahie fuel, firewood.

wahī 'eha bandage.

wahine (pl. *wāhine*) 1. woman, wife, lady. 2. femininity, womanliness. 3. feminine, female. [*He akua* **wahine** *'o Hina.* Hina is a **feminine** goddess.] (*wahine hi'u i'a* = mermaid) (*wahine kāne make* = widow) (*ho'owahine* = to behave like a woman, to grow into womanhood)

wahine

waho outside, beyond, outward. [*Ke wa'u nei lāua i ka 'i'o niu ma* **waho** *o ka hale ka'a.* They (three or more) are grating the coconut meat **outside** the garage.]

wai 1. water or any liquid other than sea water. (*wai 'ala* = perfume, cologne; *wai ea* = aerated water, mineral water; *wai ho'āno* = holy water; *wai ho'oma'ema'e* = disinfectant, any kind of cleaning liquid; *wai hua 'ai* = juice; *wai kai* = brackish water, salty water; *wai meli* = honey; *wai niu* = coconut milk; *wai puna* = spring water) 2. any liquid discharged from the body. (*hana wai* = menstrual period; syn. *ma'i wahine*) 3. to flow like water. (*waipahū* = geyser) 4. who, whom. [*'O **wai** kēlā?* Who's that?]

waia 1. dishonor, shame. 2 disgraced. [*Ua **waia** ko ke keiki lapuwale 'ohana.* The wastrel child's family is **disgraced**.]

wai 'ala perfume, cologne.

wai 'apo water caught in taro leaf, considered sacred because it hasn't touched the ground (*fig.* beloved mate).

waiehu file for grinding, polishing.

waiho 1. to deposit, leave something. (*waiho wale* = to leave without reason, to leave about carelessly) 2. internal organs of the body. 3. funds, treasury. (*hale waihona puke* = library) 4. to quit, resign, abandon something.

waihona 1. depository, closet. (*waihona 'āina* = lay of land) (*waihona ho'omana'o* = memory) (*waihona kālā* = treasury; syn. *waihona waiwai*) (*waihona meli* = honeycomb) [*Ua kī 'ia ka mahi'ai i nānao i kona lima i loko o ka pūnana meli e lālau i ka **waihona meli**.* The farmer who thrust his arm into the beehive to grab the **honeycomb** was stung.]

waiho'olu'u dye, color. [*He aha nā **waiho'olu'u** kapu i nā ali'i? 'O ka 'ula'ula, ka melemele a me ka 'ele'ele.* What were the **colors** sacred to the chiefs? Red, yellow and black.]

wailana calm, quiet (like a calm sea). [*I ka 'olu o **Wailana**.* In the pleasant **calm** of Wailana. (song, "Wailana," by M. Kaleikoa)]

wailele waterfall.

wailele

waili'ulā 1. mirage. 2. of changing color, as an opal.

wailua 1. ghost, spirit. 2. corpse (syn. *kupapa'u*). 3. two waters, a common place name probably used for an area where two freshwater streams mingle.

waimaka tears. [*Kulu ko kona makuahine mau **waimaka**.* His mother's **tears** flow.]

waina 1. place with water. 2. (from English) wine .

waiolina (from English) violin. (*waiolina kū nui* = bass)

wai 'olu pleasant, attractive, gentle. [*kou piko **wai 'olu**, ua kapu na ka mea waiwai,* your **attractive** center, reserved for the worthy person (song, "Aloha Nō Au I Kou Maka," by Leleiōhoku)]

waipahē courteous, gentlemanly, polite, agreeable. [*He mau keonimana **waipahē** nā 'ōlapa ma kāna hālau hula.* The dancers in his hula *hālau* are **courteous** gentlemen.]

waipu'ilani waterspout.

waiū 1. milk. 2. breast. (*waiū kini* = canned milk) (*waiū paka* = butter) (*waiū paka pa'a* = cheese)

waiwai 1. property, goods, worth, value. 2. rich, valuable, financial. (*waiwai ho'oilina* = inherited property, heritage) [*He **waiwai** ho'oilina makamae ko nā Hawai'i.* Hawaiians have a precious **heritage**.] (*waiwai ho'opuka* = profits) (*waiwai lewa* = liquid assets) (*waiwai pa'a* = real estate, nonliquid assets) (*ho'owaiwai* = to enrich)

Wākea legendary ancestor god, sky father whose mating created the islands. [*'O **Wākea** ke kāne, 'o Papa, 'o Walinu'u ka wahine.* **Wākea** was the husband, Papa Walinu'u was the wife. (birth chant for Kauikeaouli, composer unknown)]

Wakinekona (from English) Washington.

wala to tilt backwards, fall backwards. (*wala kua* = to fall over backwards, rear up, as a horse) [*Ma ke ka'i huaka'i i **wala kua** ai ko ke Kamali'i wahine o Lāna'i lio.* It was in the parade that the Princess of Lāna'i's horse **reared**.]

wala'au to talk, chatter, converse.

walania 1. anguish, torment, burning pain. 2. agonizing, anguishing.

wale 1. slime, mucus. [*'O ka* **walewale** *ho'okumu honua ia.* It is the **slime** that established the earth. (line from first section of the *Kumulipo* creation chant)] 2. common particle following words, used for emphasis, many possible translations. [*Nani* **wale** *ka 'ikena.* The view is **simply** beautiful.] (*wale nō* = only) [*'O au* **wale** *nō kēia.* It's **only** me.] (*'o ia wale nō* = that's all) (*ho'owalewale* = decoy, temptation, to tempt)

walea to relax. [*E* **walea** *pū 'oe me a'u.* And you are **relaxing** with me. (song, "Green Rose Hula," by J. Almeida)]

walewaha perfect fluency in a language. [**Walewaha** *ko Ni'ihau i ka 'ōlelo makuahine.* Ni'ihau's people have **perfect fluency** in the mother tongue.]

wali smooth, supple, thin, fine. (*ho'owali* = to mix poi)

waliwali smooth, gentle, easygoing, good-natured. [*Kou ihu* **waliwali** *ka'u i honi.* Your **smooth** nose I have kissed. (song, "Aloha Nō Au I Kou Maka," by Leleiōhoku)]

walu 1. eight. 2. to scratch, rub, claw. 3. (following another word) many. (*makawalu* = many eyes, ubiquitous)

wana sea urchin.

wana'ao dawn. (syn. *kaiao*) [*Ma ka* **wana'ao** *lākou i ha'alele ai.* It was at **dawn** that they (three) left.]

wānana 1. prophecy, prediction. [*Kauka'i nā ali'i i nā* **wānana** *a nā kāula me nā kilo hōkū.* The *ali'i* depended on the **predictions** of the prophet and the stargazers.] 2. to predict, prophesy.

wao 1. biogeographic zone, dividing land into sections according to usage at different altitudes. (*wao akua* = distant uplands, considered to be inhabited by gods) (*wao kanaka* = lower zone where people could live) 2. *nā wao* were legendary people, said to be ancestors of *nā wā* and *nā mū*.

waokele rain forest. [*E mālama i ka* **waokele**! Protect the **rain forest**!]

wao nahele jungle, rain forest.

wao one desert.

wa'u 1. scraper, such as used to scrape out coconut meat (*mea wa'u niu*). 2. to grate, scratch, claw, to scratch an itch. [*'Oiai mane'o ko'u kua, hiki paha iā 'oe ke* **wa'u** *mai?* Since my back is itchy, can you maybe **scratch** it?]

wauke paper mulberry tree whose bark is used to make tapa.

wawā 1. roar, distant sound. 2. rumored, talked about.

wauke

wāwae leg, foot. (*lole wāwae* = pants, shorts) [*Ua pukapuka ko ka lawai'a* **lole wāwae** *pōkole.* The fisherman's **shorts** were full of holes.]

wāwahi 1. to tear down, break down, demolish. (*wāwahi hale* = burglary, housebreaking) 2. to give change for currency. [*Hiki i ka mea 'ohi kālā ke* **wāwahi** *i kāna kālā iwakālua.* The cashier can **break** his twenty dollar bill.]

we'awe'a 1. pimp, procurer. 2. to help, tempt in love affair.

wehe 1. to open, untie, undo. [*E* **wehe** *i ka pukaaniani! Ua wela kēia lā!* **Open** the window! It's hot today!] 2. to take off clothes. 3. to cleanse, solve problem.

wehewehe to explain. [*E* **wehewehe** *mai i kou mana'o!* **Explain** your idea to me!] (*puke wehewehe 'ōlelo* = dictionary) (*wehewehe 'ana* = explanation)

wehi 1. decoration. (*wehiwehi* = adorned, festive) 2. a song composed to honor someone. 3. to decorate, adorn. (*ho'owehi* = to beautify, decorate)

wehiwa 1. a choice object. 2. choice, prized.

wehiwehi adorned, festive. [**Wehiwehi** *'oe.* You are beautifully **adorned**. (song, "Wehiwehi 'Oe," by T. Kalama)]

weke 1. fish used as offering. 2. crack, narrow opening. 3. to open a crack, to separate, loosen, free.

wēkiu 1. tip, top, summit. 2. of highest rank or status. [*he pua no ka* **wēkiu**, (*'ōlelo* *no'eau*) a flower from the summit (*fig.* a person of the highest attainment)]

wela 1. heat, temperature (*fig.* lust, passion, anger). [*ahi* **wela** *mai nei loko i ka hana a ke aloha,* **hot fire** from here within in love-making (song, "Ahi Wela," M. Doirin/L. Beckley)] [*Ke 'ike 'o ia nei i kona kaikunāne, pi'i koke kona* **wela.** When this one sees her brother, her **anger** wells up.] 2. hot, burned.

wēlau tip, end, top. [*Ua 'oki 'ia ka* **wēlau** *o ka lauhala.* The **tip** of the *hala* leaf was cut off.]

Welehu month of Hawaiian calendar (approximately mid-November to mid-December). (*lit.* warm ashes of fire, indicating the weather is cold and rainy)

weleweka (from English) velvet. [*Komo ka wahine male hou i ka holokū* **weleweka.** The bride wears a **velvet** *holokū* (formal fitted *mu'u* with a long train).]

weli 1. fears, terror. (*ho'oweli* = to frighten, terrify) 2. fearful, afraid.

welina greeting of affection, poetic opening of speech or salutation in letter (used in addressing an audience, formal rather than intimate).

weliweli terrifying, terrible. [**Weliweli** *kau mai* (a well-known phrase in chants for Pele, indicating both dread and reverence at the destructive and creative power of the fire goddess embodied in an active volcano)]

welo 1. to float, flutter (like a flag), to set (sun). [**Welo** *ana e ka hae Hawai'i.* The Hawaiian flag **flutters.** (song, "Kaleleonālani," by Nu'uanu)] 2. family custom or trait.

Welo name of month in Hawaiian calendar, approximately February-March.

welu 1. rag. [*Loa'a ka* **welu**? *Ua hanini ke koloaka.* Got a **rag**? The soda spilled.] 2. ragged.

weluwelu shredded to bits.

wena 1. glow of lava, fire, sunrise. 2. blood relative, close relation.

weuweu 1. grass. 2. bushy, fuzzy. [**Weuweu** *ka'u pōpoki keiki!* My kitten is **fuzzy.**]

wī 1. famine. [*I ka wā* **wī,** *ua 'ai 'ia ka poi 'ulu.* In **famine** times, breadfruit *poi* was eaten.] 2. syn. for *hīhīwai,* freshwater snail. 3. any high, shrill sound. 4. to squeal, tinkle.

wiki 1. to hurry, hasten. 2 quick.

wikiō (from English) video.

wili 1. mill, drill. (*ka hale wili kō* = sugar mill) (*wili kope* = coffee grinder) (*wili makani* = windmill) 2. to twist, turn, drill, mix, dial phone. [*i* **wili** *'ia me maile lauli'i,* **twined** with small-leaf *maile* (common line in songs celebrating love)] (*wili pua'a* = corkscrew)

wilikī (from English) engineer, engineering.

wiliwai whirlpool.

wiliwili 1. to twist, turn, appliqué in quilting. 2. a tree with light wood used for canoe outriggers, fishing floats, and surfboards; its seeds are made into seed *lei.* 3. wind blowing in all directions.

wini 1. sharp, pointed (*fig.* impudent). 2. wind.

wīwī skinny, emaciated. [**Wīwī** *ke kāne i lanakila i ka heihei holo wāwae.* The man who won the foot race is **thin.**]

wiwo fearful, afraid, modest, timid, obedient.

wiwo 'ole fearless, courageous, intrepid.

wohi a chiefly rank.

Notes

Notes

Notes

English–Hawaiian

a, an *he*. [*He Hawaiʻi haʻaheo au*. I am **a** proud Hawaiian.]

abandon *haʻalele* (also means **to quit a bad habit**, **quit a job** or **leave a place**). [*Ua haʻalele ka wahine i kāna kāne.* The wife **abandoned** her husband.] [*Ua haʻalele ʻo Palikū i ka puhi paka.* Palikū **abandoned** (**quit**) smoking.]

able to, can *hiki*. [*Hiki i kona kupuna kāne ke ʻōlelo Pākē.* His grandfather **can** speak Chinese.]

about 1. *no*. [*He moʻolelo kēia no ʻUmialīloa.* This is a story **about** ʻUmialīloa.] 2. phrase: *e pili ana*. [*Ua noʻonoʻo au e pili ana i kāna mea i haʻi mai ai.* I thought **about** what he told me.]

above 1. *luna* (also means **top**, or in locative phrase, **on top of**). [*E pena ʻoe i ka paia mai luna a i lalo.* Paint the wall from **above** to below (from **top** to bottom).] Note: Locative phrases are frequently used to indicate where something is. [*Aia ko ke kauka keʻena ma luna o ka puʻu o Mauʻumae ma Kaimukī.* The doctor's office is **on top of** Mauʻumae Hill in Kaimukī.]

abscess *pūhā*. [*He pūhā ko kona niho huʻi.* Her sore tooth has an **abscess**.]

absent *ma kahi ʻē* (*lit.* someplace else).

absorbed (in an activity) 1. *papau*. 2. *lilo*. [*Lilo ke keiki i ka pāʻani lolouila.* The child is **absorbed** in the computer game.]

abundant *nui* (also means **many**, **plenty of**, **lots of**). [*Nui ka ua ma ka ʻaoʻao Koʻolau i ka hoʻoilo.* There is **abundant** rain on the windward side in the rainy season.]

abuse [*n*] *hana ʻino*. [*Minamina, ʻaʻole ka hana ʻino he mea laha ʻole ma nā ʻohana.* Regretfully, **abuse** is not a rare thing in families.] [*v*] 1. *hoʻomāino*. 2. *hana ʻino*.

accident 1. *ulia*. [*Nui nā ulia kaʻa ma kēlā huina alanui.* There are lots of **accidents** at that intersection.] 2. *pilikia*.

accomplish *holo pono* (also means **to succeed**).

accustomed to *maʻa* (also means **used to**, **skilled at**). [*Maʻa kēia mau wāhine no Kona i ka ulana pāpale lauhala.* These women from Kona are **accustomed to** weaving *lauhala* hats.]

acne 1. *huehue*. 2. *puʻu*.

acquainted with 1. *kamaʻāina*. [*Kamaʻāina kēia hoahana ona i nā lula palekana.* This workmate of his is **acquainted with** the safety rules.]

across *ma kēlā ʻaoʻao* (*lit.* on that side).

active 1. *ʻeleu*. 2. *miki*. [*ʻEleu kaʻu ʻīlio.* My dog is **active**.]

add 1. *hoʻokuʻi* (add numbers). 2. *pākuʻi, hoʻokuʻi* (add on another piece).

administrator 1. *kahu*. [*Ua lilo kāna kaikamahine i kahu no kā kona makua kāne kālā.* His daughter became an **administrator** for her father's money.] 2. *luna hoʻoponopono*. (executor = *kahu waiwai*)

admirable *lehiwa*.

admiration *makahehi*.

admire *makahehi*. [*Makahehi nā ʻōpiopio i ka uʻi.* Young people **admire** physical beauty.]

adorn *wehi*.

adorned *wehiwehi*.

adornment 1. *wehi*. [a he **wehi** no koʻu kino, an **adornment** for my body (song, "Pua Wehiwa," by P. Vaughn)] 2. *kāhiko*.

adult *kanaka makua.* [*Ke piha nā makahiki he iwakāluakūmākahi iā ʻoe, he **kanaka makua** ʻoe wahi a ke kānāwai.* When you reach 21 years old, you're an **adult** according to law.]

advertise *hoʻolaha.*

advertisement *hoʻolaha.* [*Ua ʻike anei ʻoukou i ka **hoʻolaha** a OHA i hōʻike ai ma ke kīwī?* Have you folks seen the **advertisement** OHA showed on TV?]

advice *ʻōlelo aʻo.*

adze *koʻi.* [*Me ke **koʻi** i kua ai nā kūpuna i nā kumukoa?* Was it with an **adze** that the ancestors cut down *koa* trees?]

affection *aloha* (also has many other meanings, including **sympathy, feeling, greetings**).

affliction *pōʻino.*

afraid 1. *makaʻu.* [***Makaʻu** ka pōpoki i ka uaki hoʻāla.* The cat is **afraid** of the alarm clock.] 2. *wiwo.* 3. *weli.*

after *ma hope o* (also means **behind**). [*Holopeki koʻu hoahana **ma hope o** ka hana.* My buddy at work runs **after** work.]

afternoon *ʻauinalā* (lit. descent of sun). [*Auē ua wale kēia **ʻauinalā**!* Wow, it's so rainy this **afternoon**!]

again *hou* (added after verb). [*E hana **hou**!* Do it again!] [*A hui **hou** kākou!* Until we all meet **again** (see you later).]

age [n] *makahiki.* [v] *kūnewa.* [*Ua **kūnewa** ko Malu ʻanakē! He kanawalu ona **makahiki**.* Malu's auntie has **aged**! She's 80 **years old**.]

aggressive *mahaʻoi* (also means **aggression, aggressiveness**). [*Auē ka **mahaʻoi** o ka malihini!* Gosh, the **aggressiveness** of the newcomer!]

agitated 1. *piʻoloke.* [***Piʻoloke** ka moho ma mua o ka nīnauele.* The candidate is **agitated** before the interview.] 2. *luliluli.* 3. *nū.*

agonizing *walania.*

agony *walania.*

agree *ʻae.*

agreeable *waipahē.*

agreement 1. *ʻaelike* (contract). [*Ua pūlima ʻo Ipo i ka **ʻaelike** e unuhi i nā palapala hoʻoilina kahiko.* Ipo signed the **contract** to translate old wills.] 2. *lōkahi* (unity).

aid 1. *kākoʻo* (also means **support** or **to support**). [*Nui ke **kākoʻo** o nā mākuahūnōai i ka makuahine hou.* Plentiful is the **aid** of the parents-in-law for the new mother.] 2. *kōkua* (also means **help,** or **to help**). [***Kōkua** ka hope pelekikena i ke alakaʻi ʻana i ka hui ʻoihana.* The vice-president **aids** in leading the corporation.]

AIDS *maʻi hana ei* (refers to all sexually transmitted diseases).

aim at *kākiʻi.* [***Kākiʻi** ka mea pana pua i ke kiʻi ma ka mauʻu.* The archer **aims at** the picture on the grass.]

air 1. *(ke) ea.* [*Paoa **ke ea** i ka puakenikeni.* The **air** is strong with the scent of *puakenikeni* flowers.] Note: *Ea* has many other meanings, including **breath, life force, sovereignty.** 2. *lewa* (also means **sky, to sway**).

air-conditioner *mīkini hōʻoluʻolu ea.*

airplane *mokulele.*

airport *kahua mokulele.* [*Ma ka hola ʻehia ana e pae ai ka mokulele ma ke **kahua mokulele**?* What time will the plane land at the **airport**?]

airplane

alarm clock *uaki hoʻāla.*

alcohol 1. *ʻalekohola.* 2. *lama.* [*Mai inu i ka **lama** a kalaiwa ma hope!* Don't drink [**alcohol**] and drive later!]

alert [adj] 1. *makaʻala.* 2. *miki ʻala.* (Be alert! Watch out! = *E makaʻala!*)

alike 1. *like.* [*E **like** me Likelike,* just **like** Likelike (Kalākaua's sister, mother of Kaʻiulani) (song, "Sānoe," by Liliʻuokalani)] 2. *kohu.* 3. *kūlike.*

alive *ola.*

all *nā mea a pau* (also means **everyone, everything**). [*Ua haʻalele **nā mea a pau** ma hope o ka ʻaha mele.* **Everyone** left after the concert.]

allegiance *kūpaʻa.* [***kūpaʻa** ma hope o ka ʻāina,* **allegiance** to the land (song, "Kaulana Nā Pua," by E. Prendergast)]

allow *ʻae* (also means **yes**). [*E **ʻae** mai ʻoe i* *kāu kelepona.* **Allow** me to use your phone.]

alluring *'ume.*

almost 1. *'ane'ane.* 2. *kokoke.* (almost finished = *kokoke e pau*)

along *ma.* [*Holo nā keiki ma ka'e pā.* The children run **along** the edge of the wall.]

aloud *ma ka leo nui.*

alphabet *pī 'ā pā.* [*He 'umikūmākolu huapalapala o ka pī 'ā pā Hawai'i.* The Hawaiian **alphabet** has thirteen letters.]

altar 1. *kuahu* (where offerings are placed in *hula hālau*). 2. *lele* (section of *heiau* where sacrifices were laid).

although *'oiai.* [*'Oiai hiki ia'u ke hele, pono au e noho.* **Although** I can go, I must stay.]

always 1. *nā manawa a pau.* 2. *mau.* [*Kelepona ko Ha'upu 'anakala iā ia i ka Lāpule a kama'ilio lāua e pili ana i ko lāua mo'okū'auhau i nā manawa a pau.* Ha'upu's uncle calls him on Sundays and they (two) **always** talk about their genealogy.]

amazement 1. *pū'iwa.* 2. *kupaianaha.* (Both have other meanings, such as **mysterious, awesome, shocking**.)

amazing *kupaianaha.* [*He hana kupaianaha ka hua'i 'ana o ka pele ma ka pō.* The bubbling up of lava at night is an **amazing** thing.]

ambassador *kuhina.* (cabinet minister under monarchy = *kuhina nui*)

ambition *'i'ini.* [*He 'i'ini kona e hoe ma ke kōā 'o Kaiwi.* He has an **ambition** to paddle the Kaiwi Channel.]

ambulance *ka'a lawe ma'i.*

America 1. *'Amelika.* 2. *'Amelika Hui Pū 'ia* (USA).

amount *heluna* (also means **sum total**). [*'Ehia kālā ka heluna o ke kālā i uku 'ia mai?* What is the **amount** of the money that was paid?]

amputated 1. *mumuku.* 2. *muku.* 3. *mu'umu'u.*

amputee *mu'umu'u* (also means **long women's dress** adopted under missionary influence).

amuse *ho'ole'ale'a.*

ancestors *kūpuna.* [*Nani ke no'eau o ko kākou mau kūpuna i ka holo Moana.* The skill of our **ancestors** in ocean voyaging was magnificent.]

anchor 1. *heleuma.* 2. *hekau.*

ancient *kahiko.* [*I ke au kahiko, nui nā heiau like 'ole.* In **ancient** days there were many different kinds of *heiau.*]

angel *'ānela.* [*He 'ānela kia'i 'o Gabriel.* Gabriel is a guardian **angel**.]

anger 1. *huhū.* 2. *wela.* 3. *inaina.*

angry 1. *huhū.* [*Inā 'oe ho'ohenehene iā ia, hele kāu 'īlio a huhū.* If you tease him, your dog gets **angry**.] 2. *wela.* [*Pi'i kona wela a 'ōlelo pelapela ihola.* His **anger** rises up and then he swears.]

anguish *walania.*

animal *holoholona.* [*'A'ole nui nā holoholona maoli ma kēia moku 'āina.* There are not many native **animals** in this state.]

animal

animated *'īnana.*

ankle *ku'eku'e wāwae.*

annexation *ho'ohui 'āina.* [*Na wai e 'ole ke ho'āhewa i ka ho'ohui 'āina o Hawai'i?* Who would not condemn the **annexation** of Hawai'i?]

anniversary 1. *lā ho'omana'o.* 2. *piha makahiki.* [*Hau'oli lā piha makahiki!* Happy **anniversary**!]

announce 1. *hō'ike.* 2. *kūkala.* (to broadcast news = *kūkala nūhou*)

announcement 1. *hō'ike.* 2. *kūkala.*

annoy *ho'onāukiuki* (also means **to irritate**). [*Mai ho'onāukiuki i kou pōki'i!* Don't **annoy** your younger sibling!]

annoyed 1. *ukiuki.* 2. *uluhua* (also means **frustrated**).

anoint *poni.* (coronation, carnation = *poni mō'ī*)

another *kekahi.* [*Loa'a kekahi puke iā kāua?* Do we (you and I) have **another** book?] *Kekahi* has other uses, including as a pronoun. [*Aloha kekahi i kekahi.* Love one **another**.]

answer 1. *pane.* 2. *ha'ina.* [v] 1. *pane.* [*Ke kani ke kelepona,* **pane** *mau ka pēpē.* Whenever the telephone rings, the baby always **answers.**] 2. *eō* (respond to name being called).

ant *naonao.* [*Kū ka paila o* **nā naonao** *e halihali aku nei i nā huna laiki.* Tons of **ants** are carrying away the grains of rice.]

Antarctic *'Anealika.*

anthurium *pua haka.* [*'O ka "obake" kekahi 'ano* **pua haka** *nunui hou.* The "obake" is a new, very large type of **anthurium.**]

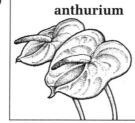

anthurium

anxiety *hopohopo* (also means **worry, to worry, nervous**). [*Pi'i wale a'e ko'u* **hopohopo** *ke komo au i ka haukapila.* My **anxiety** rises when I enter a hospital.]

any *kekahi.* (*Kekahi* is used before nouns and can also mean **a, one of the, another.**) [*Loa'a* **kekahi** *hua 'ai i ka pahu hau?* Is there **any** fruit in the icebox?]

apart *ka'awale* (also means **separated, to separate, free,** as in free time = *manawa ka'awale*).

apartment 1. *ke'ena hale.* 2. *hale papa'i.*

apiece *pākahi* (also means **individually**). [*E helu* **pākahi** *'olua i nā pila kīko'o a me ke kālā.* You (two) **individually** count the checks and the cash money.]

apologize *mihi.* [*Ke* **mihi** *a'e nei ke kāne 'ona i ho'oku'i i ko ka hope kia'āina ka'a.* The drunk man who hit the lieutenant governor's car is **apologizing.**]

appeal [n] *noi.* [v] 1. *kāhoahoa.* [*No ke aha lā e pono ai nā mākua Hawai'i e* **kāhoahoa** *mau i ka 'aha 'ōlelo e kāko'o i ka ho'ona'auao 'ana?* Why should Hawaiian parents always have to **appeal** to the legislature to support education?] 2. *ui* (also means **to question, a query, question**).

appear 1. *puka.* 2. *kū.* [*Ua* **kū** *a'ela 'o Kamapua'a ma ka pali hāweo.* Kamapua'a then **appeared** on the glowing cliff.]

applaud *pa'ipa'i lima.*

applause *pa'ipa'i lima.*

apple *'āpala.* [*I* **'āpana pai 'āpala** *nāna, a i 'āpana pai 'ōhelo na'u, ke 'olu'olu 'oe.* A piece of **apple** pie for her and a piece of *'ōhelo* berry pie for me, please.] (mountain apple = *'ōhi'a 'ai*)

appoint *ho'okohu.* [*Na Pelekikena Roosevelt i* **ho'okohu** *iā Samuel Wilder King e lilo i kia'āina a ma kona poni 'ana i 'ōlelo ai ke kia'āina hou ma ka 'ōlelo 'ōiwi o ka 'āina.* It was President Roosevelt who **appointed** Samuel Wilder King to be governor, and at his swearing-in ceremony, the new governor spoke in the native language of the land.]

appreciate 1. *mahalo.* 2. *ho'omaika'i* (also means **to congratulate**).

appropriate [adj] *kūpono.* [*E ho'opa'a manawa kāua i ka lā* **kūpono.** Let's (you and me) make an appointment for the **appropriate** day.]

approve *'āpono.* [*Ua* **'āpono** *'ia kāu noi.* Your request has been **approved.**]

April *'Apelila* (from English).

apron *'epanelole.*

aquarium *pahu i'a.*

arbitrate *'uao* (also means **to negotiate**). [*Na wai e* **'uao** *i ka 'aelike hou?* Who should **arbitrate** the new contract?]

arbitrator *'uao.*

arch *pi'o* (also means **arched, curved**). [*Pi'o ke ānuenue.* The **rainbow** arches above.]

archer *mea pana pua.*

archery *pana pua.*

archipelago *pae 'āina.* [*Nui wale nō nā mokupuni li'ili'i o ka* **pae 'āina.** There are many small islands in the **archipelago.**]

archipelago

architect *kaha ki'i hale.* [*'Imi māua 'o Lahela i ke* **kaha ki'i hale** *e kaha ki'i hou i ko māua hale mahikō.* Lahela and I are looking for an **architect** to redesign our plantation house.]

Arctic *'Ālika.*

area 1. *kahua* (also means **field**). 2. *nui* (also means **size**). [*'Ehia kapu'ai ke ākea o kēia* *nui?* How many feet is the width of this **area**?]

argue 1. *ho'opa'apa'a.* 2. *ho'owahapa'a.*

arise (command) *E ala!* (also means **get up**).

arm *lima* (also means **hand**).

army *pū'ali koa.* [*Ma hope o kona ho'oku'u 'ia 'ana e ka **pū'ali koa**, e ho'i ana kā lāua kaikamahine i ke kula?* After being released from the **army**, will their (two) daughter go back to school?]

arrest *hopu* (also means **seize**). [***Hopu** nā māka'ikiu i nā kānaka kū'ai lā'au 'ino.* The detectives **arrest** drug dealers.]

arrive 1. *hō'ea* [*Ua **hō'ea** aku nā wa'a pe'a i ko Hāna hono.* The sailing canoes **arrived** in Hāna's bay.] 2. *hiki.*

art *hana no'eau.*

artist *mea kaha ki'i.*

ashamed *hilahila* (also means **embarrassed**). (bashful, shy = *maka hilahila*)

ashes *lehu.* [*Hū a'e nā **lehu** o ka lua i ke kahe 'ana o ka pele?* Do **ashes** of the pit rise up when lava flows?]

Asia 1. *'Ākia.* 2. *'Āsia.*

aside *ma ka 'ao'ao* (*lit.* on the side).

ask (favor) 1. *noi.* 2. *nonoi.* [*E **nonoi** i ka Haku e kōkua iā 'oe.* **Ask** the Lord to help you. (traditional hymn)]

ask (question) *nīnau.* [*He **nīnau** a he noi ka'u iā 'oe.* I have a question and a favor to **ask** of you.]

asleep *hiamoe* (also means **to sleep**). [*Ke **hiamoe** nei 'o ia nei.* This one here is **asleep**.]

assign 1. *hā'awi.* 2. *kauoha.*

astonishing *kupaianaha.*

athlete *'ālapa.* [*He mau **'ālapa** ikaika nā wāhine hoe wa'a.* Women canoe paddlers are strong **athletes**.]

attend *hele.* [*Ua **hele** 'oe i ka 'aha mele?* Did you **attend** the concert?]

attention 1. *nānā.* 2. *maliu.* [*E **maliu** mai, e ku'u ipo.* Pay **attention**, sweetheart.]

attractive (person/scene) *1. māhiehie.* [*Ulu **māhiehie** ka nani o ka mesia.* The glory of the Messiah grows like an **attractive** garden. (traditional hymn)] 2. *nohea.*

audience *anaina.* [*Hū ka 'aka o ke **anaina**.* The **audience**'s laughter burst out.]

August *'Aukake* (from English).

aunt *'anakē.*

Australia *'Aukekulia.*

average *'awelika.* [*He aha ka **'awelika** o kāu uku hana ma ka mahina?* What's the **average** of your monthly salary?]

awake *ala.* [*Ua **ala** 'oukou?* Are you all **awake**?]

away 1. *aku.* 2. *'ē.* [*E hele ma kahi **'ē**!* Go **away**! (also *Hele pēlā!*)]

awesome *'e'ehia.* [***'E'ehia** ka hū 'ana a'e o ka pele a, i kekahi manawa, weliweli nō ho'i.* A volcanic eruption is **awesome** and sometimes also terrible.]

awful *weliweli* (also means **terrible, terrifying**). [*ke kaua **weliweli** ma Europa,* the **terrible** war in Europe (song, "Ke Kaua Weliweli," composer unknown)]

awkward 1. *hemahema.* [***Hemahema** wale nō ko'u hula 'ana.* My hula dancing is totally **awkward**.] 2. *hāwāwā.*

axe *ko'i* (also means **adze**).

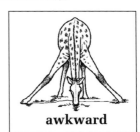

awkward

baby *pēpē.* [*He **pēpē** hou kā lāua.* They (two) have a new **baby**.]

back *kua.* [*'Eha anei kou **kua**?* Is your **back** sore?]

backbone 1. *kuamo'o.* 2. *iwi kuamo'o.*

backpack *'eke kua.* [*Na wai ke **'eke kua** 'ōma'oma'o?* Who does the green **backpack** belong to?]

bad *'ino.* [*Mai mana'o **'ino** mai!* Don't think **bad** things about me!]

bad-smelling 1. *hohono* (body odor). 2. *hauna* (rotting fish). [*Hō ka **hauna** o ka 'ōpala!* Gosh, how **bad-smelling** the garbage is!]

bag 1. *'eke.* 2. *pū'olo.*

bail 1. *kā* (to scoop water out of a canoe). [*E **kā** wa'a!* **Bail** out the canoe!] 2. *[n] pela* (from English; legal term).

bait *maunu.*

baker *mea puhi palaoa.*

bakery *hale puhi palaoa.*

ball *kinipōpō.* [*E hopu i ke **kinipōpō**!* Catch the **ball**!]

balloon *pāluna* (from English). [*E loa'a ana nā pāluna i nā keiki ma ke kaniwala.* The children will get **balloons** at the carnival.]

bamboo 1. *'ohe.* 2. *'ohe kāpala* (carved pieces of bamboo used for printing designs on tapa cloth). [*Me 'elua wale nō **'ohe kāpala** e ho'onani 'ia ai kēia kapa.* It is with only two **bamboo printers** that this tapa cloth should be decorated.]

banana *mai'a.*

band 1. *pāna.* 2. *pāna puhi 'ohe.* [*Ho'okani pinepine ka **pāna puhi 'ohe** 'o Royal Hawaiian i nā mele a nā ali'i i haku ai.* The Royal Hawaiian **band** often plays songs the royalty composed.]

bandage *wahī 'eha.* [*E Māmā, loa'a ka **wahī 'eha** ma ka wane? Ua moku ko'u wāwae i ka puna.* Mom, got **bandages** in the van? My foot was cut on the coral.]

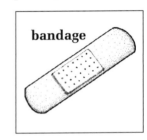

bang (sound of fireworks or gun) 1. *pohā.* 2. *pahū.*

bank *panakō.* [*Waiho 'oukou i kā 'oukou mau pila kīko'o uku ma ka **panakō**?* Do you all deposit your pay checks in the **bank**?]

banner 1. *lepa.* [*Ua kau ka **lepa** ma nā kihi o ka pā.* **Banners** were placed in the corners of the lot.] 2. *hae* (also means **flag**). 3. *bana* (from English).

barbeque *pūlehu.* [*Hiki ke **pūlehu** 'ia ka 'opihi?* Can 'opihi (shellfish) be **barbequed**?]

bark *[n] 'ili. [v] 'aoa.* [***'Aoa** nā 'īlio i ka pōpoki e pāhe'e nei i ka **'ili** o ke kumulā'au.* The dogs **bark** at the cat that's slipping on the **bark** of the tree.]

base 1. *kumu* (also means **intellectual or physical foundation, basis**). [*Inā maopopo iā 'oe ka makemakika, he **kumu** maika'i ia 'ike no ka hana ho'okani pila.* If you understand math, that knowledge is a good **foundation** for playing music.] 2. *kahua.*

baseball *pōhili.*

basket 1. *hīnaʻi* (also refers to a kind of **fish trap**). 2. *ʻie.* 3. *ʻeke* (also means **bag**).

basketball *pōhinaʻi.*

bat (animal) *ʻōpeʻapeʻa.* [*ʻAno ʻē ka lele ʻana o ka* **ʻōpeʻapeʻa.** A **bat**'s flying is odd.]

bat (sports) *lāʻau kinipōpō.*

basket

bathe *ʻauʻau* (also means **to swim**).

bathroom 1. *lua.* 2 *lumi hoʻopau pilikia.* [*Aia ka* **lumi hoʻopau pilikia** *no nā wāhine ma ka ʻaoʻao hema o ka hale kiʻi ʻoniʻoni?* Is the ladies' **bathroom** on the left side of the movie theater?]

bathtub *kapu ʻauʻau* (also means **sink, wash basin**).

battery *pākali.* [*E kūʻai mai i nā* **pākali** *kūpono o hoʻā ʻole ka lekiō.* Buy the appropriate **batteries** or else the radio won't turn on.]

battle *kaua* (also means **war**). (World War II = *Ke Kaua Honua ʻElua*)

beach *kahakai.* [*Ma ke* **kahakai** *ʻo Keawaʻula e ʻike ʻia ai nā naiʻa.* It's at the **beach** called Keawaʻula that dolphins are seen.]

beak (bird, snout of fish, animal) *nuku.*

beard *ʻumiʻumi* (also means **mustache, whiskers**).

beard

beat up *pepehi.*

beautiful 1. *nani.* [*He* **nani** *Kaʻala lae lā lae lae.* Kaʻala (mountain on Oʻahu) is **beautiful**. (song, "Nani Kaʻala," composer unknown)] 2. *uʻi* (usually refers to humans only).

because *no ka mea.* [*No ke aha e nuku ai ke poʻo kumu i ke keiki?* **No ka mea,** *ua ʻōlelo pelapela ke keiki.* Why should the principal scold the boy? **Because** the child swore.]

bed 1. *moe.* 2. *kahi moe.*

bedroom *lumi moe.* [*E hoʻi e hiamoe i kou* **lumi moe** *ponoʻī, e Nāleipua.* Go to sleep in your own **bedroom**, Nāleipua.]

bee *nalomele.*

beef (meat) *ʻiʻo pipi.*

before, in front of *ma mua o.* [**Ma mua o** *ka Natatorium kāua e hui ai ma kēia ahiahi.* It's **in front of** the Natatorium that you and I should meet this evening.]

bedroom

begin *hoʻomaka.* [**Hoʻomaka** *ka hālāwai ma ka hola ʻehia?* What time does the meeting **begin**?]

behind *hope* (also means **in back of**). [*Aia kāu puke wehewehe ma* **hope** *ou.* Your dictionary is **behind** you.]

belief *manaʻo* (also means **thought, opinion, meaning, to think**).

below *lalo* (also means **under**). [*Aia paha ke ʻō ma* **lalo** *o ke puna?* Is the fork **under** the spoon maybe?]

belt *kuapo* (also means **to swap, trade**).

bend *pelu* (also means **to fold** [paper]).

bend down *ʻaui.*

bend over *loʻu.*

berry *hua liʻiliʻi.*

best *ka ʻoi.* [*Maui nō* **ka ʻoi!** Maui indeed is the **best**!]

better *ʻoi aku ka maikaʻi.* [**ʻOi aku ka maikaʻi** *o kāna kiʻi ma mua o kāu.* Her picture (that she drew/painted) is **better** than yours.]

beyond *ma ʻō aku o.* [**ma ʻō aku o** *ka laupapa,* **beyond** the reef]

Bible *Paipala.* [*E heluhelu i kekahi mau paukū mai ke Kauoha Hou o ka* **Paipala.** Read some verses from the New Testament of the **Bible**.]

bicycle *paikikala.* [*Holo* **paikikala** *kekahi mau kānaka a puni ka mokupuni nui.* Some people ride **bicycles** around the Big Island.]

big *nui.*

Big Dipper *Nā Hiku* (*lit.* "the seven").

bigot *ho'okae 'ili* (also means **racial prejudice**).

bill *pila* (from English). [*Pono ka 'ohana e uku i nā **pila** me kēlā mahina kēia mahina.* The family has to pay the **bills** each and every month.]

bird *manu*. [*Ua loa'a ke ko'e i ka **manu**.* The **bird** caught the worm.]

birthday card *kāleka lā hānau*. [*Ua ho'ouna mai kou mau hoahānau i nā **kāleka lā hānau**?* Did your cousins send **birthday cards** to you?]

bite *nahu*.

bitter 1. *mu'emu'e*. [***Mu'mu'e** paha ka lā'au Pākē?* Are Chinese herbal medicines **bitter** tasting?] 2. *'awa'awa*.

black *'ele'ele*. [***Ele'ele** loa ka pō'ele'ele o ka pō Muku.* The darkness of the night Muku (the last night of the waning moon) is really **black**.]

blackboard *papa 'ele'ele*.

blanket *kapa*. (traditional Hawaiian blanket made of five pieces of tapa sewn together, the top layer [*kilohana*] decorated = *kapa moe*)

bleed *kahe koko* (also means **blood flows**). [*Ua moku ko ka malihini wāwae i ka 'a'ā a ua **kahe koko** nō.* The tourist's foot was cut on the sharp lava and there was lots of **bleeding**.]

bless 1. *ho'omaika'i* (to bless things). 2. *ho'opōmaika'i* (to bless people). [*Ua **ho'opōmaika'i** ke kahunapule i ka pēpē hou.* The minister **blessed** the new baby.]

blind *makapō*. [***Makapō** kēnā luahine?* Is that old lady (near you) **blind**?]

blood *koko*. [*He **koko** Hawai'i kona?* Does he have Hawaiian **blood**?]

blooming *mōhala*. (the blooming flower [often refers to young people beginning to grow up] = *ka pua mōhala*)

blow 1. *puhi*. 2. *pā*. [***Pā** mai ka makani Moa'e.* The trade winds **are blowing**.]

blowhole *puhi* (also means **eel, to be destroyed by burning**).

blue *uliuli* (also means **any dark color**, such as ocean or mountains seen from a distance).

board (transportation) *kau ma luna o*. [*Pono nā 'ōhua e **kau ma luna o** kekahi ka'a 'ōhua 'oiai ua pōloke ka peleki.* The passengers have to **board** another bus, since the brakes are broken.]

boat *wa'apā* (small boat such as a whaler). (cruise ship = *mokuahi*)

body *kino*. [*Ma'ema'e wale ke **kino** o ka palai.* The **body** of the fern is clean and chaste. (song, "Ka'ililauokekoa," by Henry Wai'au)]

body surf *kaha nalu*. [***Kaha nalu** 'nā 'ōpio ma Makapu'u.* The young people **body surf** at Makapu'u.]

body surfer *mea kaha nalu*.

bold 1. *koa*. 2. *makoa* (also means **brave**).

bone *iwi*. [*'A'ohe **iwi** o nā mū.* Bugs don't have **bones**.]

book *puke*. [*He mau **puke** ki'i kā ko'u hoaaloha no nā mokupuni like 'ole o ka Pākīpika.* My friend has picture **books** of the various islands of the Pacific.]

boots *kāma'a puti* (from English).

boots

border *palena* (also means **limit, boundary**). [*Me ke aloha **palena** 'ole.* With boundless love. (salutation)]

bored 1. *pakuā*. 2. *manakā* (also means **boring**). [***Manakā** ka hana waele nāhelehele.* Pulling weeds is a **boring** activity.]

borrow *hō'ai'ē*. [*Nele māua i ka palaoa no ka ho'omākaukau 'ana i pai pika. Hiki iā māua ke **hō'ai'ē** i 'elua kī'aha palaoa?* We (two) lack flour for preparing pizza pie. Can we **borrow** two cups of flour?]

boss 1. *haku*. 2. *luna* (also means **manager, supervisor**). [*Auē ke 'ano pa'akikī o ka'u **luna** ma ke ke'ena 'oihana!* Wow, my **boss** at work has a stubborn character!]

both *lāua 'elua* (lit. they two).

bounce *lelele*.

bowl *pola*. [*Aia ka **pola** poi ma ka pākaukau.* The poi **bowl** is on the table.]

bowl

bowling *ulu maika*

haole. [*'Ehia mau kāne ma kā 'olua hui* **ulu maika haole***?* How many men are in your (two) **bowling** group?]

box *pahu* (also means **drum, storage chest**). [*He **pahu** pepa mānoanoa ko ka hale leka?* Does the post office have cardboard **boxes**?]

boy *keiki kāne.* [*He **keiki kāne** a i 'ole he kaikamahine kā 'olua pēpē?* Is your (two) baby a **boy** or a girl?]

bra *pale waiū.*

bracelet 1. *apolima.* [*Ua hā'awi 'ia mai ke **apolima** kula Hawai'i mua loa iā Ka'iulani e kona 'anakē 'o Lydia (Lili'uokalani).* The first Hawaiian gold **bracelet** was given to Ka'iulani by her aunt Lydia (Lili'uokalani).] 2. *kūpe'e.*

brag *kaena.* [*Mai **kaena** ma mua o kāu ipo!* Don't **brag** in front of your sweetheart!]

braid 1. *hili* (in *lei* making, braiding one type of plant). [*I ko Kalei **hili** 'ana i ka pala'ā, piha ka lumi i ke 'ala anuhea o ke kuahiwi.* When Kalei **braids** the pala'ā fern, the room is filled with cool mountain fragrance.] 2. *haku* (in *lei* making, braiding together several types of plants).

brain *lolo.* [*Ho'iho'i ke a'a koko i ke koko i ka **lolo**.* The veins return blood to the **brain**.]

brake *peleki* (from English). [*Hehi 'o ia i ko kona paikikala **peleki**.* He steps on his bicycle's **brake**.]

branch *lālā* (also means **member of group, club**). [*Ua hā'ule iho kekahi **lālā** i ka pō'ino.* A **branch** fell down because of the storm.]

bread *palaoa* (also means **flour, dough**). (slice of bread = *pāpa'a palaoa*)

breadfruit *'ulu.* [*'A'ole 'o ia ala i 'ai mua i ka **'ulu**.* That one over there (that person) hasn't eaten **breadfruit** before.]

break 1. *haki* (break something; syn. *ha'i*). [*Ināhea i **haki** ai nā pipi i ka pā lā'au?* When did the cattle **break** the wooden fence?] 2. *nahā.* 3. *wāwahi.* 4. *'a'e* (to break a *kapu*). 5. *po'i* (waves).

breakfast *'aina kakahiaka.* [*'O ka hē'ī me ka mai'a kāna **'aina kakahiaka**.* Papaya and banana are his **breakfast**.]

breakwater *pale kai.*

breast 1. *waiū.* 2. *ū.*

breath 1. *hanu.* 2. *ea.* 3. *aho.*

breathe 1. *hanu.* [**Hanu** *ka i'a i kona pihapiha.* Fish **breathe** through their gills.] 2. *aho.* 3. *hā.*

breeze 1. *makani* (also means **wind**). 2. *aheahe.*

bright (shiny) 1. *hinuhinu.* [**Hinuhinu** *ko kēlā wahine lauoho 'ele'ele.* That woman's black hair is **shiny**.] 2. *mālamalama.* 3. *'ōlinolino.* 4. *'alohi.*

bring *lawe mai.* [*E **lawe mai** i kā 'olua palapala male, ke 'olu'olu.* **Bring** your (two) marriage license, please.]

broad 1. *ākea.* 2. *laulā.* (Both *ākea* and *laulā* also mean **breadth, width, wide.**)

broadcast (news) 1. *kūkala.* [**Kūkala** *nūhou lākou ma ka hola 'eono.* They **broadcast** the news at 6 o'clock.] 2. *ho'olono.*

broil *pūlehu.*

broken 1. *poloke* (from English). 2. *nahā.* 3. *haki.* [*Iā Pānānā i hā'ule ai, ua **haki** 'ia kona ku'eku'e wāwae.* When Pānānā fell, her ankle was **broken**.]

broom *pūlumi* (also means **to sweep up**). (broom made of coconut midribs tied together = *pūlumi nī'au*)

brother *kaikunāne* (refers to brother of a woman. A man has *kaikua'ana* [older brother] and *kaikaina* [younger brother] while a woman uses these same terms to refer to her older and younger sisters.).

brown *palaunu* (from English).

brown skin *'ili 'ula.*

bruise *pohole.*

bruised *pohole.* [**Pohole** *ko ka mea he'e nalu wāwae i ka nalu i po'i ma luna ona.* The surfer's leg is **bruised** due to the wave that broke on top of him.]

brush *palaki* (from English). [*Ke **palaki** nei 'oe i kou mau niho?* Are you **brushing** your teeth?]

bubble [n] *hu'ahu'a.* [v] 1. *pua'i.* [*Nui nā **hu'ahu'a** e **pua'i** ana i ka wai puna.* There are lots of **bubbles** that **bubble** up in spring water.] 2. *hua'i.*

bucket *pākeke* (also means **pocket**). [*Piha ka*

pākeke a ka lawai'a i nā 'opihi. The fisherman's **bucket** is full of *'opihi*.]

bud *'ōpu'u* (used as a symbol of new growth, a young person about to "blossom").

bug 1. *mū*. 2. *iniseka* (from English).

build *kūkulu* (also means **to set up tent**).

building *hale* (also means **house**). [*He **hale** hāiki a lō'ihi nō 'o Aloha Tower nani.* Beautiful Aloha Tower is a narrow and tall **building**.]

bump *pu'u* (also means **hill, pimple**, many other meanings).

bunch *pū'ā* (also means **bundle, clump, flock**). [*He **pū'ā** hulu manu ko ka mea hana lei hulu.* The feather *lei* maker has a **bunch** of bird feathers.]

burn 1. *ho'ā* (also means **to light a fire, turn on electrical appliance**). 2. *'ā*.

burned *pāpa'a.* [*Ua **pāpa'a** kona manamana lima i ke ahi.* His finger was **burned** in the fire.]

bury *kanu* (also means **to plant**). [*Mai **kanu** i nā pūpū o nalowale.* Don't **bury** the shells or else they will be lost.]

bus *ka'a 'ōhua.* [*Ke kau nei nā 'ōhua ma luna o ke **ka'a 'ōhua**.* The passengers are boarding the **bus**.]

bush *lā'au* (also means **medicine**). (Hawaiian herbal medicine = *lā'au lapa'au*) (vine = *lā'auhihi*)

business *'oihana.* [*He ho'okele **'oihana** kēlā wahine.* That woman is a **business** leader.]

but *akā.* [*'A'aka ka wiliki **akā** akamai 'o ia.* The engineer is grouchy, **but** she is smart.]

butter *waiū paka.*

butterfly *pulelehua* (also means **moth**).

buttocks *'ēlemu.* [*'Eha ko ka haumāna **'ēlemu** i ka noho 'ana ma mua o ka lolouila.* The student's **buttocks** are sore due to sitting in front of the computer.]

butterfly

button *(ke) pihi.* [*Mai kaomi i ke **pihi**!* Don't push the **button**!]

buy *kū'ai mai.* (to shop around = *kū'ai hele*) [*Ke **kū'ai hele** nei ka makuahine a me kāna kaikamahine e **kū'ai mai** i lole pipi'i no ka hulahula 'ana ma ka Prom.* The mother and her daughter are **shopping around** to **buy** an expensive dress for dancing at the Prom.]

C

cage 1. *pahu holoholona* (*lit.* animal box). 2. *pahu manu* (*lit.* bird box).

cake *mea 'ono* (also means **dessert, any sweet or pastry**).

calabash 1. *'umeke*. [*I ke au kahiko, ua ho'olewalewa 'ia ka '**umeke** i ke kōkō ma ka 'auamo*. In the old days, a **calabash** was made to sway in a net of the carrying pole.] 2. *ipu*.

calculate *ho'onohonoho helu*. [***Ho'onohonoho helu** wikiwiki nā 'uao i nā helu 'ai ma ka pā'ani pōhina'i*. Referees quickly **calculate** the scores in basketball games.]

calendar *'alemanaka*. [*Helu ka '**alemenaka** kahiko i nā pō mahina*. The ancient **calendar** counts the nights of the moon.]

April						
SUN	MON	TUE	WED	THU	FRI	SAT
	1	2	3	4	5	6
7	8	9	10	11	12	13
14	15	16	17	18	19	20
21	22	23	24	25	26	27
28	29	30				

calendar

calico *kalakoa*. [*'O ke **kalakoa** kekahi 'ano lole a kekahi 'ano pōpoki nō ho'i*. **Calico** is a kind of cloth and a kind of cat, too.]

call (phone) *kelepona* (from English).

call out *kāhea*.

calm *mālie*. [***Mālie** wale ka wana'ao*. Dawn is very **calm** (implies peaceful).]

calmness *la'i* (also means **quiet**).

camera *pahu pa'i ki'i*. [*Hiki anei iā 'oe ke pa'i ki'i iā māua i kā māua **pahu pa'i ki'i** hou? Can you take our (two, not you) picture with our new **camera**?]

camp *ho'omoana*.

campground *kahua ho'omoana*. [*Ua ho'okapu 'o 'Anakala i ke **kahua ho'omoana** ma Mokulē'ia no kēia hopenapule a'e*. Uncle reserved the **campground** at Mokulē'ia for next weekend.]

can [v] *hiki*. [***Hiki** iā 'oukou ke kōkua mai ia'u? **Can** you all help me?]

canal 1. *alawai*. 2. *'auwai*.

cancel 1. *kāpae* (skip over, delete). [*E **kāpae** i ka ho'okapu noho ma ka hana keaka, ke 'olu 'olu*. **Cancel** the reservations at the theater, please.] 2. *ho'opau* (put an end to, finish).

cancer *ma'i 'a'ai*. [*Aia ka **ma'i 'a'ai** ma kona 'ake māmā*. The **cancer** is in her lung].

candidate *moho*. [*E lilo paha ana ko ke kamanā kaikuahine i **moho** no ka Papa Alaka'i Ho'ona'auao*. The carpenter's sister may become a **candidate** for the Board of Education.]

candle *ihoiho*.

candy *kanakē*. [*'A'ole paha 'ono ke **kanakē** kōpa'a 'ole*. Sugarless **candy** may not be delicious.]

cane *ko'oko'o*. [*He **ko'oko'o** ko ke kāne 'o'opa*. The lame man has a **cane**.]

canoe 1. *wa'a*. 2. *wa'a kaukahi* (single hulled). 3. *wa'a kaulua* (double hulled).

canoe

canoe club *hui wa'a*.

cape 1. *lae* (peninsula or point). 2. *'ahu'ula* (feather cloak or cape, symbol of high nobility).

capitol *kapikala* (from English). [*Kohu like ke **kapikala** moku 'āina me ka lua pele ke nānā aku*. The state **capitol** looks like a volcano.]

captain *kāpena*. [*He **kāpena** moku*

māka'ika'i 'o Kanalunui. Kanalunui is a **captain** of a sightseeing boat.]

captive *pio.*

capture 1. *hopu* (also means **to catch, grab**). 2. *lawe pio* (*lit.* take prisoner).

car *ka'a.* [*'Ehia ka'a o kou 'ohana?* How many **cars** does your family have?]

car

card *kāleka.* [*E ho'ouna aku ana 'oukou i nā kāleka Kalikimaka ma kēia makahiki a'e?* Will you all send out Christmas **cards** next year?]

career *'oihana* (also means **business, profession**).

careful *akahele.* [*E akahele!* Be **careful**!]

carpenter *kamanā.* [*He aha kāu 'oihana? He kamanā kūkulu hale au.* What is your career? I'm a house-building **carpenter**.]

carpet *moena* (also means **mat, bed**).

carrot *kāloke.* [*'Ono ka lio i ke kāloke.* Horses crave **carrots**.]

carrot

carry, transport *halihali.*

carton *pahu.*

carve *kālai.* (to carve a canoe = *kālai wa'a* [also means canoe builder]) (to carve an image = *kālai ki'i* [also means image carver])

cashier *kanaka 'ohi kālā.* [*He hana kā ka'u keiki ma ke 'ano he kanaka 'ohi kālā ma ka hale kū'ai puke.* My son has a job as a **cashier** at the bookstore.]

cassette tape *lola.*

cat *pōpoki.*

catch 1. *hopu.* [*Mai ho'ā'o e hopu i nā pipi 'āhiu o pilikia auane'i 'oe.* Don't try to **catch** wild cattle or you'll have trouble sooner or later.] 2. *'apo.* (catch fish = *lawai'a*)

cassette tape

category 1. *māhele* (also means **part, section,** **to divide, share**). [*Nui nā māhele hana i ka hana hulu.* There are lots of **categories** of work in featherwork.] 2. *'ano* (also means **type, brand**).

cattle *pipi.*

cave *ana.* [*Ua komo nā po'e kahiko i ke ana kahakai e noho i laila i ka wā kaua.* The ancestors entered the sea **cave** to live there in times of war.]

cavity 1. *puka niho* (tooth cavity). 2. *po'o* (also means **head, whole note**).

ceiling *kaupoku.*

celebrate *ho'olaule'a* (also means **festival, celebration**). [*E ho'olaule'a kākou ma kou lā hope ma ka hana.* Let's all **celebrate** on your last day at work.]

cement *kimeki.*

cemetery *pā ilina.* [*Aia ka ho'olewa ma ka pā ilina ma ka Pō'aono.* The funeral is at the **cemetery** on Saturday.]

cent *keneka.*

center *kikowaena.*

centipede *kanapī.*

century *kenekulia.* [*I kēlā kenekulia aku nei i lilo ai ke aupuni mō'ī.* It was in the last **century** that the monarchy disappeared.]

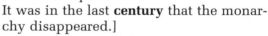
cemetery

ceramics *ka hana pālolo.*

cereal *sereala* (from English).

chain *kaula.* (chain-link fence = *pā kaula hao*) (chain of islands = *pae 'āina*)

chair *noho.*

chalk *poho.*

change [*n*] 1. *kenikeni* (loose coins). 2. *koena* (change from purchase). [*Eia kou koena, e ke kaikamahine.* Here's your **change**, girl.] [*v*] 3. *ho'ololi.* [*E ho'ololi lole a e komo i ka lole 'au'au.* **Change** clothes and put on your swimsuit.] 2. *loli.* [*Hō ua loli kona mana'o e pili ana i ka huaka'i i Aotearoa!* Gosh, he **changed** his mind about the trip to New Zealand!]

channel *kōā* (ocean or TV channel or space between objects).

chant *oli.* [*Kaulana ke oli 'o "'Au'a 'Ia."* "'*Au'a 'Ia*" is a well-known **chant**.]

chanter *mea oli.*

chase 1. *alualu.* 2. *hāhai* (also means **to follow**).

chase off *kipaku* (also means **to kick out**).

cheap *emi.* [*'A'ole* **emi** *ke kakalina.* Gasoline isn't **cheap**.]

cheat 1. *kikiki* (from English). 2. *'āpuka* (implies fraud, deceit, much more serious harm than *kikiki*).

check (bank) *pila kīko'o.* [*Hiki anei ia'u ke uku i ka* **pila kīko'o**? Can I pay with a **check**?]

cherish 1. *pūlama.* [**Pūlama** *'ia nō 'oe me ke aloha.* You are **cherished** with love. (song, "He Punahele Nō 'Oe," by A. Nāhale'ā)] 2. *ho'oheno.*

check

chest 1. *houpo.* 2. *poli.* 3. *umauma.*

chicken *moa.* [*Hānai* **moa** *kāne ko'u hoahānau no nā hakakā moa.* My cousin raises roosters for **chicken** fights.]

chief 1. *ali'i* (also means **nobility, royalty, noble/royal**). 2. *lani.*

child *keiki.* [*He lei poina 'ole ke* **keiki**. ('ōlelo no'eau) A **child** is a *lei* that cannot be forgotten.] (*pl.* **children** = *nā keiki;* my children = *kā'u mau keiki*)

chilly *hu'ihu'i* (also means **chilled**). [*He kuahiwi* **hu'ihu'i** *'o Mauna Kea.* Mauna Kea is a **chilly** mountain.]

chime *kani.*

chin *'auwae.* [*I ke kahi 'ana ona i kona 'umi'umi, ua kalakala ko kona* **'auwae** *'ili.* When he shaved his beard, the skin on his **chin** was rough.]

China *Kina.*

Chinese *Pākē.* [*He hapa* **Pākē** *paha 'olua?* Are you two part-**Chinese** maybe?]

chocolate *kokoleka.* [*Inu kā'u mau keiki i ke* **kokoleka** *ma ka pō.* My children drink **chocolate** at night.]

choke 1. *'umi* (to choke someone). 2. *kalea* (choke or cough). 3. *ha'u* (choke with sobs).

choose *koho* (also means **choice**). [*'O kēia pālule aloha ka i* **koho** *'ia? He nani ia!* Is this aloha shirt the one that was **chosen**? It's pretty!]

choppy (seas) 1. *hānupanupa.* [**Hānupanupa** *ke kai ma Hāna.* The sea is **choppy** at Hāna.] 2. *'ōkaikai.*

Christmas *Kalikimaka.* (Christmas Day = *ka lā Kalikimaka*)

church *hale pule.* (church congregation = *'ekalesia*) [*Ua kipa aku mākou i ka* **hale pule** *'o Kaumakapili a ua ho'okipa mai ka* **'ekalesia**. We visited Kaumakapili **church** and the **congregation** welcomed us.]

church

circle 1. *pō'ai.* 2. *pōhai.* [**pōhai** *ke aloha,* encircling love (song, "Pōhai Ke Aloha," by L. Machado/M. Kealakai)] 3. *lina poepoe.*

circle

circumference *anapuni.* [*'Ehia kapua'i ke* **anapuni** *o kēia pō'ai?* How many feet is the **circumference** of this circle?]

circus *hō'ike'ike.*

citizen *maka'āinana* (also means **commoner, a person not of chiefly rank**). (representative = *luna maka'āinana*) [*'O Kūhiō ka* **luna maka'āinana** *i aloha nui 'ia.* Kūhiō (Kalaniana'ole) was a **representative** of the people who was greatly loved.]

city *kūlanakauhale.* [*He* **kūlanakauhale** *'o Kahului ma Maui.* Kahului is a **city** on Maui.]

civil rights *pono kiwila.* [*Ua 'a'e 'ia nā* **pono kiwila** *o nā Hawai'i i ka hō'ole i ka hapanui o lākou e koho pāloka.* The **civil rights** of Hawaiians were violated by denying the majority of them the right to vote.]

clap [*v*] *pa'ipa'i lima* (clap hands, applaud).

class *papa* (also means **wood, any flat surface, stratum**, many other meanings). [*Aia i hea kā ke kumu kula* **papa** *ma kēia lā?* Where is the schoolteacher's **class** today?]

claw 1. *miki'ao* (also means **fingernail**). 2.

māiʻuʻu (bird; also means **fingernail, toenail, hoof**).

clay *pālolo*.

clean *maʻemaʻe*. *[v] hoʻomaʻemaʻe*.
[*Hoʻomaʻemaʻe pinepine ke kāne iā loko o kona kalaka*. The man often **cleans** the inside of his truck.]

clear 1. *ahuwale* (clear view). 2. *mao* (clear weather after rain). 3. *mōakāka* (easily understood). [*Mōakāka ko ke kauka niho wehewehe ʻana pehea e palaki niho ai*. The dentist's explanation on how to brush your teeth is **clear**.]

cliff *pali*. [*Pulu pinepine nā pali Koʻolau i ka ua*. The Koʻolau **cliffs** are often soaked wet with rain.]

climb 1. *piʻi*. 2. *pinana*. [*Mai pinana i ka pā kaula hao!* Don't **climb** the chain link fence!]

clock *uaki* (also means **watch**). [*Kani ka uaki nui ma waho o ka hale pule ma ka hapahā hola*. The large **clock** outside the church chimes on the quarter hour.]

clock

close *[v] pani*. [*E pani i ka pukaaniani o anuanu ʻoe ma hope*. **Close** the window or you'll be cold later.]

close (proximity) *kokoke*. [*Aia ka hale leka kokoke i ka Hale Aliʻi ʻo ʻIolani*. The post office is **close** to ʻIolani Palace.]

close (relationship) *pili*. [*E hoʻi mai kāua lā e pili*. Let's come back together and be **close**. (common line in love songs)]

closed *paʻa* (also means **firm, completed**, many other meanings). [*Auē! Paʻa ka panakō!* Oh, dear! The bank is **closed**!]

clothes *lole*. [*Pipiʻi ko ka puʻukani lole?* Are the singer's **clothes** expensive?] (clothes washer = *mīkini holoi lole*)

cloud *ao* (also means **light, enlightenment, daytime**, many other meanings).

cloud

cloudy *ʻōmalumalu*.

clown *kalauna* (from English).

club 1. *hui*. 2. *kalapu* (from English).

clumsy 1. *hemahema*. 2. *hāwāwā*.

coast *kapakai*. [*Eia mākou, kou kapakai*. Here we are, your **coast**. (song, "Queen's Jubilee," Liliʻuokalani)]

coat *kuka*. (raincoat = *kuka ua*)

coconut *niu*.

coconut husk *pulu* (used to make *ʻaha*, sennit rope).

coconut leaf *lau niu*.

coconut milk *wai niu*.

coconut tree *kumuniu*.

coffee *kope* (also means **copy**). [*Ke hana kope ke kākau ʻōlelo, inu ʻo ia i ke kope*. When the secretary makes **copies**, he drinks **coffee**.]

coffee

coin 1. *kenikeni* (pocket change). 2. *kālā paʻa*.

cold 1. *anuanu*. 2. *anu*. [*Hō ke anu o ka uka ʻiuʻiu!* Goodness, the high uplands are **cold**!]

collect 1. *hōʻiliʻili*. [*Laha ʻole a pipiʻi nā poʻoleka Hawaiʻi i hōʻiliʻili ʻia e ia*. The Hawaiian stamps which were **collected** by her are rare and expensive.] 2. *ʻohi*. 3. *hōʻahu*.

collection 1. *hōʻiliʻili*. 2. *hōʻahu*.

color *[n]* 1. *waihoʻoluʻu*. 2. *kala* (from English; also means to color). [*He aha kāu waihoʻoluʻu punahele no ke kala kiʻi ʻana?* What is your favorite **color** for **coloring** pictures?]

comb *[n] kahi* (also means **the place**, many other meanings).[*ʻO ka ʻāina hoʻopulapula i kapa ʻia ʻo Hoʻolehua kahi āna i hanai ʻia ai*. The Hawaiian Homes land named Hoʻolehua is **the place** she was raised.] *[v] kahi* (also means **to shave, scrape down poi bowl**). [*E kahi i kou lauoho ma mua o ka haʻalele ʻana i ka hale*. **Comb** your hair before leaving the house.]

combine *hoʻohui*. [*E hoʻohui i ke kōpaʻa, ka wai niu a me ka palaoa*. **Combine** the sugar, coconut milk and flour.]

come *hele mai*.

come back *hoʻi mai*. [*E hoʻi mai, e kuʻu ipo.* **Come back** to me, my sweetheart. (song, "Poliʻahu," by F. Hewett)]

comfortable *ʻoluʻolu* (also means **kind, nice**). [*ʻOluʻolu ko ko ʻolua mau mākua hale kahiko?* Is your (two) parents' old house **comfortable**?]

command *kauoha*. [*Kauoha ko lākou alakaʻi i nā koa.* Their leader **commands** the soldiers.]

common *laha*. (ant. rare = *laha ʻole*) [*Laha ka maʻi koko piʻi.* High blood pressure is a **common** ailment.]

community *kaiaulu*.

community college *kula nui kaiaulu*.

compact disc (CD) *sēdē, cēdē*.

compare *hoʻohālike*. [*Inā hoʻohālike ʻoe i nā pūpū, hiki ke ʻike i ka ʻokoʻa ma waena o ka pūpū laiki a me ka pūpū Kahelelani.* If you **compare** shells, you can recognize the difference between a "rice" shell and a Kahelelani shell.]

complain 1. *namunamu*. [*ʻAʻole hiki iā ʻoe ke kūnānā wale a namunamu mai.* You can't just stand there undecided and **complain** to me.] 2. *ʻōhumu*.

complete *paʻa* (has many other meanings). [*Ua paʻa ka palapala kauoha.* The will is **completed**.]

compose (words/music) *haku*. [*Na Kalākaua i haku iā "Hawaiʻi Ponoʻī."* It was Kalākaua who **composed** "Hawaiʻi Ponoʻī."] (poet, composer = *haku mele*) (author = *haku puke*)

compost *pulu*.

computer 1. *lolouila* (*lit.* electric brain). 2. *kamepiula* (from English).

concept *manaʻo* (also means **thought, idea, meaning, opinion, to think, consider**).

concern *kuleana* (also means **rights, responsibility**).

concert *ʻaha mele*. [*ʻEhia mele Hawaiʻi i hīmeni ʻia ma ka ʻaha mele ʻo Kanikapila?* How many Hawaiian songs were sung at the Kanikapila **concert**?]

conclusion *hopena* (also means **result, consequence**). [*E hana pono o ʻike ana ʻoe i ka hopena.* Work properly or you will suffer the **consequences**.]

condom *uhi ule*.

confirm *hōʻoia*. (syn. *hōʻoiaʻiʻo*)

confused 1. *huikau*. 2. *pohihihi*. [*ʻAʻole mōakāka ko ka haku puke manaʻo a pohihihi ka mea heluhelu puke.* The author's thought isn't clear and the reader is **confused**.]

confusion 1. *huikau*. 2. *pohihihi*.

congratulate *hoʻomaikaʻi*.

congratulations *hoʻomaikaʻi*. [*Hoʻomaikaʻi iā ʻolua i ko ʻolua piha makahiki! Congratulations* on your (two) anniversary!]

Congress *ʻAhaʻōlelo Pekelala*. (syn. *ʻAhaʻōlelo lāhui*)

connect 1. *hoʻohui*. 2. *hoʻokuʻi*.

conquer *naʻi*.

conscience *lunawaemanaʻo*. (syn. *lunaʻikehala*)

consciousness *ʻike hoʻomaopopo*. (lose consciousness = *pau ka ʻike, kauhola*; regain consciousness = *pohala, ao*)

consent *ʻae* (also means **to agree, allow, say yes to**). [*Ua ʻae ka paʻa male i ka ʻaelike male.* The married couple **consented** to the marriage contract.]

consider 1. *manaʻo*. 2. *noʻonoʻo*.

considerate *noʻonoʻo*.

constant *mau* (also means **enduring, ongoing**, many other meanings). [*Mau nō ke aloha o ka makua i kāna keiki.* The love of a parent for his child is **constant**.]

constellation 1. *huihui*. [*ʻO Nāhiku ka huihui e kuhi ana i ka Hōkū Paʻa.* The Big Dipper is the **constellation** that points to the North Star.] 2. *ulu hōkū*.

constitution (legal document) *kumu kānāwai*.

construct *kūkulu*.

construction worker *lima hana*.

contact lenses *pilimaka*.

container 1. *ipu*. 2. *pūʻolo*.

contest *hoʻokūkū* (also means **competition**). [*ʻO ka Merrie Monarch ka hoʻokūkū hula kaulana loa o Hawaiʻi nei.* The Merrie Monarch is the most famous hula **contest**

here in Hawai'i]. (spelling bee = *ho'okūkū hua 'ōlelo*)

continent *'āina puni 'ole.*

continue *ho'omau.*

conversation *kama'ilio.*

converse *[v]* 1. *kama'ilio.* 2. *wala'au* (informally).

cook 1. *kuke.* 2. *kālua* (in an *imu*).

cooked (food) *mo'a* (also means **done**). [*Ua mo'a ka 'i'o moa.* The chicken is **done**.]

cool *hu'ihu'i* (also means **chilly**).

cooled down *ma'alili* (refers to cooked food that has cooled, also to cooled passion).

copy *[n]* *kope* (from English). *[v]* *hana kope* (also means **to photocopy**). [*Hiki ke* **hana kope** *'ia kēia 'ao'ao.* This page can be **copied**.]

coral 1. *puna.* 2. *'ako'ako'a.* (coral head = *pūkoa*) Note: There are many names for individual corals.

cord 1. *kaula* (also means **rope**). 2. *'aha* (coconut fiber). 3. *aho.* 4. *piko* (umbilical).

corner 1. *kihi* (outside). 2. *kū'ono* (inside). [*mai luna a lalo, mai kekahi* **kihi** *a i kekahi* **kihi**, from top to bottom, from one **corner** (of house) to another (common line in house-blessing chants)]

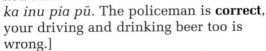

corner

correct *pololei.* [**Pololei** *ka māka'i, ua hewa kou kalaiwa 'ana me ka inu pia pū.* The policeman is **correct**, your driving and drinking beer too is wrong.]

cost *kumu kū'ai* (also means **price**).

cotton 1. *pulu.* 2. *ma'o.* [*Komo ko'u makuahine i nā lole* **ma'o** *wale nō ma ke kauwela.* My mother wears only **cotton** clothes in the summer.]

cough *kunu.* [*He anu ko kāna pēpē a* **kunu** *mau ka pēpē.* His baby has a cold and the baby constantly **coughs**.]

count *helu.* [*E* **helu** *i kāu mau puke ma mua o ka ho'okomo 'ana i loko o nā pahu.* **Count** your books before inserting them in the boxes.]

country *'āina.* [*'O Keālia kou* **'āina**? Is Keālia your **country** (the place where you are from)?]

country person *kua'āina.*

county *kalana.* [*Aia ma lalo o ke* **kalana** *'o Maui nā mokupuni 'o Lāna'i, Kaho'olawe, Maui a me Moloka'i.* Under the **county** of Maui are the islands of Lāna'i, Kaho'olawe, Maui and Moloka'i.]

courageous *koa* (also means **long-lived, soldier**).

court 1. *aloali'i* (royal). [*Kā'alo ke* **aloali'i** *o ka ho'olaule'a ma ka lā mua o Mei i ke anaina.* The **royal court** of the May Day festival goes past the audience.] 2. *'aha ho'okolokolo* (trial court).

cousin *hoahānau.*

cove *kū'ono* (also means **bay**).

cover *[n]* 1. *po'i* (lid). [*Aia i hea ke* **po'i** *o kēia 'umeke?* Where is the **cover** of this calabash?] 2. *uhi* (veil, spread, film). *[v]* *uhi.*

cow *pipi wahine.*

cowboy *paniolo.* [*Holo lio nā* **paniolo** *ma ke kahua hānai pipi.* **Cowboys** ride horses on the ranch.]

cow

crab *pāpa'i.*

crack *[n]* *māwae* (opening in rocks). *[v]* *naka* (also means **to split open, break**).

cracked *nahā.*

cracker *palena* (also means **border, boundary**). [*Ho'olu'u 'o Pāpā i ka* **palena** *i kāna kope.* Dad dips the **cracker** in his coffee.]

cracking noise *'u'ina* (*'u'i* means **to roar, rumble**). [*'U'i, 'u'i 'u'ina lā ka wai a'o Nā Molokama.* The waters of Nā Molokama (mountains at Hanalei, Kaua'i) **rumble and roar**. (song, "Nā Molokama," by A. Alohikea)]

craft *hana no'eau* (also means **art, artwork**). [*Nani maoli nō nā* **hana no'eau** *of Hawai'i kahiko, e like me ke kuku kapa a me ka hana hulu manu.* The **crafts** of old Hawai'i, like tapa beating and featherwork, were truly beautiful.]

craftsman *mea hana noʻeau.*

cramp *huki* (also means **convulsion, stroke**). [*Ua loaʻa ka ʻelemakule i ka **huki** i kona wāwae.* The old man had a **cramp** in his leg.]

crash *hoʻokuʻi.* [*E **hoʻokuʻi** ʻia ana ka pukaaniani e ka lāʻau ke hao mai ka makani?* Will the window be **crashed** into by the board when the wind blasts?]

crater *lua pele.* [*Noho ʻo Pele ma ka **lua pele** ʻo Halemaʻumaʻu.* Pele lives in the Halemaʻumaʻu **crater**.]

crawl *kolo.* [*Ke hoʻomaka nei kāu pēpē e **kolo**. E nānā!* Your baby is starting to **crawl** now. Look!]

crayon *kala.* [*ʻElima wale nō āna **kala** e kaha kiʻi ai.* She has only five **crayons** to draw with.]

crayon

crazy 1. *pupule.* 2. *hehena.*

cream *kalima* (from English).

create 1. *hoʻokumu* (also means **to establish, found**). [*Na nā mikionele i **hoʻokumu** i ke kula mua o Hawaiʻi, ʻo Lahainaluna.* It was the missionaries who **founded** the first school of Hawaiʻi, Lahainaluna.] 2. *hana* (also means **to work, make, do an activity, job**, many other meanings).

creep along *nihi.* [*E **nihi** ka hele, mai hoʻopā.* **Creep along** carefully, don't touch. (song "E Nihi ka Hele," written by Kalākaua warning his wife Kapiʻolani to be diplomatic in her travels, not to offend)]

crew *poʻe hoʻokele moku* (lit. people who navigate a ship).

crime *kalaima* (from English).

crooked *kapakahi* (also means **off center**). [*ke alanui **kapakahi** e,* the **crooked** street (song, "Tūtū Ē," composer unknown)]

crowd *lehulehu* (also means **public, multitudes**).

crowded 1. *piha kuʻi.* 2. *paʻapū.*

crown *kalaunu* (from English). [*He kalo ko ko Kalākaua **kalaunu**.* Kalākaua's **crown** has a taro plant.]

crutches *koʻokoʻo.* [*Ma muli o ka haki ʻia ʻana o ko ke kahunapule kuʻekuʻe wāwae, ʻaʻole hiki iā ia ke hele wāwae, koe wale me ke **koʻokoʻo**.* Due to the minister's ankle being broken, she can't walk, except with **crutches**.]

cry *uē.* [*Nui ko ka pepe **uē** ʻana ke pulu kona kaiapa.* The baby **cries** a lot whenever his diaper is wet.]

cube *poke.* [*He mau **poke** hau ko ka pahu hau?* Does the icebox (refrigerator) have ice **cubes**?]

cultivate *mahi* (see farm, farmer).

culture *moʻomeheu.* [*Nui nā loina o ka **moʻomeheu** kahiko.* There are many traditions in the ancient **culture**.]

cup *kīaha* (also means **drinking glass**). [*Aia iā wai kāu **kīaha**?* Who has your **cup**?]

cure *hoʻōla* (also means **heal**). [*Hiki paha ke **hoʻōla** ʻia ko nā mākua mau puʻu ʻeha?* Can the parents' sore throats perhaps be **healed**?]

curiosity *nīele.* [*Nui ko ka ʻelepaio **nīele**. ʻElepaio* birds have lots of **curiosity**.]

curious *nīele.*

curly (hair) 1. *milo.* 2. *piʻipiʻi.*

custom *loina.* [*He mau **loina** ko ke kālai waʻa.* Canoe carving has **customs**.]

cut *ʻoki.* (divorce, to divorce = *ʻoki male*)

dagger *pāhoa.*

dainty 1. *'auli'i* (also means **neat, cute**). 2. *mikioi* (also means **fine work, excellently made**).

damp *ma'ū.* [*Ma'ū* ka mau'u i ke kēhau. The grass is **damp** with dew.]

dampness *ma'ū.*

dance 1. *hula* (Hawaiian dance). 2. *hulahula* (ballet, disco, non-Hawaiian dance).

dangerous *maka'u* (also means **afraid, frightening**). [*Maka'u* ka pi'i kuahiwi ma ka pō. Hiking at night is **dangerous**.]

dark *pō'ele'ele.* [*Pō'ele'ele* ke kakahiaka nui. The early morning is **dark**.]

darling 1. *eia nei* (this phrase is used to call politely to someone whose name you don't know and can be translated in a variety of ways such as, "hello there," "hey," "you there," "dear one"). [*Eia nei, aia i hea ka hale leka?* **Hello there**, where is the post office?] 2. *makamae* (also means **precious, treasured**).

daughter *kaikamahine* (also means **girl**). (*pl. kaikamāhine*) ['*O kēnā kaikamahine no'eau kā 'olua kaikamahine?* Is that skilled **girl** (by you) your folks' **daughter**?]

daughter

dawn 1. *wana'ao.* [*Ua ao ka wana'ao.* Day has **dawned**.] 2. *kaiao.* (all night = *a ao ka pō*) [*Hana 'o ia a ao ka pō.* She works **all night** (*lit.* until light the dark).]

day *ao* (also means **daytime, daylight**). (all day = *a pō ke ao*)

daylight 1. *ao* (also means **light, wisdom,** many other meanings). [*Ikaika ke ao ma Hawai'i nei.* **Daylight** is strong here in Hawai'i.] 2. *lā.*

dead 1. *make* (also means **to pass away, die**). 2. *hala* (also means **to pass away, die, pass by**). [*Ua pau, ua hala lākou, a koe nō nā pua.* They are finished, they have **passed away**, and their descendants remain. (song, "Nā Ali'i," by S. Kuahiwi)]

deaf *kuli.* [*Kuli* kona pepeiao. Her ear is **deaf**.] (be quiet [you're making noise] = *kulikuli*)

dear 1. *aloha* (greeting in letter). 2. *auē* (exclamation "Oh, dear!"). [*E ke Kenekoa, Aloha kāua.* **Dear** Senator, hello to you and me.]

death *make.*

debt *'ai'ē.* [*Pōpilikia maoli nō ka 'āina i nā 'ai'ē o nā ali'i i nā malihini.* The country was greatly troubled due to the **debts** of the chiefs to the newcomers.] (to pay off debt = *ho'oka'a*)

deceive 1. *ho'opunipuni.* 2. *'āpiki.*

December Kēkēmapa (from English).

decide *ho'oholo.* [*Ināhea 'oukou i ho'oholo ai e 'ai i ka 'ai Wai'anae?* When did you all **decide** to eat the Wai'anae diet?]

decimal *kekimala* (from English).

declare 1. *ha'i* (also means **to tell**). 2. *hō'ike* (also means **to reveal, to demonstrate**). 3. *'ōlelo* (also means t**o speak, speech, language**).

decline *hō'ole* (to say no to).

decorated 1. *kāhiko.* [*Ua kāhiko 'ia ka Hale Ali'i no ka poni 'ana o ke kia'āina.* The Palace was **decorated** for the governor's inauguration.] 2. *ho'onani.*

dedicate *ho'ola'a.*

deep *hohonu* (means both deep water and complex thought, meaning). [***Hohonu** ka mana'o o nā mele kahiko.* The meanings of ancient poetry are **deep**.]

defecate 1. *ki'o.* 2. *hana lepo* (euphemism).

defend 1. *pale.* 2. *kūpale.*

defiled *haumia* (also means **unclean, vile, polluted**).

degree *kekele* (means both educational degree and temperature). [*Ke 'imi nei kou hoa-hānau i kāna **kekele** loea?* Is your cousin seeking her M.A. **degree**?]

delicate 1. *lahilahi* (also means **thin, frail**). 2. *'auli'i.*

delicious *'ono.* [***'Ono** nō ka poke i ka ina-mona.* The raw fish is **delicious** due to the *kukui* nut condiment.] (Used as a verb, *'ono* means to crave a specific food.) [***'Ono** nā keiki i ka haukōhi.* Kids **crave** shave ice.]

delighted, pleased *ohohia* (also means **enthusiastic**). [***Ohohia** nā keiki ma ke kula Hawai'i hou.* The children at the new Hawaiian school are **delighted**.]

deliver 1. *hā'awi* (also means **to give**). 2. *lawe* (also means **to bring, to take**).

delusion *mana'o kuhihewa.*

demonstrate *hō'ike.* [*Ke **hō'ike** aku nei 'o Malu'ihi i kāna hana ulana pāpale lauhala.* Malu'ihi is **demonstrating** her *lauhala* hat weaving now.]

demonstration *hō'ike* (also means **show**). [*Ma ka pāka e nānā ana nā māka'ika'i i ka **hō'ike** hula.* It's at the park that the tourists will watch the hula **show**.]

dented *'ōpaha.* [***'Ōpaha** ke kini.* The tin can is **dented**.]

dentist *kauka niho.*

depend on *kauka'i.* [*Hiki ke **kauka'i** i kā kāu kaikamahine kāne?* Can you **depend on** your daughter's husband?]

deposit *waiho.*

depository *waihona.* (treasury = *waihona kālā*) (archives = *waihona palapala kahiko*)

depth *hohonu.* [*'Elua kapua'i ka **hohonu** o ke kai ma ka laupapa ma ke kai piha.* Two feet is the **depth** of the sea on the reef at high tide.]

deranged 1. *hehena.* 2. *kūpikipiki'ō.*

descend *iho.* [*E nauē kākou a **iho** ma uka a ke kai.* Let's all get a move on and **descend** from the mountains to the sea.]

descendant *mamo.* [*Nā **mamo** a Hāloa.* The **descendants** of Hāloa (first human, younger brother of the first taro of same name, according to ancient legend).]

describe *huliko'a.*

description *huliko'a.* [*'Auli'i kāna **huliko'a** i ko ka 'aihue helehelena.* His **description** of the thief's facial features is precise and clear.]

desert *'āina pānoa.* [*He **'āina pānoa** ko Ka'ū.* Ka'ū has a **desert**.]

desk *pākaukau.*

dessert *mea 'ono.* [*'Ono māua i ka **mea 'ono** kokoleka a me ka haupia, e ke kuene.* We're craving a chocolate **dessert** and *haupia* (coconut pudding), waitress.]

dessert

destroy *luku.* [*Ma 'Iao i **luku** 'ia ai ko Maui koa e ka na'i aupuni.* It was at 'Iao that Maui's soldiers were **destroyed** by the conqueror.]

detective *māka'ikiu.*

detergent *wai ho'oma'ema'e.* [*'O ka **wai ho'oma'ema'e** hea ka mea e wehe ana i ka lepo?* Which **detergent** is the one that will remove dirt?]

detest *ho'okae.* [*Minamina, **ho'okae** 'o ia i kona hoanoho.* It's too bad he **detests** his roommate.] (racial prejudice = *ho'okae 'ili*)

develop *ho'omōhala* (lit. to cause to bloom). [***Ho'omōhala** ha'awina nā kumu ma ka hālāwai.* Teachers **develop** curriculum at the meeting.]

devil *kepalō* (from English).

devotion *aloha.*

diabetes *mimikō.*

diameter *anawaena.* [*'A'ohe **anawaena** o ka huinakolu. Loa'a ke anawaena i ka pō'ai.* Triangles don't have **diameters**. Circles do.]

Diamond Head 1. Kaimana Hila (from English). 2. Lēʻahi.

diaper *kaiapa* (from English).

die 1. *hala* (also means **to pass by**). 2. *hāʻule* (also means **to fall down**). 3. *make*.

diet *hoʻēmi kino* (also means **to lose weight**). [*Inā ʻoe i hoʻoikaika kino, inā ua **hoʻēmi kino** pū*. If you had exercised, you would have **lost weight** as well.]

difficult *paʻakikī* (also means **hard**). [*ʻAʻole **paʻakikī** ka hāpai paona*. Lifting weights is not **difficult**.]

dig *ʻeli*. [*Makemake ka ʻīlio e **ʻeli** i ke one*. Dogs like to **dig** in sand.]

dinner *ʻaina ahiahi*.

direction 1. *ʻōlelo kuhikuhi* (instructions). [*Ke kūkulu ʻoe i ka mea pāʻani hou, e heluhelu mua i nā **ʻōlelo kuhikuhi**. Whenever you put together a new toy, first read the **directions**.] 2. *ʻaoʻao* (compass direction).

dirt *lepo*.

dirty *lepo*. [*E waiho i ko kāua mau lole **lepo** i ka mīkini holoi*. Leave our (your and my) **dirty** clothes in the washing machine.]

disaster *pōpilikia*. [*He **pōpilikia** maoli ka makani pāhili*. A hurricane is a real **disaster**.]

discard *kiloi* (also means **to throw away**). [*Mai **kiloi** aku i nā palapala kahiko!* Don't **discard** the old documents.]

discipline *aʻo ikaika*.

discover *ʻimi a loaʻa*. [*Ua **ʻimi a loaʻa** ʻo ia i kekahi lāʻau hou*. He **discovered** a new medicine.]

discuss *kūkākūkā*.

disease *maʻi*. [*He maʻi ahulau pōpilikia ka **maʻi** hana ei*. Sexually transmitted **diseases** are a disastrous epidemic.]

dish *pā*. [*Aia nā **pā** ma ka hakakau*. The dishes are on the shelf.] (plate lunch = *pā mea ʻai*)

dishwasher *mīkini holoi pā*.

disinfectant *wai hoʻomaʻemaʻe*.

disk *pā*. [*Loaʻa ka polokalamu lolouila hou ma ka **pā** hea?* Which **disk** has the new computer program on it?] (CD = *sēdē, cēdē*)

dismiss *hoʻokuʻu* (also means **to release, let go**). [*E **hoʻokuʻu** hikiwawe i kāu papa i kēia ʻauinalā*. **Dismiss** your class early this afternoon.]

display *hōʻike*.

distance *mamao*. [*ʻEhia mile ka **mamao** mai kou hale aku i kou keʻena hana?* How many miles is the **distance** from your house to your office?]

distant *mamao*.

distinguished *hanohano*. [***Hanohano** wale ʻoe, e Haleʻiwa Pāka*. You are so **distinguished**, Haleʻiwa Park. (song, "Haleʻiwa Pāka," by A. Nāmakelua)]

distribute *hoʻomāhelehele* (also means **to divide up**).

district 1. *moku*. [*Nui nā pali kai i ka **moku** o Hāmākua ma Hawaiʻi*. There are many ocean cliffs in the **district** of Hāmākua on Hawaiʻi.] 2. *ʻāpana*.

distrust *kānalua* (also means **doubt**).

distrustful *kānalua*. [***Kānalua** ka mea maʻi i ko ke kauka manaʻo*. The patient is **distrustful** of the doctor's opinion.]

ditch *ʻauwai* (also means **canal, sewer**). Note: *ʻAuwai* were man-made ditches used to divert water from streams into taro patches.

divide 1. *māhele* (share things). 2. *hoʻonaue* (math).

divorce *ʻoki male*. [*ʻAʻole i **ʻoki male** pinepine ko koʻu mau mākua hānauna*. My parents' generation didn't often get **divorced**.]

dizzy *pōniuniu*.

doctor *kauka*. [*Lōʻihi ke kali ʻana i ko ke **kauka** keʻena*. The wait in the **doctor**'s office is long.]

dog

dog *ʻīlio*. [*He aha ke ʻano o kāna **ʻīlio**? He* "poi dog" *kāna*. What kind of **dog** does he have? He has a "poi dog" (mixed breed).)]

doll *kiʻi pēpē*. [*ʻO wai kāu **kiʻi pēpē** Pāʻele?* What's the name of your African-American **doll**?]

dolphin *naiʻa*. [*Holo anei nā **naiʻa** me nā koholā i ka hoʻoilo?* Do **dolphins** swim with humpback whales in the rainy season?]

domesticated *laka* (also means **tame**). [*'Ano laka a i 'ole 'āhiu kāu pua'a?* Is your pig kind of **tame** or wild?]

donkey *'ēkake*. [*'Āhiu nā 'ēkake ma Kona.* The **donkeys** in Kona are wild.]

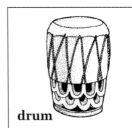
donkey

don't *mai* before verb. [*Mai hana pēlā!* **Don't** do that!]

door *puka*. [*E pani i ka puka, ke 'olu'olu.* Close the **door**, please.]

dormitory *hale noho haumāna*.

dorsal fin *kualā*. [*Kainō 'o ka nai'a ka i holo i ko'u 'ike 'ana i ke kualā.* I thought (but I was mistaken) that a dolphin was the thing that was swimming by when I saw the **dorsal fin**.]

down *iho* after verb. [*Ua noho iho ke kupuna.* The grandparent sat **down**.]

downtown *kaona* (from English).

drag *kaualakō*. [*Kaualakō ka mea ulana lauhala i nā lau i piha i ke kōkala.* The *lauhala* weaver **drags** the leaves full of thorns.]

dragon *mo'o*.

dragonfly *pinao* (also means **damselfly**). [*Nui nā 'ano pinao me nā waiho'olu'u nani ma Hawai'i.* There are many kinds of **dragonflies** with lovely colors in Hawai'i.]

draw picture *kaha ki'i*.

dream *moe 'uhane*. [*He hō'ailona ka moe 'uhane i nā Hawai'i.* **Dreams** have symbolic meaning for Hawaiians.]

drenched *pulu* (also means **soaked with rain**). [*Pulu nō nā keiki i ka ua Kanilehua o Hilo.* The children are really **drenched** due to Hilo's Kanilehua rain.]

dress *lole* (also means **cloth, clothes**). [*He lole 'olu'olu ka lole palaka. Palaka* **clothes** are comfortable **clothes**.] (*Palaka* is a checkered cotton cloth previously used for work clothes on sugar plantations.)

drink *[n] mea inu. [v] inu.* [*Ke loa'a 'oe i ka pu'u 'eha, e inu i ka mea inu wela me ka meli.* If you get a sore throat, **drink** a hot **drink** with honey.]

drinking glass *kī'aha* (also means **measuring cup**).

drip *kulu*. [*Kulu ka pakapaka ua mai ka 'ōhi'a.* Raindrops **drip** from the *'ōhi'a* tree.] (tears fall = *kulu waimaka*)

drive *kalaiwa*. [*'Oiai 'o ia e kalaiwa ana, ua kulu kona waimaka.* While she was **driving**, her tears fell.]

droop *luhe*. [*Luhe i lalo ke po'o o ke kanaka maka hiamoe.* The head of the sleepy person **droops** down.]

drop of rain *paka ua*. [*Li'ili'i nā paka ua o ka ua Kilihune.* The **raindrops** of the Kilihune rain are small.]

drown *piholo* (also means **to sink down**). [*Ua piholo 'o Hala'ea i kona 'ānunu.* Hala'ea **drowned** because of greediness. (traditional story of greedy *ali'i* whose people heaped his canoe with fish until it sank)]

drowsy *maka hiamoe*. [*Ua maka hiamoe ka 'ōpio i holo wāwae i ka heihei.* The young person who ran in the race was **drowsy**.]

drug *lā'au 'ino*.

drum *[n] pahu*. [*Ho'opa'a ke kumu hula i ka pahu.* The hula teacher beats the **drum**.] (to drum = 1. *ho'opa'a* 2. *ho'okani pahu*)

drum

drunk *'ona* (also means **"high" on drugs**). [*E nānā! Kūlanalana ke kanaka 'ona.* Look! The **drunk** person is staggering.]

dry *[v] ho'omalo'o*. [*E ho'omalo'o i nā kāwele i ka mīkini ho'omalo'o.* **Dry** the towels in the dryer.] *[adj] malo'o*. [*Ulu ke kiawe ma ka 'āina malo'o.* Kiawe trees grow on **dry** land.] (to dry in the sun, e.g. fish salted and dried in the sun to preserve them = *kaula'i*)

dryer *mīkini ho'omalo'o*.

dual *pālua*.

duet *leokū pālua*. [*Hīmeni leokū pālua nā ipo.* The sweethearts sing a **duet** together.]

dull (not interesting) 1. *manakā*. 2. *pāmalō*. 3. *pākūā*.

dull (not sharp) *kūmūmū.* [*E hoʻokala i ka pahi* **kūmūmū** *ma mua o ka ʻokiʻoki ʻana aku i nā lau ʻai.* Sharpen the **dull** knives before chopping up the vegetables.]

dumb 1. *leo paʻa* (mute). 2. *mū* (mute). 3. *hūpō* (stupid).

dump *[n] kahua waiho ʻōpala.* [*Nāu e halihali i nā lau popopo i ke* **kahua waiho ʻōpala**. You are the one to haul the rotten leaves to the **dump**.]

dust *ʻehu lepo.* (sea foam = *ʻehu kai*). [*Nui ka* **ʻehu lepo** *ma ke alanui mahikō.* There's lots of **dust** on the plantation road.] (syn. *ehu*)

dusty *ʻehu* (also means **pollen, dark red Hawaiian hair, spray, foam**).

duty *kuleana* (also means **rights, responsibility**).

dye *waihoʻoluʻu* (also means **color**). [*ʻO ke ʻōlena kekahi mea kanu* **waihoʻoluʻu**. The *ʻōlena* is a **dye** plant.] (Many plants were used to dye or to add fragrance to tapa cloth.) (to dye = *hoʻoluʻu*)

ear *pepeiao.*

early *hikiwawe.* [***Hikiwawe** ka hō'ea 'ana o ka wa'a mua ma ka heihei.* The first canoe in the race arrived **early.**]

early morning *kakahiaka nui.* [*Ala mau ka lawai'a i ke **kakahiaka nui**.* The fisherman always gets up in the **early morning.**]

earn *loa'a.* (Note: *Loa'a* has many other meanings.)

Earth *honua.* [*E mālama i ka **honua**.* Take care of the **Earth.**]

Earth

earthquake *ōla'i.* [*Nāueue ka honua i ke **ōla'i**.* The earth shakes due to the **earthquake.**]

east *hikina.* [*Puka ka lā ma ka **hikina**.* The sun emerges in the **east.** (chant)]

Easter *Lā Pākoa.* [*Ho'olu'u a ho'onani nā keiki i nā hua moa no ka **lā Pākoa**.* The children dye and decorate eggs for **Easter.**]

easy *ma'alahi.* [***Ma'alahi** ka unahi a me ka ho'oma'ema'e i'a.* Scaling and cleaning fish is **easy.**]

eat *'ai.* [*Pōloli mau ka 'ōpio a **'ai** pinepine 'o ia.* The young person is always hungry and **eats** often.]

echo 1. *wawā.* 2. *kūpina'i* (also means **to mourn**).

edge 1. *ka'e.* [*Ma **ka'e** kahawai māua i pikiniki ai.* It was at the **edge** of the stream that we picnicked.] 2. *kapa.* [***kapa** wai lana mālie,* the **edge** of the slow-moving water] 3. *lihi.*

educate *ho'ona'auao.* [*Na wai e **ho'ona'auao** i nā keiki Hawai'i?* Who should **educate** Hawaiian children?]

educated *na'auao* (also means **enlightened, wise**).

education *ho'ona'auao.*

eel *puhi.*

effort *ho'ā'o* (also means **experiment, to try**).

egg 1. *hua* (refers to any offspring or product of animal, plant, human; also means **to reproduce**). 2. *hua moa* (egg of chicken). (fruit = *hua 'ai*)

elbow *ku'e lima.*

elder *kupuna.*

eldest *hiapo.* [*'O kou kaikua'ana ka **hiapo**, e Kawaiola?* Is your older sibling the **eldest,** Kawaiola?]

elect *koho pāloka* (from English "ballot"). [*Mai poina e **koho pāloka** i ka moho e kāko'o 'ana i ka ho'ona'auao.* Don't forget to **elect** the candidate who will support education.]

election *koho pāloka.* (election day = *lā koho pāloka*)

electric *uila.* [*He mīkini **uila** ko Tūtū no ka wa'u 'ana i ka niu.* Grandpa (Grandma) has an **electric** machine for grating coconut.]

electrical outlet *puka uila.* [*Pono e pāpā i nā keiki e ho'opā i ka **puka uila**.* (You) have to forbid children to touch **electrical outlets.**]

elephant

electricity *uila.*

elementary school *kula ha'aha'a.*

elephant *'elepani* (from English).

embarrassed *hilahila* (also means **ashamed**).

[**Hilahila** *kona mau kūpuna e komo i loko o ke kula ha'aha'a.* His grandparents are **ashamed** to enter the elementary school.]

emergency 1. *ulia pōpilikia.* 2. *pilikia kūhewa.*

employ 1. *ho'ohana* (also means **to use**). 2. *hai* (also means **to hire**; probably from English "hire"; original Hawaiian word means offering, sacrifice, to sacrifice, to follow).

empty *hakahaka* (also means **blank**). [**Hakahaka** *nā hakakau o ka hale kanaka 'ole.* The shelves of the house without people in it are **empty**.]

enchanted by *ho'ohihi.* [**Ho'ohihi** *ka mana'o i ka nani o Nu'uanu.* My thoughts are **enchanted by** the beauty of Nu'uanu.]

encourage *ho'opaipai.* [*Pono kākou e* **ho'opaipai** *kekahi i kekahi e mālama i ke ola kino.* We have to **encourage** each other to take care of our health.]

encouragement *ho'opaipai.*

end [*n*] 1. *panina.* [*I ka* **panina** *o ka hālāwai, pule lākou.* At the **end** of the meeting, they pray.] 2. *pau 'ana.* [*v*] *ho'opau* (also means **to finish**). [*Ke* **ho'opau** *ka mekanika i ka ho'oponopono i ko kāua ka'a, e uku iā ia.* When the mechanic **finishes** fixing our (your and my) car, pay him.]

endangered *'ane make loa* (*lit.* almost extinct). [**'Ane make loa** *ka hapanui o nā manu 'ōiwi o Hawai'i.* Most of the native birds of Hawai'i are **endangered**.]

enemy 1. *hoa paio.* 2. *'enemi* (from English).

energetic *'eleu.*

engineer *wilikī.* [*Kūkulu ka* **wilikī** *i ka uapo.* **Engineers** build bridges.]

English (language) 1. *'ōlelo haole.* 2. *'ōlelo Pelekane.* [*He 'ōlelo laha ka* **'ōlelo Pelekane**. **English** is a common language.]

enjoy 1. *luana* (also means **to relax, socialize**). 2. *ho'onanea* (also means **enjoyable**).

enlighten *ho'omālamalama.*

enlightened *na'auao* (also means **educated, wise, wisdom**).

enough *lawa.* [*Ua kui a* **lawa** *ko'u lei.* (**Enough** flowers have been strung so that my *lei* is completed. (song, "Wehiwehi

'Oe," by S. Kalama)]

enroll *kākau inoa* (sometimes shortened to *kau inoa*). [*Inā no'ono'o 'oukou e koho pāloka, pono 'oukou e* **kākau inoa** *ma mua.* If you all are thinking about voting, you have to **enroll** beforehand.]

entangled (in problems) *hihia.*

enter *komo.* [*"E* **komo** *mai," i heahea aku ka mea ho'okipa.* "**Enter**," the hostess called out.]

entertain *ho'okipa* (also means **to welcome, extend hospitality**). [*E* **ho'okipa** *ana mākou i nā malihini mai Aotearoa mai.* We (three or more, not you) will welcome and **entertain** the guests from New Zealand.]

enthusiasm *ohohia* (also means **delight**). [*Nui ke* **ohohia** *o nā kelamoku hou.* New sailors have great **enthusiasm**.]

envelope *wahī leka.* [*Hiki iā ia ke ku'ai mai i* **wahī leka** *ma ka hale leka?* Can he buy an **envelope** at the post office?]

envelope

epidemic *ma'i ahulau.*

equal 1. *like.* 2. *like nō a like.*

era *wā* (also means **time period**). [*I ka* **wā** *a Kuali'i i noho ali'i ai, ua hui pū 'ia nā mokupuni a pau.* At the **time** that Kuali'i was ruling, all the islands were united.]

erase *holoi* (also means **to wash something**).

eraser *mea holoi.*

erect *kū* (also means **upright**). [**Kū** *kekahi kumuniu, hina kekahi.* Some coconut trees are **erect**, others fall over.]

err *hewa.*

error *hewa* (also means **mistake, guilt, sin, guilty, mistaken**). [*'A'ohe āna* **hewa** *ma ka hō'ike kalaiwa ka'a.* He had no **errors** on the driver's license exam.]

erupt *hū ka pele.* [*Ua* **hū ka pele** *ma Kalapana a uhi 'ia 'o Kaimū.* The lava **erupted** at Kalapana until Kaimū beach was covered.]

eruption *ka hū 'ana o ka pele.*

escape *pākele.* [*Ma ka mahina 'o Iune e*

pākele *ai nā keiki mai ke kula aku.* It is in the month of June that children **escape** from school.]

establish *hoʻokumu.* [*Na kā Pauahi kāne i* ***hoʻokumu*** *i ka Hale Hōʻikeʻike ʻo Pīhopa.* It was Pauahi's husband who **established** Bishop Museum.]

estimate *koho* (also means **guess, choice, to choose**).

Europe *ʻEuropa.*

evening *ahiahi.* [*Ke pāʻani pepa nei mākou ma kēia* ***ahiahi.*** We all (not you) are playing cards this **evening.**]

event *hanana.*

ever *mau.* (forever = *a mau loa aku*)

every *a pau.* [*Mahalo iā ʻoukou* ***a pau!*** Thanks to **every** one of you!]

exactly *pono* (also means **directly**, many other meanings). [*E kuhi* ***pono*** *ana māua i ka haʻina!* We (two, not you) are going to point **exactly** to the answer!] [*ʻO wai kēnā ma hope* ***pono*** *ou?* Who is that **directly** behind you?]

exam *hōʻike.*

example 1. *hoʻohālike.* 2. *laʻana.*

excel *poʻokela* (also means **outstanding, champion**).

excellence *maikaʻi loa.*

excellent 1. *kilohana.* 2. *maikaʻi loa.*

except *koe wale.* [*Ua piha ko kāu moʻopuna kāne hauʻoli i kona pāʻina lā hānau,* ***koe wale*** *kēia, ʻeha kona puʻu i kona uā mau ʻana.* Your grandson was completely happy at his birthday party, **except** for this, his throat was sore due to his constant shouting.]

excessive *pākela.* (gluttony = *pākela ʻai*) (heavy drinker, to drink to excess = *pākela inu*)

excited, exciting 1. *pīhoihoi.* [***Pīhoihoi*** *ʻo ia i kāna hana hou.* She's **excited** by her new job.] 2. *ʻeuʻeu.*

excrement 1. *kūkae.* 2. *lepo* (also means **dirt,** used in place of *kūkae* to be more polite).

excuse 1. *kala* (also means **forgive**). [*E* ***kala*** *mai iaʻu!* **Excuse** me, I'm sorry! (Response is *Ua huikala ʻia* or *kala ʻia.* You are forgiven.)] 2. *huikala* (also means **forgive**). 3. *kumu* (also means **reason, basis**).

exercise *hoʻoikaika kino.* [*ʻOiai* ***hoʻoikaika kino*** *koʻu makuahine a piula, ʻaʻole ʻo ia e hoʻēmi kino nei.* Although my mother **exercises** until she's exhausted, she's not losing weight.]

exercise

exhausted 1. *paupauaho* (also means **out of breath**). 2. *piula.*

exhibit *hōʻike.*

exit [n] *puka.* [v] *puka* (also means **to emerge**). [*Ua* ***puka*** *aku nā mea hanohano mai ka* ***puka*** *ma ka ʻaoʻao hema.* The distinguished people **emerged** from the **exit** on the left.]

expel *kipaku.* [*Ma muli o ko ke kanaka waha wale* ***kipaku*** *ʻia ʻana mai ka hale inu aku, ua kuʻi ʻo ia i ke kiaʻi.* Due to the loudmouth's being **expelled** from the bar, she hit the guard.]

expensive *pipiʻi.* [***Pipiʻi*** *ke ʻeke poi ma ka hale kūʻai mea ʻai.* A bag of poi at the grocery store is **expensive.**]

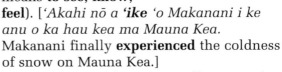
expensive
· $5000.⁰⁰

experience *ʻike* (also means **to see, know, feel**). [*ʻAkahi nō a* ***ʻike*** *ʻo Makanani i ke anu o ka hau kea ma Mauna Kea.* Makanani finally **experienced** the coldness of snow on Mauna Kea.]

experiment *hoʻāʻo* (also means **effort, to try**). [*Ke holopono nei ka* ***hoʻāʻo.*** The **experiment** is succeeding.]

expert 1. *kahuna.* 2. *loea.* [*He* ***loea*** *hula ʻo Lokalia Montgomery.* Lokalia Montgomery was a hula **expert.**] 3. *lehia.*

explain *wehewehe.* [*E* ***wehewehe*** *mai i ko ʻoukou mau manaʻo.* **Explain** your (all) opinions to me.]

explode 1. *hoʻopahū* (to cause an explosion). [*Na wai i* ***hoʻopahū*** *i nā mea hoʻopahū ma Kahoʻolawe?* Who **exploded** the bombs on Kahoʻolawe?] 2. *pahū.* 3. *pohā.*

explore *ʻimi loa.*

explosion *halulu* (also means **to roar, rumble**).

extend 1. *hoʻoloa* (to prolong, lengthen, stretch). 2. *kīkoʻo* (to extend hands, draw money from bank, stretch) (to stick out tongue = *kīkoʻo alelo*)

extinct *make loa.* [*E* ***make loa*** *ana ka ʻalalā a me ke kāhuli?* Will the Hawaiian crow and the Hawaiian tree snail become **extinct**?]

extinguish *hoʻopio* (also means **to turn off electrical appliance**). [*Ma hope o kāu pāʻani, e* ***hoʻopio*** *i ka lolouila.* After your game, **turn off** the computer.]

extinguished *pio* (also means **turned off**). [*Ua* ***pio*** *ke ahi ma ka hale.* The fire in the house is **extinguished**.]

extremity 1. *welelau* (tip of leaf). 2. *wēlau.* 3. *wēkiu* (mountain summit).

eye *maka* (also means **face, fresh, raw, beloved**).

eyeball *ʻōnohi maka.*

eyebrow *kuʻe maka.*

eyelash *lihilihi.*

face *maka* (also means **eye, fresh, raw, beloved**).

face powder *pauka maka*.

faint *maʻule*. [*Inā **maʻule** ke kanaka maʻi, he aha kā ke kahu maʻi hana?* If the patient **faints**, what does the nurse do?]

fair (just) *kaulike*. [*Pono e hoʻoponopono i ka hana a ke keʻena ʻāina hoʻopulapula a **kaulike**.* The work of the Hawaiian Homes office has to be fixed until it is **fair**.]

fall *hāʻule*. [*Ma hope o ko ka pēpē **hāʻule** ʻana iho, ua kū aʻe ʻo ia.* After the baby **fell** down, she stood up again.]

fallen over *hina*.

false *hoʻopunipuni* (also means **to lie**).

fame *kaulana*.

familiar *kamaʻāina*. [***Kamaʻāina** paha ʻoe i ke kahua hānai pipi ʻo ʻUlupalakua?* Are you perhaps **familiar** with ʻUlupalakua ranch?]

family *ʻohana*.

famous *kaulana*. [*Aia nō a **kaulana** ko kona makuahine inoa, pau ko māua pili.* As soon as his mother's name becomes **famous**, our (his and my) closeness is over.]

fan

fan *peʻahi*. (wave hand = *peʻahi lima*).

far *mamao*. [***Mamao** ke kahakai ʻo Lumahaʻi mai ʻAnini aku?* Is Lumahaʻi beach **far** from ʻAnini?]

farm *mahiʻai* (also means **farmer**).

fast 1. *wikiwiki*. 2. *ʻāwīwī*.

fasten *hoʻopaʻa*. [***Hoʻopaʻa** ka paniolo i ke kaula hao ma ka ʻīpuka.* The cowboy **fastened** the chain on the gate.]

fat [n] *aila*. [*He mea ʻai **aila** iki ko ka hale ʻaina?* Does the restaurant have low-**fat** food?] [adj] *momona* (also means **sweet-** or **rich-tasting, fertile land**). [*Hō ka **momona** o kēia kūlolo!* Boy, how **sweet-tasting** this *kūlolo* (traditional dessert made with taro, sugar, coconut milk steamed in *imu*) is!]

father *makua kāne*. [*Haʻaheo ka **makua kāne** i kāna keiki.* The **father** is proud of his son.]

fault *hewa*.

favor 1. *hana lokomaikaʻi* (to do a favor). 2. *makemake* (to prefer).

favorite *punahele*. [*ʻO "Sānoe" kaʻu mele **punahele**.* "Sānoe" is my **favorite**. (song composed by Liliʻuokalani)]

feather cloak *ʻahuʻula*. [*He hōʻailona ka **ʻahuʻula** no ke aliʻi.* The **feather cloak** is a symbol of noble rank.]

fear *makaʻu*. [*Mai **makaʻu** i ka lanalana.* Don't **be afraid of** spiders.]

February *Pepeluali* (from English).

federal *pekelala* (from English).

feed *hānai* (refers to feeding animals or people, also means **to raise a child**, including the traditional Hawaiian "adoption").

feel 1. *hāhā* (an object). [***Hāhā** ke kauka i ka puʻu ma ko Kunihi ʻāʻī.* The doctor **feels** the lump on Kunihi's neck.] 2. *ʻike* (an emotion). Note: There are many specific words that deal with feelings, which are often expressed poetically.

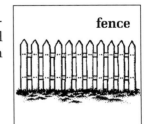

fence

fence *pā* (also means **any enclosed area**).

(hula mound = *pā hula*) (house lot, yard = *pā hale*)

fern *palapalai* (1. fragrant fern often used by hula dancers for leis, offerings 2. general name for all ferns).

festival *hoʻolauleʻa.*

few *kakaʻikahi.* [***Kakaʻikahi*** *nā wāhine kuku kapa o ke au nei.* There are **few** women beating tapa (tapa makers) these days.]

field 1. *mahina.* 2. *kīhāpai* (cultivated field). 3. *kahua.* (playing field = *kahua pāʻani*) (school campus = *kahua kula*)

fight *hakakā.* [*E Pāpā, ke **hakakā** nei kou mau kaikaina ma ʻō aku o ka pā!* Daddy, your younger brothers are **fighting** on the other side of the fence!]

fight

Fiji *Pīkī.*

Filipino *Pilipino.*

fill *hoʻopihapiha.* [*E **hoʻopihapiha** i nā haka- haka.* **Fill** in the blanks.]

fin (fish) *pewa.*

final *hope loa.* [*ʻO kāna hoʻāʻo **hope loa** kēia.* This is his **final** try.]

find *loaʻa.* [*Ua kaha ke kuke i ka iʻa a ua **loaʻa** kekahi komo lima kaimana iā ia.* The cook sliced open the fish and **found** a diamond ring.]

fine 1. *hunehune* (minute). [***Hunehune*** *ka ʻehu o ka wailele.* The waterfall's spray is very **fine**.] 2. *maikaʻi* (well).

finger *manamanalima.*

fingernail *mikiʻao* (also means **claw**). [*Pohole ko ka mea hoʻopaʻahao **mikiʻao** i kona pakele ʻana.* The prisoner's **fingernail** was bruised in her escape.]

finish *hoʻopau* (also means **put an end to, cancel**).

finished *pau* (also means **destroyed**). [*Ua **pau** ka hana ma ka hola ʻehā o ka ʻauinalā.* Work was **finished** at four p.m.] Note: idiomatic expressions such as *pau ka hana* (work is finished) and *pau ka papa* (class is finished) are common. [*Ua **pau** ka hana* ma ka hola ʻehā o ka ʻauinalā. **Work was finished** at four p.m.] The fol-

lowing example shows the more usual meaning: [*Ua **pau** nā hale i ke ahi.* The houses were **destroyed** in the fire.] *Pau au i ka papa* means "I am destroyed by the class" and not "I have finished the class."

fire *ahi.*

firefighter *kinai ahi.*

fireplace *kapuahi.*

fireworks *kao lele* (also means **rocket**). (syn. *ahikao*)

fire

first *mua* (also means **in front, before**). [*Ua holoi **mua** ke kauka holoholona i kona mau lima a laila ua hamohamo i kaʻu pōpoki.* The vet **first** washed his hands and then he petted my cat.]

first birthday party *pāʻina lā hānau mua.*

first time *makamua.* [*ʻO ka **makamua** kēlā ʻo ko lāua ʻike i ka ʻeha o ke aloha.* That was the very **first time** they (two) knew the pain of love.]

fish [n] *iʻa.* [*Aloha ka manini me ka pōpolo, he **iʻa** noho ia i ka laupapa,* Love for the *manini* and the *pōpolo* **fishes** that live on the reef (song, "Aloha ka Manini," by L. Kauwe)] [v] *lawaiʻa.*

fisherman *lawaiʻa.* [*Ua kāmākoi ka **lawaiʻa** a lawa nā iʻa i loaʻa iā ia.* The **fisherman** fished with a pole until he had enough fish.]

fishing pole *kāmākoi.*

fix *hoʻoponopono.*

flag *hae.* [*Ua welo ka **hae** kalaunu ma luna o ka hale aliʻi.* The crown **flag** waved above the palace.]

flashlight *kukui paʻa lima.*

flat *pālahalaha.* [*ʻAʻole **pālahalaha** kēia kahua kolepa ma uka nei.* This golf course here in the uplands isn't **flat**.]

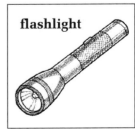
flashlight

flea *ʻuku.* [*Loaʻa ka **ʻuku** i ka moena?* Are there **fleas** in the carpet?]

fledgling *pūnua.* [*He **pūnua** ko ka ʻalalā?*

Does the *'alalā* have a **fledgling**?]

flight *lele.* [*Mamao ka* **lele** *o ke kōlea.* The plover's **flight** is a long distance.]

flight attendant *kuene.*

float *lana.* [*nā wa'a kālua* **lana** *mālie,* the double-hulled canoes **floating** calmly (song, "Song of Hōkūle'a," by K. Tauā and R. Cazimero)]

flood *kai a ka Hinali'i.*

floor *papahele.* [*Aia nā wikiō Hawai'i ma ka* **papahele** *hea?* Which **floor** are the Hawaiian videos on?] (first floor = *papahele mua*)

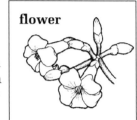

flower

flower *pua* (also means **descendant, child**). [*'A'ala ka hapanui o nā* **pua** *lei.* Most of the *lei* **flowers** are fragrant.]

flush (toilet) *ho'oholo i ka wai* (also means **to run the water**). [*Mai poina e* **ho'oholo i ka wai**! Don't forget to **flush the toilet**!]

flute *puhi 'ohe.* (Hawaiian nose flute = *'ohe hano ihu*)

flutter *welo.* [**Welo** *ka hae i ka makani.* The flag **flutters** in the wind.]

fly *lele* (also means **to jump**). [**Lele** *a'e ka mālolo.* The *mālolo* (flying fish) fish **jumps**.]

fly (something) *ho'olele.* [**Ho'olele** *ka pailaka i ka mokulele.* The pilot **flies** the plane.] (fly a kite = *ho'olele lupe*)

foam 1. *'ehu* (also means **spray, mist**). 2. *hu'a* (also means **bubble, froth**).

fold 1. *pelu* (to fold paper). 2. *'ope'ope* (to fold cloth or clothes).

follow *hahai.* [*Mai* **hahai** *mai ia'u! E* **hahai** *aku iā ia!* Don't **follow** me! **Follow** her!]

food *mea 'ai.* [*Ke ho'omākaukau mākou i ka lū'au, nui nā 'ano* **mea 'ai** *Hawai'i like 'ole.* When we (us all, not you) prepare a *lū'au*, there are all different kinds of Hawaiian **food**.]

foolish 1. *hūpō* (also means **stupid**).

foot *wāwae* (also means **leg**).

foot (measurement) *kapua'i.* [*'Ehia* **kapua'i** *ke ākea o ko 'oukou lumi ho'okipa?* How many **feet** wide is your (all) living room?]

football *pōpeku.* [*'O ke kime hea ke kime i*

lanakila i ka pā'ani **pōpeku** *i ka pō nei?* Which team won the **football** game last night?]

forbid 1. *ho'okapu.* 2. *pāpā.* Note: *Ho'okapu* means to restrict access to a place or object, implying its use is reserved for special people or activities. *Pāpā* means to prohibit an activity, such as smoking or a hula dancer's cutting her hair.

forbidden 1. *kapu* (also means **restricted, reserved**). [*He wahi* **kapu** *ka heiau.* The religious site is a **restricted** area.] 2. *pāpā 'ia.* [*Ua* **pāpā 'ia** *ke kuha 'ana i loko.* Spitting indoors is **forbidden**.]

forehead *lae* (also means **peninsula, spit of land surrounded by ocean**). [*Kahe ka hou o ka* **lae**. Sweat pours off the **forehead**.]

foreign *'ē* (also means **strange**). [*nā 'āina* **'ē**, the **foreign** lands, not Hawai'i] 2. *malihini* (used to denote someone or something not from Hawai'i).

foreign lands *nā 'āina 'ē.*

foreigner *malihini* (also means **newcomer, guest**).

forest *ulu lā'au.* [*Laha 'ole ka* **ulu lā'au** *koa i kēia mau lā. Koa* **forests** are rare these days.]

forest

foretell *wānana.*

forever *a mau loa aku.*

forget *poina.* [*Ua* **poina** *'oe e ho'opa'a manawa me ke kauka niho?* Did you **forget** to make an appointment with the dentist?]

forgive 1. *kala.* [*E* **kala** *mai ia'u!* **Forgive** me, I'm sorry!] 2. *huikala.*

fork *'ō.* [*Aia ke* **'ō** *ma lalo o ke puna?* Is the **fork** under the spoon?]

fort *pāpū.*

fraction *hakina.* [*He hana pohihihi ka ho'onaue 'ana i nā* **hakina**. Dividing with **fractions** is confusing.]

fracture *haki* (also means **to break**). [*E* **haki** *'ia ana paha ko ka 'ālapa manamana lima i ka pā'ani pōpa'i lima.* The athlete's finger might be **broken** in the volleyball game.]

fragrant *'a'ala.* [*Nani pua 'a'ala onaona i ka ihu e moani nei.* Beautiful is the **sweet-smelling** flower whose attractive scent is borne to me on the breeze (song, "Kamalani 'o Keaukaha," by L. Machado)]

France Palani (also means **French, Frances, Frank**).

free 1. *manuahi* (no charge). [*Manuahi nā manakō i hā'ule i lalo.* The mangoes that fell down are **free**.] 2. *ka'awale* (not in use). [*He manawa ka'awale kou ma ka hopenapule?* Do you have **free** time on the weekend?] 3. *noa* (free from *kapu*, indicating end of imposed period of *kapu* restrictions).

freedom *kū'oko'a* (also means **independence, sovereignty**).

fresh *maka* (also means **raw**). [*'Ai nā Hawai'i i ka i'a maka a me ka limu maka.* Hawaiians eat **raw** fish and **fresh** seaweed.]

friend *hoaaloha.* [*He hoaaloha maika'i 'oe na'u.* You are a good **friend** to me.]

friend

frog *poloka.* [*He leo ha'aha'a ko ka poloka.* **Frogs** have low (bass) voices.]

front *mua.* (in front of, before = *ma mua o*) [*E komo kāua i ke kāma'a puti ma mua o ka pi'i kuahiwi 'ana ma Mauna Loa.* Let's put on boots **before** hiking on Mauna Loa.]

fruit *hua 'ai.*

fruit juice *wai hua 'ai.*

frustrated *uluhua.* [*'A'ole i uluhua iki kēia kaikamahine i kona a'o 'ana ma ka lolouila.* This girl isn't even a little **frustrated** when she learns on the computer.]

fry *palai* (from English). [*'Ono ka 'ōpelu i palai 'ia.* The *'ōpelu* fish that was **fried** is delicious!]

fulfill (command or desire) *ho'okō.* [*'A'ole na ke aupuni e ho'okō i ko Hawai'i 'i'ini e mālama i ka 'āina.* It is not the government that will **fulfill** Hawai'i's people's desire to protect the land.]

full 1. *piha.* [*Piha ka pahu hau i nā pala-palai.* The icebox (refrigerator) is **full** of ferns.] 2. *mā'ona* (refers to someone who has just eaten).

fun *le'ale'a* (refers to all kinds of joyous activities, including sex).

funeral *ho'olewa.*

fur *huluhulu* (also refers to **body hair** as opposed to *lauoho*, hair on head).

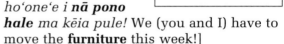

fur

furniture *nā pono hale.* [*Pono kāua e ho'one'e i nā pono hale ma kēia pule!* We (you and I) have to move the **furniture** this week!]

future *ma kēia mua aku.* [*E ho'omāhuahua a'e ana nā kānaka 'ōlelo Hawai'i ma kēia mua aku.* The number of people who speak Hawaiian will greatly increase in the **future**.]

fuzzy *weuweu.* [*Lō'ihi ko ka pōpoki keiki huluhulu a weuweu maoli ia.* The kitten's fur is long and it is truly **fuzzy**.]

gain *[n]* 1. *loaʻa.* [*He **loaʻa** liʻiliʻi ka uku pāneʻe ma ka panakō.* The interest at the bank is a small **gain.**] 2. *puka.*

gallon *kālani* (from English).

gamble *piliwaiwai.* [*Piliwaiwai nā wāhine Pākē e pāʻani ana i ka Mah-Jongg.* The Chinese women who are playing Mah-Jongg **gamble.**]

game *[n] pāʻani. [v] pāʻani* (to play a game, sport). [*Pāʻani kāua i ka **pāʻani** kahiko i kapa ʻia ʻo kōnane.* Let's **play** the ancient **game** called *kōnane* (like checkers).]

garage *hale kaʻa.*

garbage *ʻōpala.* [*Pono kākou e ʻohi i ka **ʻōpala** ma kapa alanui.* We must gather up the **garbage** from the side of the road.]

garbage can *kini ʻōpala.*

garbageperson *kanaka halihali ʻōpala.*

garden 1. *māla.* [*kou mau **māla** pua nani ē,* your beautiful flower **gardens** (song, "Hawaiʻi Aloha," by L. Lyons)] 2. *kīhāpai* (cultivated field). 3. *māla pua* (flower). 4. *māla ʻai* (vegetable).

garden

gas *ea* (also means **life force, sovereignty,** many other meanings).

gasoline *kakalina.* [*ʻEhia kālā ke kumu kūʻai o ke **kakalina** ma Kohala?* What is the price of **gasoline** in Kohala?]

gate *ʻīpuka.*

gather *ʻohi.*

gecko *moʻo* (also means any **reptile, succession or lineage**).

gecko

genealogy *moʻokūʻauhau.* [*Ma o kona **moʻokūʻauhau** i hōʻike aʻe ai ke aliʻi i kona kūlana aliʻi.* It was through his **genealogy** that a noble revealed his chiefly status.]

general *laulā* (also means **broad, widespread**). [*He aha ka manaʻo **laulā?*** What's the **general** idea?]

generation *hanauna.* (auntie = *makuahine hanauna*) (nephew = *keiki kāne hanauna*)

generous *lokomaikaʻi.* [*Nui ko ko Nihipali Tutukāne **lokomaikaʻi.*** Nihipali's grandpa is very **generous.**]

genesis *kinohi* (also means **origin, beginning**). [*Aia ka moʻolelo no Adamu me ʻEwa ma ka puke ʻo **Kinohi** ma ka Paipala.* The story about Adam and Eve is in the book of **Genesis** in the Bible.]

genitals *maʻi.* [*he mele **maʻi** no Kalākaua,* a song praising Kalākaua's **genitals** (*Mele maʻi* are traditional at the end of a hula performance, as a chief gave life to his entire nation)]

gentle *akahai.* [*He poʻe **akahai** maoli nō nā Hawaiʻi.* Hawaiians are a truly **gentle** people.]

genuine 1. *maoli.* 2. *maoli nō.* [*He poʻoleka aupuni Hawaiʻi **maoli** kāu poʻoleka i kūʻai mai ai?* Is the stamp you bought a **genuine** Hawaiian kingdom stamp?]

germ *mū* (also means **insect**).

German *Kelemania.*

Germany *Kelemania.*

gesture *kuhi.* [*Kuhi ka lima, hele ka maka.* Where the hands **gesture,** the eyes follow. (*ʻōlelo noʻeau* stating a rule in hula)]

get *loaʻa* (also means **to find, discover, receive,** many other meanings).

ghost 1. *lapu.* 2. *akua.* 3. *'uhane.* [*Ka makua, ke keiki a me ka **'uhane** hemolele,* Father, Son and Holy **Ghost** (prayer)]

gift *makana.*

gill *pihapiha.*

ginger *'awapuhi.*

gird *pū'ali* (also means **grooved, compressed in middle, to compress, warrior**).

girl *kaikamahine.* pl. *kaikamāhine.*

give *hā'awi.* [*Aia nā makana i **hā'awi** 'ia aku e nā kaikamāhine ma luna o ke pākaukau.* The gifts which were **given** away by the girls are on top of the table.]

give birth *hānau.* [*Āhea ana kou kaikuahine e **hānau** ai, e ke kāne?* When will your sister **give birth**, mister?] (to be born = *hānau 'ia*) [*Aia i hea i **hānau** 'ia ai kou kupuna kāne?* Where was your grandfather **born**?]

glad *hau'oli.*

glass 1. *aniani* (material). 2. *kī'aha* (drinking glass).

glasses (eyeglasses) 1. *makaaniani.* 2. *makaaniani pale lā* (sunglasses).

glad

glide *kīkaha.* [***Kīkaha** ka 'iwa, he lā mālie.* ('ōlelo no'eau) The *'iwa* bird glides on the wind, it's a calm day.]

gloomy 1. *kaumaha* (also means **depressed**). 2. *pō'ele'ele* (dark).

glowing 1. *hāweo* (fig. distinguished). [***Hāweo** ka wena o ka pele.* The reflection of the lava is **glowing**.] 2. *'ena* (fig. angry).

glue *tuko* (apparently from Duco, a brand name of glue; also means **paste**). [*'Oki a **tuko** nā mākua kaiapuni Hawai'i i nā puke hou.* The Hawaiian Immersion school parents cut and **glue** new books.]

go 1. *hele.* 2. *hele aku* (move away from speaker). [*E **hele** aku! E **hele** pēlā!* **Go away**, get out!]

goal *pahuhopu* (also means **goalpost**).

goat *kao.*

go get (fetch) *ki'i.*

go home *ho'i.* [*E **ho'i** kāua.* Let's **go home**.]

gold *kula.* [*Nui ko kēlā wahine mau apolima **kula**.* That lady has many **gold** bracelets.]

golf *kolepa* (from English). [*Nui nō nā kahua **kolepa** ma O'ahu nei.* There are lots of **golf** courses here on O'ahu.]

good *maika'i* (also means **fine, well**). [***Maika'i** wale 'o Kaua'i.* Kaua'i is very **fine**. (traditional chant, "Maika'i Wale 'o Kaua'i," melody by H. Wai'au)]

good-looking *nohea* (also means **handsome**). [*'Ano **nohea** paha kāu kāne?* Is your husband maybe sort of **handsome**?]

goose *nēnē* (endangered native Hawaiian goose). [*Ua 'ōlelo 'ia, loa'a nā pūnua i nā **nēnē** i ho'oku'u 'ia ma Nualolo.* It is said that the **nēnē** geese which were released at Nualolo have got fledglings.]

got (in possession of) *loa'a* (also means **get, have**). [***Loa'a** ka poi ma ka hale hana poi ma Waiāhole i kēia lā?* Does the poi factory at Waiāhole **have** poi today?]

gourd *ipu.* [*E ho'opa'a i kā 'oukou mau **ipu**, e nā haumāna hula.* Beat your **gourds**, hula students.]

govern *ho'omalu* (lit. to protect). [***Ho'omalu** pono ke aupuni?* Does the government **govern** well?]

government *aupuni* (also means **kingdom, country**).

governor *kia'āina.* (lieutenant governor = *hope kia'āina*)

grab *hopu* (also means **to catch, take, arrest**). [*Ua **hopu** 'ia kā ko'u 'anakala lio e ke kinai ahi.* My uncle's horse was **caught** by the fireman.]

graduate *puka* (also means **to emerge, come out**). [*Ināhea i **puka** ai kāna kaikamahine 'ohana mai ke kula ki'eki'e mai?* When did her niece **graduate** from high school?]

grain *huna* (small speck of something; also means **secret, hidden, sea spray**). (grain of rice = *huna laiki*)

grand *kilakila* (also means **majestic, royal**). [*he nani kū **kilakila**, 'alo lua i nā pali,* a beauty **grand** in appearance, the two faces of the cliff. ("Moloka'i Waltz," by M. Kane)]

grandchild *mo'opuna.*

granddaughter *mo'opuna wahine.*

grandfather *kupuna kāne.* [*Ha'aheo ke **kupuna kāne** hou.* The new **grandfather** is proud.]

grandmother *kupuna wahine.*

grandparent *kupuna* (also means **ancestor**). (*pl. kūpuna; nā kūpuna* = the grandparents, the ancestors; *kou mau kūpuna* = your grandparents) [*Ua maʻa ko kākou mau kūpuna i ka holo moana.* Our **ancestors** were familiar with ocean voyaging.]

grandmother

grandson *moʻopuna kāne.*

grape *hua waina.* (grape juice = *ka wai hua ʻai hua waina*)

grass *mauʻu.* [*Mae ka mauʻu i ka wela o ka lā.* The **grass** wilts in the heat of the sun.]

grate *waʻu* (also means **to scratch, scrape, scraper**). (coconut grater = *waʻu niu*)

gratitude *mahalo* (also means **respect, admiration**). [*Mau nō ka mahalo o nā Hawaiʻi i nā aliʻi o ke au i hala.* The **gratitude** of Hawaiians to the chiefs of times past still continues.]

graveyard *pā ilina.*

greasy *ʻaila.*

great 1. *nui* (also means **large, big**). 2. *piha* (also means **full**). [*Ua piha ko ke kāne hauʻoli i kona male ʻana.* The bridegroom's happiness was **great** at his wedding.]

green *ʻōmaʻomaʻo.*

grief 1. *kaumaha.* 2. *kūmākena.* 3. *luʻuluʻu.*

grieve (also means **mourn**) 1. *uē.* 2. *kanikau.*

grieving (also means **mourning**) 1. *kaumaha.* 2. *mākena.* 3. *luʻuluʻu.* 4. *kanikau.* [*Auē ke kanikau ma ka hoʻolewa!* Gosh, the **grieving** at the funeral!] Note: *Kanikau* refers to a chant of grief (a dirge or lament) and also means "grieving."

groan 1. *ʻū* (also means **to moan, wail**). 2. *ʻuhū* (also means **to moan, sigh, grunt**).

grocer *kanaka kūʻai mea ʻai.*

gross (slang) *hoʻopailua.* [*Hoʻopailua maoli kekahi mau mea e ʻike ʻia ma ke kūkala nūhou.* Some things seen on the news are really **gross**.]

grouchy *ʻaʻaka.* [*Ke hele ʻo Māmā a ʻaʻaka, e akahele!* Whenever Mom gets **grouchy**, watch out!]

ground *honua* (also means **earth**).

group 1. *pūʻulu.* 2. *hui.*

grow *ulu.* [*he kīhāpai pua ulu māhiehie,* the delightfully **growing** flower garden (song, "Kimo Henderson Hula," by H. D. Beamer)]

grumble 1. *namunamu.* 2. *ʻōhumu.* [*Mai ʻōhumu aku iā ia!* Don't **grumble** to him.]

guard (protect) *kiaʻi.* [*Nāu e kiaʻi a e mālama mai iā mākou.* May you **guard** and take care of us. (a common line in prayers)]

guava *kuawa.*

guess 1. *koho* (also means **to choose**). [*E koho ʻoe i ka haʻina!* **Guess** the answer!] 2. *mahuʻi* (also means **to suspect**).

guest 1. *hoakipa.* 2. *malihini.*

guide *alakaʻi* (also means **to lead, leader**). [*Ke alakaʻi nei ke alakaʻi hula i ka papa hoʻomaʻamaʻa.* The hula **guide** is **leading** the practice class.]

guilty *hewa* (also means **wrong, sin**). [*Hewa ke kanaka ma ka hale paʻahao?* Is the person in jail **guilty**?]

gulch 1. *ʻoawa.* 2. *awāwa* (also means **valley**).

gum *kēpau* (also means **tar, pitch, resin, lead.** Sap from breadfruit, *pāpala* and other trees was used to catch birds, as glue or caulking, and so forth.) [*Ua hoʻohana nā kāpili manu i ka pāpala kēpau.* Bird catchers used gum (sap) from the *pāpala* tree.]

gum (chewing) *kamu* (from English).

gun *pū.* (to shoot a gun = *kī pū*)

guts *naʻau* (considered to be the seat of emotions, the Hawaiian "heart").

habit *hana maʻa.* [*He* **hana maʻa** *hoʻonāuk-iuki ka nonolo.* Snoring is an irritating **habit.**]

hair 1. *lauoho* (on head). [*Pono ʻoe e kahi mua i kou* **lauoho** *a laila palaki ma hope.* You have to first comb your **hair** and then brush (it) afterwards.] 2. *huluhulu* (body hair; also means **fur**).

hairbrush *palaki lauoho.*

half *hapalua.* [*He* **hapalua** *koko Pilipino ko ko ʻoukou makuahine.* Your (all) mother has half Filipino blood.]

hairbrush

Halloween Heleuī. (trick or treat = *kili-ki o lapu* [*lit.* treat or be haunted]) (Halloween costume = *ʻaʻahu Heleuī*)

hammer *hāmale.* [*Kuʻi ke kamanā i ke kuʻi i ka* **hāmale.** The carpenter hits the nail with the **hammer.**]

hand *lima* (also means **arm**).

handkerchief *hainakā.* (facial tissue = *hainakā pepa*) [*Ke kulu nei ka hūpē mai ko ka pēpē ihu aku, akā ʻaʻohe* **hainakā pepa** *a kona makua.* Nasal discharge is dripping from the baby's nose, but his parent doesn't have a **tissue.**]

handle *ʻau.* [*E makaʻala! Wela loa ke* **ʻau** *o ka ipuhao!* Watch out! The **handle** of the pot is really hot!]

handy 1. *mākaukau* (ready, prepared). 2. *noʻeau* (clever, skillful).

hang *lī* (also means **shoelace, to lace shoe, gird, furl sail**).

happiness *hauʻoli.*

happy *hauʻoli.* [**Hauʻoli** *Lā Hoʻomaikaʻi.* **Happy** Thanksgiving.]

harbor *awa kū moku.* [*Kū nā moku kaua ma ke* **awa kū moku** *ʻo Puʻuloa.* Battleships anchor in the **harbor** named Pearl Harbor.]

hard 1. *paʻakikī* (difficult, stubborn). 2. *ʻoʻoleʻa* (tough condition, not soft). [*He poʻo* **paʻakikī** *ko ko Malulani kupuna wahine.* Malulani's grandmother has a **hard** head.]

hardware (metal) *mea hao.*

harm 1. *pōpilikia* (also means **misfortune, emergency**). 2. *hana ʻino.* 3. *hoʻopōpilikia.*

hat *pāpale.* (lauhala hat = *pāpale lauhala*)

hate *inaina.*

Hawaiian Hawaiʻi. [*He mau kānaka haʻaheo nā* **Hawaiʻi.** **Hawaiians** are proud people.] [*He mau hana noʻeau* **Hawaiʻi** *ke kuku kapa a me ka ulana lauhala.* Beating tapa and weaving *lauhala* are **Hawaiian** crafts.]

Hawaiian hawk *ʻio* (endangered native hawk). [*Ke ʻike maka ʻoe i ko ka* **ʻio** *lele ʻana, maopopo iā ʻoe no ke aha i kapa ʻia ai nā aliʻi ma hope o ia manu kelakela.* When you witness the flight of the **Hawaiian hawk**, you understand why the chiefs were named after that majestic bird.]

Hawaiian hawk

haze (vog) *uauahi.*

hazy *uauahi.* [*Mai puka i waho ke hū ka pele o pilikia kou hanu ʻana i ka lā* **uauahi.** Don't go outside when lava erupts or you'll have trouble breathing due to the **hazy** day.]

he *'o ia* (also means **she**).

head (Use with *ke.*) *po'o.*

headache *ke po'o 'eha.*

heal *ho'ōla* (also means **salvation**, many other meanings).

health *ola kino.*

healthy *ola* (also means **alive**). [*Ola kā ka makuahine hou pēpē.* The new mother's baby is **healthy**.]

heap 1. *paila* (from English "pile," often used in the idiomatic expression *kū ka paila* as an exclamation of surprise at a large amount). [*Kū ka **paila** o nā niu!* Gosh, what a **heap** of coconuts!] 2. *pu'u.* 3. *ahu.*

hear *lohe.*

hearing aid *mea ho'olohe.*

heart *pu'uwai.*

heart disease *ma'i pu'uwai.*

heart (shape) *haka.* [*E ho'ouna aku ana lāua i **haka** kokoleka kekahi i kekahi ma ka Lā Aloha.* They (two) are going to send each other chocolate **hearts** on Valentine's Day.]

heat *wela.*

heaven 1. *lani.* 2. *lewa.* [*Nā akua o ka **lewalani**, o ka **lewanu'u**.* Gods of the **lower stratum of the sky**, gods of the **upper stratum**. (a common line in ancient prayers)] Both *lani* and *lewa* also mean **sky**. *Lewa* also connotes space, while *lani* can refer to a noble or royal rank or person. Ancient Hawaiians divided the sky into various sections from the horizon to the zenith, each having a name, just as they labeled the diverse biogeographic zones of the islands. *Lewalani* refers to the highest stratum, while *lewanu'u* is lower, where birds fly. See Malo, *Hawaiian Antiquities.*

heavy *kaumaha* (can refer to physical weight or emotional sadness/depression). [***Kaumaha** ka pahu lā'au.* The wooden chest is **heavy**.]

heel *ku'eku'e wāwae* (also means **ankle**).

height *ki'eki'e* (also means **high, tall, altitude, majestic**). [*'Ehia 'īniha ke **ki'eki'e** o ke ki'i kū?* How many inches is the **height** of the statue?]

heir *ho'oilina* (also means **heritage, inheritance**). [*'O Ka'iulani ka **ho'oilina** mō'ī hope loa o ke aupuni mō'ī.* Ka'iulani was the last royal **heir** of the Hawaiian kingdom.]

help *kōkua.* [*Mai **kōkua** mai ia'u! E **kōkua** aku iā ia!* Don't **help** me! **Help** him!]

hemisphere *'ao'ao.* [*Aia 'o Nuku Hiva i ka **'ao'ao** hema.* The Marquesas are in the southern **hemisphere**.]

her (also means **his**) 1. *kona.* 2. *kāna.* (See explanation at entry for **my**. *Kona* is used in the same instances as *ko'u*; *kāna* is used in the same instances as *ka'u*.)

herbs (medicinal) *lā'au lapa'au* (also means **person who practices herbal medicine**).

here 1. *ma 'ane'i* (place). [*Aia nā manakō **ma 'ane'i**.* The mangoes are **here**.] 2. *eia* (handing something over). [***Eia** kāu kī.* **Here**'s your tea.] (here comes someone = *eia a'e*) [***Eia a'e** 'o Moke.* **Here comes** Moke.]

heritage *waiwai ho'oilina* (also means **inheritance**). [*He **waiwai ho'olina** makamae ko kākou.* We have a precious **heritage**.]

hero 1. *me'e.* 2. *kupu'eu.* [*Hō nā hana kupaianaha a nā **kupu'eu** ma nā ka'ao kahiko.* My goodness, how astonishing are the feats of the **heroes** of ancient stories.] 3. *koa.*

hero

hew *kua* (also means **to chop down**).

hibiscus *puaaloalo.*

hidden *huna* (also means **fine particle, sea spray**).

hide 1. *pe'e* (hide yourself). 2. *ho'ohūnā* (to hide something). [*Ke **pe'e** nei ka 'īlio pēpē ma lalo o ke kalaka a ma laila i **ho'ohūnā** 'ia kāna iwi.* The puppy is **hiding** under the truck and that's where his bone was **hidden**.]

high *ki'eki'e.*

high school *kula ki'eki'e.* [*Āhea ana e puka ai kāu mo'opuna mai ke **kula ki'eki'e**?* When will your grandchild graduate from **high school**?]

high tide *kai piha.*

highway *alaloa.* [*Pa'apū ke **alaloa** i nā kalaka.* The **highway** is crowded with trucks.]

high tide

hike *pi'i kuahiwi.* [***Pi'i kuahiwi** pinepine ka hui a ma'a lākou i ka lepo 'ūkele ma ke alahele.* The club often **hikes** and they all are used to mud on the trail.]

hiking trail *alahele* (also means **trail, pathway**).

hill *pu'u.*

hip *kīkala.* [*'Oni ke **kīkala** o ka 'ōlapa i ka 'ami.* The dancer's **hips** move in the 'ami (hula step with hip movements).]

his (also means **her**) 1. *kona.* 2. *kāna.* (See explanation at entry for **my**. *Kona* is used in the same instances as *ko'u*; *kāna* is used in the same instances as *ka'u.*)

hiss *hīhī* (also means **to purge**).

history *mo'olelo* (also refers to a story believed to be true, as opposed to *ka'ao*, fictional stories). [*Pono nā Hawai'i e no'ono'o hou no ko ko kākou lāhui **mo'olelo**.* Hawaiians have to rethink our nationality's **history**.]

hit 1. *ku'i* (punch, crash). 2. *pa'i* (slap).

hobby *hana ho'ohau'oli.* [*He aha kāna **hana ho'ohau'oli**? 'O ke kuiki kapa Hawai'i kāna **hana ho'ohau'oli**.* What's her **hobby**? Hawaiian quilting is her **hobby**.]

hoe [n] *hō.* [v] 1. *hō.* 2. *kālai* (also means **to carve**). (slang used on sugar plantation for hoeing rows of sugarcane = *hō hana*)

hold *ho'opa'a.* [***Ho'opa'a** ke kaikamahine i ka ho'okupu lā'ī.* The girl **holds** the *tī* leaf offering.]

hole 1. *lua* (in ground; also means **toilet, grave, two**). 2. *puka* (hole through something; also means **door, to emerge**).

holiday *lā nui.* [*He **lā nui** ka lā 'apōpō?* Is tomorrow a **holiday**?]

holy *hemolele* (also means **pure, pristine, perfect**). [*ka 'uhane **hemolele**,* the **holy** ghost]

home *home* (from English). Note: Ancient houses consisted of several separate build-ings called *kauhale*. *Pūnana* (*lit.* bird's nest) or "nest" conveys the idea of emotional attachment to a house, although "*home*" is undoubtedly used more often today.

homeland 1. *one hānau.* 2. *'āina hānau.* [*Aia i hea kou **'āina hānau**?* Where is your **birthplace**?]

honest *kūpono.* [*He pu'ukū **kūpono** 'o ia ala ma ke kalapu.* That one (over there) is an **honest** treasurer in the club.]

honey *meli.*

honeybee *nalo meli.* [*Mumulu nā **nalo meli** i nā pua mōhala.* **Bees** swarm around the blooming flowers.]

honor (someone) 1. *ho'ohanohano.* [*Ma kēia mahina a'e e **ho'ohanohano** 'ia ana nā haku mele Hawai'i.* It is next month that Hawaiian composers will be **honored**. 2. *ho'ohiwahiwa.*

hoof *māi'u'u* (also means **claw**). [*Pehu ko ka pipi wahine **māi'u'u**.* The cow's **hoof** is swollen.]

hook [n] *lou* (also means **picking pole**). [v] *lou* (also means **to pick with a picking pole**). [*E lou i ka manakō i ka **lou**.* **Pick** the mango with the **picking pole**.]

hope *mana'olana.* [***Mana'olana** au e kipa aku i ka 'āina o nā Maori ma Aotearoa.* I **hope** to visit the land of the Maori in New Zealand.]

horizon 1. *hālāwai.* 2. *kūkulu.* 3. *'alihi lani.* [*Nānā pinepine ka ho'okele i ka **'alihi lani**.* The navigator often looks at the **horizon**.]

horn 1. *kiwi* (animal horn). 2. *pū* (musical instrument, also conch shell).

horrible *weliweli* (also means **horrified, terrible, terrifying**).

horrified *mā'e'ele* (also means **numb**). [*'Aia nō a 'ike mākou i ke ōla'i ma ke kīwī, ua hele mākou a **mā'e'ele**.* As soon as we saw the earthquake on TV, we became **horrified**.]

horse

horse *lio.* [*Kīau ka **lio** ma ke kahua mau'u.* The **horse** gallops on the grassy field.]

hospital 1. *haukapila.*

2. *hale maʻi*. Some Hawaiian speakers object to the literal meaning of *hale maʻi* (sick house), since calling a place "sick" is counter to Hawaiian thinking about health. However, this is a commonly used term. Perhaps *hale hoʻōla* (house of healing) would be more appropriate.

hospitality *hoʻokipa* (also means **to welcome, entertain**).

hostile *kūʻē* (also means **to oppose, opposite**). [*He aha ka hua ʻōlelo **kūʻē** iā "pōkole"?* What word is the **opposite** of "short"?]

hot 1. *wela*. 2. *ikīki* (hot and humid). [***Ikīki** loa ka mahina ʻo Kepakemapa.* September is a very **hot and humid** month.]

hotel *hōkele* (from English).

hour *hola* (from English). [*Hoʻomaka ka hālāwai ma ka **hola** ʻehia?* What **time** does the meeting start?]

hotel

house *hale* (also means **building**). [*He **hale** kahiko a kaulana ʻo Washington Place.* Washington Place is an old and well-known **house**.]

howl *uō*. [*ʻAoa nā ʻīlio a **uō** nā kānaka ma ka pō Māhealani.* Dogs bark and people **howl** on the night of the full moon.]

house

hug 1. *ʻapo*. 2. *pūliki*. [*Mai poina e **pūliki** kekahi i kekahi.* Don't forget to **hug** one another.]

hula *hula*. (non-Hawaiian dance, including ballet = *hulahula*)

hula dancer *ʻōlapa* (after tree of same name whose leaves shake in the wind; also means **to flash**, as lightning).

hula school *hālau hula*.

hula teacher *kumu hula*. [*Hoʻopololei ke **kumu hula** i ko nā ʻōlapa hehi ʻana.* The **hula teacher** corrects the dancers' steps.]

hull *kaʻele* (also means **empty, hollow like a bowl or canoe hull**).

human *kanaka. pl. kānaka* (also means **person, people**). [*ʻAʻole au he ʻānela, he **kanaka** au.* (*ʻōlelo noʻeau*) I am not an angel, I'm **human** (I'm not perfect).]

humble *haʻahaʻa* (also means **low in height, humility**). [***Haʻahaʻa** ka mea lehia maoli.* A true expert is **humble**.]

humid 1. *maʻū*. 2. *paʻapū* (also means **crowded**). [*ʻOiai ke pā mai nei ka makani Kona, **paʻapū** ka lā.* Since the Kona wind is blowing, the day is **humid**.] 3. *ikīki* (hot and humid).

hundred *haneli*. [*i hoʻokahi **haneli** makahiki ma kēia mua aku,* one **hundred** years in the future]

hungry *pōloli*. [*I koʻu wā kamaliʻi, ke **pōloli** mākou, ʻai mākou i ka ʻuala.* In my childhood, when we were **hungry**, we ate sweet potatoes.]

hunt 1. *hahai* (also means **to follow**). 2. *alualu* (also means **to chase**).

hurray [exclamation] *hulō*. [*Hipa, hipa, **hulō** no nā kamaliʻi wahine pāʻū ma ke kaʻi huakaʻi!* Hip, hip, **hurray** for the *pāʻū* princesses in the parade!]

hurricane *makani pāhili*. [*ʻEhia manawa ʻoe i ʻike maka ai i ka **makani pāhili**? Hoʻokahi manawa, ua lawa.* How many times have you experienced a **hurricane**? Once is enough.]

hurry *ʻāwīwī* (also means **quick, fast**).

hurt *ʻeha* (also means **sore, painful**). [*ʻEha kou puʻu, e ke keiki?* Is your throat **sore**, child?]

husband *kāne*. [*ʻAʻohe **kāne** hānai nalo.* (*ʻōlelo noʻeau*) There is no **husband** who feeds his wife flies (husbands did the cooking in old Hawaiʻi).]

hymn *hīmeni* (from English; also means **to sing**).

hypocrite *hoʻokamani*. [*Inā ʻoe i hoʻokō i kāu mea i hoʻohiki ai, ʻaʻole ʻoe e lilo i **hoʻokamani**.* If you had fulfilled the promise you made, you wouldn't have become a **hypocrite**.]

ice *hau.*

icebox (refrigerator) *pahu hau.* (ice cube = *poke hau*) [*Aia nō a hoʻopio ʻoe i ka **pahu hau**, heheʻe nā **poke hau**.* As soon as you turn off the **icebox**, the **ice cubes** melt.]

ice cream 1. *ʻaikalima.* 2. *haukalima.* (shave ice = *haukōhi, hau momona*)

idea *manaʻo* (also means **thought, opinion, mentality**). [*He **manaʻo** maʻalea kēlā.* That's a cunning **idea**.]

identical *kūlike* (also means **alike, resembling**). [***Kūlike** nā makalike o nā koa.* The soldiers' uniforms are **identical**.] (exactly alike = *kūlike loa*; idiomatic phrase *ua like nō a like*, lit. just alike, is more common) [***Ua like nō a like** au me kuʻu one hānau.* I'm **just like** my birthplace. (song, "Molokaʻi Nui a Hina," by M. Kāne)]

identify *hōʻoia* (also means **to verify, prove, confirm**; syn. *hōʻoiaʻiʻo*). [*Ke **hōʻoia** nei ʻo Kawelo i ko kona mau mākua male ʻana ma o ka ʻimi ʻana i ka palapala male.* Kawelo is **verifying** his parents' marriage by searching for the marriage certificate.]

ignorance *naʻaupō* (also means **ignorant, uneducated**). [*ʻAʻohe waiwai o ka **naʻaupō**.* **Ignorance** has no value.]

ignore *nānā ʻole.*

ill *maʻi.*

illegal *kū ʻole i ke kānāwai.* [***Kū ʻole i ke kānāwai** ke ʻano o kāu hana?* Is your activity **illegal**?]

illness 1. *maʻi* (also means **disease, menstruation**). 2. *kaʻa maʻi* (chronic illness). 3. *maʻi ahulau* (chronic illness; also

ill

means **epidemic**). 4. *ʻea* (common illness).

image *kiʻi* (also means **picture, idol, memorial, statue**, many other meanings).

imagine *kuhi* (also means **to point, to suppose**). [*E **kuhi** kākou i ka hoʻomaluhia i ka honua holoʻokoʻa.* Let's all **imagine** the creation of peace on the whole earth.]

imitate *hoʻopili* (also means **to repeat after the teacher**). [*E **hoʻopili** mai iaʻu.* **Repeat** after me.]

immediately 1. *koke.* [*Na ke kauka e pane **koke** i ke kelepona paʻa lima.* The doctor is the one who should **immediately** answer the cellular phone.] 2. *ʻānō.*

impatient *ahonui ʻole.*

imperfect *kīnā* (also means **blemish, flaw, any physical defect**). (syn. *keʻe*)

implement *mea hoʻohana* (also means **tool**). [*He **mea hoʻohana** nui ke koʻi i ke au kahiko a ua nui nā ʻano koʻi like ʻole a nā kūpuna i hoʻohana ai.* The adze was an important **implement** in ancient days and there were many different types of adzes that the ancestors used.]

important *nui.* (VIP = *maka nui* or *mea nui*)

impossible *hiki ʻole.* [***Hiki ʻole** kou lilo ʻana i manu lele.* It's **impossible** for you to turn into a flying bird.]

imprison *hoʻopaʻahao.* [*I hoʻokahi haneli makahiki aku nei, ua **hoʻopaʻahao** ʻia ka mōʻī wahine ʻo Liliʻuokalani i ka Hale Aliʻi ʻo ʻIolani.* One hundred years ago, Queen Liliʻuokalani was **imprisoned** in ʻIolani Palace.]

improper *kūpono ʻole.*

improve *holomua* (also means **to go forward, make progress**). [*Ke **holomua** nei ke aʻo ʻana aku i ka ʻōlelo makuahine ma* *ke kīwī.* The teaching of the mother tongue on TV is **improving.**]

improvement *holomua* (also means **progress**).

inappropriate *kohu 'ole.*

in between *ma waena* (also means **among**). [*Ma waena o nā holokai i kū a'e ai ko'u hoaaloha ma ka hana ho'ohanohano.* It was **in between** the ocean voyagers that my friend stood at the ceremony.]

inch *'īniha.*

incident *hanana.* [*Ua kohu 'ole kā ka 'ōpio 'ōlelo ma ka hanana pōpilikia.* The young person's words at the unfortunate **incident** were inappropriate.]

incompetent *mākaukau 'ole* (also means **unprepared, incapable**).

incomplete *hapapū.* [*Hapapū nō kāna hana.* His work is really **incomplete.**]

increase *ho'onui.* [*E ho'onui a'e ana nā keiki hapa Hawai'i.* The number of part-Hawaiian children will **increase.**]

indecent *haumia* (also means **contaminated, defiled, unclean**).

independence 1. *ea* (also means **life force, gas, sovereignty**, many other meanings). 2. *kū'oko'a* (also means **freedom**).

independent *kū'oko'a* (also means **free**). [*Kū'oko'a ko ko'u hoaaloha mau mana'o.* My friend's opinions are **independent.**] (independent [private] school = *kula kū'oko'a*) (government [public] school = *kula aupuni*)

index *papa kuhikuhi.* [*He papa kuhikuhi ko ka puke mea kanu Hawai'i maoli?* Does the Hawaiian native plants book have an **index**?]

indigenous *maoli* (also means **native, real**). [*'A'ole ka uhi he lā'au maoli.* The yam is not a **native** plant.]

indulge *pailani* (also means **to spoil someone**). [*'O ke kuleana o nā kūpuna ka pailani 'ana i nā mo'opuna?* Is **spoiling** grandchildren the privilege of grandparents?]

inexpensive *emi.* [*'A'ole kēnā 'ano uaki he*

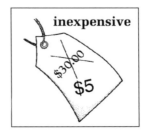
inexpensive

$30.00 $5

uaki emi. That kind of watch (near you) isn't **inexpensive.**]

inherit *ho'olina* (also means **heritage, inheritance**). [*He 'āina ho'oilina kēia kahua hānai pipi.* This ranch is **inherited** land.]

initiate 1. *ho'okumu* (also means **to establish business, school**, etc.). 2. *ho'omaka* (also means **to start, begin**). [*Na wai i ho'okumu i nā kula kaiapuni Hawai'i i ho'omaka i 'umi makahiki aku nei?* Who **established** the Hawaiian Immersion schools that **began** 10 years ago?] 3. *ho'olilo i lālā* (also means **to make someone a member of an organization**).

inject 1. *hou* (also means **to shove, stab, pierce**, etc.). 2. *hano.*

injection *hoene* (also means **medicine, enema, abortion, soft sound, rustle**).

injure *hana 'ino* (also means **to abuse, harm**). [*Ke hana 'ino 'oe iā ha'i, hana 'ino ho'i 'oe iā 'oe iho.* When you **injure** others, you also **injure** yourself.]

injustice *kaulike 'ole.* [*Ua 'ike ka lāhui Hawai'i i ka 'eha o ke kaulike 'ole.* The Hawaiian race has known the pain of **injustice.**]

ink *'īnika.* [*Aia nō a mākaukau ka 'īnika, ho'omaka ke kahunapule Pākē e kākau iho me ke kaha ki'i pū.* As soon as the **ink** is ready, the Chinese priest starts to write and draw at the same time.]

innocent 1. *hewa 'ole.* 2. *hala 'ole.*

insect *mū.* (syn. *iniseka* [from English])

insecticide *lā'au make* (also means **poison, pesticide**). [*I ke aupuni e kīkī ana i ka lā'au make ma kapa alanui, nalowale nā lā'au maoli.* When the government sprays **insecticide** on the roadside, native plants disappear.]

insert *ho'okomo.* [*E ho'okomo 'oe i ka pā lolouila i ka lolouila.* **Insert** the computer diskette into the computer.]

inside *ma loko o.* [*Ikīki ma loko o ke ka'a.* It's hot and stuffy **inside** the car.]

inside

insomnia *hia'ā* (also means **insomniac, unable to sleep**). [*Hia'ā paha 'oe i kēia pō, e Māmā?* Do you have **insomnia** tonight, Mom?]

inspect *nānā.*

inspired *ulu* (also means **to grow**). (to grow a plant, inspire = *ho'oulu*) [*E ho'oulu ana 'o Laka i ke kumu hula.* Laka (goddess of hula) will **inspire** the hula teacher.]

instant *manawa pōkole loa* (*lit.* very short time).

instantly 1. *koke.* 2. *'emo 'ole.*

instead *ma kahi o* (also means **approximately**). [*E hula ana au ma kahi o ko'u kaikaina i ka hō'ike hula.* I will dance **instead** of my younger brother at the hula show.]

instrument *pila ho'okani.* [*Ho'okani kēia kāne i nā pila ho'okani hula kahiko wale nō.* This man plays only ancient hula **instruments**.]

insult 1. *kūamuamu.* [*Kūamuamu ka 'ōpiopio na'aupō i kona kaikua'ana.* The ignorant youth **insults** his older brother.] 2. *hō'ino.*

insurance *'inikua* (from English). [*Ke pi'i a'e nei ka 'inikua no ke kalaiwa ka'a.* **Insurance** for driving your car is rising in cost.]

intelligence *na'auao* (also means **wisdom, enlightenment**).

intelligent *na'auao* (also means **educated, wise**). [*Na'auao ka 'elemakule e a'o nei i ka lomilomi.* The old man who is teaching Hawaiian massage is **intelligent**.]

interesting *hoihoi.* [*Hoihoi wale nō ka mo'olelo Hawai'i.* Hawaiian history is very **interesting**.]

interfere 1. *'āke'ake'a* (also means **obstruction, to block, hinder**). [*Ua 'āke'ake'a nā kānaka kū'ē i ka hālāwai.* The protestors **interfered** with the meeting.] 2. *hōkake.* (to disturb).

interior *loko* (also means **inside**). [*Hiki ke 'ai 'ia ka na'au o ka manini. Loa'a ka limu ma loko.* The intestines of the *manini* fish can be eaten. There's seaweed **inside**.] [*Aia kāu mau niho hou i loko o kēnā kī'aha?* Are your new teeth **inside** that glass (by you)?]

intermediate school *kula waena.*

international (phrase) *o nā 'āina 'ē.* [*He 'ahahui o nā 'āina 'ē ka UN.* The UN is an **international** organization.]

interpret *unuhi.*

interrupt *kahamaha.* [*Kahamaha ke keiki i kā kona 'anakala kama'ilio 'ana.* The child **interrupts** his uncle's conversation.]

intersection *huina alanui.*

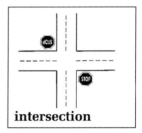

intersection

intestines *na'au* (seat of emotions in Hawaiian thinking). [*Mālie ko'u na'au.* My **"heart"** is calm.]

intoxicated *'ona.* [*'Ona anei 'oe i ka lā'au 'ino?* Are you **"high"** on drugs?] (Note: *'ona* encompasses both alcoholic intoxication and drug "high.")

introduce *ho'olauna.* [*Makemake au e ho'olauna iā 'oe me ka haku puke.* I'd like to **introduce** you to the author.]

invade *ho'ouka* (also means **to attack, battle**).

in vain 1. *makehewa* (also means **useless**). 2. *pohō* (also means loss, damage). [*Pohō ka 'imi 'ana i ke kanaka ku'i 'opihi o ka nalu i po'i ai.* Looking for the *'opihi* picker that the wave broke over was **in vain**.]

invest *ho'opuka* (also means **make profit**). [*Ua ho'opuka 'olua i ka pili waiwai?* Did you (two) **make a profit** gambling?]

investigate *kolokolo.* [*Kolokolo ka māka'ikiu i ko ke kelamoku kū'ai 'ana aku i nā kaimana.* The detective **investigates** the sailor's selling diamonds.]

invitation *kono.* [*Ua hiki mai ke kono i ka Holokū Ball i kākau 'ia ma ka 'ōlelo makuahine.* The **invitation** to the Holokū Ball which was written in Hawaiian (the mother tongue) has arrived.]

invite *kono.* [*Ua kono 'ia 'oukou i ka 'aha pā'ina?* Were you all **invited** to the banquet?]

inward *i loko.*

Ireland *ka 'āina 'Ailiki.*

Irish *'Ailiki.*

iron 1. *'aiana* (clothes iron). 2. *hao* (metal,

also general name for **hardware**).

irrigate *hanawai* (also means **irrigation, urination, menstrual period, to urinate**).

irritable 1. *ho'onāukiuki.* 2. *'a'aka.*

irritate 1. *ho'onāukiuki* (also means **tease**). [*Mai **ho'onāukiuki** i kāu hānaiāhuhu o nahu 'ia mai auane'i.* Don't **tease** your pet or else you'll be bitten after a while.] 2. *ho'ouluhua.*

irritated *nāukiuki.*

island *mokupuni.*

island chain *pae 'āina.* [*Nui nā mokupuni li'ili'i ma ka **pae 'āina** 'o Tuamotu.* There are lots of small islands in the Tuamotu **island chain**.]

island

itchy *mane'o* (slang for sexually stimulated, "horny"). [***Mane'o** kona lima i ka 'ōhune.* His skin is **itchy** due to the rash.]

jacket *lakeke.* [*'O ka lakeke mehana ka lole kūpono ma nā wēkiu.* A warm **jacket** is the appropriate clothing on the summits.]

jagged *nihoniho* (also means **serrated, scalloped**). [*Nihoniho ka wēlau o ka pahi.* The tip of the knife is **jagged**.]

jail *hale pa'ahao* (also means **prison**). [*Aia kekahi mau kānaka hewa 'ole ma ka hale pa'ahao.* There are some innocent people in **jail**.]

jail

jam *kele* (also means **jelly**). [*'Ono loa ke kele pōhā.* Pōhā berry **jam** is yummy.]

January *Iānuali* (from English). [*Ho'omaka kāna hana hou ma ka mahina 'o Iānulai.* His new job starts in the month of **January**.]

Japan *Iāpana* (from English). [*Huaka'i pinepine kāna hālau hula i Iāpana.* His hula troupe frequently voyages to **Japan**.]

Japanese *Kepanī.*

jasmine *pīkake* (lit. peacock, named for the peacock birds in Ka'iulani's garden at 'Āinahau in Waikīkī, where the first jasmines imported to Hawai'i by her father, Alexander Cleghorn, were planted.)

jaw *ā.* [*Ua ku'i 'ia ko kēia loio ā luna e kekahi hoaloio i kū'ē i kāna e 'ōlelo ana.* This lawyer's upper **jaw** was punched by a fellow lawyer who opposed what she was saying.]

jealousy *lili.*

jellyfish *pololia.* [*Mai hehi i ka pololia o 'eha koke kou wāwae.* Don't step on the **jellyfish** or else your foot will be sore immediately.]

jiggle 1. *'oni'oni.* 2. *hō'oni'oni* (to jiggle something). [*Hō'oni'oni mau ka pēpē i kāna ki'i pēpē.* The baby constantly **jiggles** his doll.]

job 1. *hana* (also means any **activity**). [*He aha kāu hana i ka pō nei?* What **(activity)** did you do last night?] 2. *'oihana* (also means **profession, career, business**). [*He aha kāu 'oihana?* What is your **profession**?]

join 1. *kāpili* (to put together). [*Ua kāpili 'ia nā 'āpana o ka nane 'āpana.* The pieces of the jigsaw puzzle were **joined** together.] 2. *pili* (become emotionally close). (my intimate friend = *ko'u hoapili*) 3. *hui* (become a member of a group or club).

joint (of body) 1. *ku'ina.* 2. *ku'eku'e.* [*Mālo'elo'e ko Nohea ku'eku'e lima i ka pā'ani kenika.* Nohea's elbow **joint** is stiff due to playing tennis.]

joke *'ōlelo ho'omake'aka.*

journey *huaka'i* (also means **trip, voyage, parade, to travel, take a trip**). [*Ua huaka'i 'o Kila i Polapola e ki'i iā La'amaikahiki.* Kila **journeyed** to Tahiti to get La'amaikahiki.]

joy *'oli* (also means **rejoice, joyous, joyful**).

judge [n] *luna kānāwai* (court judge). [v] 1. *ho'okolokolo* (in law). 2. *loiloi* (evaluate, judge contest). (judge in contest = *luna loiloi*)

judgment *'ōlelo ho'oholo* (also means **verdict**). [*'Oiai he mea nui ke kuleana i ka wai, na wai e pakele aku i ka 'ōlelo ho'oholo a ka luna kānāwai e ho'okolokolo ai?* Since water rights are important, who can help but be affected by the **judgment** that the judge will make?]

juggle *ho'oleilei.*

juice *wai hua 'ai.* [*Inu mau kāu pēpē i ka **wai hua 'ai** kuawa?* Does your baby always drink guava **juice**?]

July Iulai (from English).

jump 1. *lele* (also means **to fly**). 2. *lelele* (jump continuously).

jump

June Iune (from English). [*E male ana māua 'o ka'u ipo ma kēia **Iune** a'e.* My sweetheart and I will marry next **June**.]

jungle *wao nahele* (also means **rain forest**). [*Laha 'ole nā mū a me nā mea kanu ma ka **wao nahele** Hawai'i.* The insects and plants in the Hawaiian **jungle** are rare.]

just (fair) *kaulike.* [***Kaulike** ka 'ōlelo ho'oholo a ke kiule.* The verdict of the jury is **just**.]

justice *kaulike.* [*E loa'a ana ke **kaulike** ma lalo o ka malu o ke aupuni hou.* There will be **justice** under the protection of the new government.]

juvenile *keiki.* [*He mau **keiki** lāua, 'a'ole he mau kānaka makua.* They (two) are **juveniles**, not adults.]

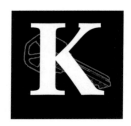

kayak *kaiaka.*

keel *kuamoʻo* (also means **spine, backbone, genealogy**). [*ʻAno like ke **kuamoʻo** o ke kino a me ka waʻa.* The **"backbone"** of the body and of the canoe are sort of similar.]

keep *mālama* (also means **to protect, take care of**). [*E **mālama** i nā wao kele.* **Protect** the rain forests.]

keeper *kahu* (also means **caretaker**). [*He **kahu** ko ka pā ilina o nā aliʻi.* The royal cemetery has a **caretaker**.]

key *kī* (also means **tea, tī leaf plant**). [*Aia iā wai ke **kī**?* Who has the **key**?]

kick *peku.* [*E **peku** i ke kinipōpō.* **Kick** the ball.]

kidney *puʻupaʻa* (also means **virgin**).

kill 1. *hoʻomake.* 2. *pepehi* (also means **to beat up**).

kind [n] *ʻano* (type). [*He aha ke **ʻano** o kēia kī aʻu e inu nei?* What **kind** of tea am I drinking?] [adj] *ʻoluʻolu* (good natured).

kindergarten *māla aʻo.* [*He kumu **māla aʻo** ʻo Moana.* Moana is a **kindergarten** teacher.]

king *mōʻī* (also means **sovereign**).

kingdom *aupuni mōʻī* (also means **monarchy**). [*Ua lilo ke **aupuni mōʻī** i lepupalika.* The **kingdom** became a republic.]

kiss *honi* (also means **to smell**). [*E **honi** kāua wikiwiki.* Let's **kiss** quickly).

kitchen *lumi kuke.* [*He **lumi kuke** nui ko koʻu mau hoahānau hale kahiko.* My cousins' old house has a big **kitchen**.]

kite *lupe.* [*Nui nā **lupe** e hoʻolele ʻia ai ma ka pāka ʻo Kapiʻolani.* There are lots of **kites** flown at Kapiʻolani Park.]

knee *kuli.*

kneel *kukuli.* [*Ke pule ʻoe, **kukuli** ʻoe i lalo?* When you pray, do you **kneel**?]

knife *pahi.*

knock *kīkēkē.* [*Ua lohe ʻia ke **kīkēkē** ʻana ma ke kulu aumoe a piʻi aʻela koʻu manene.* **Knocking** was heard at midnight, and I got that creepy feeling.]

knot *hīpuʻupuʻu.*

knowledge *ʻike.* [*He **ʻike** ko Tui e pili ana i ka hei Hawaiʻi?* Does Tui have **knowledge** about Hawaiian string figures?]

knuckle *puʻupuʻu* (also means **lumps, lumpy**). [*Moku kou **puʻupuʻu** i ka lau kō.* Your **knuckle** is cut by the sugarcane leaf.]

Korea *Kōlea.*

Korean *Kōlea.* [*Nani nō nā lole o nā wāhine **Kōlea**.* The clothes of **Korean** women are beautiful.]

machine *mīkini.*

mad 1. *huhū* (angry). [*Ua hele 'o Tūtū a* **huhū** *i kāna mau mo'opuna i ho'ohene-hene mai ia'u.* Tūtū became **angry** at her grandchildren who teased me.] 2. *pupule* (crazy). 3. *hehena* (crazy).

made *hana 'ia.* [*Ua* **hana 'ia** *ka lei hua kukui ma Moloka'i.* The *kukui* nut *lei* was **made** on Moloka'i.]

magic *ho'okalakupua.*

magician *ho'okalakupua.* [*He* **ho'okalakupua** *ko ka hō'ike'ike.* The circus has a **magician**.]

magnet *mākēneki.* [*Aia paha he* **mākēneki** *e ho'opili ai i ka pānānā i ke kalaka?* Is there maybe a **magnet** that would stick the compass to the truck?]

maidenhair fern *'iwa 'iwa.*

mail [n] *leka* (letters).

mailbox *pahu leka.*

mail carrier *lawe leka.* [*E lawe mai ana paha ka* **lawe leka** *i kekahi leka iā 'oe i kēia lā?* Will the **mail carrier** perhaps bring a letter to you today?]

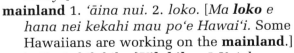
mailbox

mainland 1. *'āina nui.* 2. *loko.* [*Ma* **loko** *e hana nei kekahi mau po'e Hawai'i.* Some Hawaiians are working on the **mainland**.]

majestic 1. *kilakila.* [**Kilakila** *nā Ko'olau.* The Ko'olau mountains are **majestic**.] 2. *kelakela.* 3. *'ihi'ihi.*

majority *hapanui.* [*'A'ole 'ōlelo Hawai'i ka* **hapanui** *o nā Hawai'i.* The **majority** of Hawaiians don't speak Hawaiian.]

make (a thing) *hana* (also means **to work,** any activity, job). [*Na ka'u kāne i* **hana** *i ko 'olua mau noho paipai koa.* My husband is the one who **makes** your (two) *koa* rocking chairs.] (make a joke = *ho'omāke'aka*) (make a video = *ho'opa'a wikiō*) (make a fine appearance = *ulumāhiehie*) (make a tour around the island = *ka'ahele, ka'apuni*) (make a circuit, go around = *ho'opō'ai*) (make noise = *hanakuli, kani, ho'owā*)

male *kāne.* [*'O kēlā koloa ke kakā* **kāne**. That *koloa* bird is the **male** duck.]

malicious *na'au 'ino.* (malicious gossip or accusation = *ni'a*)

malignant *'a'ai.*

man *kāne* (male). [*He* **kāne** *kāko'o i nā 'ilihune ke kia 'āina hou?* Is the new governor a **man** who supports poor people?]

manager 1. *mea ho'oponopono.* 2. *luna.* [*Alaka'i maika'i ka'u* **luna** *i nā limahana.* My **manager** leads the employees well.]

mange *kāki'o.* [*Auē! Loa'a kēia 'īlio i ke* **kāki'o**. Gosh! This dog has **mange**.]

mango *manakō.*

mangrove *kukuna o ka lā* (*lit.* rays of the sun).

mango

mankind *kanaka.* [*Mai nānā 'ino'ino nā hewa o* **kanaka**. Don't look severely on the sins of **mankind**. (song, "Queen's Prayer," by Lili'uokalani)]

manslaughter *lawe ola.*

manual (book) 1. *puke kuhikuhi.* [*Aia ka wehewehe 'ana i ka ho'ā 'ana i ka mīkini ma ka 'ao'ao hea o ka* **puke kuhikuhi**?

On which page of the **manual** do they explain how to turn on the machine?] 2. *puke kumu.*

manuscript *palapala* (also means **document, writing**, many other meanings).

many 1. *lau.* 2. *nui.* 3. *lehu.* 4. *kini.* [*E nā kini maka o ka ʻāina.* Oh the **many** friends of the land. (traditional greeting)]

map *palapala ʻāina.* [*Iā ʻoe e hoʻomākaukau ana no ka piʻi kuahiwi, mai poina i ka palapala ʻāina.* When you prepare for the hike, don't forget the **map**.]

mar *māʻinoʻino.* [*Mai māʻinoʻino i nā palapala kahiko!* Don't **mar** the old documents!]

marbles *kinikini.*

march 1. *paikau* (often refers to military parade). 2. *kaʻi huakaʻi.* 3. *naue.* [*E naue i mua, hema, ʻākau, hema.* **March** forward, left, right, left.]

March Malaki (from English).

marijuana *pakalōlō.* [*Hoʻoulu ʻia ka pakalōlō ma nā mokupuni a pau.* **Marijuana** is grown on all the islands.]

mark *kaha.*

market *mākeke.* (farmers' market = *mākeke mahiʻai*) [*ʻO kaʻu wahi punahele no ke kūʻai ʻana mai i nā lau ʻai me nā hua ʻai, ʻo ia ka mākeke mahiʻai.* My favorite place for buying vegetables and fruits is the **farmers' market**.

marlin (fish) *aʻu.*

Marquesas Nuʻu Hiwa. [*Kūnihi nā pali ma Nuʻu Hiwa.* The cliffs of the **Marquesas** are steep.]

marriage *male ʻana* (also means **wedding**). [*Kipa mai kekahi mau malihini Kepanī no ka male ʻana.* Some Japanese tourists visit here in order to have a **wedding**.]

marriage license *palapala male.*

married couple *paʻa male.*

marry 1. *male* (from English). 2. *hoʻāo.*

marsh *nenelu* (also means **bog, swamp, swampy, soft plumpness**).

marshall *ilāmuku.*

martial arts (Hawaiian) *lua.* [*Kohu like anei ka lua me ke ʻano hula haʻahaʻa?* Is **Hawaiian martial arts** like low-style hula?]

mash [v] 1. *hoʻowali* (also means **to mix poi**). 2. *kuʻi* (also means **to smash, crush**, other meanings).

mask *makakiʻi* (mask that covers eyes or face only). 2. *poʻokiʻi* (mask that fits over head, such as head of lion in Chinese lion dance). [*Loaʻa i koʻu hoahānau kekahi mau poʻokiʻi Pākē no ka hulahula liona.* My cousin has some Chinese **masks** for the lion dance.]

massage *lomilomi.* [*Hiki ke lomilomi ʻia koʻu poʻohiwi ʻeha?* Can my sore shoulder be **massaged**?]

mast of ship *kia.* [*kahi moku kia kahi, loaʻa ʻo ka fea wini,* a **single-masted** ship (which) has a fair wind (song, "Moku Kia Kahi," by L. Bray)]

masturbate *ʻuʻu.*

mat *moena* (also means **carpet, bed**).

match 1. *hoʻokūkū* (sports or contest). 2. *ahipele* (for lighting fire).

matching 1. *like* (also means **alike**). [*Komo ka paʻa male i ka lole like.* The married couple wear **matching** clothes.] 2. *kohu.*

mate [n] *pili ʻaoʻao.* [*ʻImi mau ke kanaka i kāna pili ʻaoʻao.* Humans always seek a **mate**.] [v] 1. *male.* 2. *hoʻāo.* 3. *hoʻomau.*

math *makemakika* (from English). (math terms: add = *hoʻohui*; subtract = *lawe*; multiply = *hoʻonui*; divide = *puʻunaue*) (to count = *helu*)

mattress *pela.*

mature 1. *kanaka makua.* [*Kohu kanaka makua ke ʻano o kēnā makuahine ʻōpiopio.* The character of that young mother (by you) is like that of a **mature** person.] 2. *oʻo.*

May Mei (from English).

maybe *paha.* Note: Unlike "maybe" or "perhaps" in English, *paha* cannot be used alone, but must always follow another word. In sentences, *paha* directly follows the verb. The idiomatic phrase *malia* *paha* can start a sentence and indicates that maybe the action following will happen, as in the example. [***Malia paha* e kelepona mai ana ke kauka i kēia ahiahi. Maybe** (perhaps) the doctor will call tonight.] *Paha* is often added to *'ae* or *'a'ole* to convey the ideas of "probably so" and "probably not." [*E ho'oikaika kino ana 'oe i ka lā 'apōpō?* ***'Ae paha.*** Will you exercise tomorrow? **Probably so** (*lit.,* yes, maybe)]

mayor *meia* (from English).

meal 1. *'aina.* 2. *pā'ina* (also means **party, to eat**).

mean (disposition) *mākonā* (also means **hard-hearted**). [***Mākonā* kekahi mau luna mahikō.** Some sugar plantation supervisors were **mean.**]

meaning *mana'o.* [*He **mana'o** ko nā 'ano ao like 'ole i ke kahuna kilokilo.* All different kinds of clouds have **meaning** to the weather expert.]

measure *ana.*

measurement *ana.* (the immeasurable heaven = Kalaniana'ole, a descendant of royalty and a representative to Congress famed for helping establish Hawaiian Homes lands)

meat *'i'o* (also means **flesh**, **muscle**, figurative reference to the "heart" or core of the matter). (beef = *'i'o pipi*) (pork = *'i'o pua'a*)

meat

mechanic *mekanika* (from English). [*Ua hiki anei i ka **mekanika** ke ho'oponopono i ko Kanani mokokaikala?* Was the **mechanic** able to fix Kanani's motorcycle?]

medal *mekala* (also means **metal**).

medical practice, herbal medicine *lā'au lapa'au.*

medicine *lā'au.*

meditate *no'ono'o* (also means **to think**). [*Noho mālie ka'u kahunapule a **no'ono'o** ihola.* My minister sits calmly and then **meditates.**]

meet 1. *hui.* 2. *launa.*

meeting *hālāwai.* [*Ua launa hau'oli nā lālā o ka hui ho'oulu 'okika i ka **hālāwai** mua.* Members of the orchid-growing club happily interacted at the first **meeting.**]

melody *leo* (also means **voice**). [*He nani wale ka **leo** o "Makalapua."* The **melody** of "Makalapua" is just beautiful.]

melt *hehe'e.* [*Ke **hehe'e** nei ka haukalima i waiho 'ia ma ka pākaukau.* The ice cream that was left on the table is **melting.**]

memento *paumauno'ono'o.* [*Kau 'o Mehana i kona mau lei i ka 'umeke me he **paumauno'ono'o** lā.* Mehana places her leis in the calabash as a **memento.**]

memorial *ki'i ho'omana'o.*

memorize *ho'opa'ana'au.* [***Ho'opa'ana'au** ka ho'opa'a i ka mele oli āna e oli ai.* The hula drummer **memorizes** the chant he will chant.]

memory *waihona ho'omana'o* (*lit.* depository of memories). [*Miki kou **waihona ho'omana'o**?* Is your **memory** sharp?] Note: *Waihona ho'omana'o* refers to one's collection of memories or memory bank. *Hali'a*, *haili*, and *ho'omana'o* refer to a single memory of an event, place, or person.

men's eating house *mua.* Note: Traditionally, men prepared the food and ate separately from women.

menstrual house *hale pe'a.* Note: In ancient Hawai'i menstruating women retired to a separate house.

menstruate 1. *pe'a.* 2. *hana wai.*

menstruation 1. *ma'i wahine.* 2. *hanawai.*

menu *papa kuhikuhi mea 'ai.* [*E ke kuene, makemake au e 'ike i ka **papa kuhikuhi mea 'ai.*** Waiter, I'd like to see the **menu.**]

merciless *loko 'ino.*

mercy *aloha.*

merry *le'ale'a* (also means **fun, funny, enjoyable,** including **sexual pleasures**).

Merry Christmas Mele Kalikimaka (from English; *mele* means "song" or "poem" in Hawaiian, but in "Merry Christmas" it is used because it is the closest sound in Hawaiian to "merry").

message *mana'o* (Note: There is no exact equivalent for "message." *Mana'o* means **thought, idea**, many other meanings.)

messenger *'elele* (also means **delegate, representative**). [*Ua ho'ouna 'ia 'o Konela Iaukea i 'Enelani ma ke 'ano he '**elele** mai ke aupuni o Kalākaua.* Colonel Iaukea was sent to England as a **messenger** of the Kalākaua government.]

messy *kāpulu*. [*Kāpulu loa ka lumi kuke i ke kuke 'ana ou i ka mea 'ono?* Is the kitchen **messy** due to your cooking dessert?]

metal. 1. *mekala*. 2. *hao* (iron).

method *'ano hana*. [*He aha ke '**ano hana** kūpono e a'o aku i ka heluhelu 'ana?* What is the proper **method** to teach reading?]

meticulous *maiau*. [*Maiau ka hana a ka lehia.* The expert's work is **meticulous**.]

midday *awakea* (also means **noon**). [*'A'ohe ou aka ma ke **awakea**.* You have no shadow at **midday**.] Note: House blessings and other ceremonies are often done during midday, the time of the greatest light.

middle *waena*.

midnight *kulu aumoe*. [*ke 'ala a'u i honi i ke **kulu aumoe**,* the scent I smelled at **midnight**. (song, "Pua Ala Aumoe," by I. Beniamina)]

mild *'ūpalu*.

mile *mile* (from English; also means **mileage**). [*'Ehia **mile** āu e holopeki ai?* How many **miles** should you jog?]

military *pū'ali koa*.

milk 1. *waiū*. 2. *waiū kini* (canned milk). [*'O ka **waiū kini** a i 'ole ka wai niu ka mea e ho'omomona ai i ke kūlolo?* Is it **canned milk** or coconut milk that sweetens *kūlolo* (a dessert made with taro)?]

Milky Way *I'a*. [*Ua huli ka **I'a**.* The **Milky Way** has turned (it's past midnight).]

mill *wili*. (sugar mill = *hale wili kō*)

mine (belonging to me) 1. *ko'u*. 2. *ka'u*. 3. *no'u* 4. *na'u*. *Ko'u* and *ka'u* are possessive pronouns and can be used before nouns (*ka'u kālā* = my money) or in possessive sentences: (*He mana'o ko'u.* I have an idea/opinion.) *No'u* and *na'u* are used to indicate ownership and by extension *kuleana*, responsibility for and guardianship of an object, intellectual property, or even a person. (*No'u kēia 'āina* = This land is mine.) (*Na wai ka pēpē e uē nei? Na'u!* = Who does the baby who is crying belong to? To me!)

mine (pit) *lua 'eli*. (gold mine = *lua 'eli kula*)

minister *kahunapule*. [*Kaulana paha ke **kahunapule** i kona akahai.* The **minister** is well known for her gentleness.]

minister

minus *ho'olawe* (to subtract).

minute *minuke*. [*'O ka iwakālua **minuke** i hala ka hola 'ehā kēia.* It's twenty **minutes** past four.]

miracle *hana mana*. [*'O ke aloha ka **hana mana** e kū a'e mau ana.* Love is an ever-present **miracle**.]

mirage *waili'ulā*. [*Ma ke one wela nō i 'ike 'ia ai ka **waili'ulā** e ka lawai'a.* It was on the very hot sand that the **mirage** was seen by the fisherman.]

mirror *aniani*. [*Loa'a kekahi **aniani** kū koa kahiko i ko Līhau mau mākua.* Līhau's parents have an old *koa* standing **mirror**.] (hand-held mirror = *aniani pa'a lima*)

mischievous *kolohe* (also means **rascal**). [*Inā 'oe hana **kolohe**, 'a'ole e 'ae ana 'o Tūtū iā 'oe e 'ohi limu me ia.* If you are **mischievous**, Tūtū won't let you gather seaweed with her.]

misprint *pa'i hewa*. [*Hō kū ka paila o nā **pa'i hewa** ma ka palapala ho'oilina!* My, there are a great many **misprints** in the will!]

miss (someone) *ha'o*. [*Ha'o au iā ia. Ha'o anei paha 'o ia ala ia'u?* I **miss** him! Does he (over there) maybe **miss** me?]

missionary 1. *mikionele*. 2. *mikanele*.

misstep 1. *kāhehi*. 2. *hehi hewa*.

mist 1. *noe*. 2. *uhiwai*. (the misty rain = *ka ua noe*)

mistake 1. *hewa*. [He **hewa** *kāna pane*. Her answer is a **mistake**.] 2. *kuhi hewa*. (if I am not mistaken = *inā 'a'ole au i kuhi hewa*) [*Inā 'a'ole au i kuhi hewa*, *ua lohe mua au i kou inoa*. If I am not mistaken, I have heard your name before.] 3. *lalau*.

mistreat 1. *hana 'ino* (abuse). 2. *ho'omāuna* (waste, injure). [*E akahele kākou i 'ole e ho'omāuna i ka 'āina*. We all should be careful so we don't **mistreat** the land.]

mix 1. *kāwili* (to mix ingredients in food preparation). [*I ke kāwili 'ana ou i ke kōpa'a me ka palaoa, ho'ohana 'oe i ke puna?* When you **mix** the sugar and flour, do you use a spoon?] 2. *ho'owali* (poi). 3. *wili*.

mixed (colors or textures) *kipona*. [*Kui ko Ni'ihau i ke kaila lei pūpū i kapa 'ia ka lei kipona*. Ni'ihau's people string the style of shell *lei* called a **mixed** *lei*.]

mixed up (confused) *huikau*.

moan 1. *'ūhū*. 2. *kani'ūhū*. 3. *'ū*. 4. *kani'ū*.

mob 1. *uluāo'a*. 2. *po'e ho'ohaunaele*.

modest 1. *waipahē* (also means **courteous, gracious**). [*Waipahē kou 'ano, e ka mea ho'okipa*. You have a **modest** personality, host.] 2. *wiwo*.

moist 1. *ma'ū* (damp). [*Ma'ū i ka pu'u ke moni*. It's **moist** when you swallow it. (song, "Niu Haohao," by B. Mossman)] 2. *pulu* (soaked, drenched in moisture). 3. *līhau*.

monarchy *aupuni mō'ī*. [*E kū hou a'e ana ke aupuni mō'ī ma Hawai'i?* Will there appear a new **monarchy** in Hawai'i?]

Monday Pō'akahi. [*Hui kekahi mau papa ho'oikaika kino ma ke ahiahi o ka Pō'akahi*. Some exercise classes meet on **Monday** evenings.]

money *kālā*. (one dollar = *ho'okahi kālā*) [*Ho'okahi wale nō āna kālā. 'Ehia āu kālā?* He only has **one dollar**. How much **money** do you have?]

mongoose *manakuke*. [*He 'aihue akamai ka manakuke*. The **mongoose** is a clever thief.]

monkey *keko*. [*He mau keko nā keiki e pā'ani nei ma waho*. The children who are playing outside are (acting like) **monkeys**.]

monster 1. *pilikua nui*. 2. *tutua* (idiom).

month 1. *mahina*. [*'Elima Lāpule o kēia mahina a'e*. Next **month** has five Sundays.] 2. *malama*.

mood *'ano* (also means **personality, type, brand**).

moon *mahina*. (full moon = 1. Māhealani [name of night of full moon in ancient calendar]. 2. *mahina piha*) [*He mahina piha ko ka pō Māhealani*. The night **Māhealani** has a **full moon**.] (new moon = 1. *mahina hou*. 2. *hilo* [name of crescent moon, name of first month in ancient calendar].)

moral *pono* (also means **righteous, proper**, many other meanings).

more *hou* (also means **new, again**). [*Hiki iā lākou ke 'ai hou i ka haupia?* Can they (three) eat **more** coconut pudding?]

morning 1. *kakahiaka*. 2. *kakahiaka nui* (early morning). [*Holoholo ko'u 'anakala i ke kakahiaka nui*. My uncle goes out in the **early morning**.]

morning glory (plant) 1. *pōhuehue* (beach morning glory). 2. *koali*.

mosquito *makika*.

moth *pulelehua*. [*Ma nā pō ikīki e mumulu ana nā makika a me nā pulelehua a ānehe aku ka mo'o*. It is on hot and humid nights that mosquitoes and **moths** swarm and the gecko sneaks up (on them).]

mother *makuahine*.

mother-in-law *makuahūnōai wahine*.

Mother's Day Lā Makuahine. [*E waiho ana paha 'oe i nā loke ma ka pā ilina ma ka Lā Makuahine?* Will you perhaps leave roses at the cemetery on **Mother's Day**?]

motorcycle *mokokaikala*. [*Le'ale'a a maka'u ka holo mokokaikala*. Riding **motorcycles** is fun and dangerous.]

motorcycle

motto *mākia*. [*'O "Ho'oulu Lāhui" ka* **mākia** *kaulana a Kalākaua*. "Increase the nation" was Kalākaua's well-known **motto**.]

mountain 1. *kuahiwi* (considered to be older, more eroded than *mauna*). 2. *mauna*. [**kuahiwi** *kū kilakila i ka la'i*, **mountain** that stands majestic in the calm (song, "La'i Au Ē," by Lili'uokalani)]

mountainside *uka* (also means **uplands, upslope**). [*I* **uka** *lā, i* **uka**, *ka ulu lā'au*. There in the **uplands**, in the **uplands** is the forest. (song, "He Nani Ke Ao Nei," by M. K. Pukui)]

mourn 1. *makena*. 2. *uē*. 3. *kanikau*.

mouse *'iole* (refers to any rodent).

mousetrap *'ūmi'i 'iole*.

mouth *waha*. [*'Oiai he niho hu'i ko'u, 'a'ole pehu ko'u* **waha** *holo'oko'a*. Although I have a sore tooth, my whole **mouth** isn't swollen.]

mouse

move 1. *ho'one'e* (furniture, goods). 2. *ne'e* (move yourself). 3. *'oni* (wiggle, squirm). (moving smoothly, silently = *niau*).

movie *ki'i 'oni'oni*. [*Ma ka hola 'ehia e ho'omaka ai ke* **ki'i 'oni'oni** *a Eddie Kamae mā i ho'opa'a ai?* What time does the **movie** that Eddie Kamae folks made start?]

much *nui* (also means **big, large size, great importance**).

mucus *hūpē*.

mud 1. *kelekele*. 2. *lepo 'ūkele*. 3. *pālolo* (sticky mud [such as clay]).

muddy *'ūkele*. [*He alahele* **'ūkele** *ke alahele ma ka naele*. The trail in the swamp is a **muddy** trail.]

mug 1. *pola* (also means **bowl**). [*E 'olu'olu e ho'opiha hou i ko'u* **pola** *i ke kope*. Please fill my **mug** with coffee once more.] 2. *kī'aha* (also means **drinking glass**).

mulch *pulu* (also means **soaked with rain, coconut fiber**).

multiply 1. *ho'onui*. 2. *ho'omāhua*.

multitude 1. *lehulehu*. 2. *kini*. 3. *makamaka*. [*E nā* **kini**, *nā* **makamaka**, *ka* **lehulehu**. Oh **multitudes, friends, public** (common line at beginning of speeches).]

mumble *namunamu* (also means **to complain**). [*Ua ho'onui ka lehulehu* **namunamu** *a lilo i uluaō'a*. The **complaining** multitudes multiplied until they became a mob.]

munch 1. *nau* (chew). 2. *nome*. [*'O Pele ka wahine* **nome** *honua ma Puna*. Pele is the woman who **munches** the earth at Puna.]

murder *pepehi kanaka*.

murderer *lima koko* (*lit.* bloody hand).

muscle 1. *'i'o* (also means **meat, flesh**). [*'Ehia mau* **'i'o** *o ke kino?* How many **muscles** does the body have?] 2. *olonā* (also refers to a native shrub that yields a very strong fiber used for making cordage).

museum *hale hō'ike'ike*. [*Aia ke kalaunu Hawai'i ma ka* **hale hō'ike'ike** *a i 'ole ua ho'iho'i 'ia i ka Hale Ali'i?* Is the Hawaiian crown at the **museum** or was it returned to the Palace?]

mushroom *kūkaelio*.

music *mele* (also means **poetry**).

musician *mea ho'okani pila*.

muslin *ke'oke'o* (also means **white**).

must *pono* (also means **have to, should**). [**Pono** *nā kānaka maoli e mālama i nā lo'i kalo*. The native people **must** take care of the taro patches.]

mustache *'umi'umi*. [*Mai kahi i kou* **'umi'umi**. Don't shave your **mustache**.]

musty *pelekunu*.

mute 1. *hāmau*. 2. *mū*. 3. *mumule*.

mutual *like*. [*He kuleana* **like** *ko kāua e hānai pono i kā kāua keiki*. We (you and I) have a **mutual** responsibility for properly raising our child.]

my 1. *ko'u* (used in front of nouns that are things you can't help having, such as family born before you and including your generation, your name, land, friends, chiefs, gods, feelings, illnesses.

Also used for anything one can enter into or put on, including any building, mode of transportation, clothes). 2. *ka'u* (used in front of nouns that are things that can be acquired, including family born after you, your husband or wife, your work or any action, any tool [including computers and televisions], money, anything you make or create, food, drink, books). [*'O Maile **ka'u** mo'opuna*. Maile is **my** grandchild.]

mysterious 1. *āiwaiwa* (also means **fantastic, incomprehensible, amazing**). [***Āiwaiwa** nā ki'i pōhaku i kālai 'ia e ko kākou mau kūpuna*. The petroglyphs that were carved by our ancestors are **mysterious**.] 2. *pāha'oha'o*.

myth *ka'ao*.

nail 1. *kui.* [*'O ke **kui**, ka hāmale a me ka pahiolo nā mea ho'ohana a ke kamanā.* **Nails**, hammers and saws are the carpenter's tools.] 2. *miki'ao* (fingernail or toenail).

naked 1. *kohana.* 2. *'ōlohelohe.*

name [n] *inoa.* [*He **inoa** kaulana anei paha ko kou 'ohana?* Does your family perhaps have a well-known **name**?] [v] *kapa.*

nap *hiamoe iki.*

napkin *kāwele* (also means **towel, to dry**). [*Lawa nā **kāwele** i lawe 'ia mai i kahakai?* Are there enough **napkins** that were brought to the beach?]

napkin

narrate *ha'i* (also means **to tell, to break**). (show and tell = *hō'ike a ha'i*)

narrow *hāiki.* [*Hāiki maoli nō ke alahele ma ka wēkiu.* The trail is really **narrow** at the summit. (fine points, details [or narrow-minded] = *mana'o hāiki*) (main idea, general idea [or broad-minded] = *mana'o laulā*)

nation *aupuni* (also means **kingdom, government, country**).

nationality *lāhui* (also means **ethnic group**).

native [n] 1. *kupa.* 2. *'ōiwi.* 3. *kama'āina.* 4. *kanaka maoli* (*lit.* native person, a recent addition to the language). [adj] *maoli.* [*He holoholona Hawai'i **maoli** ka 'ōpe'ape'a.* The Hawaiian bat is a **native** Hawaiian animal.]

native country 1. *'āina hānau.* 2. *one hānau* (also means **birthplace**).

nauseated 1. *poluea* (from motion; seasick). [***Poluea** nā 'ōhua i ka holu 'ana o ka holo mokulele.* The passengers are **nauseated** due to the bumpiness of plane travel.] 2. *liliha* (from eating rich food).

navel *piko* (also means **umbilical cord**, *fig.* fontanel [top of head where *'aumakua* sits], **genitals, summit, center**, many other meanings). [*Ua hamohamo ke kahu ma'i i ka **piko** o ka pēpē hou.* The nurse rubbed the new baby's **navel**.]

navigator *ho'okele* (*fig.* business leader, administrator).

near *kokoke.* [***Kokoke** ko ko'u kaiko'eke wahine hale i ke kikowaena kū'ai.* My sister-in-law's house is **near** the shopping center.]

neat 1. *'auli'i* (also means **cute, dainty**). [***'Auli'i** ko kāna kaikamahine lole.* Her daughter's clothes are **neat**.] 2. *maiau* (also means **meticulous work, speech**).

necessary *pono.*

neck *'ā'ī.* [*'O nā pua melia nā pua ma ko Kana'ina lei **'ā'ī**.* Plumerias are the flowers in Kana'ina's **neck** lei.]

need 1. *pono* (also means **necessity**). 2. *nele* (literally means **lacking**; used by some native speakers in place of need). [***Nele** lākou i ke kaula sugi.* They **need** sugi fishing line.] Note: *Makemake*, which means "like" or "want," can also be used to convey the idea of needing something. *Makemake au i ke kālā* can mean either "I want," "I like," or "I need money," while *Nele au i ke kālā* means "I lack money" and can be used to imply that since I don't have any I therefore need some.

needle *kui* (also means **nail**). [*He **kui** 'oi kā ka wahine e kuiki nei?* Does the woman who is quilting now have a sharp **needle**?]

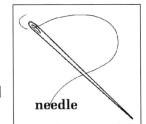
needle

negate *hō'ole* (also means to **refuse, deny, protest, contradict**). [*Mai **hō'ole** i ke kuluma mai ke au kahiko mai.* Don't **negate** traditions from the old days.]

negative (photographic) *aka ki'i*. [*Hiki ke pa'i hou 'ia ke **aka ki'i**.* A **negative** can be reprinted.]

neglect *malama 'ole*. [*Hewa ka luahine i **malama 'ole** i kāna mau pōpoki.* The old lady who **neglected** her cats was wrong.]

neighbor 1. *hoa noho*. [*'Olu'olu ko'u mau **hoa noho** ma kēia kaiaulu.* My **neighbors** in this community are nice.] 2. *hoalauna*.

nephew 1. *keiki 'ohana*. 2. *keiki hanauna*.

nerve 1. *a'a*. 2. *a'alolo*.

nervous 1. *ha'alulu*. [*Ma'a 'o Kaleo i ke kū 'ana ma mua o ke anaina a 'a'ole 'o ia **ha'alulu**.* Kaleo is used to standing before an audience and he isn't **nervous**.] 2. *pīhoihoi* (also means **excited**).

nest *pūnana* (also means **hive, shelter**, *fig.* **home**). [*E komo mai i ko mākou wahi **pūnana**.* Come into our little **nest**.]

net *'upena* (also means **web**). [*He **'upena** nae, 'a'ohe mea hei 'ole. ('ōlelo no'eau)* It's a fine-meshed **net**, there is nothing that is not caught (refers to a beautiful woman attractive to all).]

new *hou*. [*He aha ka mea **hou**?* What's **new**?]

newcomer *malihini* (also means **stranger, guest**). [*He **malihini** 'oe i ka 'ao'ao Ko'olau o ka mokupuni nei?* Are you a **newcomer** to the windward side of this island?]

newspaper *nūpepa*. [*Nui nā **nūpepa** 'ōlelo Hawai'i i kēlā kenekulia aku nei.* There were lots of Hawaiian language **newspapers** in the last century.]

newspaper
Daily News

New Zealand Aotearoa.

next month *i kēia mahina a'e*.

next week *i kēia pule a'e*.

next year *i kēia makahiki a'e*. [*I **kēia makahiki a'e** paha ana 'o ia e ho'omaha loa ai.* It is **next year** that he may retire.]

nice 1. *maika'i* (good quality). 2. *'olu'olu* (kind, comfortable).

niece 1. *kaikamahine 'ohana*. (pl. *kaikamāhine 'ohana*) [*E lawe aku ana ko'u 'anakē iā mākou **kaikamāhine 'ohana** i ka hale hō'ike'ike.* My auntie will take us **nieces** to the museum.] 2. *kaikamahine hanauna*.

night *pō* (also means **darkness, nighttime**, many other meanings). [*Pō'ele'ele ka **pō** Kāne.* The **night** called Kāne (ancient lunar calendar) is dark.]

nimble *'eleu* (also means **lively**).

nine *'eiwa*. [***'Eiwa** mahina o kā ka'u kaikamahine pēpē.* My daughter's baby is **nine** months old.]

no *'a'ole* (also means **not**). [*Pehea 'olua? Hau'oli paha 'olua? **'A'ole** loa. Kaumaha nō māua.* How are you two? Are you folks happy? **Not** at all. We two are very sad.]

noble [n] 1. *ali'i*. 2. *lani*. [adj] *ali'i*.

nobody *'a'ohe mea*. [***'A'ohe mea** e hō'ole i kāna noi.* **Nobody** can refuse her request.]

nod *kūnou*.

noise 1. *hana kuli*. 2. *kulikuli*. 3. *wawā*.

noisy 1. *kulikuli*. 2. *wawā*. [*I ka pō 'ino, he **wawā** nō ke ku'i a ka hekili.* On a stormy night, the thunder is really **noisy**.]

noon *awakea*.

normal *'ano mau*. [*Ulu kēia kalo malo'o ma ke **'ano mau**?* Does this dry land taro grow in the **normal** way?]

north *'ākau* (also means **right** [direction]). [*Aia 'o Kaua'i ma ka **'ākau** o Ni'ihau.* Kaua'i is to the **north** of Ni'ihau.]

nose *ihu*.

nose flute *'ohe hano ihu*.

nosy *nīele* (implies asking too many questions, considered rude). [*Mai **nīele** aku

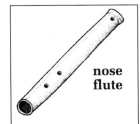
nose flute

i kou 'anakala. Mai poina "Pa'a ka waha, hana ka lima." Don't ask **nosy** questions of your uncle. Don't forget, "Close your mouth and your hands do the work." (traditional Hawaiian concept of learning)]

nothing 1. *[n] mea 'ole.* [*He **mea 'ole** ia.* It's **nothing.**] 2. *'ole* (when added after a word, means someone has none of that thing: *niho 'ole* = toothless; *waiwai 'ole* = worthless).

notice *[n] 'ōlelo hō'ike* (notification). 2. *[v] nānā* (to observe something). [***Nānā** nā mea kilo hōkū i ka hōkū welowelo ma ka 'ohe nānā.* The astronomers **observe** the comet through the telescope.]

November Nowemapa (from English).

now *i kēia manawa.* [*Ke hō'au'au ke kauka holoholona i kāna mau lio **i kēia manawa**.* The vet is bathing his horses **now.**]

nowadays *i kēia mau lā* (also means **these days**).

numb *mā'e'ele* (can mean numb with shock).

number *helu.*

numerous 1. *nui.* 2. *lau.*

nurse *kahu ma'i.*

nut *hua* (also means **fruit of plant, offspring of animal, human, egg, produce**). [*Hō ka 'ono o ka **hua** "macadamia"!* Wow, how delicious macadamia **nuts** are!]

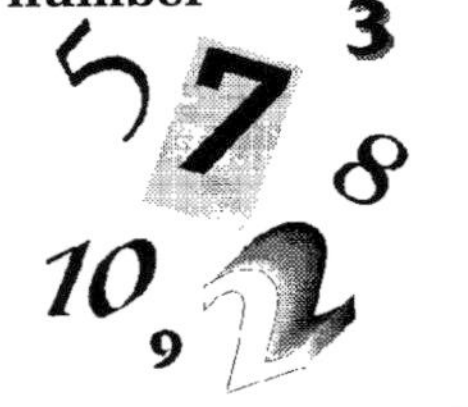

oar *hoe.* [*'Ano kaumaha ka **hoe** koa.* A koa **oar** is rather heavy.]

oath *ho'ohiki* (also means **promise, swear an oath**). [*Pono e ho'okō i kāu mea i **ho'ohiki** ai.* (You) have to fulfill the thing you **swore an oath** to do.]

obey 1. *ho'olono.* 2. *lohe.*

observatory (astronomical) *hale kilo lani.* [*Ke māhuahua nei nā **hale kilo lani** ma luna o Mauna Kea.* The **observatories** on top of Mauna Kea are multiplying.]

observe 1. *nānā.* 2. *hākilo.*

obsession *pulakaumaka.* [*He **pulakaumaka** ka hāpai hao i kekahi mau kānaka.* Lifting weights is an **obsession** to some people.]

obstruct *ālai.* [*Ālai 'ia e Nounou,* **obstructed** by Nounou (mountain on Kaua'i) (line from "Kūnihi ka Mauna," a chant asking permission to enter *hula hālau*)]

obstruction *ālai.*

obtain *loa'a* (also means **to find, catch, receive, have possession of**). [*Loa'a anei ke ahipele iā 'oe?* Do you **have** a match?]

occur *kupu.* [*Ua **kupu** a'e ka ulia pōpilikia ma ko'u ke'ena i 'elua manawa, a i ka hanana 'elua, ua ālai 'ia ka puka.* Emergencies **occurred** at my office two times, and on the second occurrence, the door was blocked.]

occurrence *hanana.*

ocean *moana* (refers to deep, open ocean, whereas *kai* refers to all seas, channels between islands, etc.). [*Holo **moana** nā wa'a kaulua.* Double-hulled canoes sail the open **ocean**.]

ocean side *ma kai.*

o'clock *hola* (also means **time**). [*'O ka **hola** 'ehia kēia? 'O ka **hola** 'umikūmākahi o ke aumoe!* What **time** is it? It's eleven **o'clock** at night!]

October *'Okakopa* (from English).

octopus *he'e.* [*'Ono ka **he'e** i ka leho a no laila he pūpū leho ko ka lūhe'e.* **Octopus** crave cowrie and therefore the octopus lure has a cowrie shell.]

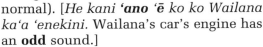
octopus

odd *'ano 'ē* (idiomatic phrase meaning strange, bizarre, not normal). [*He kani **'ano 'ē** ko ko Wailana ka'a 'enekini.* Wailana's car's engine has an **odd** sound.]

off *pio* (also means **extinguished**). (to turn off = *ho'opio*) [*E **ho'opio** i ka mīkini.* **Turn off** the machine.]

offend *ho'onāukiuki* (also means **to irritate, provoke**). [*'A'ole 'oe e **ho'onāukiuki** i kāu luna 'oihana o pilikia auane'i.* You shouldn't **offend** your boss at work or there'll be trouble later.]

offering *ho'okupu* (*lit.* to cause to sprout; spiritual offering at sacred site).

office *ke'ena.* [*Aia i hea kou **ke'ena**?* Where's your **office**?]

often *pinepine.* [*Waiho **pinepine** ka lehu-lehu i nā 'ano ho'okupu like 'ole ma Halema'uma'u.* The public **often** leave all sorts of offerings at Halema'uma'u (crater considered to be Pele's dwelling place).]

oil *'aila* (also means **tar, grease, greasy**). [*Kau nā wāhine Polapola i ka **'aila** niu i ko lākou mau lauoho a hinuhinu.* The women of Tahiti put coconut **oil** on their hair until it's shiny.]

oily 1. *hinuhinu.* 2. *kelekele.*

ointment *'aila hamo* (also means **massage oil**).

old *kahiko.*

old man *'elemakule.* (*pl. 'elemākule*)

old woman *luahine.* (*pl. luāhine*) [*Na nā luāhine e alaka'i i ko lākou mau 'ohana.* The **old women** are the ones who lead their families.]

omen *hō'ailona* (also means **sign, symbol**).

omit *kāpae* (also means **skip, pass**). [*E kāpae i ko'u manawa.* **Omit** my turn.]

one 1. *'ekahi* (used for counting). 2. *ho'okahi* (used to indicate possession of one item). [*No laila, ho'okahi ou kaikunāne? Pololei, ho'okahi wale nō o'u kaikunāne.* Therefore, you have **one** brother? Correct, I have only **one** brother (woman speaking).]

onion 1. *'aka'akai.* 2. *'aka'akai lau* (green onions).

only *wale nō* (follows word it modifies; an intensifier that can also be translated **just, very**). [*'O nā kumuniu wale nō nā kumulā'au e ulu ana ma ke one.* **Only** coconut trees are growing in the sand.]

open [v] *wehe* (also means **to remove, take off**). [adj] 1. *mōhala* (open blossom). 2. *hāmama* (open door, open-hearted). [*Hāmama nā hale kū'ai ma ke ahiahi pō'alima?* Are the stores **open** on Friday evenings?]

operate 1. *hana* (to operate machinery, do or make something). 2. *kaha* (to cut open, perform surgery).

oppose *kū'ē* (also means **to protest**).

opposite *kū'ē.* [*'O wai ka hua 'ōlelo kū'ē iā "waho"? 'O "loko" ka pane pololei.* What is the **opposite** word of "outside"? "Inside" is the right answer.]

or *a i 'ole* (phrase, *lit.* "and if not"). [*I wai hua 'ai a i 'ole i koloaka nāu?* Would you like juice **or** soda?]

orange *'alani* (refers to fruit and color).

ordeal *pōpilikia* (also means **trouble, problem, misfortune**). [*Inā*

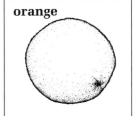
orange

ua ulu a'e 'oe a he 'elemakule, ua 'ike maka 'oe i nā pōpilikia. If you have lived to be an old man, you have experienced **ordeals**.]

order 1. *ka'ina* (succession, sequence of action, logic). [*He aha ke ka'ina hana pololei i ka ho'opakele ola?* What is the correct **order** of action in saving a life?] 2. *kauoha* (command, to command).

ordinary 1. *ma'a mau* (also means **usual**). [*He mea ma'a mau ke kaula'i 'ōpelu ma Kona.* Drying 'ōpelu fish in the sun is an **ordinary** thing in Kona.]

organ 1. *māhele kino* (body part). 2. *'okana* (from English; musical instrument).

organic *maoli* (also means **native, real**).

organization *'ahahui* (also means **club**). [*Nui nā 'Ahahui Kiwila Hawai'i ma Kaleponi?* Are there lots of Hawaiian Civic **Clubs** in California?]

organize *ho'onohonoho* (also means **to edit, put in order**).

origin 1. *kinohi* (genesis). 2. *kumu* (source, foundation). [*Mai kinohi mai,* From the beginning]

other 1. *kekahi.* [*E mālama kekahi i kekahi.* Take care of each **other**.] 2. *'ē a'e.* [*Aia i hea nā ipuhao 'ē a'e?* Where are the **other** pots and pans?]

our (yours and my): 1. *ko kāua.* 2. *kā kāua.* (hers/his and my): 1. *ko māua.* 2. *kā māua.* (all of us, 3 or more): 1. *ko kākou.* 2. *kā kākou.* (3 or more, not your): 1. *ko mākou.* 2. *kā mākou. Ko kāua, ko māua, ko kākou,* and *ko mākou* are used in front of nouns that are things you can't help having, such as family born before you and including your generation, your name, land, friends, chiefs, gods, feelings, illnesses. Also used for anything one can enter into or put on, including any building, mode of transportation, clothes. *Kā kāua, kā māua, kā kākou,* and *kā mākou* are used in front of nouns that are things that can be acquired, including family born after you, your husband or wife, your work or any action, any tool [including computers and televisions], money, anything you make or create, food, drink, books.

outlet (electric) *kumu ho'opuka uila.*

outrigger boom *'iako.*

outrigger float *ama.* [*E hāpai i ka 'iako a e kau ma luna o ke* **ama.** Lift the boom and place it on the **outrigger float.**]

outside *waho.* [*Aia nā 'alani me nā lemi āna i 'ako ai ma* **waho** *o ka pahu hau i mehana lākou ke 'ai 'ia?* Are the oranges and lemons he picked **outside** of the icebox (refrigerator), so that they will be warm when eaten?]

outside

outstanding *po'okela.* [*He mau mahi'ai* **po'okela** *kēlā mau kānaka ho'oulu pua.* Those flower growers are **outstanding** farmers.]

oven 1. *'oma* (stove). 2. *imu* (pit lined with hot lava rocks in which food is cooked by steaming).

overbearing *ho'okelakela.*

overcast *'ōmalumalu.* [*Ua* **'ōmalumalu** *ka lewa ma mua o ka hō'ea 'ana o ka makani pāhili.* The sky was **overcast** before the arrival of the hurricane.]

overcome 1. *lanakila* (to win, be victorious). 2. *lo'ohia* (overwhelmed with emotion).

overthrow *ho'okāhuli.* [*He hana 'ino maoli ka* **ho'okāhuli** *aupuni i ka lāhui 'ōiwi.* **Overthrowing** the government was a great harm to the native population.]

overwhelm *po'ipū.*

overwhelmed 1. *pa'uhia.* [***Pa'uhia** ke kākau 'ōlelo i ka hana.* The secretary is **overwhelmed** with work.] 2. *lo'ohia.*

owe *'ai'ē* (also means **debt**). (to lend = *hō'ai'ē*)

oyster 1. *'ōlepe* (also means any **mussel**, any type of **bivalve**). 2. *pipi* (pearl oyster).

Pacific Pākīpika. [*Holo moana ko kākou mau kūpuna a puni ka **Pākīpika**.* Our ancestors voyaged all around the **Pacific**.]

pack 1. ho'oukana. [*I loko nō o kona **ho'oukana** 'auli'i 'ana i kāna lole i ka paiki, ua mino nā holokū ma hope.* In spite of her carefully **packing** the suitcase, the *holokū* (long formal *mu'umu'u* with a train) were wrinkled later on.] 2. ho'okomo.

package pū'olo (originally a *tī* leaf bundle tied around offerings or leis; also means **bag, bundle, parcel**). [*Na ka hoa noho i waiho i kēia **pū'olo** manakō na kākou.* It was the neighbor who left this **package** of mangoes for us all.]

pad pale (also means **to defend, protect, shield**).

paddle (canoe) hoe wa'a.

paddler mea hoe wa'a.

page 'ao'ao (also means **side, hemisphere**). [*Aia kekahi mau ki'i o ke kumu 'ōlapa ma ka **'ao'ao** kanahā o kēnā puke.* There are some pictures of an *'ōlapa* tree on **page** forty of that book (by you).]

painful 'eha (also means **hurt, sore**). [*'A'ole **'eha** ka hoene.* Injections are not **painful**.]

paint pena. [*Aia iā wai ka **pena** 'ōma'oma'o?* Who has the green **paint**?]

pair pa'a. (suit of clothes = pa'a lole) [*Ma hea 'oe i ho'olimalima ai i kou **pa'a lole** no ka 'aha ho'ohanohano?* Where did you rent your **suit of clothes** for the celebration?] (pair of shoes = pa'a kāma'a) (married couple = pa'a male)

palace hale ali'i. [*Aia ka **Hale Ali'i** 'o Hulihe'e ma kapa kai ma Kailua, Kona.* Hulihe'e **Palace** is at the edge of the sea in Kailua, Kona.]

pale hākeakea.

palm 1. pāma (from English; plant). 2. niu (plant). 3. poho (palm of hand).

pants 1. lole wāwae. 2. lole wāwae pōkole (shorts). [*E komo i kou **lole wāwae** ma mua o ka pā'ani pōpeku wāwae.* Put on your **pants** before the soccer game.]

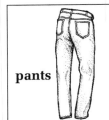

pants

papaya hē'ī.

paper 1. pepa. 2. nūpepa (newspaper).

paper napkin kāwele pepa.

paper plate pā pepa.

parade 1. ka'i huaka'i. 2. paikau (military parade).

Paradise 1. Paliuli (a legendary "heavenly" place in the uplands of Ōla'a on Hawai'i island). 2. Pihanakalani (another "heavenly" place in the uplands of Hanalei on Kaua'i).

paragraph paukū (also means **verse, section, stanza**).

parallel 1. moe like. [***Moe like** ke ala holo o nā hōkūhele?* Are the paths of the planets parallel?] 2. kaulike.

paralyzed 1. lōlō. 2. mū. [*He lima **mū** ko ke kahu ma'i.* The nurse has a **paralyzed** arm.]

parent makua. (pl. mākua) [*E Nu'ulani, 'āpono kou mau **mākua** i kou ho'i 'ana i ka hale i ke kulu 'aumoe?* Nu'ulani, do your **parents** approve of your returning home at midnight?]

park pāka. [*Kaulana ka inoa o Kapi'olani*

Pāka. The name of Kapiʻolani **Park** is well known. (song, "Kapiʻolani Park," by J. Almeida)]

party *pāʻina.* [*Ma ka hola ʻehia e hoʻomaka ai ka **pāʻina** ma kēia hopenapule aʻe a ia hopenapule aku?* What time does the **party** start on the weekend after next?]

pass 1. *hala* (also means **to die, pass away**). [***Hala** aʻe ʻo Māmala e ʻau aʻe nei ma hope.* Māmala (Honolulu Harbor) was **passed** by, swimming behind them. (song, "He Aloha Nō ʻo Honolulu," by L. Keawe)] 2. *kāʻalo.* [*Ua nānā pono ʻoe i kēlā kāne nohea i **kāʻalo** aku nei?* Did you get a good look at that handsome man who just **passed** by?] 3. *māʻalo.*

passenger *ʻōhua.* [*Ke namunamu nei ka **ʻōhua** i ke kalaiwa kaʻa **ʻōhua.*** The **passenger** is complaining to the bus driver.]

passion *kaunu.*

passionate 1. *konikoni* (love). 2. *koʻikoʻi* (also means **urgent, stressed, weighty**). [*He mea **koʻikoʻi** ka hoʻōla hou i ka ʻōlelo makuahine i ka hapanui o ka poʻe kupa o ka ʻāina.* Reviving the mother tongue is a **passionate** matter to the majority of the natives of the land.]

passport *palapala hoʻāpono.* [*Ua nalowale anei kā kāua mau **palapala hoʻāpono?*** Have our (your and my) **passports** disappeared?]

past 1. *ka wā i hala.* [*I **ka wā i hala**, ua nui ʻino nā māla nani o ke kaona nei.* In the **past**, this town had so many beautiful gardens.] 2. *ke au kahiko.*

paste [n] 1. *pauka* (also means **powder**). 2. *pauka niho* (toothpaste). (face powder = *pauka maka*) [v] 1. *hoʻopili.* 2. *tuko.*

pastry *mea ʻono* (also means **dessert**).

patched *pohopoho.*

patchwork quilt *ke kapa kuiki pohopoho.*

path *alahele* (also means **trail**). [*Nui nā **alahele** e piʻi aʻe ana i nā kuahiwi.* There are lots of **paths** that go up into the mountains.]

path

patience 1. *ahonui.* 2. *hoʻomanawanui.* [*ʻO ka **hoʻomanawanui**, ʻo ke akahai, ʻo ia ka mea e hiki pono ai.* **Patience** and gentleness are the things that make all go well. (hymn from Niʻihau, "ʻO Ka Hoʻomanawanui," by the Beazly family)]

pattern *ana* (also means **measurement, survey, cave**, many other meanings). [*Kapa ʻia ke **ana** kapa kuiki Hawaiʻi he "lau."* A Hawaiian quilt **pattern** is called a "leaf."]

pause *hoʻomaha* (also means **to rest**).

paw *wāwae* (also means **leg, foot**).

pay *uku* (also means **salary**). [*E **uku** koke i nā pila mai nā kāleka kākī mai.* Quickly **pay** the bills from charge cards.]

payday *lā uku.* [*ʻO kēia lā ka **lā uku**?* Is today **payday**?]

peace *maluhia.* [*E **maluhia** ka honua.* May there be **peace** on earth.] (make peace = *hoʻomaluhia*)

peaceful *maluhia.*

peacock *pīkake.*

peak *puʻu* (also means **hill, bump**, many other meanings).

pear *pea* (from English; slang for avocado; also means **bear**).

pebble 1. *ʻili.* 2. *ʻiliʻili.* [*nā **ʻiliʻili** nehe i ke kai,* **pebbles** rustling in the sea (song, "Kawaihae," by B. Lincoln)]

pedal *hehi wāwae.*

peddle *kālewa* (also means **trader, merchant, to sell merchandise**). [***Kālewa** nā kaikamāhine i nā mea ʻono kuki.* The girls **peddle** cookies.]

peek 1. *kiʻei.* [*Ke **kiʻei** aku ʻoe i ka puka kī, he aha kāu mea e ʻike ai?* When you **peek** into the key hole, what do you see?] 2. *hālō.*

peel *māihi.* [*E **māihi** i ka ʻili o ka ʻalani ma mua o ka ʻai ʻana.* **Peel** the skin of the orange before eating it.]

peg *kui lāʻau.*

pen 1. *peni* (writing implement). 2. *pā* (enclosure for animals).

pencil *penikala.*

penis *ule.*

people 1. *kānaka.* 2. *poʻe.*

pencil

[*He lehulehu nā **poʻe** i ʻākoʻakoʻa i ka hoʻolewa.* A multitude of **people** gathered at the funeral.]

percent *pakeneka.* [*ʻEhia **pakeneka** ka uku paneʻe ma kou panakō?* What **percent** is the interest at your bank?]

perch *hakahaka.*

perfect *hemolele* (also means **flawless, holy, many other meanings**). [*ʻAʻole **hemolele** kā kaʻu keiki heluhelu ʻana.* My child's reading isn't **perfect**.]

perform 1. *hoʻokō* (also means **to fulfill a command**). 2. *hana* (also means **to work, do something**).

perfume *wai ʻala.* [*Hū ke onaona o kēnā **wai ʻala**!* Wow, how strong your **perfume** is!]

perhaps *paha* (also means **maybe**). Note: Must be used after another word or phrase.

peril *pōʻino* (also means **misfortune, storm**).

period 1. *wā* (also means **era, epoch**). 2. *au* (also means **current**). 3. *maʻi wahine* (*lit.* woman's sickness, menstruation). 4. *kiko pau* (punctuation mark at the end of a sentence).

permanent 1. *paʻa.* 2. *loa.* 3. *mau.* (Each of these words has many other meanings; they can also be combined for added emphasis, such as in the idiomatic expression "*a mau loa aku*," which is one way of expressing the idea of "forever and ever.") [*Paʻa kēia pili **a mau loa aku.*** This close relationship is **permanent**.]

permission *ʻae.* [*Ua **ʻae** ke aupuni iā mākou e komo i ke awāwa.* The government gave us (we all, not you) **permission** to enter the valley.]

permit 1. *ʻae* (to allow, agree to). 2. *palapala ʻae* (written permit).

person *kanaka* (also means **human being**). (pl. *kānaka*)

personal 1. *pilikino.* [*He mea **pilikino** ka manaʻolana e loaʻa i ke aloha.* Hoping for love is a **personal** thing.] 2. *ponoʻī.*

perspiration *hou.*

perspire *kahe ka hou.*

pesticide *lāʻau make* (also means **poison**).

pet [*n*] *hānaiāhuhu.* [*He aha ke ʻano o kāu **hānaiāhuhu**? He lāpaki kāu?* What kind of **pet** do you have? Do you have a rabbit?]. [*v*] *hamohamo* (also means **to rub**).

petal *lihilihi.*

petition *palapala noi.* [*Nui nā **palapala noi** e loaʻa i ka ʻahaʻōlelo.* There are many **petitions** that the legislature receives.]

petroglyph *kiʻi pōhaku.*

phone *kelepona.* [*Aia a pau kāna hana, e **kelepona** mai ana ʻo Pāpā.* As soon as his work is finished, Daddy will **phone** us.]

petroglyph

photograph *kiʻi* (also means **picture, sculpture, statue, image**). (to take photo = *paʻi kiʻi*)

pick 1. *ʻako* (to pluck, gather). [***Ako** pinepine kā lākou mau moʻopuna i nā pua melia i ka pā ilina.* Their (three) grandchildren often **pick** plumerias in the graveyard.] 2. *wae* (to cull). 3. *koho* (to choose, select).

picnic *pikiniki.* [*ʻO Ala Moana kahi a lākou e **pikiniki** ai.* Ala Moana is the place where they **picnic**.]

picture *kiʻi* (also means **photograph, sculpture, image, statue**, etc.). [*He mau **kiʻi** nani nā kiʻi a Madge Tennant i pena ai.* The **pictures** that Madge Tennant painted are beautiful **pictures**.]

pie *pai* (from English). [*Ma uka loa i ʻako ai nā keiki i nā hua ʻōhelo no ka **pai**.* It was far upland that the children gathered ʻōhelo berries for a **pie**.]

piece *ʻāpana.* [*I **ʻāpana** pai nāu?* Would you like a **piece** of pie?]

pig *puaʻa.* [*Māunauna ka waokele i ka **puaʻa**.* The rain forest is laid to waste by **pigs**.]

pile 1. *ahu.* [*ʻO ke **ahu** pōhaku ka hōʻailona o ke alahele.* The **pile** of stones is the trail marker.] 2. *puʻu.*

pill *huaale.* [*Mai ale i ka **huaale** o maʻi ʻoe ma hope.* Don't swallow the **pill** or you'll be sick later on.]

pilot *pailaka.* [*ʻAʻohe mokulele o ka **pailaka**.* The **pilot** doesn't have a plane.]

pimple 1. *huehue*. 2. *puʻu* (also means **hill, lump**, many other meanings).

pin *kui* (also means **nail, needle, injection**).

pineapple *hala kahiki* (*lit.* foreign *hala* [the fruit of the pineapple and the *hala* plant look alike]).

pineapple

pink *ʻākala*. [*ʻĀkala nō ia hōkele kaulana*. That famous hotel is **pink** indeed.]

pipe *paipu*. [*Ua puhi* **paipu** *kuʻu Tūtū*. My beloved grandparent smoked a **pipe**.]

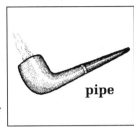

pipe

pit 1. *lua* (hole in the ground). 2. *hua* (seed). 3. *ʻīkoi* (core of some fruits, such as breadfruit, apple).

pitted *ʻālualua* (also means **rough terrain**). [*ʻĀlualua ke alanui i kīpapa ʻole ʻia*. The unpaved road is **pitted** and rough.]

pizza *pika*. [*Hiki anei ke lawe ʻia mai ka* **pika** *i kēia ahiahi?* Can a **pizza** be delivered this evening?]

place 1. *kau* (to put something some place). 2. *kūlana* (rank or position in competition). (first place = *kūlana ʻekahi*)

plain 1. *maopopo* (clear, easily understood). 2. *kula* (broad area of land between mountain and sea).

plan [v] *hoʻolālā*. [*E* **hoʻolālā** *kāua i ka ʻaha mele ʻimi kālā no ke kula ʻōlelo Hawaiʻi*. Let's (you and me) **plan** the benefit concert for the Hawaiian language school.]

plane (airplane) *mokulele*.

planet *hōkū hele*. [*ʻO ʻIao ka* **hōkū hele** *i kā ʻia e nā hōkū welowelo*. Jupiter is the planet that was hit by comets.]

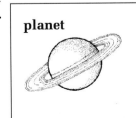

planet

plank *papa lāʻau* (*lit.* wooden board).

plant [n] *mea kanu*. [v] *kanu* (also means **to bury**). [*Ua* **kanu** *ka* *ʻīlio i kāna iwi ma lalo o ka* **mea kanu**. The dog **buried** his bone under **the plant**.]

plantation *mahikō* (sugar plantation). [*E mau ana ka* **mahikō** *ma Waialua?* Will the sugar **plantation** at Waialua continue?]

plastic *ʻea*.

plastic bag *ke ʻeke ʻea*.

plate *pā*. [*Aia iā ʻolua ke* **pā** *mea ʻai?* Do you (two) have the **plate** lunch?]

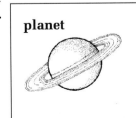

plastic bag

platform *kahua*.

play 1. *pāʻani* (game, play activity). (play football; football game = *pāʻani pōpeku*; play basketball; basketball game = *pāʻani pōhīnaʻi;* to play volleyball; volleyball game = *pāʻani pōpaʻi lima;* to play golf; golf game = *pāʻani kolepa;* to play baseball; baseball game = *pāʻani pōhili;* to play soccer; soccer game = *pāʻani pōpeku wāwae;* to play instrument = *hoʻokani pila*) 2. *hana keaka* (theatrical production). [*Leʻaleʻa ka* **hana keaka** *hou a ka Hālau Hanakeaka!* The new **play** by the Hawaiian language theater troupe is funny!]

pleasant *ʻoluʻolu*.

please (request) *e ʻoluʻolu*. [*E* **ʻoluʻolu**, *e kōkua mai*. **Please** help me.]

plump *nepunepu*. [*ʻAno* **nepunepu** *ka wahine hāpai*. The pregnant lady is sort of **plump**.]

plunge *luʻu* (also means **to dive**). [**Luʻu** *kai ka lawaiʻa e ʻō iʻa*. The fisherman **dives** in the ocean to spear fish.] (to soak, dye = *hoʻoluʻu*)

plus *a me* (*lit.* and with). [*ʻEkolu* **a me** *ʻumi*. Three **plus** ten.]

pocket *pākeke* (from English; also means **bucket**).

poet *haku mele* (syn. *mea haku mele*; also means **writer, composer**).

poetry 1. *ke mele* (also means **music**). 2. *ka mele* (song, chant).

point 1. *kuhi* (gesture). 2. *lae* (peninsula, land jutting out into sea). 3. *kiko* (dot). 4. *wēlau* (tip).

poison *lā'au make* (also means **insecticide**).

pole *pou*.

police *māka'i*.

police station *hale māka'i*. [*Aia ka* **hale māka'i** *hou ma ke alanui 'o Hale Māka'i.* The new **police station** is on Hale Māka'i Street.]

police

polite 1. *waipahē* (also means **courteous, gentle, modest**). [**Waipahē** *ke keonimana.* The gentleman is **polite**.] 2. *'olu'olu* (also means **kind, pleasant**).

polluted 1. *haumia*. 2. *pilo*. [*Mai ho'ohaumia i ke kai a* **pilo**! Don't contaminate the ocean until it's **polluted**!]

pond 1. *loko*. 2. *loko wai*. 3. *ki'o wai*.

ponder *no'ono'o*.

pool 1. *loko wai*. 2. *ki'o wai* (also means **puddle, pond**).

poor *'ilihune*.

popcorn

popcorn *kūlina pohāpohā*. [*'Ane'ane e mākaukau ke* **kūlina pohāpohā**. The **popcorn** is almost ready.]

population 1. *po'e*. 2. *lehulehu*.

porch *lānai*. [*Pale aku ka* **lānai** *nui i ka lā*. A big **porch** wards off the sun.]

pork *'i'o pua'a*. [*Inā 'ai pinepine 'oe i ka* **'i'o pua'a**, *pi'i a'e ka 'aila ma loko o kou koko*. If you often eat **pork**, the fat in your blood increases.]

porpoise 1. *nai'a*. 2. *nu'ao*.

port *awa kū moku* (*lit.* harbor where boats stop).

porter *mea hali ukana*.

Portuguese *Pukikī*.

position *kūlana* (also means **rank, status**). [*He aha kona* **kūlana** *ma ka 'ohana? 'O ka haku 'o ia?* What is his **position** in the family? Is he the head of the family?]

possess *loa'a*.

possible *hiki* (also means **to be able to, can**). [**Hiki** *ke noho ma ka wao akua?* Is it **possible** to live in the wilderness?]

postal worker *lawe leka*.

post card *kāleka po'oleka*. [*'Ehia kenikeni ke po'oleka no ke* **kāleka po'oleka** *i kēia mau lā?* How many cents is the stamp for **post cards** these days?]

poster 1. *pepa ho'olaha*. 2. *pelaha*. [*Hō'ike ka* **pelaha** *i nā i'a maoli.* The **poster** shows native fish.]

post office *hale leka*.

postpone *ho'opane'e*. [*E* **ho'opane'e** *'ia ka 'aha mele ma muli o ka makani pāhili.* The concert should be **postponed** due to the hurricane.]

pot *ipuhao* (also means **pan**). [*Malia paha o ho'oma'ema'e 'oe i kēnā* **ipuhao** *lepo i ke one*. Maybe you should clean that dirty **pot** with sand.]

pot

pouch *poho*.

pound *[n] paona* (from English). [*Pipi'i wale nō ka poi ma ka hale kū'ai: ma kahi o 'ehā kālā no ho'okahi* **paona**. Poi is really expensive at the store: around four dollars for one **pound**.] *[v] ku'i* (also means **to smash, crash**). (pound poi, poi pounder = *ku'i 'ai*)

pour (liquid) *ninini*. [**Ninini** *ka makua kāne i ka waiū na kāna kaikamahine.* The father **pours** milk for his daughter.]

pout *nuha* (also means **to sulk, sulky**).

poverty *'ilihune* (also means **poor, destitute**).

power *mana*. [*He* **mana** *nō ko ke kia'āina.* The governor has real **power**.] Note: *Mana* refers primarily to spiritual power, but is also used for political power, the power to command.

practice *ho'oma'ama'a*. [*E* **ho'oma'ama'a** *a ma'a*. **Practice** until you get used to it.]

praise 1. *ho'onani*. 2. *ho'omaika'i* (also means **congratulations**). [**Ho'onani** *ka makua mau*. **Praise** the eternal father. (Doxology)]

pray *pule*. [*Na wai e alaka'i i ka* **pule** *wehe?* Who will lead the opening **prayer**?]

precarious *kūnihi* (also means **steep**). [**Kūnihi** *ke alahele i uka?* Is the pathway toward the mountains **precarious**?]

precious *makamae*. [*'Oi aku ka **makamae** o ke aloha ma mua o ke kula*. Love is more **precious** than gold.]

precipice *pali*. [*Piha ka 'ao'ao ko'olau o Kaua'i nā **pali** kū*. The windward side of Kaua'i is full of sheer **precipices**.]

precise *miomio*. [***Miomio** wale ka humuhumu 'ana ona*. Her sewing is very **precise**.]

predict *wānana*. [*Na wai e 'ole ke makemake e **wānana** i ka hopena*? Who wouldn't want to **predict** the results?]

prefer *'oi aku ka makemake*. [***'Oi aku ka makemake** o ka hapanui o ka po'e i ka nohona 'ilihune 'ole*. Most people **prefer** not living in poverty.]

prejudice *ho'okae 'ili* (racial prejudice). [*No ke aha i ili mai ai ka **ho'okae 'ili**?* Why did we inherit racial **prejudice**?]

premonition *haili moe*. [*E kupu a'e ana ka **haili moe** i ko'u moe 'uhane?* Will a **premonition** appear in my dreams?]

prepare *ho'omākaukau*.

prepared *mākaukau*. [***Mākaukau** ka imu a wela nā pōhaku*. The *imu* (underground oven) is **prepared** and the rocks are hot.]

prescription *kuhikuhi* (also means **directions**). [*Aia nō a kelepona 'ia mai ke **kuhikuhi**, hiki ia'u ke ho'omākaukau i kāu lā'au*. As soon as the **prescription** is phoned in, I can prepare your medicine.]

presence *alo*. (face to face = *he alo a he alo*)

present *makana* (also means **scholarship, award, prize, gift**). [*'Ehia āu **makana** ma kou la hānau?* How many **presents** do you have on your birthday?]

president *pelekikena*. [*Kamaehu ka Pelekikena*. The **President** is firm of resolution and purpose.]

press *kaomi*. [*Inā **kaomi** 'ia kēia pihi, ho'ā 'ia ka lolouila*. If this button is **pressed**, the computer is turned on.]

pretend *ho'omeamea*. [*E **ho'omeamea** kāua, 'o 'oe 'o Hi'iaka a 'o au 'o Lohi'au*. Let's **pretend** you are Hi'iaka and I am Lohi'au.]

president

pretty 1. *nani*. 2. *u'i* (refers to people).

price *kumu kū'ai*. [*'Ehia kālā ke **kumu kū'ai** o nā 'ano kanakē like 'ole?* How much is the **price** of the various kinds of candy?]

pride *ha'aheo* (also means **proud**). [*'O ka lā **ha'aheo** i ka lāhui kēia lā*. Today is the day of **pride** in your ethnic heritage.]

priest *kahunapule* (also means **minister, reverend**).

prince *kamāli'i kāne*.

princess *kamāli'i wahine*.

principal *po'o kumu* (*lit*. head teacher).

print *pa'i*. [*Ua **pa'i** lima 'ia nā puke mua ma Hawai'i*. The first books in Hawai'i were **printed** by hand.]

prison *hale pa'ahao* (also means **jail**).

prisoner 1. *pio*. 2. *pa'ahao*.

private 1. *pilikino* (personal). [*He leka **pilikino** kēnā*. That (by you) is a **personal** letter.] 2. *kū'oko'a* (independent).

prize *makana* (also means **scholarship, award, gift**).

problem *pilikia* (also means **trouble**). [*He **pilikia** ko ko māua ka'a wane, e ka māka'i*. Our (her and my) van has a **problem**, officer.]

proclaim 1. *kūkala* (announce, broadcast). 2. *kuahaua*. [*Ua **kuahaua** 'o Kamehameha i ke Kānāwai Māmalahoe*. Kamehameha **proclaimed** the law of the splintered paddle.]

proclamation 1. *palapala kūkala*. 2. *kuahaua*.

produce *[v]* 1. *hua* (offspring, fruit). [*Ua **hua** ka moku a mu'o a lau a ulu*. The island **produced** life and budded and leafed and grew. (common line in name chants and creation chants)] 2. *ho'ohua*.

profession *'oihana* (also means **career, business**). [*'O ke alaka'i huaka'i kāna **'oihana***. Her **profession** is tour guide.]

profit 1. *waiwai ho'opuka*. [*Ma hope o ka uku 'ana aku i ka uku pane'e i ka panakō, 'ehia kālā ka **waiwai ho'opuka**?* After paying the interest to the bank, how much is the **profit**?] 2. *loa'a*.

profitable *makepono*. [*He 'oihana **makepono** ka hale 'aina?* Is the restaurant a **profitable** business?]

profound *kūhohonu* (syn. *hohonu;* also means **deep, complex**).

program 1. *polakalamu.* 2. *hōʻike.* 3. *papa hōʻike* (printed).

prohibit *pāpā* (also means **to forbid**). [*Nāna, na ke kumu hula i **pāpā** mai iaʻu, ʻaʻole au e ʻoki i koʻu lauoho.* It was she, it was the hula teacher who **prohibited** me from cutting my hair.]

prominent 1. *kiʻekiʻe.* 2. *ʻoi.* [***Oi** kēlā pae pali ma Molokaʻi.* That row of cliffs on Molokaʻi is **prominent**.]

pronounce *puana* (also refers to **song refrain**).

proof *hōʻoiaʻiʻo* (also means **to prove, verify**; syn. *hōʻoia*).

propaganda *hoʻolaha manaʻo.* [*He manaʻo kūpono a i ʻole he **hoʻolaha manaʻo** kāna e hoʻolohe nei ma ke kīwī?* Is it a proper opinion or is it **propaganda** that he is hearing now on TV?]

property 1. *waiwai* (also means **estate, wealth, value, rich, valuable**). 2. *kuleana* (also means **land division, rights, responsibility**).

prophecy *wānana.*

prophet *kāula.*

protection *malu* (also means **shade, government**). [*Noho mālie ka lehulehu ma lalo o ka **malu** o ke aupuni.* The public lives calmly under the **protection** of the government.]

protest *kūʻē.* [*Na kākou a pau i **kūʻē** i ka ʻaelike o ke aupuni e kākoʻo i ka hana ʻino iā Pele.* It was all of us who **protested** the government's contract to support doing harm to Pele (through geothermal development).]

proud *haʻaheo.*

provisions 1. *pono.* 2. *lako.*

prow *ihu* (also means **nose**).

pry 1. *une* (also means **lever**). 2. *ʻōhiki* (also means **to prod, pick, sand crab**).

public *[n] lehulehu. [adj] ākea.*

publish *paʻi* (also means **to slap, clap, snap**). [*E **paʻi** ʻia ana kāu puke?* Will your book be **published**?]

pudding *pūkini.* [*ʻOno ʻo Anoe i ka **pūkini** tapioca.* Anoe craves tapioca **pudding**.]

pull *huki.* [*E **huki** i ke kaula a paʻa ka peʻa.* **Pull** the rope until the sail's taut.]

punch *kuʻi* (also means **to smash, crash, hit**).

punish *hoʻopaʻi.*

pure 1. *maʻemaʻe.* 2. *hemolele.* [***Maʻemaʻe** wale ke kino o ka palai.* The body of the *palai* fern is **pure**. (song, "Ka ʻIlilauokekoa," by Waiʻau)]

purse *ʻeke.* (wallet = *ʻeke kālā*)

pursue *hahai* (also means **to follow**).

push *pahu* (also means **box, drum**). [*Mai **pahu** kekahi i kekahi, e ka lehulehu.* Don't **push** each other, friends.] (push-up = *koʻo lima*)

put *kau.*

put on *komo* (also means **enter**). [*E **komo** i kou pālule hou no ka pāʻina.* **Put on** your new shirt for the party.]

puzzle *nane.* [*Aia iā lāua ka **nane** ʻāpana.* They (two) have the jigsaw **puzzle**.]

pyramid *pūʻoʻa* (also means **tower**).

qualified 1. *mākaukau.* [*'O ia ka moho mākaukau no ia 'oihana.* She's the **qualified** candidate for that position.] 2. *kūpono.*

quality 1. *'ano.* 2. *kūlana.* [*He kūlana 'ekahi kāna hana?* Is his work top **quality**?]

quantity 1. *nui.* [*He 'ekolu haneli paona ka nui o nā lū'au a Keli'i i 'ako ai i nehinei a ia lā aku.* Three hundred pounds is the **quantity** of the taro leaves that Keli'i picked the day before yesterday.]

quarrel 1. *ho'opa'apa'a.* 2. *hukihuki.* [*Auē ka hukihuki ma waena o ke kaikua'ana a me ke kaikaina!* Wow, the **quarrel** between the older and younger siblings!]

quart *kuaka* (from English).

quarter (coin) *hapahā kālā.* [*Loa'a ka hapahā kālā iā 'oe? Pono au e kelepona aku i ka hale.* Do you have a **quarter**? I have to phone home.]

quarter [adj] *hapahā.* [*He hapahā Kāmoa kāu kāne?* Is your husband a **quarter** Samoan?]

queen *mō'ī wahine.* [*'O Kaleleonālani ka mō'ī wahine i lilo i moho i ke koho pāloka 'ana i mō'ī hou.* Kaleleonālani

queen

was the **queen** who became a candidate for the election of the new sovereign.]

quench *ho'okena.*

quenched (thirst) *kena.* [*Ke inu nei 'o ia a kena ka makewai.* He is drinking now until his thirst is **quenched**.]

question 1. *nīnau* (also means **to ask question**). 2. *uī* (also means **query, to question**)

quick *'āwīwī.*

quiet [n] *mālie.* [v] *ho'onā* (quiet someone; also means **to soothe, pacify, comfort, relieve pain**). [adj] *mālie.* [*E ho'onā a e ho'omalimali i nā māhoe uē a mālie lāua.* **Soothe** and fondle the crying twins until they (two) are quiet.]

quilt [n] 1. *kapa kuiki.* 2. *kapa kuiki pohopoho* (patchwork quilt). [v] *kuiki.*

quit *ha'alele.* [*E ha'alele ana au i ka hana i ka lā 'apōpō.* I will **quit** tomorrow!]

quilt

quiver *kapalili* (also means **quivering, fluttering, to throb, flutter** as a leaf in the wind). [*Kapalili ka pu'uwai ke 'ike ka 'ōpio i kāna ipo.* The heart **quivers** whenever the youth sees his sweetheart.] [*Ka lau kapalili.* The **quivering** leaf.]

quiz *kuisa* (from English).

quote *'ōlelo.* [*He 'ōlelo kēia maiā Kauikeaouli mai. "Na wai e 'ole ke akamai i ke alahele i hehi 'ia e o'u mau kūpuna?"* This is a **quote** from Kauikeaouli (Kamehameha III). "Who wouldn't be clever on the path that was treaded by my ancestors?"]

rabbit *lāpaki.*

race 1. *heihei* (competition). 2. *lāhui* (nationality).

racial prejudice *ho'okae 'ili.*

radiant 1. *mālamalama.* 2. *'ālohilohi.*

radio *lekiō.*

radio

raft *huinapapalana.*

rag *welu.* [*E lālau i ka **welu**! Ua hanini ka waina ma luna o ka mea hāli'i pākaukau!* Grab the **rag**! The wine spilled on the tablecloth!]

rage *inaina* (also means **anger, hatred**). [*Pi'i a'e paha kou **inaina**?* Is your **rage** rising up?]

raid *pākaha* (also means **to cheat, plunder, rob, robbery**). *He **pākaha** kā ka māka'i i nā hale piliwaiwai.* The police have **raids** in gambling houses.]

railroad *ka'aahi* (also means **train**). [*Mai Kohala a i Hilo i holo ai ke **ka'aahi** ma mua.* It was from Kohala to Hilo that the **train** used to run.]

rain *ua* (usually a specific type and/or name of rain is added). [*ka **ua** loku a'o Hanalei,* the pouring **rain** of Hanalei. (song, "Ka Ua Loku," by A. Alohikea)]

rainbow *ānuenue.* [*Pi'o mai ke **ānuenue**.* The **rainbow** arches overhead.]

raincoat *kuka ua.* [*'O ka 'ahu lā'ī ke **kuka ua** o ke au kahiko.* The *tī*-leaf cape was the **raincoat** of ancient days.]

raincoat

raindrop *pakapaka ua.*

rain forest 1. *wao kele.* 2. *wao nahele.*

rainy *ua.* [*Ua ka wao kele.* The rain forest is **rainy**.]

raise 1. *ho'oulu* (grow plants; also means **to inspire**). [*'O ka **ho'oulu** pua haka kā kāna wahine 'oihana.* His wife's business is **raising** anthuriums.] 2. *hānai* (rear a child; also means **to feed animals or people, adopt**). 3. *hāpai* (lift up, carry; also means **pregnant**). 4. *kāmau* (raise a glass, drink liquor; also means **to persevere, continue**).

rake *kopekope.*

ranch *kahua hānai pipi.* [*Kokoke ke **kahua hānai pipi** 'o Kapāpala i ka lua pele.* Kapāpala **Ranch** is close to the crater.]

rank (place, position, title) *kūlana.* [*He **kūlana** ali'i ki'eki'e ko ka na'i aupuni? 'A'ole.* Did the conqueror (Kamehameha I) have high chiefly **rank**? No.]

rape *pu'e* (also means **to attack, force, compel**).

rapture *lilo.*

rare *laha 'ole.* [*Minamina 'a'ole he mea **laha 'ole** ka pu'e.* Regrettably, rape is not a **rare** thing.]

rascal *kolohe* (also means **mischievous, naughty**).

rat *'iole* (also means **mouse,** any **rodent**).

rattle (sound) 1. *ko'ele.* 2. *nakeke.*

raw *maka* (also means **fresh, eye, face, "eye" of net**). [*'O ka poke ka i'a **maka** i ho'ohui 'ia me ka limu a me ka pa'akai. Poke* is **raw** fish that has been mixed with seaweed and Hawaiian salt.]

ray (sun) *kukuna.* [*Ho'omaka nā **kukuna** o ka lā e ne'e ma luna o ka 'āina ma* *kaiao.* The **rays** of the sun start to move over the land at dawn.]

read *heluhelu.*

ready *mākaukau.* [*Ua **mākaukau** kākou, e nā hoa? E naue i mua!* Are we all **ready**, friends? Let's move forward!]

read

real *maoli.*

realize 1. *'ike* (to understand; also means **to see, know, experience**). [*Ua **'ike** ke kanaka pī i kona hewa.* The stingy person **realized** her mistake.] 2. *ho'omaopopo* (to bring to fruition).

reason *kumu.* [*'O ia ke **kumu** a kāna mo'opuna i noho ai i ka haukapila.* That's the **reason** his grandchild stayed in the hospital.]

recede *emi* (also means **inexpensive, reduced, to reduce**). (low tide = *ke kai emi*)

receive 1. *loa'a* (also means **get, catch, find**). [*E **loa'a** ana ka uku lawelawe iā ia ma hope o kona lawe 'ana mai i nā mea inu.* She'll **receive** a tip after she serves the drinks.] 2. *loa'a mai* (also means **get, catch, find**).

recent *hou.*

receptionist *mea ho'okipa* (also means **host, hostess**).

recess *ho'omalolo* (means to adjourn temporarily, not school recess).

recipe 1. *lekapī* (from English). [*Ke huli nei au i ka **lekapī** no ke kele kuawa.* I'm searching for a **recipe** for guava jam.] 2. *'ōlelo kuhikuhi* (also means **directions**).

recite *ha'i.*

recline *kāmoe* (also means **to lie down**).

recognize *'ike* (also means **to see, know, experience**). (it has been recognized, acknowledged [phrase often used at end of chants] = *ua 'ikea* [from *ua 'ike 'ia*])

record *[n]* *pā leo* (musical album). *[v]* 1. *ho'opa'a* (story or voice). [***Ho'opa'a** wikiō 'o Puhipau i nā kūpuna.* Puhipau **records** videos of the elders.] 2. *ho'opa'a leo* (voice). [*Iā lākou e **ho'opa'a leo** ana i ka pā leo hou, na wai e ho'oholo i ke ka'ina*

hana? When they are **recording** the new album, who decides the sequence of activities?]

recover *pohala.* [*Ke **pohala** nei ko'u hoaaloha i hō'eha 'ia i ka ulia mokokaikala.* My friend who was hurt in the motorcycle accident is **recovering**.]

rectangle *huinahā loa.*

red *'ula'ula.*

red-eyed *mākole.* [***Mākole** 'o ia nei i ka piwa.* This person is **red-eyed** due to fever.]

reduce *ho'ēmi.* [***Ho'ēmi** ke kauka i kāna mau huaale e ale ai.* The doctor **reduces** the pills that she swallows.] (reduce weight = *ho'ēmi kino*)

reed *'ohe* (also means **bamboo**).

reef 1. *laupapa.* [*'O ka wana a me ka puhi kekahi o nā i'a ma ka **laupapa**.* Sea urchins and eels are some of the sea creatures on the **reef**.] 2. *pāpapa.* 3. *'āpapa.* 4. *hāpapa.*

reflection *aka.*

refrain (song) 1. *puana.*

refrigerator *pahu hau.* [*Mai poina e ho'okomo i kou lei i ka **pahu hau**.* Don't forget to put your *lei* in the **refrigerator**.]

refrigerator

refuge *pu'uhonua.* [*'O Hōnaunau Pāka ma Ke'ei, Kona Hema kahi o ka **pu'uhonua** kaulana loa o Hawai'i nei.* Hōnaunau Park in Ke'ei, South Kona, is the place of the most famous **refuge** here in Hawai'i.]

refuse *[n] 'ōpala.* *[v] hō'ole* (also means **to deny, negate**).

register *kau inoa* (syn. *kākau inoa*, write name).

regret 1. *mihi* (also means **repentance, to apologize**). 2. *minamina* (also means **to value highly**).

reign *noho ali'i.*

rejoice *'oli.*

relationship 1. *pilina.* [*He aha ka **pilina** ma waena o kēlā mau wāhine?* What is the **relationship** between those women?] 2. *pilikana.*

relax *nanea* (also means **enjoyable, relaxed, to have fun, fascinating,** many other meanings). [*Nanea nā keiki ma ke kauwela.* Children **relax** in the summer.]

relax

release *ho'oku'u* (also means **to dismiss, let go**). [*Ho'oku'u ka lawai'a i ka 'upena.* The fisherman **releases** the net.]

religion *ho'omana* (also means **to worship**).

religious site *heiau*. [*'Oiai 'o Pi'ilanihale ka heiau nui loa o ka pae 'āina, e kipa aku i laila i maopopo iā 'oukou ka ho'omana kahiko.* Since Pi'ilanihale is the largest **religious site** of the island chain, visit there so that you all can understand ancient worship.]

relish *[n] pūpū* (also means **shell, hors d'oeuvre, party snack**). *[v] 'ono* (also means **to savor**).

remain *koe*.

remainder *koena* (also means **leftovers, remnant, change from buying something**). [*Eia kāu koena: 'ekolu kālā me kanahā keneka.* Here's your **change**: three dollars and forty cents.]

remember *ho'omana'o* (also means **to remind**). [*Ho'omana'o kākou i ka lā i lilo ai 'o Hawai'i nei i moku 'āina.* We all **remember** the day Hawai'i became a state.]

remote *mamao* (also means **far, distance**).

remove *lawe aku* (also means **to take away**). [*Na ka mea holoi pā e lawe aku i ke puna lepo.* The dish washer is the one who should **remove** the dirty spoon.]

renew *hana hou*.

rent *ho'olimalima*.

repair *ho'oponopono* (also refers to **traditional family counseling/therapy**). [*E ho'oponopono 'ia ana ko ke po'o kumu paikikala i kēia Pō'akolu a'e.* The principal's bicycle will be **repaired** next Wednesday.]

repeat *ho'opili* (also means **to imitate**). [*E ho'opili mai ia'u.* **Repeat** after me.]

repent *mihi* (also means **to confess**).

reporter *kākau nūpepa*. [*'O kēlā ka leo mihi o ke kākau nūpepa i ho'opunipuni i ka luna ho'onohonoho.* That's the confessing voice of the **reporter** who lied to the editor.]

repress 1. *'umi (also 'u'umi)*. [*'U'umi i ke aloha me ka waimaka lā.* **Repress** love with tears. (song, "Kaimukī Hula." by A. Richart)] 2. *kāohi*.

reputation *kūlana* (also means **status, rank**).

request 1. *noi*. 2. *nonoi*. [*He nonoi kā Kamailelauli'i iā ia.* Kamailelauli'i has a **request** to ask of him.]

requirement *koi*.

rescue *ho'opakele*. [*I ka manawa a ka pele i hū ai ma Kalapana, ua ho'omaka nā akeakamai e ho'opakele i nā holoholona i ho'oku'u 'ia.* At the time that the lava erupted at Kalapana, the scientists started **rescuing** the animals that had been abandoned.]

research *noi'i*.

resemble *kohu like*. [*Kohu like ke kaikunāne i kona kaikuahine.* The brother **resembles** his sister.]

reserve *ho'okapu*. [*E ho'okapu i 'ehā noho ma ka hale 'aha mele no kēia ahiahi.* **Reserve** four seats in the concert hall for this evening.]

reserved *kapu* (also means **forbidden**).

residence *hale noho*.

resign *ha'alele* (also means **to leave, to quit**). [*'Akahi nō a ha'alele ka lawe leka i kana 'oihana a hū a'ela kona inaina.* The mail carrier finally **resigned** his job and then his rage spilled out.]

resist 1. *kū'ē* (also means **to oppose, opposite**). 2. *pale* (also means **to defend, ward off**).

resolute *'onipa'a* (also means **steadfast;** Queen Lili'uokalani's motto).

resources *kumu waiwai*. [*Na wai nō e ho'olilo i nā kumu waiwai makamae o ka honua nei?* Who is it that would waste the precious **resources** of this earth?]

respect *mahalo* (also means **to admire, be grateful for, thank**).

responsibility *kuleana*. [*'O ko kākou kuleana ke a'o 'ana aku i ko kākou ho'oilina i ka hanauna hou.* Our **responsibility** is to teach our heritage to the new generation.]

rest *ho'omaha.*

restaurant *hale 'aina.* [*Nui nā 'ano* **hale 'aina** *like 'ole ma ke kaona nei.* There are all kinds of **restaurants** here in town.]

restrain *kāohi* (also means **to control, repress, prevent**). [*Pono ka makua e* **kāohi** *i ka huhū.* A parent must **restrain** his anger.]

restroom 1. *lumi ho'opau pilikia.* 2. *lua.*

retarded *lohi* (also means **late, slow, backward**). [*Nā ko'u kaikua'ana e ho'olālā nei i ka papa a'o i nā haumāna* **lohi.** My older sister (woman speaking) is the one who is planning the class for the **retarded** students.]

retire 1. *hō'olu'olu* (to rest; syn. *ho'omaha*). 2. *ho'omaha loa* (to retire from work).

return 1. *ho'i* (go back; can imply going home). [*E* **ho'i** *kāua.* Let's go **(back)** home.] 2. *ho'iho'i* (return something; also means **restore**). [*Ma mua o kou ho'i 'ana e hiamoe, e* **ho'iho'i** *i nā 'upena i loko o ka hale ka'a.* Before you go to sleep, **return** the nets inside the garage.]

reveal *hō'ike* (also means **to demonstrate, show**). [*Ke* **hō'ike** *mai nei ko'u kupuna wahine i ko mākou mo'okū'auhau.* My grandmother is **revealing** our genealogy to us.]

revenge *pāna'i* (also means **substitute, reward, to revenge, pay back**). (syn. *uku*)

reverence *hō'ano* (also means **to revere**).

reverend *kahu* (also means **caretaker**; short for *kahunapule*, which also means **minister, priest**).

reverse 1. *huli* (also means **to turn, to change lifestyle or opinion**). 2. *lole* (also means **cloth, clothes**).

revolve *ka'apuni.* [**Ka'apuni** *nā hōkū hele i ka lā.* The planets **revolve** around the sun.]

reward *makana.*

rhythm 1. *pā* (also means **fence, enclosure, yard**, many other meanings). 2. *pana* (also means **beat in music, heartbeat, to shoot a bow, legendary place**).

rib *iwi 'ao'ao.* [*'Oiai 'o ia i pahe'e ai i ka 'aila, ua hā'ule iho i lalo a ua pohole nā* **iwi 'ao'ao** *ona.* Since she slid in the oil, she fell down and bruised her **ribs**.]

ribbon *lipine* (also means **tape**). [*He mau* **lipine** *nani ko kona lei.* His *lei* has pretty **ribbons**.]

rice *laiki.*

rich *waiwai* (also means **valuable, wealthy**).

riddle *'ōlelo nane.* [*'A'ole hiki ke loa'a ka pane i ka* **'ōlelo nane.** The answer to the **riddle** can't be found.]

ride 1. *holo* (also means **to travel, move**, many other meanings). [**Holo** *lio nā paniolo.* Cowboys **ride** horses.] 2. *holoholo.*

ridge *kualapa.*

ridicule *ho'ohenehene* (also means **to tease**). [**Ho'ohenehene** *nā hoa noho i ka makuahine kāpulu.* The neighbors **ridicule** the slovenly mother.]

right 1. *pono kiwila* (civil). 2. *pololei* (also means **correct, straight**). [*E kalaiwa* **pololei** *i mua ou no 'elua palaka a laila e huli hema.* Drive **straight** in front of you for two blocks then turn left.] 3. *'ākau* (right side, direction; also means **north**).

righteous *pono* (also means **correct behavior**).

rigid *'o'ole'a* (also means **physically tough, stiff, hard**, many other meanings). [**'O'ole'a** *ko ke koa kino i ka maka'u.* The soldier's body is **rigid** due to fear.]

ring [*n*] *komolima* (*lit.* wear on hand). [*v*] *kani* (also means **to sound, chime**, many other meanings). [**Kani** *nā pele o ka uaki kahiko ma ka hale pule.* The bells of the old clock at the church **chime**.]

ring

riot *haunaele.* [*He* **haunaele** *ko Polapola i ke kū'ē 'ana i ke aupuni Palani.* Tahiti had a **riot** in protest against the French government.]

rip *nāhae* (also means **to tear**).

ripe *pala.* [**Pala** *paha nā manakō? A 'o ia!* Are the mangoes perhaps **ripe**? You got it (you're right)!]

rise *ala* (also means **to wake up, awake**). [*E* **ala** *mai!* **Wake up!**]

risk *maka'u* (also means **risky, danger, dangerous, afraid**). [*Auē! He hana* **maka'u** *ka* *ho'oipoipo 'ana i kēia mau lā.* Gosh! Making love is a **risky** business these days.]

ritual *hana ho'ohanohano* (also means **ceremony**).

rival *hoa paio* (also means **opponent in combat**).

river *kahawai.* [*Hālana ke **kahawai** i ka pō'ino.* The **river** floods in a storm.]

road 1. *alanui* (street). 2. *alaloa* (freeway). 3. *alahele* (pathway, trail).

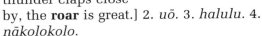

road

roar 1. *wawā.* [*Ke ku'i kokoke ka hekeli, nui ka **wawā**.* When thunder claps close by, the **roar** is great.] 2. *uō.* 3. *halulu.* 4. *nākolokolo.*

roast *'oma* (also means **stove, to bake**).

robbery *pōā* (refers to burglary, taking things from inside a location, in contrast to *'aihue,* which implies that a particular thing was stolen). [*Ua **pōā** ka panakō a ua '**aihue** 'ia ke kula.* The bank was **robbed** and the gold was **stolen**.]

rock *pōhaku* (also means **stone**). [*He pā **pōhaku** 'alā ko kona hale.* His house has a lava **rock** wall.]

roll 1. *kāka'a* (means **to turn over**). 2. *pōka'a* (bundle of *hala* leaves ready for weaving).

romantic *ho'oipiopio.* (also means **to make love**). [*'Ano **ho'oipiopio** ka mele āna e hīmeni nei?* Is the song he's singing sort of **romantic**?]

roof *kaupoku.* [*Pono e kūkulu hou i ke **kaupoku** o helele'i ka ua i loko o ka hale.* The **roof** has to be repaired or else the rain will fall inside the house.]

room *lumi.*

roommate *hoa noho.*

rooster *moa kāne.*

root *mole* (also means **foundation, source, ancestral root**). [*ka **mole** o Lehua,* the foundation **root** of Lehua (a small island off Ni'ihau, used as a symbol of the western boundary of Hawai'i. Traditional greet-

ings poetically include all islands and all people of Hawai'i, often by mentioning traditional eastern and western boundaries of the archipelago.)]

rope *kaula* (also means **string**). (lasso = *kaula 'ili*) (beef jerky = *pipi kaula*)

rose *loke.*

rotten 1. *palahū* (overripe fruit). [***Palahū** nā hē'ī a kāua i 'ako ai i kēlā lā aku nei.* The papayas that you and I picked the other day are **rotten**.]

rose

2. *palahē* (fragile, easily torn, as paper). 3. *popopo* (wood, decayed leaves).

rough 1. *'ōkaikai* (choppy sea). 2. *mālualua* (pitted road, rough terrain). 3. *kalakala* (rough texture). [*Ua 'ānai 'ia ka wa'a i ka lau **kalakala** o ka 'ulu a i 'ole i ka pōhaku poepoe i ke au kahiko.* Canoes were rubbed (sanded down) with the **rough-textured** breadfruit leaf or with round stones in olden days.]

round *poepoe.* (the globe = *ka poepoe honua*)

row 1. *lālani.* 2. *pae.*

royal *ali'i* (also means **chief, noble**).

rub 1. *'ānai* (with friction, to sand). [*'**Ānai** ke kālai ki'i i ka lā'au i ka pōhaku hamo.* The image carver **rubs** the wood with the rubbing stone.] 2. *hamo* (with oil, as in massage).

rubber band *lahalio.*

rubbish *'ōpala.* [*Na ke ka'a halihali 'ōpala e lawe aku i ka '**ōpala**.* Garbage trucks are the ones that haul away **rubbish**.]

rubbish can *kini 'ōpala.*

rudder *hoe uli.*

rude 1. *kiko'olā.* [***Kiko'olā** kā ka mea na'aupō 'ōlelo.* The ignorant person's speech is **rude**.] 2. *kalakala* (also means **rough texture**).

rule 1. *lula* (from English; regulation). 2. *kānāwai* (law, code, many other meanings). 3. *ho'omalu* (to govern). 4. *noho ali'i* (to reign as a noble or king).

rumble, reverberate *nākolo.*

run *holo*. Note: *Holo* is a general term for movement, and its English meanings include to travel, to move, to sail, to swim (fish). *Holo wāwae* specifies running;  *holo peki*, jogging; *holoholo*, going around, "cruising."

rural *kuaʻāina*. [*Kamaʻāina ʻo Lilia i nā ahupuaʻa* **kuaʻāina** *o Koʻolaupoko*. Lilia is familiar with the **rural** *ahupuaʻa* (land sections from mountain to ocean) of the Koʻolaupoko district.]

rush *pūlale*. [*No ke aha ʻoe e* **pūlale** *mai?* Why do you **rush** up to me? (song, "Hōkio," by M. Pukui and M. Lam)]

rust *kūkaehao* (also means **rusty**).

rustle 1. *nehe*. [*ke kai* **nehe** *ʻōlelo me ka ʻiliʻili*, the **rustling** sea talking to the pebbles (song, "Kawaihae," by B. Lincoln).] 2. *nākolo*.

rut *napoʻo* (also means **cavity, armpit, to sink down**). (sunset = *napoʻo ka lā*)

sacred 1. *la'a*. [***La'a** ka heiau i ho'ola'a 'ia iā Lono*. The *heiau* dedicated to Lono is **sacred**.] 2. *kapu*.

sacrifice *mōhai*. [*'O ka ulua kekahi 'ano **mōhai**. The *ulua* fish is a type of **sacrifice**.]

sad *kaumaha* (also means **depressed, heavy**).

saddle *noho lio*.

safety *palekana*. [*'O ka **palekana** ka mea nui i ka holo 'ana*. **Safety** is the important thing in sailing.]

sail *holo*. (to sail to leeward = *ka'alalo*; to sail to windward = *ka'aluna*)

sailboat *moku pe'a*.

sailor 1. *kelamoku*. 2. *'aukai*. 3. *'aumoana*.

salary *uku hana*.

sale *kū'ai emi*.

salesperson *kālepa* (also means **merchant, peddler**). [*'Oiai he kū'ai emi kēia, 'oi aku paha ka li'ili'i o kā ke **kālepa** uku hana?* Since this is a sale, is the **salesperson**'s salary smaller?]

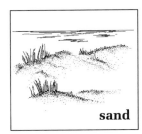
sailboat

salt *pa'akai*.

salted *miko*. [*Ua **miko** ka 'i'o i ka pa'akai*. The meat was **salted**.]

same *like*. [*'Ano **like** ko ke keiki 'ano me ko kona makua kāne*. The character of the child is the **same** as his father's.]

Samoa *Kāmoa*.

sanctuary *pu'uhonua*. [*'O ke ali'i nō kekahi 'ano **pu'uhonua**. The chiefs themselves were one kind of **sanctuary**.]

sand *one*. [*Ke **one** wela i ka lā ke hehi a'e*. When you step on it, the **sand** is hot due

to the sun. (song, "Ka Uluwehi o Ke Kai," by E. Kanaka'ole)]

sandwich *kanuwika* (from English).

sarcastic *kīko'olā* (also means **rude, impertinent**).

satiated *mā'ona* (means full of food, when one has eaten enough).

satisfy *hō'olu'olu*.

sauce *kai* (also means **gravy, condiment, dressing**). [*Loa'a ke **kai** nīoi?* Got **chili pepper water**?]

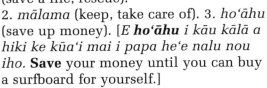
sand

sauce

sausage *na'aukake*.

save 1. *ho'opakele* (save a life, rescue). 2. *mālama* (keep, take care of). 3. *ho'āhu* (save up money). [*E **ho'āhu** i kāu kālā a hiki ke kūa'i mai i papa he'e nalu nou iho*. **Save** your money until you can buy a surfboard for yourself.]

saw 1. *pahiolo*. 2. *pahiolo ulia* (electric saw).

say *'ōlelo*. [*Mai **'ōlelo** pēlā!* Don't **say** that!]

scab *pāpa'a* (also means **burned, overdone, slice of bread** [*pāpa'a palaoa*], other meanings).

scale [n] 1. *ana paona* (for measuring weight). 2. *unahi* (fish scale). [v] *unahi*. [*Me ke puna i **unahi** ai ko Momi kupuna wahine i ka i'a*. It was with the spoon that Momi's grandmother **scaled** the fish.]

scar *'ālina*. [*E Tūtū, e hō'ike mai i kou mau*

'*ālina* kaua. Grandpa, show us your battle **scars**.]

scarce *kaka'ikahi* (also means **seldom, infrequently, few**). [*Kaka'ikahi* nā keiki kama'āina 'ole i ka lolouila. There are **few** children who are not familiar with the computer.]

scare *ho'omaka'u* (also means **to frighten**).

scatter *ho'opuehu* (also means **to disperse, blow away, blown away**). [*Ke ho'opuehu 'ia nei nā huna laiki e ka makani.* The grains of rice are being **scattered** by the wind.]

scenic view point *'ikena* (also means **vista, panorama, view**). [*ka 'ikena iā Hi'ilawe,* the **view** of Hi'ilawe falls (song, "Hi'ilawe," by Kuakini/Li'a)]

schedule *papahana*. [*Loa'a ka papahana mokulele iā ia?* Does she have the airplane **schedule**?]

scholarship *makana* (also means **prize, gift**). [*E loa'a ana ka makana 'o "Nā Ho'okama" i kāna mo'opuna wahine.* His granddaughter will receive the "Nā Ho'okama" **scholarship**.]

school *kula*. (elementary school = *kula ha'aha'a*; high school = *kula ki'eki'e*; university = *kula nui*)

school campus *kahua kula*.

schoolhouse *hale kula*.

schoolmate *hoa kula*.

school semester *kau kula*.

science *akeakamai* (also means **philosophy**).

scientist *akeakamai* (also means **philosopher, seeker of knowledge**). [*Alaka'i nā akeakamai kilo hōkū i ka hana ma nā hale kilo hōkū ma Mauna Kea.* **Astronomers** (*lit.* scientists who observe stars) lead the work at the astronomical observatories on Mauna Kea.]

scissors *'ūpā*. [*Aia nō a ho'okala 'ia ka 'ūpā, hiki ke 'oki i ka ana kuiki.* As soon as the **scissors** are sharpened, the quilt pattern can be cut.]

scold *nuku*. [*Mai nuku aku i nā keiki, e ahonui.* Don't **scold** the children, be patient.]

scrape *kahi*. [*Ke kahi nei ka hiapo i ke pola poi.* The eldest child is **scraping** the poi bowl.]

scratch *wa'u* (also means **to grate**). [*E wa'u mai i ko ka pēpē kua.* **Scratch** the baby's back.]

scream [*n*] *'alalā* (also means **Hawaiian crow**). [*v*] 1. *'alalā*. 2. *uā* (also means **to shout, yell out**).

screen *pākū* (also means **curtain, veil, partition**).

screwdriver *kuikala*.

screwdriver

sea 1. *kai*. 2. *moana* (refers to deep ocean far from land).

sea foam 1. *hu'a* (also means **bubble, suds**). 2. *'ehu* (also means **dust**). 3. *huna kai*.

seal 1. *'īlio holo i ka uaua*. 2. *sila* (from English). [*He mea laha 'ole ka 'ikemaka i ka sila maoli.* Seeing a native Hawaiian monk **seal** is a rare thing.]

seal

seam 1. *ku'ina* (also means **joint, junction**). 2. *humuhumu* (also means **to stitch, sew**).

sear *kuni* (also means **to brand**).

search 1. *'imi*. 2. *huli*. Note: *Huli* refers to searching for something you've misplaced, while *'imi* refers to exploring or seeking something you don't have. [*Iā ia e huli ana i ka huaale, ua hele a pōniuniu.* While he was **searching** for the pill, he became dizzy.]

seashore *'ae kai*.

seasick *poluea* (also means **nausea, nauseated**).

season *kau* (also means **to place something somewhere, to board transportation** [*kau ma luna o*]. Note: Ancient Hawaiians noted two seasons in the year: *kau wela*, *lit.* hot season, or summer, and *kau ho'oilo*, the rainy season. (for ever and ever [*lit.* from season to season] = *no nā kau a kau*) [*a he lei poina 'ole no nā kau* *a kau*, and a *lei* never forgotten **from one season to the next** (song, "Hawaiian Love Song," by C. King)]

seat *noho* (also means **chair**).

sea urchin 1. *wana.* 2. *'ina.* 3. *hā'uke'uke.*

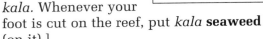

sea urchin

seaweed *limu.* [*Ke moku kou wāwae i ka pāpapa, e kau i ka limu kala.* Whenever your foot is cut on the reef, put *kala* **seaweed** (on it).]

second 1. *kekona* (time). 2. *lua* (sequence). [*'O Manule'a ka lua o kāna mau mo'opuna.* Manule'a is the **second** of his grandchildren.] (second floor = *papahele 'elua*) 3. *kōkua* (second a motion).

secret [n] *mea huna.* [*Mai ha'i aku i ka mea huna!* Don't tell the **secret**!] [adj] *huna.*

secretary *kākau 'ōlelo.* [*'Oi aku ke akamai o ke kākau 'ōlelo ma mua o kāna haku.* The **secretary** is cleverer than his boss.]

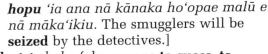

secretary

secretly *malū* (also means **illegally, stealthily, furtive**). [*Ho'olālā malū nā mea kipi.* The rebels plan **secretly**.]

section 1. *māhele* (also means **piece**). 2. *paukū* (also means **verse, stanza, paragraph**).

security guard *kia'i.* [*E aho nāna e 'ae i ke kia'i e kelepona aku i ke ka'a lawe ma'i.* It's better for her to let the **security guard** phone the ambulance.]

see *'ike* (also means **to know, feel**). [*Ua 'ike mua 'oe iā lāua?* Have you **seen** them (two) before?]

seed *'ano'ano.* [*Nui nā 'ano'ano li'ili'i o ka hē'ī.* The papaya has lots of little **seeds**.]

seek 1. *'imi* (to look for something you don't have). 2. *huli* (to search for something you've misplaced).

seer *kāula* (also means **prophet, magician**).

seize *hopu* (also means **to grab, catch**). [*E*

hopu 'ia ana nā kānaka ho'opae malū e nā māka'ikiu. The smugglers will be **seized** by the detectives.]

select 1. *koho* (also means **to guess, to choose**). 2. *wae.*

self *pono'ī* (also means **private, personal, exactly**). [*Nou pono'ī kāna mele i oli ai?* Does the chant that he chanted belong to you, your**self**?]

sell 1. *kū'ai aku.* 2. *kālewa.* [*Kālewa kēia wahine i nā mea ho'onani maka i kona mau hoaaloha.* This woman **sells** cosmetics to her friends.] 2. *kālepa.*

send *ho'ouna.* [*Pipi'i ka ho'ouna 'ana i nā pū'olo i nā 'āina 'ē.* **Sending** packages to foreign countries is expensive.]

sensitive *'eha wale* (easily hurt by criticism).

sentence 1. *hopuna 'ōlelo.* 2. *māmala 'ōlelo.*

separate *ka'awale* (also means **separately, apart**). [*Noho ka'awale ke kāne a me ka wahine.* The husband and wife live **separate** lives.] [v] *ho'oka'awale.*

September *Kepakemapa* (from English).

sequence *ka'ina.* [*He aha ke ka'ina hana pololei ke kūkulu 'oe i ka hale pe'a?* What is the right **sequence** of action when you are setting up a tent?]

serene 1. *mālie.* 2. *la'i.* 3. *maluhia.*

serrated *nihoniho* (also means **toothed, jagged**). [*'O'oi ka 'ao'ao nihoniho o ka pahiolo!* The **serrated** side of the saw is sharp!]

servant 1. *'ōhua* (also means **passenger, member of household**).

serve *lawelawe.*

settle *kau.*

severe 1. *'o'ole'a.* 2. *ko'iko'i.*

sew *humuhumu.* [*Pono paha 'o Nālei e humuhumu i ko kona mu'umu'u pelu.* Maybe Nālei should **sew** up her *mu'umu'u*'s hem.]

sewer *'auwai* (also means **irrigation ditch, taro patch, flume**). Note: *'Auwai lawe mea 'ino* specifically refers to "sewer," whereas *'auwai* by itself usually refers to the ditch used to divert stream water into taro patches.

shade *malu* (also means **protection, govern-**

ment). [*Ma luna ou ka* **malu** *o ka lani.* Above you is the **protection** of heaven. (song, "Queen's Jubilee," Lili'uokalani)]

shadow *aka.* [*I ka pouli lā, uhi ke* **aka** *a ka mahina i ka lā a pō'ele'ele ka lā holo'oko'a.* In an eclipse, the **shadow** of the moon covers the sun until the entire sun is dark.]

shake 1. *naue.* 2. *lūlū.* (shake hands = *lūlū lima*)

shallow *pāpa'u.* [*Pā'ani nā keiki i ke kai* **pāpa'u.** Children play in the **shallow** sea water.]

shame *hilahila* (also means **embarrassment, ashamed, shy, embarrassed**).

shampoo [*n*] *kopa lauoho.* [*v*] *holoi lauoho.*

shape *'ano.* [*Poepoe ke* **'ano** *o ka lei kīkā.* A cigar lei's **shape** is round.]

share [*n*] 1. *māhele.* 2. *kea* (share of stock). [*'Ehia a'u* **kea** *ma ka hui 'oihana ho'opuka?* How many **shares** do I have in the profitable business?] [*v*] 1. *māhele.* 2. *ho'omāhelehele.* (dividend = *māhele kālā*)

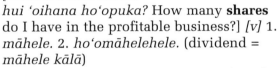

shampoo

shark *manō.* [*Kaka'ikahi nā* **manō** *'ai kanaka.* Man-eating **sharks** are rare.]

sharp 1. *'oi* (not dull). 2. *'o'oi* (prickly). 3. *'āwini* (bold, forward).

sharpen *ho'okala.*

shave *kahi* (also means **to comb, number one**, many other meanings).

shave ice 1. *haukōhi.* 2. *hau momona.*

shawl *kīhei.* [*Komo kona makuahine i ke* **kīhei** *ma ke ahiahi.* His mother puts on a **shawl** in the evening.]

she *'o ia* (also means **he**).

sheep *hipa.* [*Hānai* **hipa** *lākou ma Ni'ihau.* They raise **sheep** on Ni'ihau.]

sheet 1. *uhipela* (bed linen). 2. *'ao'ao* (sheet of paper). 3. *lau* (surface).

shelf *hakakau.* [*Aia nā uhipela pāhoehoe ma ka* **hakaukau** *o ka waihona lole.* The satin sheets are on the **shelf** of the closet.]

shell *pūpū.* [*Minamina ka nalowale 'ana o nā*

waiho'olu'u hinuhinu o ka **pūpū** *i kapa 'ia ke kāhuli ma nā wao kele.* The disappearance of the shining colors of the **shell** called the *kāhuli* (Hawaiian land snail) in the rain forest is deplorable.]

shelter *wahi lulu.*

shepherd *kahu hipa.* [*Iesu nō ke* **kahu hipa.** Jesus is indeed the **shepherd.** (traditional hymn)]

shiny 1. *hinuhinu.* [**Hinuhinu** *ko ke kāne po'o 'ōhule i ka hamohamo 'ana i ka 'aila.* The bald man's head is **shiny** due to rubbing oil on it.] 2. *mālamalama.*

ship *mokuahi* (*lit.* steamship). (sailboat = *moku pe'a*)

shirt *pālule.* [*Pipi'i nā* **pālule** *aloha kahiko i kēia mau lā.* Old aloha **shirts** are expensive these days.]

shiver *ha'ukeke.* [**Ha'ukeke** *ka 'īlio maka'u.* The frightened dog **shivers.**]

shock *hikilele* (also means **disturbance**).

shocked 1. *kūnāhihi.* [**Kūnāhihi** *ka lehulehu i ka 'elepani 'āhiu.* The crowd is **shocked** by the wild elephant.] 2. *mā'e'ele* (also means **numb**).

shoes *kāma'a.* (boots = *kāma'a puti*) (high-heeled shoes = *kāma'a lau li'ili'i*)

shoes

shoot 1. *kī* (also means **to spout up, aim at**, other meanings). [*Wai***kī**kī (*lit.* spouting fresh water, named for the many freshwater springs that were part of the extensive wetlands and taro patches there before development)] 2. *kī pū* (shoot a gun). [*Mai 'ae kākou i ke* **kī pū**! Let's not allow **shooting guns**!]

shooting star *hōkūlele.*

shopping center *kikowaena kū'ai.* [*'O ka hale kū'ai hea ka mea hou ma ke* **kikowaenakū'ai** *'o Kūhiō?* Which store is the new one at the Kūhiō **shopping center**?]

shore 1. *'ae kai.* 2. *lihikai.* [*He mau pali ko kēia* **lihikai.** This **shore** has cliffs.

short *pōkole.*

shorts *lole wāwae pōkole.*

shoulder *poʻohiwi.*

shout *hoʻōho.* [*Hoʻōho aku ka lehulehu i ka pōpaʻilima.* The public **shouts** at the volleyball game.]

shove 1. *hou.* 2. *pahu.* [*Pahu nā keiki kū laina kekahi i kekahi.* The children standing in line **shove** each other.]

shovel *kopalā* (from English). [*ʻEli ka mahiʻai i kona kīhāpai i ke kopalā.* The farmer digs his field with a **shovel**.]

show *hōʻike.* [*E hōʻike mai i kou poho.* **Show** me your palm.]

shower 1. *kiliʻau* (bathing) 2. *nāulu* (sudden rain squall).

show off *hōʻoio.* [*Hōʻoio kā Kamahele kaikamahine i kona apolima kula hou.* Kamahele's daughter **shows off** her new gold bracelet.]

shrewd *maʻalea* (also means **cunning, deceit, skilled**). [*He ʻōlelo maʻalea kā ka mea ʻāpuka.* The deceitful person has **shrewd** speech.]

shrimp *ʻōpae.* [*Aia nā ʻōpae ʻula i nā loko wai hapakai.* The red **shrimp** are in the brackish water pond.]

shut *[v] pani.* [*E pani a e laka ʻia ana ka puka ma ka hola ʻumi o ke ahiahi.* The door will be **shut** and locked at 10 in the evening.] *[adj] paʻa* (closed).

shy 1. *hilahila* (also means **embarrassed, ashamed**). 2. *ʻāhiu* (also means **unsociable, wild**).

sibling (older) *kaikuaʻana* (of the same sex as the person who has the sibling). [*He kaikuaʻana ko Lāhela.* Lāhela (woman) has an **older sister**.] [*He kaikuaʻana ko Palikū.* Palikū (man) has an **older brother**.]

sibling (younger) *kaikaina* (of the same sex as the person who has the sibling). [*He mau kaikaina ko Lāhela.* Lāhela (woman) has several **younger sisters**.] [*ʻAʻohe kaikaina o Palikū.* Palikū (man) has no **younger brothers**.]

sick 1. *maʻi.* 2. *ʻōmaʻimaʻi* (sickly).

side *ʻaoʻao* (also means **page, group, hemisphere**).

sight 1. *ʻike.* 2. *ʻikena* (view).

sign *hōʻailona.*

silent *hāmau.* [*E hāmau!* Be **silent**! (stronger than *kulikuli*)]

similar *like* (also means **like**). [*Like ke kaikaina ou me kou kaikuaʻana?* Is your younger sister **similar** to your older sister? (a woman is being asked)]

simple *maʻalahi* (also means **easy**).

sin 1. *lawehala.* 2. *hewa* (also means **wrong, guilty**).

since *no ka mea* (because). [*E holoi i ka pahi, no ka mea, ua lepo.* Wash the knife, **since** it's dirty.]

sing 1. *hīmeni.* 2. *mele.* 3. *kani* (birds).

singer *puʻukani.* [*Me he leo ʻānela lā ka leo o ka puʻukani e hīmeni nei iā "Papakōlea."* The voice of the **singer** who is singing "Papakōlea" seems like the voice of an angel.] 2. *ka mea hīmeni.*

single 1. *kuakahi* (unmarried). 2. *hoʻokahi* (one of a thing; one person).

sister (of a female) 1. *kaikuaʻana* (older sibling). 2. *kaikaina* (younger sibling). Note: *Kaikuaʻana* can refer to either a man's older brother or to a woman's older sister. *Kaikaina* is used to refer to either a man's younger brother or a woman's younger sister.

sister (of a male) *kaikuahine.*

sit *noho* (also means **to live or stay someplace**). [*E noho i lalo a e ʻai pū kāua.* Let's **sit** down and eat together.]

site 1. *kahua.* 2. *wahi.*

six *ʻeono.* (syn. *ʻaono, ono*)

size *nui.* [*Pehea ka nui o kēnā pālule T? Loaʻa anei paha kekahi ʻano "nunui"?* How's the **size** of that T-shirt (by you)? Do you maybe have an extra large?]

skeleton *paʻa iwi.*

skilled *noʻeau.* [*He kālena ko Keawe ma nā hana noʻeau Hawaiʻi.* Keawe is **skilled** in Hawaiian crafts.]

skin *ʻili* (also means **bark of tree, surface of sea**).

skip *kāpae.* [*Ke kāpae kēlā kime i ko lākou manawa, huhū ke alakaʻi pāʻani.* Whenever that team **skips** their turn, the leader of the game is mad.]

skirt *pāʻū*. (hula skirt = *pāʻū hula*)

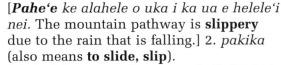
hula skirt

skull *iwi poʻo*. [*Pale aku ka **iwi poʻo** i ka lolo.* The **skull** protects the brain.]

sky 1. *lani*. 2. *lewa* (also means **space, air, upper heavens**). [*Kau mai ke ānuenue ma ka **lewa**.* Rainbows appear in the **sky**.]

slack *ʻaluʻalu* (also means **loose, baggy**). [***ʻAluʻalu** ka pālule o ka ʻelemakule.* The old man's shirt is **baggy**.]

slack key (Hawaiian guitar style) *kī hōʻalu*. [*Hoʻokani kīkā ʻo George Kuo i ke kaila **kī hōʻalu**.* George Kuo plays guitar in the **slack key** style.]

slant *hiō* (also means **diagonal, incline, to lean**).

slap *paʻi* (also means **to hit, clap, print, publish**).

slave *kauā* (also means **servant, attendant**).

sled *hōlua* (ancient sport of sledding down hills on long, narrow sled). [*Holo iho ka meʻe a lele ihola ma luna o ka **hōlua**.* The hero ran downhill and then jumped onto the **sled**.]

sleep *hiamoe*.

sleepy *maka hiamoe*. [*E ka **maka hiamoe**, e hoʻi e hiamoe.* Hey, **sleepy**head, go to sleep.]

slender *wīwī* (also means **slim, thin**).

slice open (fish) *kaha*. [*Unahi mua ka lawaiʻa i nā iʻa a pau a ma hope **kaha** i ka ʻōpū a wehe i ka pihapiha a me ka naʻau.* The fisherman first scales all the fish and later **slices open** the stomach and removes the gills and intestines.]

slime *waliwali*. [*ʻO ka **waliwali** hoʻokumu honua ia.* It was the **slime** that established the earth. (line from *Kumulipo* creation chant)]

slip *paheʻe*.

slippers *kālipa* (from English).

slippery 1. *paheʻe* (also means **to slide, slip**).

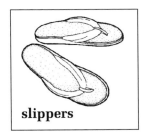
slippers

[*Paheʻe ke alahele o uka i ka ua e heleleʻi nei.* The mountain pathway is **slippery** due to the rain that is falling.] 2. *pakika* (also means **to slide, slip**).

slow *lohi* (also means **late, retarded**). [*Lohi ko ke kāne nui holo ʻana.* The large man's running is **slow**.]

small *liʻiliʻi*.

smart *akamai* (also means **skilled, clever**).

smear *pala* (daub of something, used in insults).

smell *honi* (also means **to kiss**). [*Hiki ke **honi** ʻia ke ʻala o nā pua pīkake e māpu mai nei.* The scent of the *pīkake* flowers being borne on the breeze can be **smelled**.]

smile *minoʻaka*. [*Kū kāna muli loa i kona makua kāne i kona **minoʻaka**.* Her youngest child's **smile** is like his father's.]

smoke *uahi*.

smoky *uauahi* (also means **voggy**). [*Uauahi ʻo Kona i ka hū ʻana o ka pele.* Kona is **voggy** due to the eruption of lava.]

smooth *nemonemo* (also means **polished, slick**).

smuggle *hoʻopae malū*.

snack *mea ʻai māmā*. [*ʻO ka hapahā hola ʻelua ka manawa no ka **mea ʻai māmā** ma ka Pūnana Leo.* Quarter past two is **snack** time at the Pūnana Leo preschool.]

snail *pūpū* (also means **shell, hors dʻoeuvre**).

snake *naheka*. [*ʻAʻohe **naheka** o Hawaiʻi.* Hawaiʻi has no **snakes**.]

snatch *kāʻili*.

sneeze *kihe*. [*Kihe a mauli ola.* **Sneeze** and live. (traditional response when someone sneezes, like "Gesundheit" or "Bless you"; often shortened to "*ola*")]

snout *nuku* (also means **beak, tip, mountain pass, harbor or river entrance**). [*He **nuku** ʻoi nō ko ka lau wiliwili nukunuku ʻoiʻoi.* The *lau wiliwili nukunuku ʻoiʻoi* fish has a truly sharp **snout**.]

soap

snow *hau kea*.

soak *hoʻoluʻu*.

soap *kopa* (from English).

soar *kīkaha.* [*Kīkaha ka ʻiwa, he lā mālie.* (ʻōlelo noʻeau) The ʻiwa bird **soars**, it's a calm day.]

socket *pona.*

soda *koloaka* (from English "soda water").

soda

soft *palupalu* (also means **supple, fragile, tender**). [*Palupalu ko ka makuahine hou ʻili.* The new mother's skin is **soft**.]

soil *lepo* (also means **dirt**, **dirty**, euphemism for **excrement**). (to make something dirty = *hoʻolepo*) [*Mai hoʻolepo i kou lumi moe.* Don't **dirty up** your bedroom.] (fertile soil = *lepo momona*)

solar *lā.* [*Kaulana ke kula kiʻekiʻe ʻo Konawaena i ke kaʻa lā.* Konawaena High School is well known for its **solar** car.]

soldier *koa* (also means **brave, courageous**).

solemn *kūoʻo* (also means **serious, dignified**). [*Kūoʻo ka hana hoʻohanohano ma ka hale aliʻi.* The ceremony at the palace was **solemn**.]

solid *paʻa* (also means **stuck, completed,** many other meanings).

solo *pākahi* (also means **individually, by ones**). (dual, by twos = *pālua*; by threes = *pākolu*)

solution *haʻina* (explanation). [*E haʻi mai i ka haʻina.* Tell me the **solution**.]

someone else *haʻi.* [*E hāʻawi aku i kāu ʻōlelo aʻo iā haʻi!* Give your advice to **someone else**!] Note: *Haʻi* has many other meanings, including **sacrifice, to tell, to break**.

something *kekahi mea.*

sometimes *i kekahi manawa.* [*Luʻu kai ke kamanā i kekahi manawa?* Does the carpenter go diving **sometimes**?]

son *keiki kāne* (also means **boy**; *keiki* can also imply son, boy).

song 1. *mele.* [*ʻO wai ka mele a lākou e hoʻokani nei ma ka lekiō?* What's the name of the **song** they are playing now on the radio?] 2. *hīmeni.*

soon *koke* (also means **immediately**). [*E heleleʻi koke ana kou lauoho.* Your hair will **soon** fall out.] 2. *auaneʻi.*

soothe *hoʻonā.* [*E hoʻonā i kāu keiki i maʻi i ka piwa.* **Soothe** your child who is sick with fever.]

sore *ʻeha* (also means **pain, painful**). (headache = *ke poʻo ʻeha*)

sorry 1. *minamina.* 2. *mihi.* [*Ke mihi aku nei au i kā kaʻu moʻopuna hana minamina. E kala mai.* I'm confessing my grandchild's regrettable action. **I'm sorry.**]

sort 1. *wae* (select). [*E wae i nā hua kukui a e mālama i nā hua liʻiliʻi.* **Sort** the *kukui* nuts and keep the small ones.] 2. *ʻano* (kind, type).

soul *ʻuhane* (also means **ghost, spirit**).

sound *kani* (also means **to ring, chime**). [*Kani ka uaki nui ma ka hapalua hola.* The big clock **sounds** on the half hour.]

sour *ʻawaʻawa* (also means **bitter**). [*ʻAwaʻawa ka ʻawa ke inu iho.* ʻAwa is **bitter-tasting** when you drink it. (ʻAwa is a traditional drink, mildly intoxicating, used in ceremonies honoring gods and chiefs; it is also used medicinally.)

source *kumu.*

south *hema* (also means **left**).

South Pacific *Pākīpika Hema.* [*ʻAʻole ʻo ia i holo ma ka Pākīpika Hema.* She hasn't sailed in the **South Pacific**.]

sovereignty *ea* (also means **life force, breath, gas**, many other meanings).

sow *lūlū* (also means **to shake, donate, donation**). [*Lūlū ka mahiʻai i nā ʻanoʻano kaloke ma ka māla ʻai.* The farmer **sows** carrot seeds in the vegetable garden.]

space 1. *wā* (also means **epoch** or **time period, interval**). 2. *kōwā, kōā* (intervening space between objects, such as channels between islands; also means **time interval**). 3. *lewa lilo loa* (outer space). [*Loaʻa paha kekahi mea ola ma ka lewa lilo loa?* Is there possibly something alive in **outer space**?]

spacious *ākea* (also means **broad, wide**).

sparkling *ʻōlinolino* (also means **shining, radiant**). [*ʻŌlinolino ka wai o kēia kahawai.* The water of this stream is **sparkling**.] 2. *ʻālohilohi.*

speak *ʻōlelo.* [*ʻŌlelo pinepine māua ʻo koʻu*

'anakē i nā hālāwai o ka Hui Kīwila. My aunt and I often **speak** at the Civic Club meetings.]

spear 1. *'ō* (also means **fork**). (fishing spear = *ke 'ō*). [*Hopu ko'u kaikunāne i ka he'e i ke 'ō.* My brother catches octopus with a **spear**.] 2. *ihe* (weapon).

special *kūikawā* (also means **temporary, transitional**). [*He hana kūikawā kā kēia kia'i.* This guard has a **special** job.]

speed 1. *'āwīwī* (also means **fast, quick, quickly**). 2. *wikiwiki* (also means **fast, quick, quickly**).

spelling bee *ho'okūkū hua 'ōlelo.*

spider 1. *nananana.* [*Na ka nananana i nahu iā Nu'umealani?* Was it the **spider** that bit Nu'umealani?] 2. *lanalana.*

spill *hanini.*

spin *ho'oniniu* (also means **to cause dizziness**). [*E ho'oniniu i ka hū.* **Spin** the top (toy).]

spine *kuamo'o* (refers to genealogy, since generations are counted going down the backbone, and ancestors are considered to be a living part of the spine; syn. *iwikuamo'o*).

spiral *pāka'awili.*

spirit 1. *'uhane* (also means **god, ghost**). [*He 'uhane ko nā mea a pau?* Does everything have a **spirit**?] 2. *akua.*

splash *pakī.* [*Pakī a'e ka 'ehu kai i ko ka mea he'e nalu pae 'ana i ka nalu.* The sea spray **splashes** up when the surfer catches the wave.]

spoil 1. *'ino* (decay). 2. *hōkai* (mar, deface). 3. *pailani* (pamper). [*'O kēlā mau kaikamāhine ko Momi mau kaikua'ana pailani.* Those girls are Momi's **spoiled** older sisters.] 4. *palahū* (to become overripe, rotten [fruit or food]).

sponge *'ūpī.*

spoon *puna* (use with *ke*). [*E 'ai 'oe i kēnā pūkini i ke puna, 'a'ole i ke 'ō.* Eat that pudding (near you) with the **spoon**, not with the fork.]

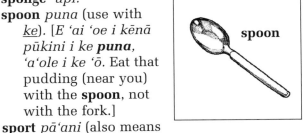
spoon

sport *pā'ani* (also means

game, to play game).

spotted *kikokiko* (also means **freckled, to type**).

spray [n] 1. *'ehu kai.* 2. *huna wai.* [v] *kīkī* (also means **to spout or shoot up**).

spread *hāli'i.* [*E hāli'i aku i ke kapa ma luna o ka mau'u no ka pikiniki.* **Spread** the blanket on the grass for the picnic.]

spread out [adj] *laha* (also means **common**).

spring (water) *pūnāwai.* [*Hāli'i ka lā'auhihi a puni ka pūnāwai.* Vines spread out around the **spring**.]

sprinkle 1. *pīpī* (to scatter about, as salt water in house blessings). 2. *kāpī* (to sprinkle fish or meat with salt for flavoring, preservative). A traditional phrase at the end of storytelling is *pīpī holo ka'ao*, lit. sprinkled around, the story travels on; that is, in being retold, a story lives on.

square *huinahālike.*

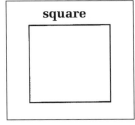
square

squeeze *'uī.* [*E 'uī hou i kāu 'ūpī a e holoi i nā kī'aha.* **Squeeze** out your sponge and wash the glasses.]

squid 1 *he'e* (octopus). 2. *mūhe'e.*

squirm *'oni* (also means **wiggle, move**).

stack *pu'u.*

stadium *kahua pā'ani* (also means playing field).

stage [n] *kahua.*

stagger *kunewa.* [*Kunewa ke kanaka pōniuniu.* The dizzy person **staggers**.]

stair (step) *'ānu'u* .

staircase *alapi'i* (also means **ladder**). [*Hinuhinu ke alapi'i koa o ka Hale Ali'i 'o 'Iolani.* The koa **staircase** of 'Iolani Palace is shiny.]

stamp [n] 1. *po'oleka* (postage). 2. *'ohe kāpala* (stamp for printing tapa). [v] *hehi.*

stand *kū* (also means **to stop, appear, upright**).

star *hōkū.* [*Kū ka hōkū ahiahi i ka lewa.* The evening **star** appears in the sky.]

start *ho'omaka.* [*Ma ka hola 'ehia e ho'omaka ai ka hālāwai?* What time does the meeting **start**?]

state *moku'āina*. [*He kanalima **moku'āina** o 'Amelika Hui Pū 'ia*. The U.S.A. has fifty **states**.]

statue 1. *ki'i* (also means **picture, image**). 2. *ki'i kū*. [*He **ki'i** kū o ka na'i aupuni ko Kohala*. Kohala has a **statue** of the conqueror.]

steadfast *'onipa'a*. Note: This is the motto of Hawai'i's last queen, Lili'uokalani.

steal *'aihue*.

steer *[n]* *pipi po'a* (*lit.* castrated cattle). (bull = *pipi kāne*) *[v]* *ho'okele* (also means **to navigate, navigator, leader**).

stem 1. *'au* (also means **handle, shaft, bone of lower arm, leg**). [*Kukū ke **'au** o ka loke*. The **stem** of a rose is thorny.] 2. *hā* (of *kalo* plant).

step *[n]* *'ānu'u*. *[v]* 1. *hehi*. 2. *ke'ehi*. [***Ke'ehi** ka mahi'ai kalo i ka 'ūkele i ka lo'i hou*. The taro farmer **steps** in the mud in the new taro patch.]

stevedore 1. *po'olā*. 2. *kipikoa* (from English). [*'O Tui ka luna **kipikoa** e hehi ana ma nā moku ma Kawaihae*. Tui is the **stevedore** supervisor stepping on the boats at Kawaiahae.]

stick *[n]* 1. *lā'au* (also means **bush, medicinal herb**). 2. *'ō'ō* (digging stick). 3. *'auamo* (carrying stick). *[v]* 1. *pili* (to adhere). 2. *ho'opili* (to adhere).

sticker 1. *mea pipili*. 2. *pepa pipili*. [*He mau **pepa pipili** ka'a Hawai'i ko kona wane*. His van has Hawaiian bumper **stickers**.]

sticky *pipili*.

stiff 1. *'o'ole'a* (rigid). 2. *mālo'elo'e* (tight-muscled, stiff from exercise).

still 1. *mālie*. 2. *lana*.

stingy *pī*. [*'Ano **pī** kāna mo'opuna? Is his grandchild kind of **stingy**?]

stir 1. *'oni* (move). 2. *hō'eu'eu* (to animate, encourage). 3. *kāwili* (to mix, as ingredients).

stomach *'ōpū*. [*'O'ole'a ko ke kinai ahi **'ōpū***. The firefighter's **stomach** is hard.]

stone *pōhaku*.

stop 1. *kū* (stop moving). [*E **kū** a e hāpai i kou mau lima! **Stop** and put your hands up!*] 2. *ho'okū* (stop a car or machinery). 3. *ho'opau* (to finish). (Stop it! = *Uoki!*)

store *hale kū'ai*.

storm *pō'ino*.

stormy 1. *'ino* (also means **bad**). 2. *'ino'ino* (also means **bad**).

story (tale) 1. *ka'ao* (story considered to be fictitious). [*He mau kinolau ko nā kupua o nā **ka'ao** kahiko*. The demigods of the old **stories** have lots of body forms.] 2. *mo'olelo* (can also mean history, story considered to be true).

stout 1. *pu'ipu'i* (also means **plump, stocky, sturdy**). 2. *poupou* (short and stocky).

straight *pololei* (also means **correct**). [*E kalaiwa **pololei** a hiki i ka huina alanui a laila, e huli hema*. Drive **straight** ahead until the intersection, then turn left.]

strange *'ano 'ē* (also means **odd behavior, bizarre**).

stranger *malihini* (also means **newcomer, guest**). [*He **malihini** a i 'ole he kama'āina 'o ia nei? Is this person here a **newcomer** or a local?*]

strangle *'u'umi*.

stream *kahawai*.

street *alanui*. [*'O wai ka inoa o kou **alanui**? What is the name of your **street**?*]

strength *ikaika*.

stretch *kīko'o* (also means **to stick out**).

strike 1. *ku'i* (hit). 2. *'olohana* (work stoppage).

string *kaula* (also means **chain, rope**). [*E huki i nā **kaula***. Pull the **ropes**.] (string a *lei* = *kui*) [*'Elima a 'olua lei i **kui** ai? Did you two **string** five *lei*?*]

strip *[n]* *'āpana* (also means **piece, section**). *[v]* 1. *'u'u* (to strip *maile*). 2. *māihi* (to peel). 3. *hole* (to peel). 4. *kīhae* (to strip thorns from *lauhala*). (to strip until naked = *wehe a kohana*)

stripe *kaha*.

striped *kahakaha*. [*He i'a **kahakaha** ka manini*. The *manini* is a **striped** fish.]

stroke *huki* (also means **cramp**).

strong *ikaika*.

struggle *'ā'ume'ume*.

stubborn *po'o pa'akikī*. [*He **po'o pa'akikī** ko kāna wahine*. His wife is **stubborn**.]

stuck *pa'a* (also means **closed, firm, completed**). [*Pa'a ka pukaaniani.* The window is **stuck**.]

student *haumāna.*

study *ho'opa'a ha'awina.*

stumble *'ōkupe* (also means **to trip**). [*E 'ōkupe ana ka mea 'oki mau'u i ka 'ili'ili.* The person cutting the grass will **stumble** on the pebbles.]

stump *'ōmuku.*

stunted 1. *'i'i.* [*'I'i ke kumu 'ōhi'a ma uka loa.* The *'ōhi'a* tree far up in the mountains is **stunted**.] 2. *'ōkumu* (implies stumpiness, shortness). 3. *kanali'i* (small growth).

stupid 1. *hūpō.* 2. *na'aupō* (ignorant).

style *kaila* (from English).

stylish *kaila.* [*Kaila nā lole i hō'ike 'ia ma ka ho'olaha.* The clothes shown in the advertisement are **stylish**.]

submarine *mokulu'u.* [*'A'ohe ona hoi e holo ma loko o ka mokulu'u.* She has no desire to travel on a **submarine**.]

substitute *pani hakahaka.* [*Hiki anei iā 'oe ke pani hakahaka nāna ma kēia Pō'aono a'e?* Can you **substitute** for him next Saturday?]

subtract *lawe* (also means **to take away**). [*'Elima lawe 'elua 'o ia 'ekolu?* Is five **subtract** two three?]

succeed *holomua.* [*E holomua ana paha anei kā kāu keiki 'oihana hou?* Will your son's new business **succeed**?]

suck *omo.*

suction *omo.* [*He omo ikaika ko ka mīkini ho'oma'ema'e moena.* The carpet cleaning machine has strong **suction**.]

suddenly *'emo 'ole* (without delay). [*'Emo 'ole ka pi'o o ke ānuenue.* A rainbow **suddenly** appeared.]

suffering *'īnea* (also means distress, hardship, to suffer). [*'A'ole paha hiki ke ho'onā i ka 'īnea o ka mea ma'i.* It may not be possible to quiet the **suffering** of the patient.]

sugar plantation *mahikō.*

suit (of clothes) *pa'a lole.*

suitcase *paiki.* [*He mau paiki a he mau ukana 'ē a'e kā ka malihini.* The guest has some **suitcases** and other baggage.]

sulky 1. *nuha.* 2. *mumule.*

summer *kauwela.* [*Ma ke kauwela e waele ana nā hoaaloha i nā lo'i.* It is in **summer** that the friends will weed the taro patches.]

sun *lā* (also means **day**).

sunbathe *'ōlala.*

sunburned *pāpa'a lā.* [*Inā he 'ili pāpa'a lā kou, e hele i ke kauka 'ili.* If you have **sunburned** skin, go to the skin doctor.]

sunglasses *makaaniani pale lā.*

sunrise 1. *kaiao.* 2. *wana'ao.* (Both words also mean **dawn**.)

sunset *napo'o ka lā.* [*Makemake nō lāua e noho ma ke one a napo'o ka lā.* They (two) like to sit on the sand until **sunset**.]

sunglasses

superior *'oi a'e.* [*'O ka hale holoi lole hea ka hale holoi lole 'oi a'e i kou mana'o?* Which launderette is the **superior** launderette in your opinion?]

supervisor *luna.*

support *kāko'o.*

supreme *po'okela.*

surf *he'e nalu.*

surface 1. *'ili* (skin, bark, surface of sea). 2. *papa* (flat surface).

surfboard *papa he'e nalu.*

surfer *mea he'e nalu.*

surge 1. *hū.* 2. *hānupanupa.* [*Ka hānupanupa o ke kai.* The **surging** of the sea. (a description of rough seas, fig. surging emotions)]

surplus *koena.* [*Loa'a nā hale kū'ai e kū'ai aku ana i ke koena pū'ali koa ma Kapalakiko.* There are stores that sell army **surplus** in San Francisco.]

surprised *pū'iwa.*

surrender *hā'awi pio* (also means **to give up**). [*Mai hā'awi pio!* Don't **give up**!]

surround *kaiapuni.* (Hawaiian Immersion school = *kula Kaiapuni Hawai'i*)

survey *ana 'āina* (land). (to measure = *ana*)

suspect *huoi.* [*Ho'omaka anei kou hoahānau e huoi i ka hana malū a kāna kāne?* Has your cousin begun to **suspect** her husband's secretive activity?]

swallow 1. *ale.* 2. *moni.*

swamp *pohō* (also means **bog, mire, useless, in vain**).

swear 1. *'ōlelo pelapela* (also means swearing). [*He hana a ka palaualelo ka '***ōlelo pelapela**. **Swearing** is what a lazy windbag does.] 2. *ho'ohiki* (a vow, promise, oath).

sweat 1. *hou* (perspiration). 2. *kahe ka hou.*

sweater *kueka.* [*Pono e komo i ke ***kueka** *mehana a me ka lakeke ke pi'i 'oe i nā hale kilo hōkū ma Mauna Kea.* You have to put on a warm **sweater** and a jacket when you go up to the observatories on Mauna Kea.]

sweep *pūlumi.*

sweetheart *ipo.* [*E ***ipo** *nohea kou?* Do you have a handsome **sweetheart**?]

sweet-smelling 1. *'a'ala.* 2. *onaona* (alluring, attractive, sweet-scented).

swept away *lilo* (has many other meanings). [*E akahele o ***lilo** *kāu ukana i ke kahawai i pehu i ka ua nui i helele'i i ka pō nei.* Be careful or else your baggage will be **swept away** by the stream swollen with the heavy rain that fell last night.]

swim *'au'au* (also means **to bathe**). (to give a bath to someone/an animal = *hō'au'au*)

swimming pool *loko 'au'au.*

swimsuit *lole 'au'au.*

swing *[n] paiō. [v] lele koali* (so called because one could swing on the twined vines of the *koali*, native morning glory).

swollen *pehu.*

symbol *hō'ailona* (also means **sign**). [*He hō'ailona ke ānuenue.* The rainbow is a **symbol**.]

swim

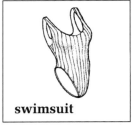

swimsuit

sympathy 1. *aloha.* [*Mai poina e ho'ouna aku i ke kāleka ***aloha**. Don't forget to send a **sympathy** card.] 2. *aloha menemene.*

table *pākaukau*.

tablespoon *puna pākaukau*. [*Loaʻa ke **puna pākaukau** i kou lumi kuke?* Does your kitchen have a **tablespoon**?]

table

taboo *kapu* (also means **sacred**). [*ʻO ka māpele ka heiau **kapu** no Lono*. The agricultural *heiau* is the religious site **sacred** to Lono.]

tack [n] *kui* (also means **nail**). [v] *pūnini* (as a sailboat; also means **to drift here and there**).

tackle [v] *lālau* (also means **to grab, seize**). [n] *lako lawaiʻa* (fishing).

Tahiti *Polapola*. (Kahiki is an ancestral homeland to the east, not Tahiti.)

tail 1. *huelo* (animal). 2. *puapua* (bird). 3. *hiʻu* (fish). [*He **hiʻu** iʻa ko ka wahine hiʻu iʻa*. The mermaid has a fish **tail**.]

take *lawe aku*. [*Nāu e **lawe aku** iā ia i ke kauka niho?* Are you the one who will **take** him to the dentist?]

take care of *mālama* (also means **keep**). [*E **mālama** i kou ola kino*. **Take care of** your health.]

tale 1. *kaʻao* (considered fictitious). [*Ua unuhi ʻia ke **kaʻao** ʻo Tazana i ka ʻōlelo Hawaiʻi*. The **tale** Tarzan was translated into Hawaiian.] 2. *moʻolelo* (considered true).

talent *kālena*.

talented *noʻeau* (also means **clever, skilled**).

talk 1. *ʻōlelo*. 2. *kamaʻilio* (to converse). [***Kamaʻilio** nā hoa hānau ma ka hui ʻohana*. The cousins **converse** at the family reunion.]

tall *lōʻihi*.

tame *laka*. [*ʻAʻole **laka** ka tika*. The tiger isn't **tame**.]

tangerine *ʻalani pākē*.

tap [v] *kīkēkē*. [*Na wai i **kīkēkē** i ka puka ma ka pō nei?* Who **tapped** on the door last night?]

tapa *kapa*. [*ʻO ke kilohana ke **kapa** mua o ke kapa moe*. The *kilohana* is the top **tapa** of the Hawaiian blanket. (In old Hawaiʻi, five pieces of tapa were bound together to make a "blanket," with the top piece beautifully decorated. When foreign merchants introduced cotton cloth, pieces of cotton were beaten into the *kilohana*, resulting in strikingly beautiful colors in the *kapa moe*. *Kilohana* became a word for anything excellently made or of highest quality.)]

tape 1. *lipine* (recording tape). 2. *leki* (cellophane tape). [*E hoʻopaʻa i ka pelaha i ka paia i ka **leki***. Put the poster on the wall with the **tape**.]

taro patch *loʻi*. (terrace of taro patches = *papa loʻi*) [*Nui nā **loʻi** ma ka **papa loʻi***. There are lots of **taro patches** in a **taro patch terrace**.]

task *hana*. [*Maʻalahi ka **hana** i ka laulima*. The **task** is easy due to many people working together.]

taste *ʻono*. [*Pehea ka **ʻono** o ka ula maka?* How does the fresh lobster **taste**?]

tasteful *kohu* (also means **tastefully**). [***Kohu** kāna hana hoʻonaninani i ka pākaukau a ʻono hoʻi ka ʻaina awakea*. Her decorating the table was **tastefully** done and the lunch was also delicious.]

tattoo 1. *kākau ʻili*. [*He hōʻailona ke **kākau**

'ili Hawai'i no ka 'aumakua? Are Hawaiian **tattoos** symbols of guardian spirits?] 2. *kākau.* 3. *uhi* (solid tattoo, like a covering).

taxes *'auhau.* [*No ke aha e uku ai 'o Pāpā i nā 'auhau 'ehā manawa o ka makahiki?* Why does Daddy pay **taxes** four times a year?]

taxi *ka'a ho'olimalima* (also means **rental car**). [*Āhea e hiki mai ai ke ka'a ho'olimalima āu i kelepona aku ai?* When will the **taxi** that you phoned arrive?]

tea *kī* (also means *tī* **leaf plant, key**). [*Ke hele ko'u 'anakē a ma'i i ka piwa, inu 'o ia i ke kī ko'oko'olau.* When my auntie becomes sick with a fever, she drinks *ko'oko'olau* **tea**.]

tea

teach *a'o aku.*

teacher *kumu.* [*A'o aku ke kumu i ka 'ōlelo no'eau i kēlā pule kēia pule.* The **teacher** teaches a wise saying every week.]

team 1. *kimi* (from English). 2. *kime* (from English). [*E lanakila ana ka mākou kime ma luna o 'oukou!* Our **team** will beat you folks!]

tear (rip) 1. *hae.* 2. *hahae.* [*E hahae ana nā kānaka 'ohi kikiki i kā 'olua mau kikiki.* The ticket takers will **tear** your (two) tickets.]

tease *ho'ohenehene* (also means **ridicule**). [*Iā ia e uē ana, ho'ohenehene kona kaikuahine iā ia.* While he cried, his sister **teased** him.]

teaspoon *puna kī.*

telephone *kelepona.*

television *kīwī.*

tell 1. *ha'i.* [*E ha'i aku ana ka māka'ikiu i ka ha'ina i kēia lā.* The detective is going to **tell** the solution today.] 2. *'ōlelo.*

temper *na'au.* [*Ua nā ko ka ho'okele na'au.* The steersman's **temper** has been soothed.]

temperature 1. *wela* (hot). [*'Ehia kekele ka wela o kēia lā 'ino?* How high is the **temperature** of this stormy day?] 2. *anu* (cold).

temple 1. *heiau.* 2. *luakini* (a specific kind of large religious site, a place of human sacrifice).

temporary *kūikawā.* [*E hai 'ia ana kekahi mea ho'okipa kūikawā e a'u.* A **temporary** receptionist will be hired by me.]

tempt *ho'owalewale.* [*'A'ole 'oukou e ho'owalewale iā ia e inu i 'ole 'o Kale e hele a 'ona.* You all shouldn't **tempt** Kale to drink so that he doesn't become drunk.]

temptation *ho'owalewale.*

tent *hale pe'a.* [*'A'ole i kūkulu 'ia ka hale pe'a ma ka lihi kai. Aia ia ma ke kahua ho'omoana.* The **tent** wasn't set up at the edge of the sea. It's on the campground.]

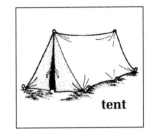

tent

terrace 1. *lānai.* 2. *'anu'u* (also means **stairs, ledge, to strain, sprain**). 3. *papa lo'i* (terrace of taro patches).

terrible *weliweli* (also means **horrible, terrifying, horrifying**). [*He pōpilikia weliweli ko kona mau mākua.* His parents had a **terrible** misfortune.]

territory *panalā'au.*

test *hō'ike* (also means **demonstration of knowledge, skill**).

testimony *'ōlelo hō'ike.* [*'Oiai e heluhelu ana ke kiule i ka 'ōlelo hō'ike, e helele'i iho ana nā waimaka.* While the jury was reading the **testimony**, their tears were falling.]

thanks *mahalo* (also means **admiration, respect**). [*Mahalo nui iā 'oukou!* Many **thanks** to you all!] [*Mahalo ka mea ho'okani 'ukulele i kā kāna kumu 'ukulele kahiko.* The 'ukulele player **admires** his teacher's old 'ukulele.]

Thanksgiving Day *Lā Ho'omaika'i.*

that 1. *kēlā* (far away). 2. *kēnā* (near person being addressed). [*He naonao kēnā ma kāu kanuwika?* Is **that** (near you) an ant on your sandwich?]

the 1. *ka* (used with most words). 2. *ke* (used with words that begin with k, e, a, o). [*Mālie ke kahu hipa akā 'eleu ka hipa.*

The shepherd is slow, but **the** sheep is nimble.]

theater *hale keaka.* (movie theater = *hale ki'i 'oni'oni*)

their (two people): 1. *ko lāua.* 2. *kā lāua.* (three or more people): 1. *ko lākou.* 2. *kā lākou. Ko lāua* and *ko lākou* are used in front of nouns that are things you can't help having, such as family born before you and including your generation, your name, land, friends, chiefs, gods, feelings, illnesses. Also used for anything one can enter into or put on, including any building, mode of transportation, clothes. *Kā lāua* and *kā lākou* are used in front of nouns that are things that can be acquired, including family born after you, your husband or wife, your work or any action, any tool [including computers and televisions], money, anything you make or create, food, drink, books.

them 1. *lāua* (two). 2. *lākou* (three or more).

theory *kumu mana'o.* [*He* **kumu mana'o** *ko ka mea kilo hōkū no ka ho'okumu honua.* The astronomer has a **theory** about the creation of the world.]

there 1. *'ō* (unspecified location). 2. *laila* (location known). (all over [*lit.* over there and over here] = *i 'ō a i 'ane'i*) [*Holo ka'u mau 'īlio pēpē* **i 'ō a i 'ane'i***. My puppies run* **all over***.*]

thermometer *ana wela.* [*Ma ka lā ikīki, pi'i a'e nā kekele ma ke* **ana wela***. On hot and humid days, the temperature rises on the* **thermometer***.*]

they 1. *lāua* (two). 2. *lākou* (three or more).

thick *mānoanoa.* [*'Ano* **mānoanoa** *ka puke a ke kumu e heluhelu ana i nā keiki.* The book that the teacher is reading to the children is kind of **thick**.]

thief *'aihue.*

thigh *'ūhā* (also means **lap**). [*Eia nei, e noho iho ma ko'u* **'ūhā***. Dearie, sit on my* **lap***.*]

thimble *komo humuhumu.*

thin 1. *wīwī* (human body). 2. *waliwali* (poi).

thing *mea* (also means **person**). [*He 'ano pono hana hou anei kēlā* **mea***? Is that* **thing** *a new kind of tool?*]

think 1. *mana'o.* 2. *no'ono'o.*

thirsty *makewai.* [**Makewai** *wale mākou keiki, e ke kahu ma'i.* We kids are really **thirsty**, nurse.]

this *kēia.*

thought *mana'o* (also means **opinion, idea**). [*'A'ole 'ae nā Hawai'i a pau i nā 'ano* **mana'o** *like 'ole no ke ea, akā 'ae kākou e a'o mai a e holomua.* All Hawaiians don't agree with the various **thoughts** about sovereignty, but we all agree to learn and to go forward.]

thread *lopi.* [*Aia iā wai ka* **lopi** *ke'oke'o a me ka mānai? Makemake au e kui lei.* Who has the white **thread** and the *lei* needle? I want to string a *lei.*]

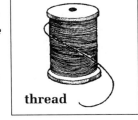

thread

three *'ekolu.* (syn. *'akolu, kolu*)

thrifty *makauli'i.* [*Mālama ka wahine* **makauli'i** *i ka lopi.* The **thrifty** woman saves thread.]

throat 1. *pu'u* (also means **hill, pimple, bump,** many other meanings).

throb 1. *konikoni.* [**Konikoni** *ka pana o kona pu'uwai i ke a'a koko.* Her heart beat is **throbbing** in her vein.] 2. *kapalili.*

throw 1. *ho'olei.* [**Ho'olei** *aku ka paniolo i ke kaula 'ili.* The cowboy **throws** the lasso.] 2. *nou.*

throw away 1. *kiloi.* 2. *kiola.* [*Mai* **kiola** *i nā nūpepa. E ho'ohana hou ana au iā lākou ma ke 'ano he pulu i ka māla pua.* Don't **throw away** the newspapers. I'll use them again as mulch in the flower garden.]

throw up *lua'i.* [*Pehea ka pēpē ma'i? Ua* **lūa'i** *'o ia?* How is the sick baby? Did he **throw up**?]

thumb *manamanalima nui.*

thunder *hekili.* [*'Ōlapa ka uila, ku'i ka* **hekili***, nāueue ka honua.* Lightning flashes, **thunder** roars, the earth shakes. (common line in chants)]

ticket 1. *likiki.* 2. *kikiki.* [*He mau* **kikiki** *kā 'olua no ka mokulele?* Do you (two) have **tickets** for the airplane?]

tickle *hoʻomaneʻo.* [*E **hoʻomaneʻo** ʻoe i ko ka pēpē wāwae a hū kona ʻaka.* **Tickle** the baby's foot until he laughs.]

tidal wave *kai eʻe.* [*ʻEhia hale i lilo i ke **kai eʻe**?* How many houses were swept away in the **tidal wave**?]

tide 1. *kai.* 2. *au.* (low tide = *kai emi/kai maloʻo*) (high tide = *kai piha*)

tidepool *kāheka.*

tidy 1. *ʻauliʻi.* [***ʻAuliʻi** kā kēia makua kāne holoi ʻana i nā pā.* The father's washing dishes is **tidy**.] 2. *maiau.*

tie *nākiʻi.* [*E **nākiʻi** i ka hoe ʻē aʻe i ka ʻiako.* **Tie** the other paddle to the outrigger boom.]

tight *māloʻeloʻe* (taut; also means **stiff from physical labor, tired**). [*Ua **māloʻeloʻe** koʻu kua ma mua o ka lomilomi ʻia ʻana.* My back was **tight** before being massaged.]

time 1. *manawa.* [*ʻO ka **manawa** pāʻani kēia.* This is play **time**.] (It's your turn = *ʻO kou manawa kēia*) 2. *hola* (telling time, o'clock). [*ʻO ka **hola** ʻehia kēia? ʻO ka hapalua **hola** ʻekolu.* What **time** is it? It's half past three.] 3. *wā* (era, epoch). [*I ka **wā** o ʻUmi.* In the **time** of ʻUmi.]

tin *kini* (also means **tin can, gin** [from English], **many, multitude**).

tiny *ʻuʻuku.* [***ʻUʻuku** kēia ʻano ʻiole.* This type of rodent is **tiny**.]

tip 1. *wēlau* (top, edge). 2. *uku lawelawe* (gratuity).

tired *māluhiluhi.*

tobacco *paka.* (to smoke a cigarette = *puhi paka*) [*Mai **puhi paka**, ke ʻoluʻolu.* Don't **smoke**, please.]

today *i kēia lā.* [*E pikiniki kāua i kahakai **i kēia lā**!* Let's picnic at the beach **today**!]

toe *manamana wāwae.* [*ʻEhia ou **manamana wāwae**, e ka pēpē?* How many **toes** do you have, baby?] (big toe = *manamana nui*)

toenail *mikiʻao* (also means **fingernail**).

together 1. *pū.* [*Hana **pū** kēia mau hoakula.* These schoolmates work **together**.] 2. *like.*

toilet *lua.*

toilet paper *pepa hēleu.*

toilet paper

(syn. *pepa hāleu*) [*Aia nō a loaʻa ka **pepa hēleu**, pono ʻo ia nei e hoʻopau pilikia.* As soon as you find **toilet paper**, she has to use the bathroom.]

tolerant *manaʻo laulā* (*lit.* broadminded; also means **main idea**).

tomato *ʻōhiʻa lomi.*

tomb *hē* (also means **grave**).

tomorrow *i ka lā ʻapōpō.* [***I ka lā ʻapōpō** kāua e holo moku peʻa ai.* It's **tomorrow** that we (you and I) may sail on the sailboat.]

tomato

tongue *alelo.* [*Mai kīkoʻo i ke **alelo**!* Don't stick out your **tongue**!]

tonight *i kēia ahiahi.*

too 1. *nō hoʻi.* 2. *pū.* [*Māloʻeloʻe kou kua? ʻO au **pū**!* Is your back tight and sore? Mine **too**!] 3. *kekahi.*

tool 1. *pono hana.* [*He **pono hana** i hoʻohana mau ʻia e ka mekanika ka mea ʻōwili.* The screwdriver is a **tool** that is always used by the mechanic.] 2. *mea hoʻohana.*

tooth *niho.* [*He mau **niho** hou kā ka luahine, akā paʻa ʻole ka ʻaoʻao "mauka."* The old woman has new **teeth**, but the "mauka" (upper) teeth aren't firmly in place.]

toothbrush *palaki niho.*

toothless *niho ʻole.*

toothpaste *pauka niho.* [*Mai pakū i ka **pauka niho** mai luna i lalo.* Don't squeeze out the **toothpaste** from top to bottom.]

toothbrush

top 1. *luna* (top section). 2. *hū* (spinning toy).

torch *lamakū.*

toss 1. *hoʻolei.* 2. *kiola.* 3. *kiloi* (toss out).

total 1. *huina.* 2. *heluna* (sum).

touch *hoʻopā* (also means **to influence**).

tough 1. *uaua* (tough to chew). 2. *paʻakikī* (difficult). [***Uaua** ka ʻiʻo kao a **paʻakikī** ka naunau ʻana no ka ʻelemakule niho ʻole.* The goat meat is **tough** and chewing (it) is **difficult** for the toothless old man.] 3.

'o'ole'a (strong condition).

tour *māka'ika'i.* [*Ua* **māka'ika'i** *lākou i nā mokupuni 'o nā Tuamotu.* They **toured** the Tuamotu islands.]

tourist 1. *mea māka'ika'i.* 2. *kanaka māka'ika'i.*

tow *kaualakō* (also means **to drag**). [*Kaualakō ke kalaka i ke ka'a.* The truck **tows** the car.]

towel *kāwele* (also means **to dry, wipe off**). (paper towel = *kāwele pepa*)

town 1. *kūlanakauhale* (also means **city, village**). 2. *kaona* (from English). [*Aia i hea ma Kaua'i ke* **kaona** *'o Kalāheo?* Where on Kaua'i is the **town** of Kalāheo?]

trace *ho'okolokolo* (also means **to investigate**). [*E hiki ana iā 'oe ke* **ho'okolokolo** *i ko kou 'ohana mo'okū'auhau?* Will you be able to **trace** your family's genealogy?]

trade 1. *kālepa* (also means **merchant, salesman, to barter**). 2. *'oihana* (occupation).

tradition 1. *loina* (also means **custom, rule**). [*He mau* **loina** *ko ka holo kai ma nā wa'a?* Does ocean traveling on canoes have **traditions**?] 2. *kuluma.*

trail *alahele.*

train *ka'aahi.* [*Ua halihali ke* **ka'aahi** *i nā 'ōhua mai 'Iwilei a i Hale'iwa ma mua.* Previously, the **train** transported passengers from 'Iwilei to Hale'iwa.]

tramp [n] *kuewa* (vagabond). [v] 1. *hehi* (also means **to step, tread on, trample**). 2. *ke'ehi* (also means **to step, tread on, trample**).

trample 1. *hehi.* [*Hehi ka lehulehu i ka hinahina ma ka pu'e one.* The public **tramples** the *hinahina* plant at the sand dune.] 2. *ke'ehi.*

transform *ho'ololi.*

transformed *loli* (also means **changed**). [*Ua loli ka waiho'olu'u o ka pua hau kahiko a 'ula'ula.* The color of the old *hau* flower **changed** to red.]

translate *unuhi.*

transparent *aniani.*

transport *halihali.* [*Mai loko mai e* **halihali** *'ia mai ka hapanui o ko Hawai'i mea 'ai.* Most of Hawai'i's food is **transported** here from the mainland.]

trap 1. *'ūmi'i* (also means **clamp, clutch, to clamp, choke**, many other meanings). 2. *pahele* (also means **deceit, snare, noose, to ensnare**). [*Loa'a* **nā pahele** *pua'a ma ka wao kele.* There are pig **traps** in the rain forest.]

trash *'ōpala* (also means **garbage**).

travel *huaka'i* (also means **trip, voyage**).

tray *pā halihali.*

treason *kipi* (also means **rebellion, treachery, rebel**). [*'O ke* **kipi** *paha, 'a'ole paha kā Wilikoki mā hana?* Were Wilcox folks doings **treason** or not?]

treasure [n] *mea makamae.* [*He* **mea makamae** *ka na'auao.* Wisdom is a **treasure**.] [v] *pūlama.* [*Pūlama 'ia nā lei pua 'a'ala.* Fragrant flower *lei* are **treasured**.]

treasurer *pu'ukū.*

treaty 1. *ku'ikahi.* 2. *palapala 'aelike.*

tree *kumulā'au.*

tree fern 1. *hāpu'u.* 2. *'ama'u.*

tremble 1. *ha'ukeke* (also means **shiver, quiver**). [*Ha'ukeke ke keiki i ke anu o ke kai, kahi āna e kāpeku nei.* The child is **shivering** due to the cold of the sea, where she is splashing around now.] 2. *ha'alulu.*

tree

trespass *komohewa.* [*Mai* **komohewa** *i ko ha'i pā hale.* Don't **trespass** in other people's yards.]

trial 1. *'aha ho'okolokolo* (court). 2. *ho'ā'o* (experiment). 3. *pōpilikia* (trouble).

triangle *huinakolu.*

tribute *ho'okupu* (also means **offerings**). [*He* **ho'okupu** *kūpono kāna mea i ha'i ai.* What he said is an appropriate **tribute**.]

trick *hana ma'alea.*

trim 1. *'oki* (to cut). 2. *'auli'i* (neat).

trip [n] *huaka'i.* [v] *'ōkupe.* [*Ke* **'ōkupe** *hou ka 'elemakule, e kōkua aku iā ia.* Whenever the old man **trips** again, help him.]

troop *hālau* (hula). 2. *pū'ali koa* (army).

trouble *pilikia.* [*Nalukai kēia luahine no ka mea ua 'ike i nā 'ano* **pilikia** *like 'ole.* This old lady is weatherworn because she has experienced all kinds of **trouble**.]

truck *kalaka* (from English).

true *'oia'i'o.* [*Eia nei,* **'oia'i'o** *ka'u i lohe ai, ua ho'omaha loa kāu kāne?* Darling, is it **true** what I've heard, that your husband retired?]

trunk 1. *kumu* (tree). 2. *pahu* (chest, box). 3. *ihu loloa* (elephant; *lit.* very long nose).

trust *hilina'i.* [*Mai* **hilina'i** *i nā kānaka e noi aku ana i kāu kālā.* Don't **trust** those who ask for your money.]

truth *'oia'i'o.* [*He aha ka* **'oia'i'o**? What is the **truth**?]

try *ho'ā'o.*

T-shirt 1. *pālule* T. 2. *pale 'ili* (undershirt).

tug *hiuhiu.* [**Hiuhiu** *ka pōpoki pēpē i ka mea pā'ani palupalu.* The kitten **tugs** at the soft toy.]

tune *[n] leo mele* (also means **melody**). [*Pehea ka* **leo mele** *o "Alekoki"? 'Āwīwī anei ka pana?* How about the **tune** of "Alekoki"? Is the beat fast?] *[v] ho'okani pono.*

turn 1. *huli.* [*E* **huli** *hema i ke kukui 'ula'ula.* **Turn** left at the red light.]

turn off machine *ho'opio.*

turn on machine *ho'ā.* [*E* **ho'ā** *ana ka pailaka i ka lolouila? Ua 'ā mua!* Will the pilot **turn on** the computer? It's already on!]

turtle 1. *honu* (common green turtle). [*Ulu nā pu'u ma nā* **honu** *a puni ka honua akā 'a'ole i maopopo 'ia ke kumu o ia ma'i weli.* Tumors grow on **turtles** around the world, but the reason for that dreadful disease is not understood.] 2. *'ea* (hawksbill turtle; *'ea* has many other meanings).

tusk *niho* (also means **tooth**).

TV *kīwī.*

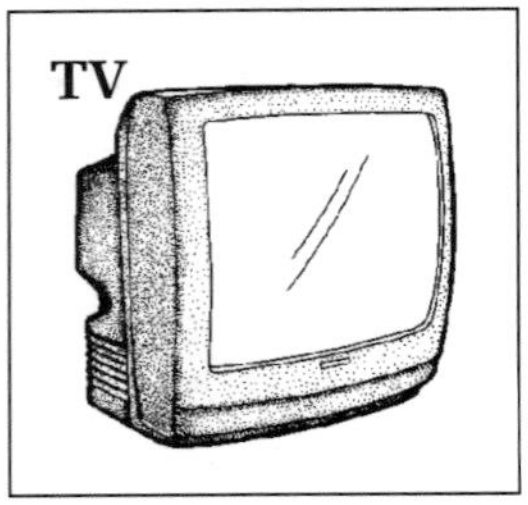

twilight *mōlehu.* [*Ma ka* **mōlehu** *e kau mai 'o 'Iao a me Venuse.* At **twilight** Jupiter and Venus appear.]

twine *[n]* 1. *kaula.* 2. *kaula kuaina* (from English). *[v] wili.*

twirl *koali.*

twist *wili* (also means **entwined, bound together**). [**wili** *'ia me ka maile lau li'ili'i,*

twisted with small-leaf *maile* (song, "Aloha Kaua'i," by M. A. Lake)]

two *'elua.* (syn. *'alua, lua*)

type *'ano.*

ugly *pupuka.* [*Inā maʻemaʻe ʻole ke kino, ʻo ia ka mea **pupuka**. A inā maʻemaʻe, nani.* If the body isn't clean, that's an **ugly** thing. And if it's clean, that's beautiful.]

ukulele *ʻukulele* (*lit.* "jumping flea," evolved from instrument introduced by Portuguese immigrants).

ukulele

ulcer *pūhā* (also means **abscess, to burst**).

ultimate *hope loa* (also means **very last**). [*ʻO ka heʻe nalu ʻana ma Koʻolauloa ka pahuhopu **hope loa** o nā mea heʻe nalu.* Surfing in the Koʻolauloa area is the ultimate goal of surfers.]

umbilical *piko.*

umbrella *māmalu.* [*ʻOiai ke heleleʻi nei ka ua, e wehe i kēnā **māmalu** āu.* Since the rain is falling, open up that (by you) **umbrella** of yours.]

uncle *ʻanakala.* [*ʻAkahi nō a hoʻomaka nā **ʻanakala** e wehe i ka pulu niu a aia nō a nahā nā niu, e waʻu ana nā ʻanakē i ka ʻiʻo.* The **uncles** have finally started to remove the coconut husks and as soon as the coconuts are cracked open, the aunties will scrape out the meat.]

uncover *wehe* (also means **to open, take off**).

undecided *kānalua* (also means **doubt, doubtful**).

under *lalo.* [*ʻAno kānalua ka haku inā he uku kaulele kā nā limahana ma **lalo** ona.* The boss is kind of doubtful whether the employees **under** him have overtime pay.]

underhanded *poholalo.*

underpants *pale maʻi.* [*He aha ke ʻano o kou **pale maʻi** e komo nei?* What kind of **underpants** are you wearing?]

understand *maopopo.* [*ʻAʻole **maopopo** iā ia pehea e hoʻopiha ai i ka palapala ʻauhau.* He doesn't **understand** how to fill out the tax form.]

undulate *hoʻānuʻunuʻu.* [***Hoʻānuʻunuʻu** nā ʻupena i ke kai piʻi.* The nets **undulate** on the incoming tide.]

unequaled 1. *lua ʻole.* [*He nani **lua ʻole** ko Nāpali.* The Nāpali coast has **unequaled** beauty.] 2. *ana ʻole.*

uneven 1. *kaulike ʻole* (also means **unjust**). 2. *lualua* (also means **rough, bumpy**).

unfair *kaulike ʻole.* [***Kaulike ʻole** ka hoʻēmi ʻana i ka uku hana a nā wāhine e hana e like nō me nā kāne.* Reducing the salaries of women who do the same work as men is **unfair**.]

unfamiliar *kamaʻāina ʻole.* [*Ua kāhāhā ke anaina i ko ka hui hīmeni **kamaʻāina ʻole** i ka mele i noi ʻia ʻo "Pua Lililehua."* The audience was surprised at the singing group's being **unfamiliar** with the song which was requested, "Pua Lililehua."]

unfavorable *kūpono ʻole.* [*Kūpono a **kūpono ʻole** paha ka hopena o ka ʻolohana?* Are the results of the strike favorable or **unfavorable**?]

unfold 1. *lole* (also means **clothes, to turn inside out**). 2. *mōhala* (as a flower).

uniform [n] *makalike.* [*Komo ko ka hōkele mau limahana i nā **makalike**.* The hotel's employees wear **uniforms**.] [adj] *like.* (syn. *kohu like*)

unimportant *mea ‘ole.* [***Mea ‘ole** ka loa o Kaimukī lā.* The distance to Kaimukī is **unimportant**. (song, "Kaimukī Hula," by A. Richart)]

unintelligible *maopopo ‘ole.* [***Maopopo ‘ole** kāna ‘ōlelo ma hope o ka ma‘i huki.* His speech is **unintelligible** after the stroke.]

uninteresting *manakā* (also means **dull, boring, uninterested**). [***Manakā** ka helu ‘ana i nā ‘ao‘ao.* Counting pages is **uninteresting**.]

union 1. *hui* (group, meeting). 2. *pilina* (close relationship). 3. *uniona* (from English; labor union).

unique *laha ‘ole* (also means **rare**).

united *hui pū‘ia.* (United States of America = ‘Amelika Hui Pū‘ia)

unity *lōkahi.* [*‘O ka laulima a me ka **lōkahi** nā mea e ho‘omaluhia mai ai.* Sharing work and **unity** are the things that bring peace.]

universe *ao holo‘oko‘a.* [*‘O ka I‘a ka inoa o ko kākou māhele o ke **ao holo‘oko‘a**.* The Milky Way is the name of our section of the **universe**.]

university *kula nui.*

unkind *loko ‘ino* (also means **merciless, heartless, cruel**). [***Loko ‘ino** maoli ‘oe e ke hoa.* You are truly **unkind**, friend. (song, "Latitu," by S. Kainoa)]

unlucky *pakalaki.* [*Mana‘o kekahi po‘e, he hō‘ailona **pakalaki** ke ao pouli.* Some people think a dark cloud is an **unlucky** sign.]

unprepared 1. *hemahema* (also means **awkward**). 2. *mākaukau ‘ole.*

unsafe *maka‘u* (also means **risk, danger, fear, dangerous, afraid**). [*I kēia mau lā, he hana **maka‘u** ka moe ipo.* These days, having an affair is **unsafe**.]

upland *uka.* [*Aia ke kula waiwai loa o ‘Amelika ma Kalihi **uka**.* The richest school in America is in **upper** Kalihi.]

upper *luna* (also means **above**).

urge 1. *koi.* [*E **koi** ana ka pelikikena i nā lālā o ka Hui Kīwila Hawai‘i e ‘imi kālā.* The president of the Hawaiian Civic Club will **urge** the members to fund-raise.] 2. *ha‘akoi.*

urgent *ko‘iko‘i* (also means **emphatic, prominent, harsh, stressed, weight**). [*He hana **ko‘iko‘i** ka ho‘ona‘auao ‘ana i ka hanauna hou.* Educating the new generation is an **urgent** thing.]

urinate *mimi.* [*Aia ia hea ka lua? Pono au e **mimi**.* Where is the toilet? I have to **urinate**.]

urine *mimi.*

us 1. *kāua* (you and I). 2. *māua* (we two, not you). 3. *kākou* (us all, three or more). 4. *mākou* (we all, not you). Note: *Māua* and *kāua* include two people only. *Māua* refers to "us" in the sense of "me and my buddy," not including the person being addressed. *Kāua* includes only the person speaking and the one being addressed, "us" here meaning "you and me." *Mākou* and *kākou* refer to three or more people. *Mākou* has the same meaning as *māua*, only now it means "me and my bud<u>dies</u>." *Kākou* includes the speaker and everyone she is talking to.

use *ho‘ohana.* [*E **ho‘ohana** i ka hamale e ku‘i i ke kui.* **Use** the hammer to hit the nail.]

used to *ma‘a* (also means **skilled at**). [***Ma‘a** ka ho‘okele wa‘a i ka hākilo ‘ana i ka ‘alihi lani.* Navigators are **used to** staring at the horizon.]

useless 1. *makehewa.* [***Makehewa** kou ku‘i ‘ana i ka ‘opihi. Pono ‘oe e noi iā ‘Anakē e a‘o mai iā ‘oe.* Your pounding ‘opihi is **useless**. You should ask Aunty to teach you.] 2. *waiwai ‘ole.*

usual *ma‘amau.*

vacant *hakahaka* (also means **empty**). [*Hakahaka ka hale hoʻolimalima.* The rental house is **vacant**.]

vacate *haʻalele.*

vacation *wā hoʻomaha.* [*Ma kona hale hoʻomaha mākou e kipa mai nei i ka wā hoʻomaha Pakoa.* It's at her vacation home that we all are visiting now during Easter **vacation**.]

vagina *kohe.*

vague *powehi.* (syn. *poehi*)

vain *1. makehewa* (useless, unsuccessful effort). *2. pohō* (useless, unsuccessful effort). *3. hoʻokano* (proud).

valley *awāwa.* [*Laukanaka ke awāwa ʻo Hālawa na Molokaʻi i ke au kahiko.* The **valley** of Hālawa on Molokaʻi was densely populated in ancient days.]

valuable *waiwai* (also means **wealth**, many other meanings).

vanish *nalowale* (also means **to disappear, lose something, lost, disappeared**). [*Pono nā Hawaiʻi e makaʻala o nalowale ko kākou hoʻoilina.* Hawaiians have to be vigilant or our heritage will **vanish**.]

vapor *ea* (also means **gas**, many other meanings).

variable *lolelua* (also means **inconsistent, unstable**). [*Lolelua ko ka moho manaʻo i kāna haʻi ʻōlelo.* The candidate's thoughts are **variable** in his speech.]

various *like ʻole.* [*Hō ka nani o nā pua poni like ʻole i wili ʻia i ka lei poʻo!* My goodness, how beautiful are the **various** purple flowers that have been bound together in the head *lei*!]

vegetable *1. lau ʻai. 2. mea kanu.*

vegetarian *1. mea ʻai lau ʻai. 2. hamu lau.*

vein *aʻa koko.*

velvet *weleweka.*

verdict *ʻōlelohoʻoholo.* [*Hiki anei ke kūkala ʻia ka ʻōlelohoʻoholo ʻo "hewa"?* Can the "guilty" **verdict** be broadcast?]

verify *1. hōʻoiaʻiʻo. 2. hōʻoia* (also means **to confirm, validate**). [*Ma o ka hoʻopaʻa ʻana i ka wikiō e hōʻoia ai ke kauka holoholona i ka hana ʻino i nā lio.* (It is) by making a video that the vet should **verify** the abuse of the horses.]

verse *paukū.*

very *1. loa.* [*Hauʻoli loa ka paʻa male hou.* The newly married couple is **very** happy.] *2. nui. 3. nō.*

veterinarian *kauka holoholona.* [*Aloha kaʻu kauka holoholona i nā ʻano pōpoki like ʻole.* My **vet** loves all kinds of cats.]

veterinarian

veto *hōʻole* (also means **to deny, refuse, negate**).

vice-president *hope pelekikena.* [*Na ka hope pelekikena e pani hakahaka ana no ka pelekikena ma ka ʻaha ʻaina.* The **vice-president** will substitute for the president at the banquet.]

vicious *ʻino.*

victim *luaahi.* [*E makaʻala o lilo ʻoe i luaahi.* Be alert so you don't become a **victim**.]

victorious *lanakila.* [*Ua lanakila ʻo Kamehameha ma luna o Kiwalaʻō ma ke kaua ʻo Mokuʻōhai.* Kamehameha was **victorious** over Kiwalaʻō at the battle of Mokuʻōhai.]

victory *lanakila.*

video *[n] wikiō.* [*E ki'i kāua i* **wikiō** *e nānā ai ma ka hopenapule.* Let's you and me go get a **video** to watch on the weekend.] *[v] ho'opa'a wikiō.*

view *'ikena* (also means **scenic view point**).

vigilant *maka'ala* (also means **watchful, alert**).

vine *lā'auhihi.* [*E 'u'u pono i ka maile i onaona ka* **lā'auhihi***.* Strip the *maile* carefully so that the **vine** will be sweetly fragrant.]

violence *hana 'ino.* [*Ma muli o ka nui o ka* **hana 'ino** *e hō'ike 'ia ma ke kīwī, hō'ole pinepine ko ko'u mau hoahānau mau mākua iā lāua e nānā.* Due to the great amount of **violence** that is shown on TV, my cousins' parents often don't allow them to watch.]

VIP 1. *maka nui.* 2. *mea nui.*

virtue *hemolele.*

visible *kūmaka* (also means **seen, eyewitness**). [**Kūmaka** *ka uluwehi o ke kuahiwi i ka noe.* The verdant beauty of the mountain in the mist is **visible**.]

vision 1. *'ike* (sight; also means **to see, to know**). 2. *akakū* (extra-sensory perception; also means **reflection, trance, hallucination**).

visit *kipa.* [**Kipa** *aku,* **kipa** *mai ka 'ohana ma ka lā nui.* The family **visits** back and (visits) forth on the holiday.]

voice *leo.* [*A he* **leo** *wale nō, 'ae.* And it is only a **voice**, (saying) yes. (line from chant granting permission to enter)]

volcano *lua pele.*

volunteer *'a'a* (also means **to dare, to challenge**). [*E* **'a'a** *ana 'oe e kōkua i nā kānaka 'ōma'ima'i?* Will you **volunteer** to help the chronically ill?]

vomit *lua'i.*

vote *koho pāloka* (also means **election, voting**; *lit.* choose ballot). [*Pehea lā e loa'a ai ke ea ma ke* **koho pāloka** *'ana?* How indeed will sovereignty be obtained through a **vote**?]

vow *ho'ohiki* (also means **promise, to swear an oath**).

voyage *huaka'i* (also means **trip, tour**). [*E* **huaka'i** *maika'i ma ka Pākīpika.* Have a good **voyage** on the Pacific.]

wade *helekū*. [**Helekū** *'o Holoua i loko o ke kāheka*. Holoua **wades** in the tidepool.]

waft *māpu* (also means **bubbling, surging [emotions], wind-borne fragrance**). [*He 'ala nei e **māpu** mai nei*. Here is a fragrance that is being **wafted** here on the wind. (song, "Ahe Lau Makani," by Lili'uokalani)]

wag *luli* (also means **to shake, sway unsteadily**). [*Luli ke kanaka mū i kona po'o a pēlā 'o ia e hō'ike nei i kona maopopo*. The mute person **wags** her head, and that's how she's showing that she understands.]

wage (pay) *uku* (also means **reward, revenge**, many other meanings). [*Ua loa'a ka **uku** iā 'oe i kēia kakahiaka?* Did you receive your **wages** this morning?]

wagon *ka'a*.

wail 1. *uē*. 2. *kanikau*.

wait 1. *kali*. 2. *alia*. [*"E alia iki" wahi a ke kuene*. The waitress said, "**Wait** a little."]

waiter *kuene* (also means **waitress, flight attendant**).

wake someone up *ho'āla*. [*'Akahi nō a hiamoe ka'u kāne akā pono au e **ho'āla** iā ia*. My husband is finally sleeping but I have to **wake him up**.]

waitress

wake up *ala* (also means **to rise up, awake**). [*E **ala** mai, e ka maka hiamoe!* **Wake up**, sleepyhead!]

walk *hele wāwae*. [*Hele wāwae ko Likolehua hoakula a puni ka pāka i nā kakahiaka a pau*. Likolehua's classmate walks around the park every morning.]

wall 1. *paia* (wall of a building). 2. *pā* (an outside wall or fence).

wander *'auana*. [*Mai kahi pae a kahi pae o ka 'āina i **'auana** ai nā kuewa*. From one end of the land to the other the tramps **wandered**.]

wane 1. *manono* (moon). [*Manono ka mahina i kēia pule*. The moon **wanes** this week.] 2. *emi*.

want *makemake* (also means **need, desire**). [*He aha kou **makemake**, e ke keiki?* What do you **want**, child?]

war *kaua*. [*Hiki anei i ka hanauna hou ke ho'opau i ke **kaua**?* Can the new generation put an end to **war**?]

warehouse *hale ho'āhu*. [*Mehana nā pahu i waiho 'ia ma ka **hale ho'āhu**. The boxes which were deposited in the **warehouse** are warm.]

warm *mehana*.

warn *a'o*.

warrior

warrior *koa* (also means **courage, brave, martial, native tree** whose wood is prized for furniture, canoes). [*E ola koa*. ('ōlelo no'eau) Live long and like a **warrior**, with courage.]

wary *'e'ena*.

wash *holoi* (also means **to erase**).

washing machine (clothes) *mīkini holoi lole*. [*'O nā lole ke'oke'o wale nō nā lole āna e ho'okomo nei i ka **mīkini holoi lole**? Is it only white clothes that he is putting into the **washing machine**?]

washing machine (dishes) *mīkini holoi pā*.

waste *hoʻomāuna.* [*ʻAʻole kākou e **hoʻomāuna** i nā waiwai o ka ʻāina o hewa loa kā kākou hana ma mua o nā kūpuna.* We shouldn't **waste** the resources of the land or else our actions will be very wrong to our ancestors.]

watch *[n] uaki* (also means **clock**). *[v]* 1. *nānā* (also means **to observe, look at**). 2. *mālama* (also means **to keep, take care of**). 3. *kiaʻi* (watch over, protect).

watch out *makaʻala* (also means **alert, vigilant**). [*E **makaʻala** o lilo ke keiki i ka pāʻani lolouila.* **Watch out** or else the child will become absorbed in the computer game.]

water *wai.*

water ditch *ʻauwai.* [*Holo ka wai ma ka **ʻauwai** a hiki i ka papa loʻi.* Water flows in the **water ditch** to the taro patch terrace.] (sewer = *ʻauwai lawe mea ʻino*)

waterfall *wailele.* [***Wailele** hune nā pali, ko kāhiko nō ia.* **Waterfall** sprinkling the cliffs, it is your adornment. (song, "Molokaʻi Waltz," by M. Kāne)]

watermelon *ipu haole.*

wave (ocean) 1. *nalu* (breaks close to shore). 2. *ʻale* (ocean swell).

way *alahele.*

we 1. *kāua* (you and I). 2. *māua* (us two, not you). 3. *kākou* (all of us; three or more). 4. *mākou* (all of us [three or more], not you).

weak *nāwaliwali.* [*ʻAno **nāwaliwali** paha ka pēpē i hānau ʻia i nehinei.* The baby which was born yesterday is possibly a bit **weak**.]

wealth *waiwai* (also means **property, benefit, valuable**, many other meanings).

weapon *mea kaua.* [*ʻAʻole ka pahi kaua he **mea kaua** kahiko ma kēia pae ʻāina.* The sword was not an ancient **weapon** in this island chain.]

weapon

wear *komo* (also means **to enter**). [***Komo** mau kaʻu luna i ka lei pua.* My supervisor always **wears** a flower *lei*.]

wearisome *hoʻoluhi* (also means **burdensome**). [*He hana **hoʻoluhi** kā ke kauka.* Doctors have a **wearisome** job.]

weary *luhi.*

weather 1. (phrase) *ke ʻano o ka manawa.* 2. *aniau* (climate). 3. *[v] nalukai* (weathered).

weave *ulana.* [*No ka hapalua kālā wale nō i kūʻai aku ai kona kupuna wahine i nā pāpale lauhala a kona ʻohana i **ulana** ai i ka hale kūʻai ma Kona i kona wā kamaliʻi.* It was for only a half dollar that his grandmother sold the *lauhala* hats her family **wove** to the store in Kona in her childhood.]

web *ʻupena* (also means **net**). [*ʻEhia ʻīniha ka lōloa o ka maka **ʻupena**?* How many inches long is the eye of the **net**?] (spider web = *ʻupena nananana*; syn. *pūnāwelewele*)

wedding *male ʻana.* [*Aia ka **male ʻana** ma waho, ma ka māla pua.* The **wedding** is outside, in the flower garden.]

weed *[n] nāhelehele.* [*Pono e waele i nā **nāhelehele** i ka loʻi i ʻole e uluwale ka loʻi.* The **weeds** in the taro patch have to be pulled so that the patch won't be overgrown.] *[v] waele.*

week *pule.* [*ʻEhia **pule** āna e holopeki ai a mākaukau no ka heihei?* How many **weeks** should she jog until she is prepared for the race?]

weep 1. *uē.* 2. *kulu waimaka.* [*Ke lohe au i ia mele, **kulu waimaka**.* Whenever I hear that song, **tears fall**.]

weight *kaumaha* (also means **sad, depressed**). [*ʻEhia paona ke **kaumaha** o kou kino?* How much do you **weigh**? (*lit.* How many pounds is the weight of your body?)]

weightlifting 1. *hāpai hao.* 2. *hāpai paona.*

welcome 1. *hoʻokipa* (to welcome, entertain as guest). [***Hoʻokipa** ʻo Malia i kona mau hoaaloha ma ke kahua mokulele.* Malia **welcomes** her friends at the airport.] 2. *aloha aku* (give greeting). [*E **aloha aku** iā Kīhei.* **Give my love** to Kīhei.]

well *maikaʻi.*

well supplied *lako.*

west *komohana* (where the sun enters the sea [*komo*] at sunset).

wet *pulu* (soaked with rain).

whale 1. *koholā* (humpback whale). 2. *palaoa* (sperm whale; also means **ivory**, especially whale ivory used to make whale-tooth pendants (*lei niho palaoa*), a symbol of high rank).

whale

wharf *uapo* (also means **bridge**).

what *he aha*. [**He aha** *kēnā? He mau pūpū nani kēia.* **What**'s that (by you)? These are pretty shells.]

wheel *huila*. [*ke ʻoni nei ka* **huila**, **wheels** turning (song, "Holoholokaʻa," by C. Kinney)]

wheelchair *noho huila*.

when *i ka manawa* (at the time). [**I ka manawa** *āu i pae ai i ka nalu, ua ʻike paha ʻoe i ka manō?* **When** you caught the wave, did you maybe see a shark?] Note: Unlike in English, there are a variety of ways to say "when" in Hawaiian, depending on the type of sentence pattern being used.

where 1. *kahi* (the place where). 2. *Aia i hea…?* (Where is…?)

which 1. *hea* (used in questions). [*ʻO ka lā* **hea** *kou lā male?* **Which** day is your wedding day?]

whirlpool 1. *mimilo*. 2. *wiliwai* (also means **eddy**).

whiskers *ʻumiʻumi* (also means **mustache, beard**). [*Kahi ke kāne i kona mau pāpālina i ʻole e ulu ka* **ʻumiʻumi**. The man shaves his cheeks so **whiskers** don't grow.]

whisper *hāwanawana*.

whispering *hāwanawana*. [*Kawaihae, i ke kai, i ke kai* **hāwanawana**, Kawaihae, the sea, the **whispering** sea (traditional song, "Hilo Hanakahi")]

whistle *hōkio*.

white *keʻokeʻo*. (white hair on head = *poʻo hina*)

whiz by *pūhalahio*. [*Ua* **pūhalahio** *aʻe ʻo Walaʻau ma kona waʻa peʻa.* Walaʻau **whizzed by** on his sailing canoe.]

who *ʻo wai*. [**ʻO wai** *kēlā?* **Who**'s that?]

whole *holoʻokoʻa* (also means **entire**). [*Ua ʻokiʻoki ʻia ka ʻulu* **holoʻokoʻa**. The **whole** breadfruit was chopped into small pieces.]

why *no ke aha*. [**No ke aha** *i hoʻohūnāʻia ai ka hula kahiko ma mua?* **Why** was ancient hula hidden in the past?]

wide 1. *ākea* (also means **spacious, unobstructed, broad, public**). 2. *laulā* (also means **liberal, publicly**).

widespread *laha*. [*Ua* **laha** *ke aloha ʻāina.* Patriotism (love for the land) is **widespread**.]

width 1. *ākea*. 2. *laulā*. [*ʻEhā kapuaʻi ka* **laulā** *o ka pākaukau koa. ʻEhia kapuaʻi ka lōʻihi?* Four feet is the **width** of the *koa* table. How many feet is its length?]

wife *wahine* (also means **woman, female, feminine**).

wild *ʻāhiu* (also means **shy**). [*ʻAʻole* **ʻāhiu** *kēia manu. Laka ia.* This bird is not **wild**. It's tame.]

will [n] 1. *palapala hoʻoilina*. 2. *palapala kauoha*. [*I kona unuhi ʻana i nā* **palapala kauoha** *kahiko, kolokolo ka loio i ka hoʻoilina ʻāina.* When she translates old **wills**, the lawyer traces the inheritance of land.]

Last Will & Testament

I, being of sound mind and body do hereby bequeath…

will

wilt *mae* (also means **wilted**). [**Mae** *nā lei pua i ka wela o ka lā.* The flower leis **wilted** in the heat of the sun.]

win *lanakila*. [*ʻO wai ka inoa o ka mea oli i* **lanakila** *i ke kūlana ʻekahi?* What is the name of the chanter who **won** first place?]

wind *makani* (also means **breeze**). [*Pā aheahe mai ana ka* **makani**. The **wind** is gently blowing.]

window *pukaaniani*.

wind surf *heʻe nalu makani*.

wing *ʻēheu*. [*ʻElua* **ʻēheu** *o ka manu.* Birds have two **wings**.]

wink *ʻimo* (also means to **twinkle**, as stars).

wink

[**'Imo**'imo kou maka, kou le'ale'a paha. Your eyes **wink**, you're maybe having fun. (song, "He Mea Ma'a Mau Ia," by J. Almeida)]

winter ho'oilo (lit. rainy season; ancient Hawaiians had no word for winter).

wipe kāwele (also means **towel, to dry**).

wire uea (also means **cable**). [E nāki'i i ka **uea** a puni ka pou. Tie the **wire** around the post.]

wisdom na'auao (also means **enlightenment, knowledge**).

wise na'auao (also means **enlightened, educated, intelligent**).

wish makemake. [Ua ho'okō ka'u ipo i ko māua **makemake** e kipa aku i Kaho'olawe. My sweetheart fulfilled our (her and my) **wish** to visit Kaho'olawe.]

with me. [Me wai i komo ai ka mea ma'i i ka haukapila? **Me ia?** **With** whom did the patient enter the hospital? **With** him?]

without 'ole. [Niho **'ole** ka pēpē. The baby is **without** teeth.]

witness 'ike maka. [Ua **'ike maka** ko'u kupuna wahine i ka ho'opahūpahū iā Pu'uloa. My grandmother **witnessed** the bombing of Pearl Harbor.]

woman wahine.

wonder [n] 1. mea kupaianaha (amazing or astonishing thing). 2. hana kupaianaha (amazing event). [v] nune (speculate, ponder). [**Nune** nā kilo hōkū inā loa'a ke ola ma nā hōkūhele 'ē a'e. Astronomers **wonder** if there's life on other planets.]

wonderful kupaianaha (also means **astonishing, mysterious, surprising**). [**Kupaianaha** ka hū 'ana o ka pele. The spouting up of lava is **astonishing**.]

wood lā'au (also means **bush, medicine**). ['Ai wale nā mū i nā hale **lā'au**. Insects and bugs eat **wood** houses.]

wool hulu hipa.

word hua 'ōlelo. [He aha ka mana'o o kēia **hua 'ōlelo**? What's the meaning of this **word**?]

work [n] hana (refers to any activity; 'oihana refers specifically to job, profession). [He aha kāu **hana** ma hope o ka hola 'elima?

What (activity) do you do after five o'clock?] [v] hana (also means **to make something**). [**Hana** kāna mo'opuna wahine kuakahi ma ko kāna kāne hale kū'ai. His great-granddaughter **works** at her husband's store.]

worker limahana (also means **employee, laborer**).

work together 1. hana like. 2. alu like. 3. laulima.

world 1. honua. (globe = poepoe honua) 2. ao.

worm ko'e.

worried hopohopo.

worried

worry hopohopo. [Mai **hopohopo**, e hau'oli! Don't **worry**, be happy!]

worship 1. ho'omana. 2. haipule. [Mālama 'ia kekahi hana **haipule** ma Mauna 'Ala i ka mahina 'o Pepeluali. A **worship** service is held at Mauna 'Ala (Royal Mausoleum) in the month of February.]

worthless 1. waiwai 'ole. 2. lapuwale (also means **foolishness, vanity, scoundrel**). 3. 'ala'uka (also means **vile conduct, dregs of society**). ['Ala'uka a poholalo kā nā kānaka loko 'ino hana 'āpuka. Nasty people's fraudulent activities are **worthless**.]

worthy kūpono (also means **proper, favorable, appropriate**).

wound palapū. [E loa'a ana paha ka **palapū** i ke koa ma ka ho'ouka kaua. The soldier might receive a **wound** in the battle.]

wrap wahī (also means **envelope, covering, case, to bundle up, cover up, dress wound**). [E **wahī** i nā pua melia a me nā kiele i ka lā'ī. **Wrap** the plumerias and gardenias in the tī leaf.]

wreck wāwahi (also means **to demolish, tear down, shatter**). [He hana kūpono ka **wāwahi** wale 'ana i nā hale kahiko? Is it a proper thing to just **wreck** old houses?]

wring 'uī. [Ua **'uī** 'ia nā welu pulu. The wet rags were **wrung** out.]

wrinkled minomino. [He hō'ailona ko ku'u kupuna lae **minomino** i ka nui o kona na'auao. The **wrinkled** brow of my

beloved grandparent is a sign of the
breadth of her wisdom.]

wrinkles *'uka.*

wrist *pūlima* (also means **to sign your name**).
[*'Eha pinepine ko ka laweleka **pūlima.***
The mail carrier's **wrist** is often sore.]

write *kākau* (also means **tattoo**).

writer *mea kākau.*

writing 1. *palapala.* 2. *kākau.*

wrong *hewa* (also means **guilt, sin**). [***Hewa***
paha nā 'ōlelo kuhikuhi i hā'awi 'ia mai
ia'u. Perhaps the directions which were
given to me are **wrong**.]

yam *uhi* (also means **cover, lid, veil, solid tattooing, to cover**).

yam

yard 1. *pā hale* (of a house). [*He mau kumuniu a he mau kumumai'a kāna ma kona **pā hale***. She has coconut trees and banana trees in her **yard**.] 2. *iā* (measurement). [*'Ehia **iā** ka lō'ihi kūpono no ka holokū?* How many **yards** is the proper length for a *holokū* (formal, figure-hugging *mu'umu'u* worn for balls and special occasions, with a long train)?

yawn *ho'ohāmama*. [*Ke **ho'ohāmama** 'oe, piha ke akemāmā i ke ea*. When you **yawn**, the lungs fill with air.]

year *makahiki*. (last year = *i kēlā makahiki aku nei*) (next year = *i kēia makahiki a'e*) [*I kēlā makahiki aku nei, 'a'ole i hiki iā La'akea ke he'e nalu makani, akā na'e, i kēia makahiki a'e ana 'o ia e he'e nalu makani ai ma Ho'okipa, Maui*. **Last year**, La'akea couldn't wind surf; however, it is **next year** that he will windsurf at Ho'okipa, Maui.]

yearn *ake*. [*Ke **ake** inu wai o ka Maluaki'iwai*. The Maluaki'iwai wind **yearns** to drink water. (song, "Kalama'ula," by H. Dudoit)]

yearning *'i'ini*. [*I loko nō o ka lō'ihi o ke ka'awale 'ana, ulu mau ko ke keiki **'i'ini** e 'ike hou i kona māu mākua*. In spite of the length of separation, the **yearning** of a child to see his parents again always grows.]

yell 1. *ho'ōho*. [*Mai **ho'ōho** i ko'u wahi pepeiao!* Don't **yell** in my dear little ear!] 2. *'uā*.

yellow 1. *melemele* (light yellow). 2. *lenalena* (orange yellow).

yes *'ae* (also means **to yield, allow**). [*E **'ae** paha ana ka'u haku 'āina i ka'u noi e loa'a i ka hānaiāhuhu*. My landlord may say **yes** to my request to have a pet.]

yesterday *i nehinei*. [*I nehinei i mālama 'ia ka ho'omaika'i 'ana i ka hale*. **Yesterday** was when the house blessing was held.]

yet 1. *na'e* (also means **however**). [*Ua luhi loa ko'u hoahānau a ua hiki **na'e** iā ia ke humuhumu i nā pā'ū hula me ka maiau*. My cousin was really tired, **yet** she could sew the hula skirts skillfully.] 2. *akā na'e*.

yield *'ae*.

you 1. *'oe* (one person). 2. *'olua* (you two). 3. *'oukou* (you all, three or more).

young *'ōpiopio*. [*Kōkua nā kāne **'ōpiopio** i nā kānaka makua*. The **young** men help the adults.]

your (one person): 1. *kou*. 2. *kāu*. (two people): 1. *ko 'olua*. 2. *kā 'olua*. (three or more people): *ko 'oukou*. 2. *kā 'oukou*. *Kou, ko 'olua*, and *ko 'oukou* are used in front of nouns that are things you can't help having, such as family born before you and including your generation, your name, land, friends, chiefs, gods, feelings, illnesses. Also used for anything one can enter into or put on, including any building, mode of transportation, clothes. *Kāu, kā 'olua,* and *kā 'oukou* are used in front of nouns that are things that can be acquired, including family born after you, your husband or wife, your work or any action, any tool [including computers and televisions], money, anything you make or create, food, drink, books.

youth *ʻōpio.* [*Haʻaheo ka lāhui i nā* **ʻōpio** *e hoʻōla nei i kā kākou ʻōlelo.* The Hawaiian people are proud of the **youth** who are reviving our language.]

zeal *mana'o ikaika.*

zero *'ole.* [*'O ko lākou helu kelepona 'o 'eiwa 'ehā 'eiwa 'elima **'ole** 'elua 'ehiku.* Their (three) phone number is nine four nine five **zero** two seven.]

zigzag *kīke'eke'e* (also means **twisting, crooked**).

zigzag

zipper *huka.* [*Mai huki ikaika i ka **huka** o poloke paha.* Don't pull strongly on the **zipper** or else it might break.]

zone 1. *māhele* (also means **portion, piece**). 2. *wao* (refers to biogeographic zones such as *wao kanaka*, the section of fertile lands where people lived).

zoo *kahua holoholona.* [*'Aka'aka aku au i nā keko ma ke **kahua holoholona**.* I laugh at the monkeys in the **zoo**.]

Notes

Notes